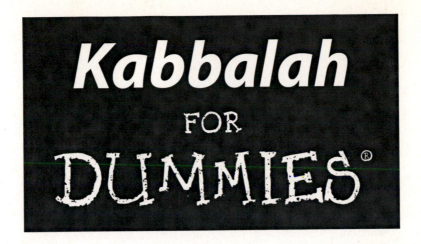

Kabbalah
FOR
DUMMIES®

by Arthur Kurzweil

BICENTENNIAL
1807
WILEY
2007
BICENTENNIAL

Wiley Publishing, Inc.

Kabbalah For Dummies®

Published by
Wiley Publishing, Inc.
111 River St.
Hoboken, NJ 07030-5774
www.wiley.com

About the Author

A direct descendant of Rabbi Chaim Yosef Gottlieb (1790–1867), Rabbi Isaiah Horowitz (1555–1630), and Rabbi Moses Isserles (1530–1572), three revered rabbis and teachers of Kabbalah, **Arthur Kurzweil** frequently teaches the Talmud and introductory classes on Kabbalah to groups of adults in synagogues and other Jewish gatherings across America. He also currently serves as publisher at *Parabola* magazine.

Arthur is the author of *On the Road with Rabbi Steinsaltz: 25 Years of Pre-Dawn Car Trips, Mind-Blowing Encounters, and Inspiring Conversations with a Man of Wisdom* (Jossey-Bass). He's also the author of the best-selling classic *From Generation to Generation: How to Trace Your Jewish Genealogy and Family History* (Jossey-Bass), co-editor of *The Hadassah Jewish Family Book of Health and Wellness* (Jossey-Bass), and editor of *Best Jewish Writing 2003* (Jossey-Bass). He has also written *My Generations: A Course in Jewish Family History* (Behrman House), which is used in synagogue schools throughout the United States.

Arthur is the recipient of the Distinguished Humanitarian Award from the Melton Center for Jewish Studies at The Ohio State University for his unique contributions to the field of Jewish education. He received a Lifetime Achievement Award from the International Association of Jewish Genealogical Societies for his trailblazing work in the field of Jewish genealogy.

A member of the Society of American Magicians and the International Brotherhood of Magicians, Arthur frequently performs his one-man show "Searching for God in a Magic Shop," in which he blends the performance of magic tricks with a serious discussion of Jewish theological ideas.

Visit Arthur's Web site at www.arthurkurzweil.com.

Dedication

To my parents, Saul and Evelyn Kurzweil,

Who in partnership with God brought me into this world, and who taught me the holy process of curiosity, ("There are three partners in man" [Talmud, Niddah 31a])

To my children, Moshe, Miriam, and Malya,

Who study and live the wisdom of Kabbalah, who have made me the wealthiest man in this world, and who are my greatest blessings. ("The Lord bless you and keep you; the Lord make His face to shine upon you and be gracious to you; the Lord lift up His countenance upon you and give you peace." [The Five Books of Moses, Bamidbar 6:24])

To my soul mate, Bobby,

My partner in all the worlds. ("In how many days did the Holy One create the world?" "Six." "And what has God been doing since then?" "Making matches, assigning this man to that woman, and this woman to that man." [Midrash, Genesis Rabbah 68:4])

To my extraordinary Teacher,

Who nourishes me with Wisdom. When God wills it, may this wisdom usher me gently into the World to Come. ("But your teacher who taught you wisdom . . ." [Talmud, Bava Metzia, 33a])

Author's Acknowledgments

Each morning I engage in a spiritual practice known for centuries to students of Kabbalah. This practice is simply the recitation of a brief prayer expressing gratitude to God, at the moment of my first conscious thoughts, for continuing to sustain my soul. I am always grateful for opportunities to express my gratitude.

I want to thank:

Chrissy Guthrie, my project editor: Thank you for your encouragement, patience, warmth, and, most of all, your guidance. You made this book better with every suggestion.

Elizabeth Rea, my copy editor: You're proof, once again, that the unsung hero of book publishing is the copy editor, who takes a manuscript and vastly improves it.

Michael Lewis, my acquisitions editor: You encouraged me and believed in me from the very beginning. Thank you.

Alan Rinzler, my friend, mentor, and colleague: You suggested me for this project. For that, and for so much more, I will always be grateful.

Simcha Prombaum: Your friendship, your support, your insights, your guidance, and your words of Torah all nourish me and feel like gifts from Above.

Goldie Milgram: You're such a gifted teacher; I admire your talents and your profound empathy for your students. Thank you for your help with this book.

Alan Zoldan: Your inspired creativity is always so impressive. Thanks for your suggestions and for your encouragement.

Gary Eisenberg, Richard Carlow, Ed Rothfarb, Marc Felix, Rick Blum, and Robin Bauer: When I add up the years that each of you has been my friend, it comes to over 200 years of love, spiritual explorations, mutual support, and countless blessings.

Mrs. Turnwall, Mrs. Combs, Miss Umanoff, Mrs. Custer, Mr. Joseph Kenneth Puglisi, Mr Stanley G. Heisey, Mr. Louis Krauss, Alida Roochvarg, Mr. David Christman, Dr.Robert Sobel, and Mr Irving Adelman: You were all beacons of light for my life, and I will remember you forever.

Rabbi Chaim Yosef Gottlieb (1790–1867), Rabbi Isaiah Horowitz (1555–1630), and Rabbi Moses Isserles (1530–1572): I have the great honor and also the awesome responsibility of being, in each case, your direct descendant. I have prayed to receive your blessings on this book, with the hope that it will be a successful part of my ongoing desire to share our inheritance with others.

My children, Malya, Miriam and Moshe: We discuss the profound ideas of Kabbalah with each other all the time. Fortunate and blessed is the father who can engage in the study of Torah with his children.

My brother, Ken Kurzweil: I'm more secure knowing that you're always there to help me with a computer problem. And special thanks for studying the great spiritual Jewish poets — B. Dylan and L. Cohen — with me.

Ruth Rothwax: Thank you for your love and for the many ways you have helped me.

My parents, Saul and Evelyn Kurzweil: Thank you for studying the Torah of life with me. Since my earliest years we've been discussing the great eternal questions together. Thank you for being my most important role models. I am grateful to be your son.

Bobby Dor, love of my life: You helped me with your insights, with our countless conversations about spiritual matters, with your suggestions, with your profound love, and with a delicious feta cheese and tomato omelet whenever I wanted one.

Blessed are You, Lord our God, King of the Universe, who keeps us alive, sustains us, and permits us to reach this season.

Rabbi Adin Steinsaltz, Ram Dass, the Bobover Rebbe, the Lubavitcher Rebbe, and Elie Wiesel: How fortunate and blessed I have been to be in your presence, to sit at your feet, and to drink up your words of Torah.

Publisher's Acknowledgments

We're proud of this book; please send us your comments through our Dummies online registration form located at www.dummies.com/register/.

Some of the people who helped bring this book to market include the following:

Acquisitions, Editorial, and Media Development

Senior Project Editor: Christina Guthrie

Acquisitions Editor: Michael Lewis

Senior Copy Editor: Elizabeth Rea

Editorial Program Coordinator: Hanna K. Scott

Technical Editor: Rabbi Simcha Prombaum

Editorial Manager: Christine Meloy Beck

Editorial Assistants: Erin Calligan, David Lutton

Cover Photos: © Rena Pearl/Alamy

Cartoons: Rich Tennant (www.the5thwave.com)

Composition Services

Project Coordinator: Patrick Redmond

Layout and Graphics: Carl Byers, Lavonne Cook, Joyce Haughey, Barbara Moore, Barry Offringa, Lynsey Osborn, Heather Ryan, Alicia B. South

Anniversary Logo Design: Richard Pacifico

Proofreaders: Aptara, Jessica Kramer, Rob Springer

Indexer: Aptara

Publishing and Editorial for Consumer Dummies

Diane Graves Steele, Vice President and Publisher, Consumer Dummies

Joyce Pepple, Acquisitions Director, Consumer Dummies

Kristin A. Cocks, Product Development Director, Consumer Dummies

Michael Spring, Vice President and Publisher, Travel

Kelly Regan, Editorial Director, Travel

Publishing for Technology Dummies

Andy Cummings, Vice President and Publisher, Dummies Technology/General User

Composition Services

Gerry Fahey, Vice President of Production Services

Debbie Stailey, Director of Composition Services

Contents at a Glance

Table of Contents

Chapter 15: Praying Like a Kabbalist 245

Chapter 16: Knowing the Unknowable God 269

Introduction

Kabbalah is the theology of the Jewish people; it is the way Judaism understands God and the relationship between God and the world. For Kabbalists, all the laws, customs, practices, holidays, and rituals of Judaism are best understood in light of the Kabbalistic teachings about God and of what it is that God wants from humans.

Over the centuries, Kabbalah has become more and more systematized. Brilliant Jewish sages have explored, developed, and refined Jewish theology to the point at which, in the last six centuries, Kabbalah has become a distinct system of ideas, beliefs, technical terminology, and values with its own history, great personalities, controversies, and vocabulary. But Kabbalah, which means "the received tradition," has always been an integral part of Jewish religious and spiritual life.

Like other studies of divinity and spirituality, Kabbalah deals with ultimate questions: Who are we? Where do we come from? Where are we going? What for? Why?

About This Book

Kabbalah is often thought to be a secret study occupying the minds of elite students throughout the ages. But the "secrets" of Kabbalah aren't the typical kind in which information is revealed to the few.

There are two kinds of secrets:

- **Secrets that are kept from the public:** When revealed, these secrets are recognized for what they are: clever illusions that, once revealed, can never fool again. Whatever "mysteries" the illusions once held disappear.

- **Real secrets that are available for all to see:** When real secrets are explored, they become deeper and more profound. They become richer and give birth to even greater secrets while their revelations illuminate the world. Such are the so-called "secrets" of Kabbalah.

My goal in writing this book is to help set the record straight and to inform the general public about what Kabbalah is — and also what Kabbalah isn't.

In recent years Kabbalah has become a pop culture phenomenon, a development that's resulted in the spread of tremendous inaccuracies and misinformation about the subject. This book is for those who are curious about the subject as well as for those who sincerely want to begin to grasp some of the profound teachings of Kabbalah and to integrate Kabbalistic wisdom into their daily lives.

Unfortunately, some books represent Kabbalah as a New Age, mystical practice dealing with amulets, obscure forms of meditation, superstition, and occult practices. Some books on Kabbalah separate Kabbalah from Judaism, misinforming well-meaning students and encouraging them to think of Kabbalah as a general philosophy of life rather than as a spiritual practice inextricably integrated into Jewish law, ritual, prayer, and study.

Kabbalah For Dummies explains in plain English both the major abstract ideas of Kabbalah as well as the Kabbalistic practices that are part of daily Jewish life. Although the study of Kabbalah can be a major commitment that influences a practitioner's entire life, a person can pick up on many profound approaches to life just by considering the ideas and perspectives of Kabbalah.

Conventions Used in This Book

Because Kabbalah is a complex and often controversial topic, I had to establish a few conventions while writing to keep things as fair and simple as possible. As you're reading *Kabbalah For Dummies,* please keep in mind my conventions regarding the following:

- ✔ **References to God:** Kabbalistic notions about God include the fundamental belief that the Almighty doesn't have a gender, so whenever possible, I refrain from referring to God using masculine pronouns. However, the primary language of Judaism, Hebrew, doesn't have a neutral gender, so most Hebrew nouns are masculine. In addition, although there's a female term that indicates God's indwelling presence in the world, the male forms of God's names have their own spiritual significance (Kabbalistic tradition has many names for God, as I explain in Chapter 16). In Jewish prayers, for example, God is referred to as "He." This isn't sexism; God is neither He nor She, so please don't be offended when God is referred to as "He."

- ✔ **The word "Kabbalist":** Throughout this book I refer to things that Kabbalists do or believe. In reality, none of the great (or even not-so-great) Kabbalists ever referred to themselves as Kabbalists. All the great Kabbalists throughout history have been Jews, more specifically traditional, observant Jews. In today's terms, they'd probably be called Orthodox Jews.

I use the term "Kabbalist" through this book to refer to those people, great sages, or everyday people like me who integrate into their lives the beautiful Jewish practices and profound ideas that are part of Jewish tradition and have explicit connection to Jewish theological — and therefore Kabbalistic — ideas.

A great sage is referred to as a Kabbalist because he wrote about or taught the theology of Judaism and was specifically interested in using the vocabulary and essential ideas contained in the theological, esoteric explorations of Judaism. Even today, teachers who are considered masters of Kabbalah aren't generally known as Kabbalists; instead, the term **mekubal** (meh-koo-*bahl*) indicates that a certain teacher is a qualified teacher of Kabbalah and is known for his or her Kabbalistic teachings.

✔ **Hasidism:** In recent centuries, there have been two streams of Kabbalah study.

- One is represented by the great rabbi born in the year 1720 known as Rabbi Elijah (also known as the Vilna Gaon). He saw Kabbalah as a subject reserved for study only by the best students.

- The other is represented by the great rabbi born around the same time, in 1698, known as Rabbi Israel (also known as the Baal Shem Tov). The thrust of his teaching was to bring the wisdom and practice of Kabbalah to the average person, not just to the elite scholar. This effort is called *Hasidism*.

In this book, many of the sages that I quote and many of the Kabbalistic practices that I address come from Hasidism, which is basically the effort during the last few centuries within Judaism to bring Kabbalah to the masses. Because *Kabbalah For Dummies* is an effort to explain Kabbalah to as many people as possible, it's filled with teachings from Hasidism, which is Kabbalah for everyone.

✔ **Dates:** I don't use the abbreviations BC and AD to indicate dates in this book because these designations measure time in relation to Christian history. Rather, I use BCE, which means "Before the Common Era" and CE, which means "Common Era." For example, the year that Columbus discovered America would be indicated as 1492 CE.

✔ **Gender equality:** Religious groups throughout history have defined participatory roles for men and women in a number of ways. Throughout this book, I've tried to approach subjects from a starting point that assumes that both men and woman can participate in all Jewish rituals. However, it's important to note that the Kabbalistic tradition isn't gender neutral; it maintains that men and women are spiritually different. When men and women honor and celebrate these differences through practices and roles unique to each gender, they fully realize the deeper spiritual dimension of their lives and the unique contributions to the world that emanate from these different spiritual places.

✔ **Pronunciation of Hebrew words:** Many Hebrew words and phrases appear throughout this book, and because not everyone's familiar with the language, I've offered pronunciation help. The syllable that has the accent is always in *italics*. But you should be aware that there are two ways to pronounce many Hebrew words:

- **Ashkenazic:** This is the Eastern European pronunciation that's used in most Orthodox synagogues. An example is **Shabbos** (*shah*-bus; Sabbath), with the accent on the first syllable.

- **Sephardic:** This is the modern Israeli pronunciation that's used in most liberal synagogues in the United States. An example is **Shabbat** (shah-*baht;* Sabbath), with the accent on the second syllable.

As you can see from the examples, not only are the pronunciations of the sounds different, but the accented syllable is also different. It isn't unusual for someone today to bounce back and forth between pronunciations. In the traditional Jewish world I've live in for the past 25 years, pronunciation of Hebrew words is generally Ashkenazic. But the modern Israeli pronunciation also has a great influence, and some of my pronunciations reflect this. For example, I sometimes find myself saying both "Shabbos" and "Shabbat" on the Sabbath, sometimes within mere moments of each other. In this book, I mostly use the transliteration and pronunciation commonly used in Israel, but sometimes, especially if it has become common usage, I give the Ashkenazic pronunciation.

By the way, another example of varied pronunciation is the word "Kabbalah." The Ashkenazic pronunciation is kuh-*bah*-lah, whereas the modern Israeli pronunciation is kah-bah-*lah.*

What You're Not to Read

If you have the time and inclination to read this book from cover to cover, by all means, get to it! However, if you're only looking for the most helpful, most essential facts and explanations, you can skip the sidebars, which appear in shaded gray boxes throughout this book. They're interesting (I hope!) anecdotes and pieces of information that supplement the text but aren't essential for an understanding of the topics being explored.

Foolish Assumptions

When writing this book, I had to make some assumptions about you, dear reader. First off, I don't assume that you're Jewish, nor do I assume that you want to be. And although Kabbalah is just as much a spiritual practice as a spiritual theory, I don't assume that you want to engage in each and every practice.

Following are some additional assumptions I've made. If you fit into any of these categories, this book is for you:

- You've heard about Kabbalah and are curious about it, perhaps because some showbiz personality has said that he or she is studying it or because it was a part of your general education but you don't have a firm grasp of what it's all about.

- You want to know more about Kabbalah, whether you're religious or not.

- You know little or nothing about Jewish religious practice, which is really the framework of Kabbalah.

- Like so many people, you've tried to understand what life is all about, and you've heard that Kabbalah has its own approach to the big, eternal questions of life.

- You've heard about some things that the media claims are part of Kabbalah (like wearing a red string around your wrist or drinking Kabbalah water), and you want to know if there's any truth or authentic basis to these things.

- You're a spiritual seeker, and you've heard that Kabbalah is a spiritual approach to life.

- You know people who are "into Kabbalah" and you want to understand them better.

- You may or may not be Jewish, but you're curious about Jews who call themselves Hasidic, which means they live a religious lifestyle based on the principles and practices of Kabbalah.

- You've been told that Kabbalah is a secret tradition, and you want to know what the secret is all about.

- You're Jewish but feel that the Judaism you know is lacking in spirituality — and you've been led to believe that Kabbalah is the spiritual path (and sometimes even called the soul) of Judaism.

How This Book Is Organized

I organized this book so that you can skip around easily. In order to help you get in, get the information you need, and get out without reading cover to cover, I divided the book into parts that give you one piece of the Kabbalah picture at a time.

Part 1: So, What's the Big Secret? Unmasking Kabbalah

This part provides you with the basics. First, you get an overview of the entire subject, in particular its major ideas and concepts. Because Kabbalah has evolved over the centuries and is populated by many key teachers throughout the ages, a history of Kabbalah is a must. Although I've taken great pains to avoid technical language, Kabbalah, like every field of study, has its own unique terms and vocabulary. This part introduces these terms with clear explanations. And because so much misinformation floats around about Kabbalah, I explore and explain what Kabbalah isn't.

Part II: Cutting to the Core of Kabbalah

Every worldview, philosophy, and religion has assumptions, and Kabbalah is no exception. This part presents what I would say are the two major assumptions at the heart of Kabbalah: The world is in need of repair, and the human soul is eternal. These two assumptions also have a connection to each other: The work of the human soul is to use its body to repair the world. This part explores how Kabbalists participate in repairing the world as well as the nature and journey of the human soul.

Part III: Livin' La Vida Kabbalah

This part puts the theory of Kabbalah into practice. Kabbalah isn't just an abstract philosophy, and it isn't just a system of ideas. Kabbalah is a way of life. There are things Kabbalists do every day, every week, every year, and throughout their lives, from birth to death. These acts and others give expression to the profound and eternal ideas taught by the great sages of Kabbalah. The chapters in this part cover the major activities, celebrations, and rituals that make up the life of a Kabbalist.

Part IV: Fine-tuning the Essential Skills of the Kabbalist

In this part, I define and explore the two almost-constant activities of Kabbalists: study and prayer. Both activities are expressions of one's relationship to God; the study of the holy books of Kabbalah and the recitation of daily prayers define the ongoing conversation that Kabbalists have with God. This part concludes with an in-depth look at the Kabbalistic view of God, known to Kabbalists as the Infinite One.

Part V: The Part of Tens

Every *For Dummies* book has a Part of Tens. This part consists of interesting lists people, places, and myths related to Kabbalah. With so much misinformation floating around about Kabbalah, I take on the ten biggest myths circulating in books and in the media. I move on to well-known Kabbalists throughout the ages, of which the cream of the crop are easily identifiable. Even though the well-known artist, Madonna, whose work I enjoy and admire, doesn't belong in such a list, she's the first person who comes to mind for many people who know little about Kabbalah, so I discuss her in this part. And because there are many places around the globe of particular interest to Kabbalists, this part contains an enlightening Kabbalistic travelogue. I wrap up this collection of lists with my top recommendations of Kabbalistic books and authors.

Part VI: Appendixes

Here I've included a few more handy items that didn't really fit elsewhere in the book but are important just the same. Appendix A is a list of books and authors related to Kabbalah, Appendix B is a breakdown of the important characters in the Torah, and Appendix C is a convenient glossary of all things Kabbalah.

Icons Used in This Book

All *For Dummies* books feature icons (little pictures that grab your attention) in the margins to serve you well. Think of them as road signs pointing to different kinds of information in the chapters.

Kabbalistic ideas are often well-documented in holy books, but an essential transmission of Kabbalah moves from teacher to student. This icon alerts you to specific teachings that I've received from my Kabbalah teachers and that I want to share with you.

This icon alerts to you concepts, terms, and ideas that are of particular importance. Keep the points marked with this icon in mind, and you can't go wrong.

This icon points out helpful information that you can use to put Kabbalah to practice into your daily life. It also points out a good way to understand a particular concept.

This icon highlights pitfalls or misconceptions about Kabbalah. Be sure to read this information!

This icon highlights instances in which I quote directly from classic Kabbalistic sources. These sources are English translations of insights and observations made by some of the greatest sages in Jewish and, therefore, Kabbalistic history.

Where to Go from Here

The classic books of Kabbalah don't begin at the beginning; throughout the ages, students of Kabbalah have jumped into a holy book at any point and started swimming through it. In fact, when studying a book of Kabbalah, it often isn't until the second time around that the reader begins to really understand the depths of the text. Often, concepts build upon each other, and it isn't until a student grasps a certain idea that he or she can start building ideas upon ideas.

Kabbalah For Dummies works in a similar way — it doesn't necessarily begin at the beginning. Like Kabbalists throughout history, why not just jump in wherever you want to begin? Although I've tried to provide a useful introduction to the entire subject in Chapter 1, you can just look through the table of contents and pick out something of special interest. For example, if you've studied Eastern religions, you know that reincarnation is a fundamental notion, and so you may be interested in the Kabbalistic take on the topic in Chapter 7.

Bob Dylan once wrote the lyric that he doesn't want to learn something that he has to "unlearn." Unfortunately, many false notions and half truths about Kabbalah circulate these days, so you may want to first clean the slate and "unlearn" what you've heard by turning to Chapter 2, which tells you what Kabbalah *isn't*. And you may want to supplement that information with Chapter 17's take on myths about studying Kabbalah.

But wherever you begin, get ready to enter a profound worldview that has inspired and sustained countless spiritual seekers since time immemorial.

Chapter 1

What *Is* Kabbalah?

Kabbalah is the part of Judaism that deals with the understanding of God, Creation, the relationship between God and God's Creation, and the nature and way of the soul. Kabbalah is concerned with questions of good and evil, death and the afterlife, and the spiritual aspects of existence. It's often described as *Jewish mysticism,* but it goes far beyond the mystical aspects of Judaism. Kabbalah is central to Jewish belief and its spiritual practices.

Contrary to popular belief, Kabbalah isn't a book. I've heard that common misconception time and time again. When I worked in a bookstore years ago, when I was a librarian, and even in recent days, I've been asked if there are any good translations of the book "Kabbalah." Some people think that just like you can study the Bible, you can study the book of Kabbalah. It's not a book, but its moral, spiritual, and ethical teachings can be found in the great spiritual books of the Jewish people.

In this chapter, I define the word "Kabbalah," allow you to get some of Kabbalah's key concepts under your belt, and explore some of the ways people today are into the subject. But perhaps the most important point that this chapter establishes, and that this book is about, is that Kabbalah is best understood by *doing* Kabbalah, not just reading about it.

Getting to Know Kabbalah, "The Received Tradition"

The word "Kabbalah," like every Hebrew word, is based on a *root*. The root usually consists of three Hebrew letters that serve as the basis for many words. Each root has a primary meaning; the meaning of the root of "Kabbalah" is "to receive."

What is the person who's engaged in the study of Kabbalah receiving? The answer is both simple and, in a sense, impossible. Kabbalists receive knowledge of God and guidance for living.

Taking the root meaning a step further, the word "Kabbalah" also means "the received tradition." I once asked one of my teachers how to perform a certain ritual. When he explained it to me, I told him that I had heard that it was done differently. He replied, "You can do it the other way too, but the way I do it is the way my teacher taught me. That's *my* Kabbalah!"

In order to receive the tradition of Kabbalah, one must open himself and make room within himself so that he's able to receive the teachings.

Is Kabbalah Jewish mysticism?

The biggest myth about Kabbalah, and one that has remarkably snuck into the definition of Kabbalah by most writers and teachers who look at Kabbalah from the outside, not the inside, is that Kabbalah is Jewish mysticism. As Professor Joseph Dan, one of the world's leading authorities on Kabbalah explains, until the 19th century there were no "Jewish mystics."

The term "mysticism" isn't even a part of Jewish culture or language. The term mysticism was borrowed from a term found in Christian thought, that of *unio mystica,* the mystical union with God. Some scholars thought that some of the central ideas of Kabbalah were parallel to this Christian notion, and so the term "Jewish mysticism" evolved and attached itself to Kabbalah.

For example, one of the primary uses of the term "mysticism" is that it describes notions and experiences that can't be put into words or language. Because Kabbalah stresses that, ultimately, God can't be described, the use of the term "mysticism" became a common one. Mysticism is also used when referring to experiences that are beyond the senses. Here too, because Kabbalah often deals with matters of faith, it seems to be useful to say that Kabbalah is "Jewish mysticism." In this book, I barely use the term "mysticism" because the Kabbalistic literature itself never uses it.

Kabbalah is Jewish theology

In a real sense, the history of Kabbalah is the history of Judaism — the two can't be separated. Throughout the centuries, the greatest sages of Judaism have been serious students of Kabbalah. You may be wondering, "If Kabbalah and Judaism are part of the same thing, what's the difference between them? Why is there even a need for the word 'Kabbalah,' let alone a book about Kabbalah? Why isn't _Kabbalah For Dummies_ simply a book about Judaism?"

Throughout this chapter, I explore the idea that Kabbalah is a _theological process central to Judaism_. That is, Kabbalah is the way in which Jewish tradition tries to grasp the Infinite and tries to communicate to each generation the ways that the sages have understood that human life — in relation to the creator — should be lived.

Asking life's ultimate questions

Kabbalah is concerned with life's ultimate questions. For example, when I look at the world, I see so much suffering of all kinds, and I'm left to wonder why God would have created a world with so much suffering. It often seems that good people suffer and that, too often, people who do evil thrive. The tradition within Judaism that deals with such issues and questions is Kabbalistic tradition.

When people come to realize that life is really a temporary journey and that life can end in a painful and difficult way, they're prompted to ask what this life is all about and wonder how this seemingly crazy design makes any sense. Kabbalah is the part of Jewish existence and belief that ponders such questions and offers answers to such immense riddles (see Chapters 5 and 6 for more about this).

Taking on the spiritual level of existence

Kabbalah is that part of Judaism that explores the nature of life and the soul and the meaning of human existence. It comes into play when people begin to perceive that they aren't just flesh and blood but seem to have a spirit, a spark of life, an aspect that rocks and minerals don't have. Kabbalists detect that the human experience may be profoundly different from that of plants and animals thanks to free will and one's consciousness of oneself. Kabbalists also realize that, as humans, they not only have bodies that are temporary but also have souls that have a greater longevity than physical things.

Kabbalah tries to perceive the metaphysics of life and tries to teach people how to use the spiritual forces that exist and how to use them wisely. Kabbalists notice that life and human existence seem to contain some working metaphysical principles, in which some things seem good and healthy while others seem bad and destructive, and in which some things seem to lift humans to sublime heights while others seem to degrade human lives.

Studying Kabbalah: First do it, then understand it

A fundamental principle among those individuals throughout the centuries who have lived their lives based on the teachings of Kabbalah is that it's impossible to grasp these teachings unless you participate in them.

Take a kiss, for example. You can read about kissing, study scientific books about kissing, understand all the facial muscles needed to form a kiss, and even watch Andy Warhol's film "Kiss," which has extreme close-ups of people kissing, but the only real way to know — to truly know — about kissing is to kiss!

The notion that one can't have external knowledge of Kabbalah goes back to a famous verse (famous among Kabbalists, that is) found in the Holy Scriptures, in the book of Exodus. The text describes Moses reading to the people the teachings that he received from God on Mount Sinai. Upon hearing the words spoken by Moses, the people said, "All that the Lord spoke we will do and we will hear" (Exodus 24:7). Jewish commentators say that this means, "We will do these things first, and afterwards we will understand them."

This approach is contrary to what people normally do; often, one first learns something and *then* does it. But not with Kabbalah. To really know Kabbalah, you have to participate.

Nevertheless, a person who wants to learn about Kabbalah can begin to study the subject without fully jumping in. But out of respect to the subject and in order to be true to its teachings, the person has to begin by acknowledging that studying about Kabbalah without participating in its teachings has its limitations.

Of course, you could say that about practically any activity. For example, you could learn quite a bit about playing chess without ever playing the game itself. But true knowledge of chess, or any subject, requires participation. Kabbalah takes this phenomenon seriously, and I feel obligated to make that point clear from the beginning.

Hey, What Are the Big Ideas?

You can't adequately summarize Kabbalah in a few sentences. On the contrary, in Kabbalah you have to build ideas, putting them together to form larger ideas. Comparing Kabbalah to math, first you learn how to add and subtract; then you learn how to multiply and divide. After that, you can start learning simple algebra, and then you can go on to advanced algebra, and so on.

The first, foremost, and central idea of Kabbalah is God. For Kabbalists, by the way, God is hardly a human idea. In fact, a Kabbalist would say that humans are an "idea" of God. How to "know" God is the primary goal of the Kabbalist. On a course of knowing, or trying to know, God are several key concepts that form the foundation of Jewish theology, known as Kabbalah.

Why did God create the world?

The question often asked is "Why did God create the world?" The great sages of Kabbalah point out that God surely didn't create the world because God needed the world. To say that God needs something implies that there's some deficiency in God, and one of Kabbalistic tradition's fundamental notions about God is that God is whole, perfect, flawless, and in need of nothing. By the way, according to Kabbalah, God didn't create the world in one moment and then stop. Rather, Kabbalah teaches that God continues to create the world every moment. Creation is an ongoing divine activity. (For more on this topic, check out Chapter 4.)

Why, then, does God create the world? As a gesture of love and because God wants humans to *receive*. Kabbalists say that God wants humans to receive the greatest pleasure possible: knowledge of God.

"Knowledge of God?" you may be asking. *"That's* the greatest pleasure?" The teachings of Kabbalah emphatically declare that indeed the greatest possible pleasure is to know God — to really know God.

The point of life is getting to know God, even if it's impossible

Kabbalah is the system of beliefs, ideas, and actions contained in Jewish tradition that help people truly know the Divine. If you don't recognize a problem at this point, you should. You've just collided with a paradox.

Now, Kabbalah is filled with paradoxes. A *paradox* is a statement that appears to contradict itself. But a paradox isn't an absurdity; it can contain awesome truths. So, the first paradox to consider is the Kabbalistic view that, although the greatest pleasure is to know God, knowledge of God is impossible.

Perhaps it's more accurate to say that *complete* knowledge of God is impossible. What Kabbalistic tradition provides are ways to glimpse God, and even a tiny glimpse contains profound pleasure.

One of Kabbalah's primary principles is an unbridgeable gap between God and humans. Although a person can make contact with God, ultimately this contact can't take place solely through the efforts of the person. No matter how hard a person tries, he or she can't reach God. Kabbalah teaches that the gap can indeed be crossed, but *only* by God. When that gap is crossed, it's because God reaches out.

It's all about receiving

God makes the gesture to reach out to a person, and it's the person's job to receive (remember that "Kabbalah" *means* "to receive"). The rituals, customs, laws, and activities of the person who lives according to Kabbalistic tradition are intended to prepare that person to receive God, to receive knowledge of God, and to receive the greatest possible pleasure.

Kabbalah is the tradition received from the Jewish sages in order to help people perceive and live in the fullness of the presence of God.

You may say, "Knowledge of God isn't the greatest pleasure." Some people think that having lots of money is the greatest pleasure. Others may think that sex is the greatest pleasure. Still others may feel that fame or food or any number of things are among the greatest pleasures of life. But Kabbalah teaches that the most profound source of pleasure is to know God.

Preparing to know God

How does one prepare to receive the knowledge of God? Many have taught that the first step is to make room for this knowledge. If one is all closed down or filled up, then knowledge of God has no way to enter and no place to reside.

If a person holds on tightly to the ideas and beliefs that he or she currently has, it's usually impossible to let new ones in. But the biblical view — first do and then understand — is a useful approach. There's no need to do everything and surely no need to do everything at once, but students of Kabbalah have found that by participating in a little study, prayer, and ritual observance, the doors begin to open, and true learning can take place.

A few more key Kabbalah concepts

The following is a list of other major concepts which require in-depth study in order to benefit from Kabbalah as a system of daily practices:

- **God is infinite:** Kabbalah understands God to be a perfect, supreme being who's infinite and both formless and changeless. You can find out more about the infinite nature of God in Chapter 16.

- **Divine contraction:** One of the questions that Kabbalah tries to answer is "If God is infinite, where is there room for God's creation?" The Kabbalistic term for the process of God contracting in order to make room for Creation is **tzimtzum** (*tzim*-tzoom). The Kabbalistic view of creation imagines that God prompted an absence of the Divine, which resulted in a "space" for creation to happen.

- **Ten utterances:** Kabbalah teaches that God creates the world through the ten utterances, which form, by their infinite combinations, all the detail of existence. These ten utterances are also congruent with another major concept, the ten *sefirot* (see Chapter 4).

  It's absolutely impossible to study Kabbalah without a grasp of the ten *sefirot*. The ten *sefirot* are ten divine powers or channels or flows of divine plenty that continuously create and nourish creation. For the Kabbalist, the mastery of the ten *sefirot* is a major life task and a major tool used to connect with God. The ten *sefirot* flow downward from God to God's creation, and human actions send the flow back "up" to the Divine.

- **The breaking of the vessels:** The Kabbalistic concept of creation includes **shevirat ha-kelim** (sheh-*vee*-raht hah-*kay*-leem; the breaking of the vessels). Some refer to it as the great catastrophic event that occurred when God poured infinite divine light into vessels that were unable to contain this light (see Chapter 5).

  The shards produced by this shattering are the stuff of creation. The divine light is embedded within every aspect of creation, and the task of humans is to release the Divine that resides in all of creation through good deeds, righteous living, and spiritual acts.

- **Tikkun:** Following from the notion of the shattering of the vessels is the Kabbalistic concept of **Tikkun** (tee-*koon*; repair). Tikkun is the purpose of human existence and the way to come to know God. Instruction for this repair is found in the Torah and specifically in the *mitzvot,* which are guidelines for healthy living found in the Torah.

- **Halachah:** Halachah (hah-lah-*khah;* the way to walk) is the sum of the laws and instruction of the Torah that will make the necessary repairs. Humans must participate in the repairing of the world and must learn the proper ways to do so in order to separate good from evil and ultimately extinguish the evil that exists in the universe. Every human being is required to do his or her part in perfecting of the world (see the chapters in Part III).

✔ **Mitzvot:** A **mitzvah** (*mitz*-vah) is a divine commandment, and "mitzvot" is the plural form of the word. These commandments are divided into two groups: positive commandments describing what one is supposed to do, and negative commandments describing what one is supposed to refrain from doing. For example, giving charity is a positive command-ment; "Do not murder" is a negative commandment.

Jewish tradition teaches that 613 commandments are found in the Five Books of Moses. But as it's taught, this number is deceptive because there are actually thousands of teachings in Jewish tradition helping us align with our highest possible selves. All commandments have two purposes: to make people conscious of God as the one and only reality and to repair the world. I discuss mitzvot in the chapters of Part III.

✔ **Everything is for the best:** One of the most difficult and profound teachings in all Kabbalistic tradition is the view that everything that happens is for the best. *(What?? Even the Holocaust? Even the death of an innocent child?)* Kabbalists live in a paradox: On the one hand, people have an obligation to repair the world, to help relieve suffering, to work to advance medical science, to cure diseases, to fight evil, and to mourn the dead. On the other hand, people have an equal obligation to cultivate the belief that ultimately the world is in God's hands, God knows what's happening, and everything has a purpose beyond anything humans can possibly imagine. For more on this topic, turn to Chapter 5.

✔ **Souls:** Kabbalah teaches that humans live in two realms: the physical world and the spiritual world. Humans are unique in this way, being the only creatures that partake of both realms. The human struggle is to make sure that one's body is the tool or instrument of the soul. The body should be ruled by the spirit. Kabbalah teaches that the soul exists before the body, and after the body dies, the soul continues on its spiri-tual journeys — sometimes by being reincarnated into another body in order to have another go at it. I examine the nature of bodies and souls in Chapter 6 and reincarnation in Chapter 7.

A Constant Search for God

The first thing Kabbalah students learn about God is that God is beyond any conception that a person can possibly imagine. As one of my teachers taught, if you think you grasp God, one thing is certain: You're wrong. In a sense, the Kabbalistic definition of God is that which is beyond any possible human conception.

Nevertheless, Kabbalah teaches that the human task in life is to look for God, reach out to God, and learn from the great spiritual masters of Jewish tradition how to undertake the search for God. Ultimately, God makes the contact with humans, but great importance lies in the human effort and reaching.

Missing the forest for the trees

Within Judaism are seemingly countless practices and rituals — things to do and things to refrain from doing. To an outsider, these dos and don'ts seem almost like a petty list of unrelated commands. In fact, many Jews alienate themselves from the practices of Judaism because they seem like such senseless details. But the situation can be compared to looking at trees: If you get up close to a tree, you see a huge number of little details and details within details. However, if you focus on the details of just one tree, you miss the magnificence of the forest.

The laws of Judaism are deeply connected to Kabbalah. The most well-known and authoritative Code of Jewish Law was complied by one of the most revered Kabbalists of Jewish history, and many people don't realize that every page of the Code of Jewish Law has a Kabbalistic commentary that spells out the spiritual meaning of each of law.

God is in the details

From awakening each morning until falling asleep, through the course of the day, week, year, and one's life, the Kabbalistic lifestyle offers countless opportunities and methods to connect with a consciousness of God.

The Kabbalist wants to be aware of God at all times. Kabbalah connects a person to God while eating, working, and doing every other human activity. The goal is to constantly have God in one's mind and heart because God is the center of existence.

A Kabbalist defines his or her life as a relationship with God. All other relationships, whether they be with friends, partners, parents, children, neighbors, employers, or even Kabbalah teachers, are seen as temporary. The only permanent relationship, the only relationship that truly defines who a person is, is the relationship he or she has with God.

Who Can Study Kabbalah?

Kabbalah is a Jewish tradition. In fact, Kabbalah *is* Jewish tradition. Although some have tried to represent Kabbalah as a philosophy or approach to life that's independent of Judaism, that simply isn't accurate. And it's not only inaccurate, it's impossible.

Every great sage of Kabbalah throughout the ages has taught that Kabbalah and Jewish tradition are part of the same whole. You can certainly extract ideas from Kabbalistic tradition, separating them from anything Jewish, but what you're left holding just isn't true Kabbalah. Just as a few Buddhist teachings don't represent the rich and ancient tradition of Buddhism, the gathering of a few notions familiar to Kabbalists in past centuries doesn't make up the tradition of Kabbalah.

True, some books written by Jewish teachers and even contemporary rabbis relegate Kabbalah to some fringe of Jewish history. You can find books written by teachers who aren't Jewish that claim that Kabbalah isn't a specifically Jewish phenomenon. You also can find books and teachers who claim that one can understand Kabbalah and even be a Kabbalist without participating in Jewish life, rituals, and celebrations.

But the simple fact is that Kabbalah is the soul of Jewish life. Every great Kabbalist and authority on Kabbalah for centuries has lived life as a Jew profoundly involved in Jewish study, Jewish prayer, Jewish ritual, and Jewish life.

Do you have to be Jewish?

One principle of Kabbalah is that Kabbalah and Jewish law are inextricably linked. One can't be a Kabbalist and abandon the guidelines for a Jewish life. Without that flow of rituals and practices, the container necessary for the profound insights of Kabbalah is simply missing One cannot be a Kabbalist and ignore Jewish ritual. To the Kabbalist, Jewish ritual without Kabbalah is an empty shell, and Kabbalah without Jewish practice is incomplete and a mere splinter of something whole and complete.

Of course, you don't have to be Jewish to *study* Kabbalah. On the contrary, in today's world, the wisdom of the great spiritual traditions is, for the first time, universally available. In the past, you may have been able to find a book here or there or spend some time with an occasional teacher from a religious or spiritual tradition that wasn't your own. But now, books, Web sites, and ease of travel afford the opportunity to encounter the world's great religious and spiritual traditions. There's certainly nothing wrong with wanting to nourish oneself at the watering hole of any source of wisdom.

It's also perfectly fine to borrow an idea or integrate a piece of wisdom from Kabbalah (or any tradition, for that matter) into your own life. When someone who isn't Jewish approaches Kabbalah, expresses an interest in its wisdom, and even incorporates that wisdom into his or her life, it's a natural phenomenon.

But it's important to know that every great Kabbalist, every important book on Kabbalah, and every law, ritual, or practice of Kabbalah that exists comes from Jews who are speaking to Jews. Kabbalah and Judaism are unlike some religious traditions that teach that everyone needs to believe what they believe and unlike many spiritual traditions or teachers who think they have a monopoly on wisdom and truth. Kabbalah is a legacy of the spiritual tradition of the Jewish people, and central to the spiritual culture of the Jewish family.

Can an atheist be a Kabbalist?

Although Kabbalah is primarily concerned with the human relationship to God, there's nothing inappropriate about someone who's a nonbeliever, or even a confirmed atheist, spending time trying to grasp the basic ideas of Kabbalah.

A well-known statement made to atheists is, "The God that you don't believe in, well, I don't believe in that God either." In other words, a person may state that he or she is a nonbeliever, but when a believer explores just what it is that the nonbeliever doesn't believe in, the believer finds that he or she also doesn't believe in that conception of God.

Some people grow up with an image of God as a man with a beard sitting on a heavenly throne. Others grow up with an idea of God as an angry, vengeful, strict dictator who punishes people with fire and brimstone. All kinds of ideas about God float around; humans are inherently seekers, and Kabbalists are full-time God seekers. But these conceptions of God all too often chase people away from God, and result in a wholesale rejection of the study of religion.

My teacher points out that many people who claim to be atheists are really not atheists at all. They simply reject old-fashioned and inaccurate views of God. They may not believe in an angry God or a vengeful God or the old man on the heavenly throne God, but they may have more in common with the Kabbalist and his or her beliefs about the "unknowable God" than they might think (see Chapter 16 for more on God as unknowable).

Different Approaches to the Study of Kabbalah

Until recently historians, including some Jewish historians, have been down-right hostile to Kabbalah, claiming that it belongs in the folklore department or as is mere superstition. Some have gone as far as to completely ignore Kabbalistic tradition in their writings.

What is the Torah?

The answer to that question isn't simple, but it's surely worth exploring and is actually crucial to an understanding of Kabbalah itself.

The Hebrew word "Torah" has the same root as the Hebrew word **hora'ah** (hoe-rah-*ah*; instruction or teaching), and "Torah" is used in a number of ways.

✔ Torah is the Five Books of Moses, the written revelation that Moses received from God at Mount Sinai. Although one can find the text (called the **Chumash** [choo-*mahsh*; five]) today in printed book form, it most commonly appears in the form of a handwritten scroll of ink on parchment that's found in the sanctuaries of synagogues throughout the world.

✔ Torah is the Holy Scriptures of the Jewish people. Outside of the Jewish world, these Holy Scriptures are sometimes referred to as the Pentateuch (five books), or the Jewish Scriptures, and sometimes the term "Old Testament" is used by those who imply a New Testament has supplanted the original.

✔ Torah is the term used to refer to the entire body of Jewish spiritual literature, including well-known works such as the Talmud and the Zohar as well as the thousands of other works written by Jewish spiritual teachers throughout the centuries. A seeker who says that he or she is studying Torah may mean the study of any work of Jewish literature that continues the endless chain of religious tradition growing out of the original revelation at Mount Sinai.

✔ Torah is what a Jewish spiritual teacher rooted in tradition teaches *tomorrow*. This interpretation of the word "Torah" reflects the traditional Jewish belief that Torah is timeless, eternal wisdom.

Throughout the ages, books that have been written by great sages sooner or later join the chain of Torah literature. These works don't become a part of that chain through a vote but rather by their wide acceptance among the Jewish people in general and the sages in particular.

In other words, regardless of whether the Zohar was written in the second century by the Talmudic sage Rabbi Shimon bar Yochai or in the 12th century by Rabbi Moses de Leon, the important fact is that every Kabbalist who ever lived studies the Zohar, studies commentaries on the Zohar, and in doing so connects with the chain of people who recognize the Zohar as an important Kabbalistic text.

The study of Kabbalah during the past century has been dominated by academics. (In the 20th century, the academic study of Kabbalah has centered around the work of Professor Gershom Sholem whose work has dominated the field for decades.) Academics often focus upon questions of history, such as "Who wrote this or that book?" or "Who influenced whom?" In addition, it's a general opinion that many of the academics who have studied and written about Kabbalah in recent generations have done so as scientists (from a secular perspective), not as active participants in the religious tradition of Judaism. The weakness of this approach, of course, is that Kabbalah, as I indicate earlier in this chapter, can't be adequately understood from the outside.

Traditional Jews generally aren't as interested in a scientific, scholarly study of Kabbalah. Rather, for the Kabbalist who is immersed in a traditional religious life, Kabbalah fits unconditionally into the timeless unfolding of God's revelation.

A closer look at the different ways in which Kabbalah is approached depending one's bias can be illustrated by the question, "Who wrote the Zohar?" The Zohar, which I cover in Chapter 13, is probably the most well-known and important book of Kabbalistic teachings. Here are three different approaches to answering that question:

- Traditionalists claim that the Zohar was written by Rabbi Shimon bar Yochai, a sage who lived in the second century and who's said to have written the book during the 13 years he spent in a cave hiding from the Romans. Many centuries of Kabbalists have accepted this view that the Zohar was written by Rabbi Shimon bar Yochai.

- Academic scholars say that the Zohar was written by Rabbi Moses de Leon in the 12th century. These scholars compare the writing style of the Zohar to other writing of Rabbi Moses de Leon and use additional academic tools to draw their conclusions. They reject the traditionalist approach.

- Mainly in the traditionalist camp but with a slightly different approach are those who don't care about questions of history too much and don't really know whether the author of the Zohar was Rabbi Moses de Leon or Rabbi Shimon bar Yochai or someone else. People who follow this approach simply join the countless students of Kabbalah throughout the centuries who study the Zohar without questioning its source and participate in a Kabbalistic exploration of life.

The study of Kabbalah is the study of timeless and eternal wisdom. Kabbalah is grounded in a part of a more general notion that Kabbalists call *Torah* (in the sense that a generic meaning of the word Torah is "instruction." As long as there has been a notion of Kabbalah, there has been "the study of Torah." Basically, anyone who is studying Kabbalah is actually a student of Torah and, in fact, would be more apt to state that he or she is a student of Torah than a student of Kabbalah.

Picking a Kabbalah that Works for You

In the year 70 CE, a cataclysm of vast proportions occurred in Jewish history. The destruction of the Holy Temple in Jerusalem by the Roman Empire still reverberates in Jewish life today. One of the results of this terrible event was the end of any central authority among the Jewish people.

With the destruction of the Temple came the end of the highest court in Jewish life, the Sanhedrin. This court, which was similar to the Supreme Court of the United States but with far more authority, decided major issues for the Jewish community worldwide. Among its powers was the authority to ordain rabbis. Since the fall of the Sanhedrin, there has been no accepted singular authority within Jewish life.

As a result, controversies within Jewish communal life went unresolved, splits occurred, differences of opinion and differing approaches proliferated, and significant disagreements on all kinds of matters arose. For example, Jewish life in the United States today contains four different *movements* representing, in some cases, vastly different beliefs.

Not only does Judaism have four major movements — Orthodox, Conservative, Reconstructionist, and Reform — but each movement is divided into different divisions. For instance, within the Orthodox world, one finds Hasidic Jews and non-Hasidic Jews. And the newest movement within Jewish life, Jewish Renewal, defines itself in part as a worldwide, transdenominational movement grounded in Judaism's prophetic and mystical traditions.

Note: In this book, I draw heavily upon Hasidism because the Hasidic movement has been, for the past few centuries, the great popularizer of Kabbalah and because it is within the Hasidic world today that the most complete form of Kabbalah is practiced. In addition, Hasidism is the most rapidly growing movement in the Jewish world, and its influence on all the other movements is clear and significant. While Hasidism is a major influence on the other movements, the opposite is not true: Hasidism is not being influenced by the other movements.

Today, those who want to pursue the study of Kabbalah have many options available.

A person who wants to study Kabbalah need not become a member of the Hasidic community or the Jewish Renewal world or pursue the offerings of the Kabbalah Centre or a university course. Many available books written for laypeople and scholars can contribute to a deep understanding of the Kabbalistic way. Nothing, however, is better than locating an authentic teacher (see Chapter 14) and becoming a student of both the theory and practice of Kabbalah.

Hasidism

Founded by Rabbi Israel (known as the Baal Shem Tov; see Chapter 18) in the early 18th century, **Hasidism** (*khah*-sid-ism) is a movement within Jewish life that seeks to bring the wisdom of Kabbalah to the masses. (The word "hasid" means pious one.) Hasidism began with its leader and his disciples, but over the generations, the movement has splintered into many Hasidic groups, each led by a leader known as a **rebbe** (*reh*-bee; spiritual mentor).

Usually, when a rebbe dies, his son, son-in-law, or another person selected by the rebbe or the community to succeed him becomes the spiritual guide of the group. Today, many Hasidic groups have headquarters or branches throughout the world, but many are found in Israel and New York City.

The Hasidic group most open to and even encouraging of newcomers is commonly known as either **Chabad** (khah-*bahd*), which is an acronym of three important terms in Kabbalah (see Chapter 3) or **Lubavitch** (loo-*bah*-vitch), after the town in Russia where the movement flowered generations ago. The lifestyles, practices, rituals, and beliefs of Chasidim today most resemble those of Kabbalists throughout the centuries.

Orthodox (non-Hasidic) Judaism

Whereas Kabbalah is openly studied in Hasidic communities, many people mistakenly think that non-Hasidic Orthodox Jews don't study Kabbalah. Actually, the average Orthodox Jew is discouraged from serious study of Kabbalah, but the most brilliant students usually are encouraged to delve into the teachings of Kabbalah. Regardless, most Orthodox Jews participate in many Kabbalistic rituals even though they may be unaware that the rituals originated among Kabbalists. More important, essentially, the basic theology accepted by Orthodox Jews is Kabbalah, although again many Orthodox Jews are unaware of its Kabbalistic roots.

Jewish Renewal

Jewish Renewal was founded in 1962 by Rabbi Zalman Schachter-Shalomi (also known as Reb Zalman), a traditionally trained Chasidic rabbi, and led by an organization called the Aleph Alliance for Jewish Renewal.

At the heart of Jewish Renewal is the notion that the generation following the destruction of European Jewry, when one out of every three Jews in the world was murdered during the Holocaust, is a rebuilding generation. One way to rebuild, of course, is to mimic the old ways and try to duplicate what was lost. This approach has been referred to as *restorative*.

Reb Zalman's approach to rebuilding is a radical one: Rather than restore Judaism to the old ways, he suggested a *renewal* of Judaism. That is, he called for a Judaism that understands the essences of the timeless teachings and is willing to find new forms of expression for those teachings in a language and style that fits with more modern sensibilities. One major trend in Jewish Renewal, for example, is egalitarianism, in which gender roles are obliterated and both genders have equal access to communal roles and ritual practices.

The Aleph Alliance for Jewish Renewal describes itself as the core institution in the Jewish Renewal movement. In addition to its publications, conferences, and classes, Aleph trains and ordains Jewish Renewal rabbis, cantors and Rabbinic pastors many of whom draw heavily upon Kabbalistic teachings. Although the vast majority of its members as well as those who affiliate with Jewish Renewal in one way or another (taking classes, attending conferences, reading its literature, and so on.) don't not lead traditional Jewish lifestyles and aren't usually participating in the formal requirements of Jewish law, many individuals who are connected in one way or another with Jewish Renewal find themselves increasingly involved with traditional Jewish practices normal to the life of a traditional Kabbalist.

Jewish Renewal has inspired many gifted teachers and has ordained many Jewish Renewal rabbis who are devoted to grasping the teachings of Kabbalah and integrating these teachings into their lives and the lives of their students. Dozens of Jewish Renewal communities of varying sizes and levels of Jewish observance exist throughout the world.

The Kabbalah Centre

The Kabbalah Centre was founded in 1969 by Rabbi Philip Berg, author of many introductory books on Kabbalah, and his wife Karen.

Drawing upon the wisdom of Kabbalah, the Kabbalah Centre and its teachers have generated a program of publishing and classes that urge Jews and others to drink from the waters of Kabbalistic tradition.

The Kabbalah Centre has received much publicity in recent years, due in large part to several high-profile celebrities (most notably the singer and actress Madonna) who have affiliated with the Kabbalah Centre and allow it to be known that they are students of Rabbi Berg and his disciples.

University and general study

Most major universities have Jewish studies departments, and an increasing number of those departments offer courses in Kabbalah. Of course, these classes are directed at neither the believer nor the practitioner. As I explain earlier in this chapter, from a Kabbalistic viewpoint, the limitation of an academic study of Kabbalah is that Kabbalah is bound up in the *practice* of Kabbalah.

Nevertheless, many excellent scholars have written books on various aspects of Kabbalah that surely aid the sincere student in an understanding of what Kabbalah is all about. Notable among these scholars are Joseph Dan and Moshe Idel, each of whom have contributed tremendous understanding of Kabbalah to those who dedicate themselves to studying their work.

Chapter 2

Magic, Mishegas, and Other Things that Kabbalah Isn't

I once attended a Jewish history lecture, and the speaker said, "Kabbalah is just **mishegas**" (pronounced mih-shih-*gahs;* a Yiddish word for craziness). But Kabbalah has gotten a bad rap, starting with the word "Kabbalah" itself. The English word "cabal" comes from the word "Kabbalah" and is defined as a secret clique that seeks power usually through intrigue. The word "cabal," by the way, was popularized in England around 1673 as a handy acronym for five ministers of King Charles II (Clifford, Arlington, Buckingham, Ashley, and Lauderdale) who were seen as a threat to the power of the throne and the monarchy. So for centuries, the word "cabal" has influenced the popular image of Kabbalah; people often think of Kabbalah as some kind of secretive philosophy of the Jews, but there's really no truth to that.

More people have learned about the word "Kabbalah" in the last few years than ever before, thanks in part to various famous personalities who've taken up the study of Kabbalah, but that doesn't mean that everything you hear about Kabbalah is true. In this chapter, I explain what Kabbalah isn't as a way of clarifying what it actually is.

Setting the Record Straight

Kabbalah has been misunderstood and distorted over the years for many reasons, including the following:

- Until the 1700s, Kabbalah was mainly studied by a few elite scholars. Everyone else had to speculate about it.

- Beginning in the 1500s, Christian scholars borrowed certain concepts and terms from Kabbalah and superimposed Christian theology onto it, resulting in what's often referred to as *Christian Cabala*.

- The study of alchemy borrowed some concepts from Kabbalah. As alchemy received its share of criticism and skepticism, so did Kabbalah.

- As with the sciences in general, there is a risk when a pure science is popularized. The popularization of most subjects usually ends up with lots of distortions.

- Kabbalah speculates about metaphysical rather than physical matters, and metaphysical matters are often rejected and scorned by rationalists. Many modern, so-called "rational" thinkers are embarrassed by such speculations.

So with all these factors contributing to the misunderstanding of Kabbalah, I want to take some time to set the record straight (or a least set it straighter) on what Kabbalah is and what it isn't.

The long way is shorter

Some people prefer to go to Kabbalistic texts to grab at esoteric, practical techniques in order to get a quick spiritual fix, while avoiding the demanding disciplines and commitments that authentic Kabbalah requires. This distortion has resulted in many people thinking that Kabbalah is really all about magic, prolonged sessions of silent meditation, chanting Hebrew words for long periods of time, and wearing good luck charms. These techniques certainly aren't nonexistent in Jewish history, but if you want to learn about Kabbalah, they are the wrong places to look to build a foundation for your spiritual practice.

Many masters of Kabbalah have pointed to a profound teaching that is found in the Talmud that "the short way is longer" and "the long way is shorter." In other words, when you want to take a shortcut, you often get lost. But the tried and true long way actually ends up being shorter than the short way. Too many modern seekers hope for a shortcut and never really get on the Kabbalistic path. It's my hope that this book will serve you well and will provide a strong foundation if you want to further your study of Kabbalah.

What Kabbalah isn't

Because you're going to be dealing with the "isn't" part of Kabbalah more often than not, at least at first, you need to know the following:

- Kabbalah isn't pop psychology or New Age philosophy.
- Kabbalah isn't superstition, a collection of secret formulas, or a bunch of mystical incantations.
- Kabbalah isn't a fad. Though it may seem like one because of the sudden rise in popularity and exposure, it's actually been around and developing for thousands of years.
- Kabbalah isn't an easy path to the eternal bliss or enlightenment.

What Kabbalah is

Now that you have a better understand of what Kabbalah isn't, it's probably a good time to summarize what Kabbalah is. Kabbalah is

- The theology of the Jewish people
- The study of the ways the great sages of Judaism understand how the universe works
- An exploration of the most profound wisdom of Jewish tradition
- The abstract understanding of the meaning and purpose of life according to Jewish tradition
- The Jewish speculations about God and God's relationship with Creation
- The abstract underpinning of Jewish law
- The explanations of the meaning and purpose of Jewish ritual practice
- The study the Jewish tradition that describes the building blocks of creation
- The Jewish study of the unseen laws that govern the universe
- The Jewish understanding of the structure and workings of the human soul

Trying to Figure Out Who's Legit and Who's Not

In the world of Kabbalah, there are individuals and groups who represent themselves as teachers of Kabbalah but whose authenticity and motives are questionable. Kabbalah has drifted into the hands of some of the snake oil peddlers of the world because Kabbalah has been distorted into a quick-fix technique. A quick and easy road to enlightenment is a perfect commodity for charlatans to try to sell. Separating legitimate students and teachers from the rest isn't an easy task, but allow me to try to give you some advice and guidance.

In the long run, I believe that providing you with some advice for how to go about making your own evaluation of Kabbalists is more useful that rattling off a list of names I do or don't endorse. The following points are actually based on the advice of one of my teachers. Here's what to look for and what to avoid. A teacher should have

- ✔ A broad and deep knowledge of the subject

- ✔ Humility and the ability to say "I don't know." (My teacher taught me to run away quickly when a teacher seems to know every answer to every question.) Sometimes the best teachers are reluctant teachers, and the converse is also often true: A teacher who is too eager to teach may have questionable motives like ego needs and the lust for power and authority. I believe that any evidence to the contrary be a real red flag for a seeker looking for a Kabbalah teacher.

- ✔ Generosity, which, for a teacher, is the love of giving and sharing

- ✔ Empathy, which is the ability to reach students on various different levels. There is a traditional title for a certain kind of Jewish teacher known as the **Maggid** (*mah*-geed), which is often translated as storyteller. The title is actually reserved for the teacher and storyteller who is able to reach students with differing levels of knowledge and understand at the same time. A Maggid can teach a class and everyone, regardless of his or her level, thinks that the teacher is directing the lesson to him or her.

- ✔ Insight, not just information. It's easy to think that a teacher who knows Hebrew, for example, or who knows a lot of terms that are unfamiliar is a master of the subject.

Beware of people who like to put others down. One of the great Kabbalists of the 20th century, Rabbi Abraham Isaac Kook, who was also the first Chief Rabbi of modern Israel, warned that there are two ways for people to raise themselves up: to actually work hard (the only way) or to put down those around them (the reprehensible way). Also beware of the teacher who thinks that he or she has a monopoly on wisdom.

An unlikely teacher

For a number of years, I visited New York City's Central Park regularly and would sit for hours by the small lake near the Hans Christian Andersen statues. At the time, it was a relatively quiet part of the park and therefore ideal for peaceful meditation and contemplation. One day, I noticed a man nearby engaged in needlepoint. He created remarkable tapestries based on classic and well-known paintings, and he did it all freehand. People wandered by in awe of this man's gift and the exquisite items that he made. He was a street person who wore tattered clothes and spent his nights in doorways around the city. His skin hung on thin bones, and he clearly looked like he had weathered many unsheltered days and nights. I often heard people offering to purchase his creations, but he always refused, explaining that he had made a promise never to sell any of his work but rather to give it all to a local church that often provided him with food, clothing, and other necessities.

I would sit next to this man and watch him work, supplying him with silk thread and even visiting Chinatown to buy him dozens of spools of thread of all thicknesses and shades of color.

I mention him because he was, in my opinion, one of the wisest and most brilliant people I've ever encountered. He didn't look the part, but almost everything he said, whether to me or to passersby, was deep and profound and wise. He had no degrees or credentials, and he didn't even have a roof over his head, and yet somehow he was one of the most special souls I've ever met. He didn't write articles or books, and he wasn't affiliated with any institution, but he taught his class each day on that park bench to anyone fortunate enough to discover him and quiet down enough to hear his words.

One doesn't have to be an expert in order to be a teacher. On the contrary, everyone has the responsibility to share what they know with others. Sometimes, one little piece of wisdom can change someone's entire life, but it's also true that one could take a class from a leading scholar and sit for hours, if not weeks, without picking up a thing. A Kabbalist is seeker, and the true seeker looks for wisdom everywhere. (For more on finding a good Kabbalah teacher, flip to Chapter 14.)

Chapter 3

Looking Back: A Brief History of Kabbalah

In This Chapter

▶ Revealing Kabbalah's roots in the Bible

▶ Getting to know history's greatest Kabbalists

▶ Understanding the way Kabbalah manifests in modern times

There's no beginning when it comes to the history of Kabbalah. As the tradition teaches, "Nine hundred and seventy-four generations before the world was created, the Torah had already been written." And as the Zohar teaches, "God looked into the Torah and created the world."

Kabbalah is the deepest level of Torah, which is the spiritual way of Judaism; it's the theology that holds up the entire spiritual tradition of Judaism. Put simply, Kabbalah is the heart and soul of Judaism.

Although Kabbalah doesn't have a beginning, one can trace its path through history starting with the book of books, the Holy Scriptures, and beginning with the opening chapters, which introduce the first human. Many biblical figures have great significance in the history of Kabbalah. In this chapter, the first thing I do is focus on the most important ones in the history of Kabbalah: Adam, Abraham, and Moses.

When the Holy Temple in Jerusalem was destroyed in the first decades of the first millennia CE, an important event that followed was the writing of the Talmud and other Rabbinic texts. This chapter introduces you to the two most important Kabbalists in the Rabbinic period: Rabbi Akiva, the extraordinary sage in the Talmud, and Rabbi Shimon bar Yochai, traditionally thought of as the author of the Zohar.

After the Rabbinic period, which ended about 500 CE, the next significant development in the history of Kabbalah was the 13th-century revelation of the Zohar, the great Kabbalistic text of Judaism. And then, a few centuries later, the brief life of the greatest Kabbalist of all time, Rabbi Isaac Luria (the Ari), changed the course of Kabbalah and Judaism forever.

In this chapter, you also meet the infamous Kabbalist, Shabtai Tzvi, whose reputation went from the greatest heights down to the depths, and you delve into the Hasidic movement, the great revival that brought Kabbalah to Jews everywhere. Finally, I tell you where Kabbalah is happening right at this moment.

Note: Many outstanding figures in addition to the ones I focus on in this chapter make up the history of Kabbalah. Knowledge of Kabbalah has been spread by so many outstanding scholars throughout history, such as Rabbi Judah, known as the Maharal of Prague (1512–1609), Rabbi Isaiah Horowitz (1565–1630), Rabbi Moshe Hayyim Luzzatto (1707–1746), and Rabbi Elijah the Gaon of Vilna (1720–1797), to name a few.

Kabbalists in the Bible

There are many biblical figures who are profoundly important to the history of Jewish spiritual thought and therefore to Kabbalah. Abraham's grandson, Jacob, for example, wrestles with an angel and becomes "Israel." And King David writes most of the book of Psalms and, in doing so, reveals his extraordinary personal relationship with God.

But Adam, Abraham, and Moses occupy the top three Kabbalistic spots when I look at the biblical period. Adam represents every person; Abraham is such an amazing visionary that he became a central figure in three world religions; and Moses is regarded in Jewish tradition as the greatest teacher who ever lived and who reached greater intimacy with God than anyone before or since.

Adam: First man, first Kabbalist

Adam, the Bible's first human, is also considered to be the first Kabbalist. Kabbalists have a traditional belief that a book containing the wisdom of Kabbalah was delivered by an angel to Adam.

Adam is significant to Kabbalists for another reason. Many Kabbalists have tended to focus on a few specific areas of the Torah more than others, and one of those areas is the story of creation in the book of Genesis. Kabbalists analyze each and every detail of the story — not only the words but also the letters that make up the words that tell the story of God's creation of the world and Adam and Eve. For Kabbalists, the tale of Adam and Eve is emblematic of human life, and the deepest mysteries of creation and the human situation are contained within the details of the language of the Torah.

Kabbalists are particularly interested in

✔ **The significance of the notion that Adam was split in two to create male and female:** In Kabbalistic tradition, the institution of marriage is seen as the primary cell of social existence; in deeper, more spiritual terms, marriage is seen as a holy act in which two halves come together to make one whole. This basic and sacred combination of male and female was designed by God and has the ability to produce life. The profound relationship between left and right and the principle of two halves forming a whole are major topics in an understanding of the ten *sefirot* (see Chapter 4). That male and female come together to form one whole unit is a basic principle of life itself for the Kabbalist.

✔ **Adam's relationship to the trees in the garden, planted by God and described in some detail:** Early in the book of Genesis is the story of Adam and Eve in the Garden of Eden. The garden, says the text, had many trees, most notably the Tree of Life, which was in the middle of the garden, and the Tree of Knowledge of Good and Evil. Kabbalists study these details and the stories that contain them in an effort to understand some of the most profound principles of life. What is evil? What is temptation? How can one overcome temptation? What is the relationship between free will and temptation? One theme found in the teachings of many Kabbalists that's reflected in the biblical verses about Adam in the garden is this: Sometimes eating from the tree of knowledge actually has the reverse effect and knowledge actually gets in the way of true knowing.

✔ **Adam's relationship to the snake in the Garden of Eden:** The snake, known in Hebrew as **nochosh** (*noh*-khosh), is often seen as a symbol of the evil inclination, the tempter, and is sometimes even referred to as the **suhtun** (*suh*-ton), from which the word "Satan" comes. In the Torah, the snake's punishment is having to eat the dust of the earth forever. Kabbalists sometimes interpret dust as the sins of humans, implying that evil in the world is fed by the misdeeds that humans commit. Kabbalists believe that evil isn't something that lives on its own, but rather they view evil as a parasite that lives off of the errors of humankind.

Kabbalistic tradition views Adam as a unique entity. He isn't just the biological ancestor of all humans; he's also the spiritual ancestor. Kabbalists believe that the soul in each person is really a fragment of one great soul — that of Adam, known among Kabbalists as **Adam HaRishon** (*ah*-dum hah-*ree*-shone, the first human.) Another Kabbalistic term, **Adam Kadmon** (*ah*-dum *kahd*-mun), is also frequently used and is translated as Primordial Man, the first being that ever emerged from creation. (For more on Adam, see Chapter 18.)

Appreciating Abraham and his Kabbalistic contributions

The patriarch Abraham lived approximately 4,000 years ago. Abraham taught and reminded the world that there is a God and that God is One. This view of God is essential to the Kabbalist, who doesn't believe that any human being is or could be a God, nor does a Kabbalist see the world as created, controlled, or influenced by a number of gods. Kabbalists believe in a fundamental oneness, a holy "one" that's unique, that's different from any other oneness, and is beyond human grasp and the source of all things.

Abraham's teachings had far-reaching influence; both Christian and Islamic traditions also look to the teachings and lineage of Abraham.

What did Abraham do for Kabbalah?

Kabbalistic tradition holds that Abraham wrote one of the fundamental books of Kabbalah, **Sefer Yetzirah** (*say*-fehr yih-*tzee*-rah; the Book of Formation). Abraham is also the source of many profound teachings contained in the legends, stories, and laws that have been passed down through the generations and were ultimately revealed by Moses in the form of the written Torah and the Oral Tradition.

So did Abraham actually write Sefer Yetzirah? Did he truly receive a Kabbalistic tradition from Adam and then pass it on to his children and grandchildren and their descendents? For the Kabbalist, the answer is surely "yes." And remember, that on the most profound level, Kabbalists live in the eternal present. In fact, serious Kabbalists throughout the centuries experienced the patriarch Abraham not as a myth or even as an historical figure but rather as a being in the eternal present. A tangible example of this belief is the holiday of **Sukkot** (sue-*coat;* see Chapter 11), when one of the fundamental rituals is inviting Abraham and other ancestors to sit with the Kabbalist and to study the Torah and break bread with him or her.

Abraham = Lovingkindness

Abraham represents *Chesed,* one of the ten *sefirot* (see Chapter 4). Abraham is the individual in Kabbalistic tradition who best represents the qualities of *Chesed:* lovingkindness, hospitality, generosity, affection, openness, and expansiveness. In today's Kabbalistic circles, a complimentary way to describe someone is as a **ba'al chesed** (bahl *keh*-sed; a master of *Chesed,* an expert at lovingkindness).

Abraham's reputation and ongoing importance

Abraham is well known among Kabbalists as a man who experienced ten severe and bitter trials. One of the questions that Kabbalists confront is the question of why there's so much suffering in the world, and Abraham is emblematic of such suffering. The ten trials of Abraham are symbolic of the trials that all people face in life.

Kabbalah scholars have long poured over the details of Abraham's life as recorded in the Torah as well as other Rabbinic literature. For example, one episode in the Torah describes the command that Abraham received from God to sacrifice his son Isaac on an altar on a mountain. This story, known as *the Binding of Isaac,* takes on profound meaning when studied through a Kabbalistic lens. Kabbalists have written about the Binding of Isaac as a deep exploration of two of the fundamental forces in the universe: *Chesed* (loving-kindness) and *Gevurah* (restraint) (see Chapter 4). For the Kabbalist, the entire Bible has many layers of meaning, but because Abraham represents one of the fundamental forces in the universe, he gets particularly close examination when Kabbalists pour over the holy books.

Moses: The greatest teacher who ever lived

Moses lived approximately 3,400 years ago. Kabbalists consider him the greatest prophet and teacher who ever lived as well as the humblest of men.

It's generally believed that the mystical-esoteric tradition that came to be called Kabbalah has its roots in the transmission of wisdom that begins with Adam and works its way on to Abraham and then on to the generation of Moses. But when the Children of Israel arrived at Mount Sinai, Moses ascended and received a unique and great transmission from the Divine that ultimately included all human knowledge, including all the details of Kabbalistic tradition.

Receiving the Torah at Mount Sinai

Moses is probably most famous for leading the Children of Israel out of slavery in Egypt, through the desert for 40 years, and eventually into the Promised Land. However, another important story sheds additional light on why Moses is so important to Kabbalah.

The story, as recorded in the Talmud, describes Moses going up Mount Sinai and finding God in the midst of writing the Torah. Moses looked at the scroll that God was writing and saw many things that he couldn't understand. God told him that one day a great man named Rabbi Akiva would understand all the things that Moses couldn't understand and would be able to teach these things to his students. As the story goes, Moses asked God if he could meet Rabbi Akiva. God asked Moses to turn around, and suddenly Moses found himself sitting in Rabbi Akiva's classroom.

As Moses sat in Rabbi Akiva's classroom many centuries later, he found that he couldn't understand what the teacher was teaching. One student asked, "From whom do we learn these secret traditions found in the Torah scroll?" To Moses's astonishment, Rabbi Akiva replied, "We received these secret traditions from Moses, who received them at Mount Sinai.

This sense of history, that in some inexplicable way everyone can live in the eternal present, transforms Moses from a man who lived in one era of history into one with whom Kabbalists can live in the eternal present. For the serious Kabbalist, the voice of Moses spoken both through the text he left in the Five Books of Moses and in the countless Oral Traditions that Kabbalists recognize as coming through him at Mount Sinai is part of the tradition that existed before the world began.

An ancient text known as the Sayings of the Fathers can be found in every traditional prayer book and is traditionally read during the afternoon of the Sabbath each week. The opening words of the text are **Moshe kibel Torah mi'Sinai** (*moe*-sheh *kee*-bail *toe*-rah meh-*see*-nye; Moses received the Torah at Sinai). The words "kibel" (received) and "Kabbalah" are grammatical forms of the same Hebrew term. This relationship ties into the idea of Kabbalah as the received tradition, which I explain in Chapter 1.

Gifts from Moses

Kabbalists believe that the tradition Moses received at Mount Sinai and passed along contains both a written form and an oral form. Kabbalists view the written Torah as the body of the divine teachings from God to Moses. and the soul of those teachings resides in the Oral Tradition. Moses passed down from Mount Sinai both the written Torah and the Oral Tradition, which contains the Kabbalistic tradition.

Kabbalah today consists of those same two elements received from God and Mount Sinai:

- ✔ The esoteric spiritual ideas, the theology taught by Kabbalah
- ✔ The Commandments, the basic rituals that help the Kabbalist connect with God and that God has commanded

Kabbalah in the Rabbinic Period

The writings produced during the Rabbinic period (the early centuries of the Common Era) by the many great sages who lived then are concerned largely with law. The Talmud was the creative scholarship of the great rabbis of the Rabbinic period and grew out of the **Mishnah** (mish-*nah*), which is the written form of the Oral Tradition from Mount Sinai (see Chapter 13). The rabbinic texts are also filled with practical wisdom, morality tales, science, and more.

But certain particular Rabbinic personalities were especially interested in theology and an abstract understanding of the relationship between humans and God. In the Rabbinic period, the study and cultivation of both the written and oral traditions was in a powerful and active stage. The Talmudic sages Rabbi Akiva, the son of Joseph, and Rabbi Shimon, the son of Yochai, were pivotal personalities in the history of Kabbalah.

Rabbi Akiva: A spiritual teacher to the last moment

Rabbi Akiva was a master of Kabbalah and the leading rabbi of his generation. He's known in Rabbinic tradition as the rabbi of his time who entered the deepest depths of spiritual exploration and managed it all without trouble. His colleagues weren't able to cope with the deepest mysteries of tradition, but Rabbi Akiva is the example of the spiritual explorer who was able to grasp the wisdom of Kabbalah in its entirety.

Kabbalists have been intimately familiar with the dramatic record of the story of Rabbi Akiva's death for nearly 2,000 years. A great teacher of Torah, Rabbi Akiva was such a role model to his generation that people considered his most mundane actions to be part of what they considered to be Torah. Teaching Torah was illegal under the oppressive Roman rule after the destruction of the Holy Temple in Jerusalem, yet Rabbi Akiva taught Torah and was arrested for it, put into prison, and ultimately tortured to death.

Rabbinic tradition records that while the Romans were raking his flesh with hot iron combs and torturing him to death, his students wept, but Rabbi Akiva offered a teaching. As his flesh was burning, Rabbi Akiva taught that each day, in prayer, people read the passages from the Torah that refer to their love of God. Rabbi Akiva said that he always wondered at the meaning of the Torah text "to love God with all your soul." He explained that he always understood this passage to mean that "even at that moment when God has decided to separate my body from my soul, I will acknowledge my love of God, and that God is One." Rabbi Akiva explained that the text asks people to love God with all their souls and that the moment of death is the opportunity to do so. As he died, Rabbi Akiva had the following words on his lips: "Hear O Israel, the Lord our God, the Lord is One." Legend has it that Rabbi Akiva said the word "one" as he died.

Rabbi Akiva's manner of death and the high level of consciousness that it describes is well known in Kabbalistic tradition and considered to be an archetype. Rabbi Akiva saw his own horrible death not as a tragedy but rather as a spiritual opportunity. The story reminds Kabbalists everywhere to see every moment as a spiritual opportunity and to know that "God is One."

Rabbi Shimon Bar Yochai writes the Zohar

Rabbi Shimon Bar Yochai was a student of Rabbi Akiva who ultimately earned a reputation as an extraordinarily important figure in the history of Kabbalah. Although the Roman Empire was successful in murdering Rabbi Akiva (see the preceding section), the Romans were unsuccessful at capturing Rabbi Shimon Bar Yochai. He and his son sought refuge in a small cave and avoided arrest by the Romans for 13 years.

Kabbalistic tradition maintains that both Moses and Elijah the Prophet appeared to Rabbi Shimon Bar Yochai while he hid in the cave. During their isolation, the rabbi and his son experienced visions of the greatest depth that led Rabbi Shimon Bar Yochai to write the great classic of Kabbalistic tradition, the Zohar, the Book of Splendor.

The multilevel nature of Kabbalistic ideas and the unique ways they influence each other make it almost impossible to translate Kabbalistic ideas into words on a page. But the Zohar is a text that expounds upon the major themes of Kabbalah. Kabbalistic tradition holds that Rabbi Shimon Bar Yochai wrote the Zohar, and it was then hidden away for centuries.

Thriving in Spain in the 13th Century

After the decimation of the Jewish community due to the oppression of the Roman Empire, Kabbalistic tradition was preserved from one generation to the next as a few highly skilled and trained individuals transmitted the tradition to a few chosen students. It wasn't until the 13th century that the teachings of Kabbalah began to spread far and wide.

In the 13th century, 1,200 years after the destruction of the Temple in Jerusalem, a Spanish Kabbalist named Moses de Leon revealed the document known as the Zohar (it had been hidden away for centuries; see the preceding section). The Zohar became such an important part of the Kabbalistic tradition that it's often considered one of the three pillars of the wisdom writings of the Children of Israel; the other two pillars are the Torah and the Talmud.

Much of the scholarship of the Kabbalists in Spain centered around the following two major threads of Kabbalistic tradition at that time, which are both mentioned in the Talmud:

✔ **Ma'aseh Bereshit** (mah-ah-*seh* ber-aye-*sheet*): The mystical understanding of the verses in the Torah in the book of Genesis describing the process of creation. Kabbalists believe that a careful look at the details of the creation in the Torah results in a deeper understanding of the fundamentals of human existence. In the most precise yet mysterious way, each letter, word, and sentence both contains and sheds light on the most profound wisdom.

In the same way that Kabbalistic tradition teaches followers not simply to acknowledge the surface of life but rather to pierce into the depths of things (see Chapter 14), Kabbalists don't look (and never did look) at the Ma'aseh Bereshit on a superficial level. Rather, Kabbalists analyze this verse in as detailed a way as possible, down to the minute nuances contained within the Torah text that are believed by Kabbalists to reveal extraordinary ideas and ideals.

✔ **Ma'aseh Merkava** (*mah*-ah-seh mer-*kah*-vah): The study of the vision in Ezekiel's prophecy and the other details in the verses contained in the book of Ezekiel found in the Holy Scriptures including images of a divine chariot. Kabbalistic tradition teaches that the fantastic visions of Ezekiel also contain the most sublime teachings and permit students a glimpse into the deepest depths of Torah. According the great Jewish philosopher and rabbi, Moses ben Maimon (Maimonides), who was born in Spain in 1135, Ma'aseh Merkava is also the general term that refers to the obligation and effort on the part of all Jews to try to grasp God and to contemplate the meaning of God and God's attributes.

The Jewish people are like a plant

Botanists know that cutting back a plan often results in a burst of growth and flowering; paradoxically, cutting or trimming a plant stimulates its growth. The observation has been made that the history of Kabbalah is, in fact, the history of a plant that continues to be cut back.

The profound teaching pertaining to the transition between the expulsion of the majority of Jewish people from Spain in 1492 and the next great period of growth in the Kabbalistic tradition observes that, throughout Jewish history, the Jewish people behave as a surviving nation in the manner of a plant that continues to bounce back after being trimmed and cut back.

✔ When the great Temple in Jerusalem was destroyed in 70 CE and the Rabbinic period was decimated at the hands of the fierce and intolerant Romans, the result was a document known as the Talmud. The Talmud represents an amazing fountain and flourishing of learning among the forebears of those who would be officially known as Kabbalists.

✔ When the Jews, including the great Kabbalists of Spain, were expelled from Spain in 1492, the result was a burst of creativity and an amazing flourishing of Kabbalistic innovation — poetry, literature, philosophy — reflecting a diversity of practices and perspectives on how best to express and engage in Kabbalah.

✔ The terrible massacres of the Jewish people starting in 1648, known as the *Chmielnicki massacres*, included as targets great Kabbalists in the Ukraine, which was home to a huge Jewish population. The birth of Hasidism occurred shortly after this horrible experience in Jewish history, reshaping Kabbalah to changing times and becoming one of the major forces active in passing Kabbalah on to current generations.

The Jewish community in Spain flourished for a number of centuries. For the most part, Jews lived peacefully with their Arab and Christian neighbors, and the Jewish community was well integrated into all levels of Spanish society. However, in the same year that King Ferdinand and Queen Isabella supported the voyage of Columbus from Spain across the Atlantic Ocean, they also threatened the conversion or expulsion of the Jews of Spain. Many Jews stayed and converted, but a large number of Jews left Spain and settled in the countries to the east of Spain and as far east as Russia. Many Eastern European Jews from the last few centuries descend from the Jews who fled from Spain at that time.

Coming of Age in the Mystical City of Tzfat

In the early 1500s, just a short span of years since the expulsion of the Jews from Spain in 1492, a community of Kabbalists sprung up in the city of Tzfat in the Holy Land. This gathering of great Kabbalists and scholars essentially formulated the way in which Kabbalah would be studied and understood then and in the future.

A gathering of great minds

The Kabbalah that serious practitioners study and practice today is the Kabbalah of the great sages of the city of Tzfat in the 16th century. Primary among these sages was the great Kabbalist Rabbi Isaac Luria, known as the Ari, who single-handedly transformed the study of Kabbalah. Kabbalists from then until now know that their Kabbalah is the Kabbalah of the Ari (see Chapter 18).

In Tzfat, a congregation of rabbis and holy teachers flourished for a brief but significant time. Rabbi Isaac Luria died before he reached the age of 40, and he barely wrote anything. But much of his teachings were put into writing, in a work called **Etz Chayim** (ayts *chah*-yeem; the Tree of Life). In 1570, Rabbi Chaim Vital became a student of the Ari, and when the Ari died in 1572, Rabbi Vital began to write down everything he had learned from his master.

In 1570, the Ari arrived in Tzfat from Egypt and found a gathering of some of the finest Jewish minds in history. These outstanding Kabbalists included

✔ **Rabbi Joseph Karo,** who was not only a great Kabbalist but also the author of the famous Code of Jewish Law, the Shulchan Aruch

✔ **Shlomo Alkabetz,** one the greatest poets of Spanish culture who, among other things, composed a song called "L'cha Dodi," which is sung to this day by Jews throughout the world who participate in the Friday night ritual known as Kabbalat Shabbat. Kabbalat Shabbat is a series of prayers developed by the Kabbalists of Tzfat that became one of the cornerstones of Jewish Sabbath observance.

✔ **Israel Najara,** a great poet in this Kabbalistic community

✔ **Moses Cordovero,** often considered the leader of all the primary Kabbalists of his time

Important principles taught and revealed by the Ari

The hundreds or perhaps thousands of books of Kabbalah that have been written over the generations are mostly attempts to clarify, expand, and develop the teachings found in the Zohar. Through the writings of his disciple Rabbi Chaim Vital, the Ari continued that process and expressed much of what ultimately came to be called the heart and soul of Kabbalah for centuries and until today.

Some teachings of the Ari

Here are some of the pivotal ideas that can be found in the Ari's teachings:

✔ God acts in the world through ten emanations of divine influence called the ten *sefirot*.

✔ These ten *sefirot* serve as instruments of the Divine.

✔ Even though God is infinite and has no limits or attributes in worldly terms, God chooses to be revealed to the world through the ten *sefirot*.

✔ The *sefirot* disseminate into the world in a wide variety of combinations, and these combinations determine the workings of the world.

✔ Humans act upon the combinations of *sefirot* through their actions, thoughts, and words.

✔ The evil in the world is the result of a distortion of the *sefirot* prompted by evil thoughts, words, and deeds among humans.

✔ The Torah is a revelation of the proper way to live so that the divine plenty in the form of the ten *sefirot* will nourish the world properly.

✔ A deed known as a **mitzvah** (*mitz*-vah) helps to cause the proper combination among *sefirot* in order to prompt the proper amount of **shefa** (*sheh*-fah; divine plenty) in the world.

✔ A sin or a transgression contributes to the forces of pollution in the world.

✔ Kabbalah is that innermost part of the teachings of the Torah that explains the significance of every movement and thought in metaphysical terms.

> ✔ The person who acquires authentic Kabbalistic wisdom can use the ability that this wisdom provides to become closer to God and to establish a deeper relationship with God. When this connection occurs, a Kabbalist is able to repair the world and become a partner with God in the process of perfecting the world.

The creation of the world

Included among the teachings of the Ari is one that became pivotal among Kabbalists forever: his understanding of the creation of the world. The Ari taught that the world was created by an act of divine contraction known as **tzimtzum** (*tzim*-tzoom). According to this teaching, the Infinite hid or contracted itself, resulting in a "place" in which God could create the finite world.

Kabbalists often say that the world exists and is built on "an absence of being" and that this nonbeing comes from God. For the concept of the world's existence, the Ari also offered the image of the shattering of the vessel. Some say that the best way to describe the Ari's image of the shattering of the vessel is to imagine a vessel in which the infinite light of God poured in; needless to say, this infinite light couldn't be contained by a finite vessel, and therefore the vessel shattered. The teachings go on to declare that the light of God is covered over by shards of the shattered vessel, and it's the role of the Kabbalist to find these shards, sometimes called "husks," and release the divine sparks trapped inside of them. In this way, the Kabbalist becomes a partner with God by repairing the world.

The Kabbalistic view of creation then, as taught by the Ari, is that the world that Kabbalists now know and live in is made up of elements that contradict each other and are incomplete, chaotic, and confusing due to the breaking of the vessel. The fragments of the pure vessel are scattered throughout the world and throughout existence. Some of the shattered pieces are clear, bright, reliable, and formed the foundation of the world. Others are distorted and became forces of evil that humans need to repair.

The need to repair the world

The Ari taught that life in its entirety is an endless struggle to form light out of darkness, to repair the broken world. Through self-discipline, high moral behavior, proper intention, prayer, study, and good deeds, the Kabbalist helps to repair the world and restore it to its proper place. Kabbalists don't wait for the Messiah but rather work to *bring* the Messiah. Each proper thought, word, and deed (as described in the holy books) bring more rapid redemption of the world as a whole.

This vision is at the heart of the teachings of the Ari. His teachings ultimately became Kabbalah; all Kabbalistic traditions before it funnel through the teachings of the Ari, and all Kabbalistic tradition that came after the Ari grew out of the Kabbalah of the Ari himself. The teachings of the Ari are the foundation upon which Hasidic approaches to Kabbalah are based (see Chapter 1).

The Bigger You Are, The Harder You Fall: The Shabbatai Tzvi Affair

Shabbatai Tzvi is an influential figure in Jewish history (and specifically in the history of Kabbalah) whose legacy continues today in its impact on the very image of Kabbalah in the world.

Shabbatai Tzvi was born in 1626 and had a traditional religious education. As a young man, he was well versed in Talmudic studies and took a particular liking to Kabbalah. Shabbatai Tzvi settled in Salonica, Greece, wherefrom he was expelled for his abuse of power and holy symbols. One story reports that the expulsion was punishment for a wedding that he staged with himself as the groom and the Torah as the bride.

Shabbatai Tzvi had a remarkably charismatic personality and was a captivating teacher, given his mastery of the Talmud, the Zohar, and other mystical texts. In 1663, Shabbatai Tzvi went to Egypt and studied with the Kabbalah scholars in residence there.

At that same time, a man named Nathan from a place called Gaza was known as a great spiritual personality who bestowed blessings on others with remarkable outcomes. Shabbatai Tzvi visited Nathan, and the result of the encounter was that Nathan of Gaza became Shabbatai Tzvi's ardent disciple. In 1665, reportedly at the encouragement of Nathan of Gaza, Shabbatai Tzvi declared himself to be the messiah.

Shabbatai Tzvi had a great impact on many, including some of the greatest rabbis of the time who were swept up in his pseudo-messianic fervor, and he attracted a vast number of followers. His great Talmudic scholarship and skillful manipulation of Kabbalistic text held sway over Rabbinic leaders as well as the masses. After declaring himself to be the Messiah, Shabbatai Tzvi's abuse of power escalated; he even made proclamations claiming the authority to change the Torah law.

The rabbis of Jerusalem weren't among those who were swayed by Shabbatai Tzvi's skill set and charm, and they banned him from the holy city of Jerusalem. The rabbis of Jerusalem generated a letter-writing campaign warning leading rabbis throughout the world of his unfounded claims. Shabbatai Tzvi and Nathan of Gaza then traveled together far and wide, and through travels and public appearances, Shabbatai Tzvi continued to gain popularity.

As the tidal wave of support for Shabbatai Tzvi increased, the Turkish authorities became curious. They also became alarmed by the growing movement of followers of Shabbatai Tzvi and the fact that over 100,000 followers had sold their businesses in preparation to follow him, in his role as messiah, back to Israel. The economic disruption was intense, and the Turkish authorities issued an ultimatum to Shabbatai Tzvi: He should either convert to Islam or be executed.

That unique personality Shabbatai Tzvi, whose charisma swept Europe and Asia influencing the masses in general and students of Kabbalah in particular, disappointed his public when he converted to Islam. He took a Muslim name, was given a job, and was accepted into Islam. It's said that sometimes Shabbatai Tzvi lived the life of a Muslim and sometimes he attempted to reclaim power within local Jewish communities. He died at age 50. Nathan of Gaza continued to spread belief in Shabbatai Tzvi.

Shabbatai Tzvi's popularity was so great and his reputation reached such heights that his fall was dramatic and damaged the reputation of Kabbalah phenomenally. Shabbatai Tzvi's focus on Kabbalah and his ultimate downfall came to be seen as a great example of how Kabbalah in the wrong hands leads to tragedy.

The Great Revival: Hasidism

As I mention in the sidebar "The Jewish people are like a plant," terrible massacres known as the Chmielnicki massacres occurred in the Ukraine in the 1600s. The destruction of Jewish families, including many of the great Kabbalists of that generation, during these events was vast. In the midst of the despair, and during the trauma experienced by the survivors in the decades after this terrible cataclysm, a teacher emerged who caused nothing short of a revolution in Jewish life that would change Judaism forever.

This teacher founded a movement that would rediscover the wisdom of Kabbalah and would dedicate itself to spreading this wisdom to everyone.

The rise of the Baal Shem Tov

In 1698, a boy named Israel was born in Okop, a tiny village in the Ukraine on the border between Russia and Poland. Israel's parents, Eliezer and Sarah, were deeply spiritual people. They were quite old at the time of Israel's birth and died when he was still a boy. Legend tells that Eliezer's last words to his son Israel were "Fear nothing other than God."

As an orphan, Israel was cared for by the community. He earned a reputation for walking through woods and fields, staying by himself, and praying to God — not in formal prayer, but in spontaneous prayer that poured out from his heart. As he grew up, he became a local teacher as well as a caretaker in a synagogue, which provided him with the time he needed to attain an extraordinary level of knowledge, particularly of the mysteries and secrets of Kabbalah.

In 1734, Rabbi Israel changed his approach to life radically. Rather than keep to himself, he became a great teacher, and his reputation spread far and wide as an amazing holy man who understood the secret names of God and could use them properly in blessings and to entreat God on behalf of supplicants who asked for intercession. He became known as the **Baal Shem Tov** (bah-*ahl* shem towv; Master of the Good Name), and to this day, more people know him as the Baal Shem Tov than as Rabbi Israel. The Baal Shem Tov's teachings were based on the Kabbalistic teachings, and in particular, the teachings of the Ari (see the section "Important principles taught and revealed by the Ari" earlier in this chapter).

What the Baal Shem Tov offered that was different from the teachings of the Ari was an ability and desire to spread Kabbalistic teachings to all levels of the community. The Baal Shem Tov was able to communicate the most profound ideas through stories and parables, sayings, and teachings that shed light on the greatest and most fundamental of Kabbalistic principles in a way that almost anyone could understand.

Over the years, the Baal Shem Tov became more and more famous, and great scholars became his scholars and disciples. The Baal Shem Tov also represented the principle of reaching out to others to spread blessing and knowledge to all. From the mid-1700s to the present, Kabbalah manifested itself in a living way through the lives of the followers of the Baal Shem Tov, the founder of the movement of Hasidism.

The Baal Shem Tov didn't record his teachings in books, so most of what Kabbalists know about his teachings come from a book called *Toldos Yaakov Yosef,* written by Rabbi Yaakov Yosef Hakohen of Polnoye. Rabbi Yaakov Yosef wrote this and some other volumes that contain hundreds of quotes from the Baal Shem Tov — some short and some long, but all coming together to form the basis of the Kabbalistic lifestyle known as Hasidism.

A contemporary opponent

In the years that overlapped the life of the Baal Shem Tov, another great student and leader of Kabbalah appeared. His name was Rabbi Eliyahu of Vilna, and he was known as the Vilna Gaon. Living in the 18th century, the Vilna Gaon became known as an opponent of Hasidism and the followers of the Baal Shem Tov, but like the Baal Shem Tov, the Vilna Gaon was also a great student of Kabbalah. One of their differences is that the Vilna Gaon saw Kabbalah as a subject for the few, whereas the Baal Shem Tov wanted to spread knowledge of Kabbalah to the masses.

The slandering of Kabbalah among historians

For years, Kabbalah has gotten a bad rap among historians — even Jewish historians. In their histories of the Jewish people, a few key Jewish historians relegated Kabbalah to a narrow or fringe aspect of the tradition from Moses at Mount Sinai and viewed it as having been drowned out.

These historians, swept up by the Enlightenment and the modern scientific age, were squeamish about the spiritual ideas contained in Kabbalah. Largely because they couldn't understand the concepts themselves and didn't grasp the deep significance of Kabbalistic teachings as the very soul of Torah, these influential historians missed the point. As a result, a tremendous amount of ignorance and misinformation about Kabbalah has been disseminated by otherwise seemingly reliable sources.

The good news is that scholars are now widely recognizing and writing about the central role of Kabbalah as the very soul of Judaism.

A movement is born

When the Baal Shem Tov died, leadership of his movement of spreading Kabbalah to the masses was handed over to Rabbi Dov Ber, known as the Maggid of Mezrich. The Maggid of Mezrich was the Baal Shem Tov's primary disciple, but he'd also been a student of the teachings of the Ari as well as of another great Kabbalist in history, Rabbi Moshe Chaim Luzzatto.

The disciples of the Maggid of Mezrich and their disciples through history to the present comprise the *Hasidic movement,* that group of people in the world whose lives are primarily based on the same beliefs and the same rhythms as Kabbalists throughout the centuries. Up until the time of the Baal Shem Tov, only a very small number of people were concerned with Kabbalah. For the last few centuries, the Hasidic world has continued to spread the message of Kabbalah. Hasidic groups today such as Lubavitch, Bobov, Satmar, and Breslov all base their beliefs and lives on Kabbalistic practices and assumptions that they trace back to the Baal Shem Tov.

Kabbalah Today

Active interest in Kabbalah exists today in four main veins, which I explore in this section. In all cases, today's Kabbalists are influenced by the Kabbalah of the Ari (see the section "Coming of Age in the Mystical City of Tzfat" earlier in this chapter).

In addition, Kabbalah teachers aren't always a part of any defined group but may have a depth of knowledge, an understanding heart, a reluctance to teach, and the willingness to guide regardless. Such teachers join the many individuals, well-known and anonymous, who have continued to probe the depths of the profound questions of life through the way of Kabbalah.

Kabbalah and Hasidism

Kabbalah is alive and well in the Hasidic precincts of the Jewish community. Although severely damaged by the Holocaust, demographics indicate that the worldwide Hasidic population is flourishing and will continue to flourish. Additionally, this segment of the Jewish population is clearly growing at a greater rate than any other.

The Baal Shem Tov, founder of Hasidism, brought Kabbalah to the masses. Through straight talk as well as instructive parables and the gifts of a master teacher, the Baal Shem Tov and his disciples through the generations were able to translate the wisdom of Kabbalah from a difficult and abstract science of existence into a way of life that all can live.

Kabbalah and Jewish Renewal

Founded by Rabbi Zalman Schachter Shalomi and also greatly influenced by the teachings and spirit of the late Rabbi Shlomo Carlebach, the phenomenon known as *Jewish Renewal* is a nontraditional, loosely networked group who have a great affinity for Kabbalistic ideas and approaches to life.

The use of the word "renewal" in this movement's title is meant to imply that, after the Holocaust, when the old forms of spiritual expression in the Jewish community (Kabbalah) were once again silenced, it became necessary not simply to reproduce the old but to renew it. By looking at old paradigms and old forms of spiritual and Kabbalistic expression, Jewish Renewal develops new, modern ways to give expression to those ideas and ideals without necessarily being committed to the choreography of traditional Jewish life as it has been manifested in traditional communities.

Conservative, Reform, and Reconstructionist Judaism

With the popularization of Kabbalah in our times, every denomination and many Jewish community centers have brought teachers versed in Kabbalah into their seminaries and programs. Prayer book and bible commentaries across all denominations now highlight the influence of the Kabbalists on the development of Jewish prayer and thinking.

Kabbalah and the Kabbalah Centre

The Kabbalah Centre, led by Rabbi Philip Berg, has a widespread public profile due largely to Madonna and other celebrities who have publicly announced their interest in Kabbalah Centre programs. The Centre has offices around the world that often attract media attention when famous people are seen coming or going. According to its Web site (www.kabbalah.com), "The Kabbalah Centre is a spiritual and educational organization dedicated to bringing the wisdom of Kabbalah to the world."

The Kabbalah Centre has produced many books written mostly by its founder and his family members. It markets its books, products, and activities as "the practical tools and spiritual teachings of Kabbalah" and states that Kabbalah is "accessible to everyone for personal change and transformation." The Centre's approach has been widely criticized in the Jewish world, with critics claiming that the Kabbalah Centre separates Kabbalah from Judaism and from Jewish laws and obligations.

Part I

So, What's the Big Secret? Unmasking Kabbalah

The 5th Wave   By Rich Tennant

"I'm thinking of taking a spiritual journey, but I want to make sure I look right for the trip."

In this part . . .

Sometimes it's essential to find out what a topic *isn't* before finding out what it *is*. Without a doubt, a lot of misconceptions are floating around about Kabbalah; some have been misleading people for centuries, and others have popped up more recently. To help you start to really understand Kabbalah and what makes Kabbalists tick, this part lets you get some fundamentals under your belt, look back at the history of Kabbalah, and sweep away some of the big myths that are just downright distracting.

Chapter 4

The Link between Heaven and Earth: Kabbalah's Own Top-Ten Countdown

Kabbalists believe that a superficial look at the world is simply that — a narrow and limited grasp of reality. They believe that a lot more is going on beneath the surface of what people see.

In this chapter, you discover the Kabbalistic belief in ten fundamental forces that drive everything, and you find out that humans can manipulate those forces. In fact, the heart of the life of the Kabbalist is the manipulation of these ten fundamental forces that God uses to create and sustain the world.

Seeing below the World's Surface

Some people believe that a person is born, lives, and dies. In other words some people think that you begin at the moment of conception and cease to exist when your body merges into the earth. But according to the great Kabbalists throughout history, there's more to life than often meets the eye.

The Kabbalist's task is to pierce the seemingly hard surface of the reality of the world and glimpse the reality of God. Through deeds and prayer, study, and intense contemplation on the abstract, unknowable God, the Kabbalist has faith that a more clear and real apprehension of reality is possible.

Kabbalah provides the student with the tools he or she needs to break through the surface of the hard and concrete reality. In the same way that a molecular biologist has tools allowing him to see electrons, protons, and neutrons and the spaces between objects, so too the Kabbalist has tools in the form of knowledge of the ten **sefirot** (seh-*fear*-oat), the four worlds (see Chapter 6), and the teachings of the Torah that allow for a vision of the reality within all the perceived reality.

Kabbalists know that the human mind and perceptions are often distracted by the material world to such an extent that God isn't seen and, more extreme, God's existence is denied. The goal of the Kabbalist is to see God as the center of all reality. Kabbalah teaches the student how to know God and reminds the student that often what one sees is an illusion.

It's tempting to say that Kabbalists don't trust surfaces, but that isn't entirely true. More accurately, a Kabbalist sees the surface of things and recognizes it for what it is — a surface. Think of the human body. You look at the human body and see all its external features. If you were to simply stop there, you'd get an accurate view of the external form of the body. Yet beneath that external form are major and minor organs, veins and arteries, different kinds of cells, and all kinds of bodily functions happening simultaneously.

A Kabbalist makes the same assumption about the world: The surface that one sees certainly exists and provides lots of information about the world itself, but beneath that surface are all kinds of activities vital to a more complete understanding of God's universe.

The world is filled with God

A few ideas and assumptions made by Kabbalists come together and offer a very different view of reality. First and foremost, the tradition of Kabbalah teaches that everything in the world is filled with God. This is a basic assumption of Kabbalah, but of course, it can't be proven. In fact, Kabbalists don't even think of proving it. For a Kabbalist, the world *is* filled with God, and this is as plain and as evident as anything else. A Kabbalist *experiences* the world as filled with God.

Everything that happens in the world, even the most seemingly trivial details, all occur because God allows it. Everything is from God. Pleasure, pain, beauty, harmony, evil — *everything*. God knows what is best, so if something doesn't work out the way you want it to, the assumption is that this is ultimately the way God wants it. In a sense, Kabbalah is based on a paradox: As fundamental a belief as the fact that everything that happens is ultimately from God is the belief that humans have free will and choose freely.

God is constantly creating and sustaining the world

Another primary assumption in the tradition of Kabbalah is that God constantly creates the world for the purpose of bestowing good to the world. You might say, "How do we know that?" The Kabbalistic answer is that this isn't a matter of belief; it's the reality that's perceived by the Kabbalist. Kabbalists believe that by diligent study, prayer, and proper action, you can see reality more clearly and know that God is indeed *in* everything and that God *does* give divine goodness to the world.

How does God constantly sustain the world and bestow goodness to it? Kabbalists point to what they actually perceive in the reality of the world: ten fundamental forces, the ten *sefirot*. These ten forces flow in two directions: God creates and sustains the world through these ten forces, and humans take these ten forces, combine them, mix them, utilize them, and try to learn how to use them properly. One way we communicate with God is in the ways we use or abuse the ten *sefirot*.

Kabbalists believe that the world humans exist in isn't the harmonious world that it could be. When Kabbalists refer to **Gan Eden** (gahn *ayden;* the Garden of Eden), they conjure up a view of a world of harmony. It is, in fact, the task of each person to do what he or she can to repair the disharmony and put things in their right order. Kabbalists teach that the proper human use of the fundamental forces in the world is the task of humans. Kabbalists learn to recognize the ten forces and see reality in terms of their functioning.

A new creation every moment

At least one traditional observer puts it this way: God continues to create the world, and if God were to hesitate for a moment and glance in another direction, the entire universe and everything in it would disappear. Kabbalists believe the world is being created anew at every moment, and thinking that time flows uninterrupted is an illusion. Every moment is an entirely brand-new moment for the universe; although the world looks the same at this moment as it did a moment before, that's simply an illusion.

One of the fundamental implications of this notion of God's continued creation is that God is involved with everything that goes on in the universe. As the Baal Shem Tov, the founder of Hasidism, stated, "Even the movement of a single blade of grass occurs because God wills it to occur."

According to Kabbalah, God doesn't form the universe out of nothing. Rather, creation is really an act of revelation. As one Kabbalist put it, creation is an emanation from the divine light. Kabbalists believe that God shines this divine light and forms it, limits it, and transmutes it into the world. As Kabbalists frequently note, the world couldn't possibly exist within the actual light of the Divine, so one of the mysteries of creation is that God hides or contracts, limiting God's infiniteness and withholding light, in order to continuously create the world.

The Ten Fundamental Forces that Sustain the World

A primary notion within Kabbalah is the belief that the world is created and sustained by ten channels of divine plenty. These ten channels are referred to as the ten *sefirot*.

The ten *sefirot* are not simple. Kabbalists point out that each of the ten *sefirot* has many different meanings and gradations, and they appear in various Kabbalistic texts using varying and alternate terminology. In one of the basic Kabbalistic texts, Sefer Yetzirah (see Chapter 13), the *sefirot* are described as numbers. But generally speaking, the *sefirot* are referred to as emanations, or qualities of God. In the 12th century Kabbalistic text Sefer Ha Bahir, the ten *sefirot* are related to the ten words or sayings by which the world was created. In the major Kabbalistic text, the Zohar, other words such as "powers," "gates," "lights," and even "garments" refer to the ten *sefirot*.

Kabbalists throughout the centuries have developed a system that views the ten *sefirot* as the fundamental building blocks of the world and of the human soul. God creates the universe continuously by emanating the ten *sefirot* and combining them. An important view of Kabbalists is that humans are a microcosm of the world, and just as the world is created and sustained through the ten *sefirot,* the soul of each individual consists of the ten *sefirot*.

The Bible says "Ten Utterances," not "Ten Commandments"

In the Kabbalistic tradition, there's no such phrase as "The Ten Commandments." The term in Hebrew is **Aseret Hadibrot** (ah-*ser*-et hah-*dib*-rote), which translates to the Ten Utterances. (Not quite as catchy as "commandments". . . .)

Kabbalists have linked these ten utterances to the ten *sefirot* and conclude that the world was created and continues to be created through ten divine expressions.

The Zohar contains a remarkable statement that God looked into the Torah before he created the world. The implication of this image is that the Torah holds the blueprint of reality. More specifically, the chart of the ten *sefirot* is considered the blueprint of the world and the blueprint of the human soul.

The chart of the ten *sefirot* has appeared in many documents throughout the centuries. Frequently, the ten *sefirot* are drawn as an arrangement or a configuration resembling a human being, with each of the ten *sefirot* corresponding to one of the organs or limbs of the body. This illustration is sometimes known as the *Tree of Life* (see Figure 4-1). In this section, I describe each of the ten *sefirot* individually using the Tree of Life configuration.

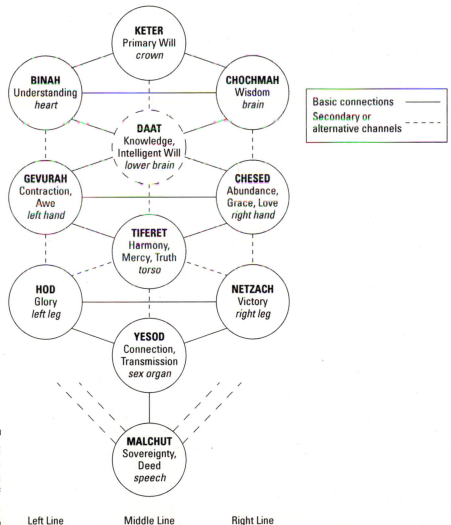

Figure 4-1:
The ten
sefirot as
the Tree of
Life.

If you're paying attention, you see that eleven *sefirot* actually appear on the Tree of Life. The reason is that two of the *sefirot*, *Keter* (crown) and *Da'at* (knowledge) are interchangeable, as I explain later in this section.

The crown

The uppermost *sefirah* on the chart of the Tree of Life is **Keter** (*keh*-tehr; crown). Unlike the other *sefirot*, which have parts of the human body as reference points, *Keter* doesn't refer to a human body part but rather refers to a royal crown sitting on top of a head. This depiction offers a hint at the meaning behind *Keter*.

Keter is often referred to as the divine will and the source of all delight and pleasure. *Keter* contains all the other *sefirot* in it, and it's often said that *Keter* activates the soul from above. Kabbalists suggest that one should picture God sending divine light and power down through the top of the head, infusing the entire body with all of its abilities and qualities.

Keter is considered to be the link between the infinite world of God and the finite world in which people live. *Keter* starts the flow of each of the *sefirot* into the next, and the *sefirah* on the bottom returns to *Keter* at the top and completes the circle.

In response to the commonly asked question "Why did God create the world?," Kabbalists agree that God didn't create the world because God needs it. To say that God *needs* anything implies a deficiency, and one can never say that God is deficient in any way. Many Kabbalists indicate that God created the world in order to create the human being and that God created the human being in order to give the human being pleasure. It follows, then, that the greatest pleasure that a human can experience is knowledge of God. Nevertheless, in the final analysis, Kabbalists agree that God creates the world through *Keter*, the divine will. In other words, God "wills" the world, and it is through God's will that the world is created.

Each of the ten *sefirot* has a name of God corresponding to it. The name of God that corresponds to *Keter* is **Ehveh** (*eh*-veh), which is a form of "I shall be."

Wisdom: The intuitive mind

The second *sefirah*, **Chochmah** (*khokh*-mah), translates as wisdom and is often referred to as intuition. *Chochmah* is the basis of the human's ability to grasp things intuitively. By coming from *Keter*, *Chochmah* is considered to be a higher wisdom — the wisdom that's somehow inborn.

In my experience raising birds, I've seen intuition firsthand. Many birds have laid eggs in cages in my living room, and I've had the privilege of watching baby birds emerge from those eggs many times. I often marvel that the birds seem to know what to do without being taught; they know how to eat, bathe, preen themselves, and do many other things without benefit of a school, class, or book. The higher wisdom within them knows how to be and how to manifest as a bird.

Chochmah represents the beginning of thought and the beginning of mental activity. It takes the pure energy of *Keter* and transforms it into something useful, creating the intellect.

Note that *Chochmah,* a top *sefirah* on the right side of the Tree of Life, is sometimes referred to as conception. Kabbalists often refer to *right side* and *left side* when looking at the configuration of *sefirot* in this diagram. The right vertical line is considered masculine and sometimes is referred to as father or **abba.** The left side is considered feminine and is referred to as the mother or **ema.**

The name of God often associated with *Chochmah* is **Yah.** Kabbalists have also associated biblical figures with several of the *sefirot,* and the biblical figure corresponding to *Chochmah* is King Solomon. This connection isn't surprising, of course, because wisdom is associated with the archetype of King Solomon, the wisest man who ever lived.

Understanding: The analytical mind

The *sefirah* of **Binah** (*bee*-nah) means understanding. *Binah* manifests the ability of logical analysis. For example, simple algebra indicates that if A = B and B = C, then A = C. One's *Binah* allows for easy understanding of this simple set of equations.

In a way, *Binah* is seen as *Chochmah*'s partner (see the preceding section for an explanation of *Chochmah*). These two *sefirot,* often referred to as father and mother, male and female, and "two beloved friends" and the interaction between them are often described in erotic language. *Binah,* as the *sefirah* that takes information and figures it out internally, is sometimes referred to as the divine womb. Some Kabbalists go so far as to say that *Binah* gives birth to all the *sefirot* that come after it.

Another way that *Chochmah* and *Binah* are a pair is that *Binah* probes the meaning of that which comes from *Chochmah.* Kabbalists often refer to *Binah* as the ability to make distinctions between and among things. They relate the word "Binah" to the Hebrew word **livnot** (liv-*note;* to build). *Binah* takes the abstract wisdom from *Chochmah* and builds on it, expanding and developing it.

Scientific *sefirot*

Modern theorists observe that *Binah* and *Chochmah* correspond neatly with left-brain and right-brain thinking. Of course, the notions of *Chochmah* and *Binah* predate such theories by many centuries, but it's not unusual for Kabbalistic insights made generations ago to foreshadow scientific discoveries.

Another observation is that the Tree of Life looks very much like the double helix of DNA. In addition, the combination of masculine and feminine result in the creation of the *sefirot* that follow them.

The name of God connected to the *sefirah* of *Binah* is **Elohim** (eh-low-heem), and the biblical figure that's often connected with *Binah* is the matriarch Leah.

Da'at: The crystallization of awareness

The *sefirah* of **Da'at** (*dah*-aht) is referred to as knowledge.

Da'at is interchangeable with *Keter,* the crown. When referring to exactly ten *sefirot,* one either counts the ten including *Keter* and leaving out *Da'at* or the other way around. Why? Simply put, *Keter* is an emanation from God, whereas *Da'at* is the experience of man. *Da'at* is specifically experienced knowledge, and *Da'at* is a view of reality from the point of view of the human being and his or her accumulated experiences. In its ultimate form, *Da'at* is knowledge of God.

Da'at is different from *Chochmah* and *Binah.* Whereas *Chochmah* is intuition and *Binah* is understanding or the ability to grasp concepts, knowledge is an accumulation of experience. In other words, there are three ways in which a person knows the functions of the mind or of consciousness: through the intuitive grasp of *Chochmah,* through the analytical powers of *Binah,* and through the accumulation of one's experiences, known as one's *Da'at.*

Imagine putting your finger into a hot flame. In some ways, you hesitate to put your finger into a flame because your intuition tells you that the dancing blue, yellow, and red flame offers some danger. In another way, your *Binah* prompts you to avoid putting your finger in the flame because you figure that if the flame is sufficiently hot, then putting your flesh into the heat will not serve it well. Your powers of figuring things out are at your service. Additionally, your experience of flames in the past — your *Da'at* — tells you not to put your finger into the heat.

Expansion: The impulse to give

The *sefirah* of **Chesed** (*keh*-sed), which translates as grace, is the fourth *sefirah*. It's characterized by an expanding impulse and is sometimes referred to as *Gedulah* (geh-*doo*-lah), which means greatness. (Sometimes, the entire right vertical line of the Tree of Life is referred to as the side of *Chesed,* which makes sense because the right side is known as the masculine side, and *Chesed*'s nature as an outgoing force corresponds to that male reference.)

Kabbalists also refer to *Chesed* as love, the inclination towards things, the attraction to things, the outgoing flow, an opening up, and a giving of itself. On the configuration of the ten *sefirot* as a human figure in the Tree of Life (see Figure 4-1), *Chesed* is associated with the right arm. The right arm reaches out and gives, and *Chesed* represents a love that's given freely.

Chesed also refers to kindness and benevolence, but it's a lovingkindness that knows no restraint. The third verse of Psalm 89 says that the world was built with *Chesed*. Whereas the preceding three *sefirot* of *Chochmah, Binah,* and *Da'at* are intellectual *sefirot, Chesed* is the first of the emotional *sefirot*.

The name of God that's connected to the *sefirah* of *Chesed* is **El** (ehl), and the biblical figure associated with this *sefirah* is Abraham the patriarch. Abraham is the legendary figure of love and expansion, which explains his connection with *Chesed*. Abraham was known to live in a tent that was open on all four sides so that he could easily see visitors and invite them into his tent as guests. This outward thrust of welcoming visitors and guests so easily associates *Chesed* with both Abraham and the masculine.

A helpful way to understand a *sefirah* is by examining its relationship with another *sefirah*. In this case, a Kabbalist can increase her understanding of *Chesed* by deepening her understanding of its partner, *Gevurah,* which I talk about in the next section.

Contraction: The impulse to receive

Gevurah (geh-*voo*-rah), often known as power, is also sometimes referred to with the Hebrew word **din,** meaning judgment, justice, or law. *Gevurah* also can mean restraint, concentration, fear, control, or awe.

Kabbalists teach that every *sefirah* has both a positive and negative aspect, and this duality is perhaps most clear in the *sefirah* of *Gevurah*. The discipline and restraint side of *Gevurah* can manifest itself in a positive or negative way. *Gevurah* is contraction, and too much contraction or too much judgment can result in squashing or in something disruptive. On the other hand, the strength aspect of this *sefirah* is an inward withdrawal, a concentration of power; that concentration of power can result in hate or fear but also in justice and control.

The *sefirot* of *Chesed* and *Gevurah* represent two opposing poles: *Chesed* reflects love that's free and lacking in restraint, whereas *Gevurah* represents discipline and a limitation. Yet *Chesed* and *Gevurah* balance each other because *Chesed* is on the right (masculine) side of the Tree of Life, and *Gevurah* resides on the left (feminine) side.

Love is often considered feminine (like maternal love), and toughness is considered masculine. But in the Kabbalistic cosmology, the opposite is the case. *Chesed* is expansive and therefore male, and *Gevurah* encloses and constricts and is therefore feminine. Kabbalists note that *Gevurah* is strength, and yet the path to *Gevurah* is the path from *Chesed.* In other words, true strength comes through giving. *Gevurah* harnesses the energy of *Chesed.*

One can easily see *Chesed* and *Gevurah* at work in the world. Child rearing, for instance, is an artful combination of expressions of *Chesed* and *Gevurah.* If a parent is too permissive, the result can be disastrous for a developing child. Similarly, if a parent is too repressive and restrictive, the result is again sad and unhealthy. But in combination, *Chesed* and *Gevurah* serve a parent well. At almost every moment of a parent's relationship with his or her child, he or she faces the question of just how much *Chesed* and just how much *Gevurah* to offer. A combination of the two results in a healthy child.

The name of God associated with *Gevurah* is **Elohim** (eh-low-*heem*), and the biblical figure associated with *Gevurah* is the patriarch Isaac. Isaac is a far more passive personality in the Torah than Abraham, who's associated with *Chesed* (see the preceding section). Although *Gevurah* is sometimes seen as negative, it isn't negative to the Kabbalist, and instead is often referred to as an aspect of God's kindness. The divine light pours down from God, and it would be impossible to exist if that light weren't restricted, controlled, and harnessed. The *Gevurah* aspect restricts the divine light and allows for the world to exist. Both *Chesed* and *Gevurah* express different aspects of God's love and of love in the world.

Harmony: The desire for balance

The *sefirah* of **Tiferet** (tee-*fehr*-et; beauty) is a combination of harmony, truth, and compassion. *Tiferet* is also a balancing of the two *sefirot* that precede it, *Chesed* and *Gevurah.* The word "Tiferet" comes from the Hebrew word **pa'ear** (pah-*air;* beauty). *Tiferet* is the ability to merge the flow of *Chesed,* which is open and outpouring, with the restrictive nature of *Gevurah* and achieve an appropriate mixture of the two. *Tiferet* is sometimes referred to as **Rachamim** (*rah*-khah-meem; compassion or mercy).

On the chart of the Tree of Life shown in Figure 4-1, notice that *Tiferet* is at the center. It's the central *sefirah* between right and left and between top and bottom. The part of the body that corresponds to *Tiferet* is the upper torso.

Perhaps most important to Kabbalists is the fact that *Tiferet* is also a symbol of the Torah. As a way of life, the Torah teaches the Kabbalist how to achieve the right balance in life. *Tiferet* manifests the ability to create the proper balance between *Chesed* and *Gevurah*. Often the expression of *Chesed*, which is lovingkindness, may be a grievous error if a situation doesn't call for such kindness. Similarly, the severity of *Gevurah* is sometimes too fierce for a particular moment or occasion.

Kabbalists believe that the perfect harmony to be achieved through a synthesis of *Chesed* and *Gevurah* isn't absolutely equal but rather a bit more of *Chesed* than *Gevurah*. The extra dose of lovingkindness results in the ideal kind of harmony as found on the Tree of Life.

The name of God that's connected with the *sefirah* of *Tiferet* is the most sacred of all God's names in Kabbalistic tradition, the Tetragrammaton (also known as the four-letter name of God), **Y-H-V-H.** This connection isn't surprising given that *Tiferet* is a symbol of the Torah.

The Biblical figure associated with *Tiferet* is Yaakov (Jacob), who's known in the Torah as Israel. The three patriarchs Abraham, Isaac, and Jacob correspond to the three central *sefirot* on the Tree of Life: *Chesed*, *Gevurah*, and *Tiferet*. Just as the first triad on the Tree of Life, *Chochmah*, *Binah*, and *Da'at* are often referred to in Kabbalistic literature as a unit, so too is the second triad on the Tree of Life, *Chesed*, *Gevurah*, and *Tiferet* (lovingkindness, judgment, and harmony) a unit. Whereas Kabbalists consider the first three *sefirot* of *Chochmah*, *Binah*, and *Da'at* mental processes or processes of consciousness, the lower *sefirot*, *Chesed*, *Gevurah*, and *Tiferet*, are the *sefirot* that act directly upon the world. In some ways, each person is constantly navigating life through these *sefirot*.

Victory: The urge to get things done

The *sefirah* of **Netzach** (*neh*-tzakh) may be referred to as victory or eternity. *Netzach* is the *sefirah* of conquest; it's also the capacity for overcoming. My Kabbalah teacher likes to say that *Netzach* is the profound urge to get things done.

Kabbalistic literature frequently points out that all the *sefirot* are pure in their essence but that each has a positive aspect and a negative aspect. In the case of *Netzach,* it's the urge to get things done, but its negative manifestation may be workaholism, when the urge to get things done is out of control. Another example of *Netzach* is when something is put into the marketplace before it's ready, a sort of overenthusiasm.

The name of God that's connected to the *sefirah* of *Netzach* is **Y-H-V-H Tzvaot** (tzih-vah-*oat*; the Lord of Hosts). The biblical figure associated with *Netzach* is Moses. As an accomplished leader, it stands to reason that Moses is associated with the *sefirah* of victory and the urge to conquer.

Glory: The way of persistence

The *sefirah* of **Hod** (hode), often referred to as splendor, is sometimes described as persistence or holding on. *Hod* is also the power to repudiate obstacles (a reference to persistence).

Just as the three *sefirot* before *Netzach* (*Chesed, Gevurah,* and *Tiferet*) are *sefirot* that act directly on the world, the next three (*Netzach, Hod,* and *Yesod*) are even more directly connected to the real world in which people live.

Think of *Netzach* and *Hod* as a progression from the urge to get things done to persistence or holding on. When you want to participate in a task, you begin with *Netzach.* When you're in the midst of doing something and want to continue to do the task at hand and not poop out, you need to exercise your persistence, your ability to hold on. Suppose you want to climb a mountain, for example. The urge to climb that mountain is *Netzach.* During the climb, your desire to muster up enough discipline to continue the trek is *Hod.* You can't be successful with just one and not the other.

One contemporary teacher sees *Hod* as incubation and the place where you design the wrapping for the idea or let it percolate to a deeper level; it's the place of enhancement, deeper inspiration, of completing something with full consciousness for it to be the best that it can be before it gets out there.

When you look at the chart of the Tree of Life (see Figure 4-1), you may notice that *Netzach* is below *Chesed,* and *Hod* is below *Gevurah.* Keep in mind that the right side, which is sometimes generally referred to as *Chesed,* is masculine and outgoing, so that just as *Chesed* is an outward gesture of lovingkindness, *Netzach* is an outward gesture of getting something done. Similarly on the left side, just as *Gevurah* is the ability to discipline oneself, *Hod* is a bearing down, an inner thrust to persist and persevere.

Mark your calendar!

Each of the seven lower *sefirot,* beginning with *Chesed,* corresponds to a day of the week. The day of the week associated with *Yesod* is Friday. Friday night is the inauguration of the Sabbath, when the Kabbalist actually takes part in a kind of wedding ceremony, marrying the divine presence in the world. A Kabbalist even calls the Sabbath a bride. According to the Kabbalistic sages, Friday night is also the best time for a husband and wife to make love.

The name of God associated with *Hod,* **Elohim Tzvaot** (eh-low-*heem* tzih-vah-*oat;* the God of Hosts), also indicates the close similarity between *Netzach* and *Hod,* which is connected to the name of God **Y-H-W-H Tzvaot.** *Hod* is usually associated with the biblical personality of Aaron, who was Moses's brother and the first High Priest of the Jewish people.

Yesod: The bridge-builder

The *sefirah* of **Yesod** (yeh-*sowd;* foundation) is thought to be the vehicle or carrier from one thing, person, or condition to another.

One of my Kabbalah teachers tells me that *Yesod* is the power of connection as well as the capacity and the desire to build bridges or make contacts. *Yesod* is also the ability to establish relationships, whether they be with teachers, parents, or lovers.

The organ of the body associated with *Yesod* is the penis or phallus, which is appropriate when one considers that the essence of *Yesod* is the ability to make connections. Keep in mind that these associations are symbolic, so the connection that one makes with one's teacher, friend, or parent must never be a sexual one but is nonetheless a reaching out in a desire to connect.

In the same way that *Tiferet* is a balance of *Chesed* and *Gevurah,* so too is *Yesod* a balance between *Netzach* and *Hod. Yesod* stimulates the desire to connect, receive, and give. On the Tree of Life chart (see Figure 4-1), *Yesod* also appears between the central *sefirah* of *Tiferet* and the last *sefirah* of *Malchut* (see the next section). *Yesod* is the channel through which the central *sefirah* of *Tiferet* can unite with the ultimate, concluding *sefirah* of *Malchut.*

One of the names of God connected with the *sefirah* of *Yesod* is **El Shaddai** (el shah-*die;* the Almighty God, or God Almighty). The biblical character associated with *Yesod* is Yosef (Joseph), Jacob's son. Just as the *sefirah* of Jacob comes after Abraham and Isaac on the Tree of Life, *Yesod* comes right below *Tiferet*, or Jacob, resulting in Jacob's favorite son, Yosef. *Yesod* is sometimes referred to as the foundation of the world, known in Hebrew as **Yesod olam,** and is seen as the balance of the productive energies of *Netzach* and *Hod.*

Sovereignty: The ultimate receptacle

The last of the ten *sefirot* on the Tree of Life is **Malchut** (mahl-*khoot;* kingdom). The word "Malchut" in Hebrew is **melech** (*meh*-lekh; king).

One of my Kabbalah teachers explains that *Malchut* is the realization of all human potential. It's a summation of all the *sefirot* that appear above it, and the word "kingdom" certainly refers to the ultimate and final gathering of all resources. As the bottom *sefirah* on the chart, *Malchut* receives everything from the *sefirot* above it, which is why it's referred to as the ultimate receptacle.

Malchut can be seen as the fruits of all one's labor. Whereas *Yesod* is the *sefirah* that corresponds to the penis or phallus (see the preceding section), *Malchut* corresponds to the feminine form of the divine. The connection between the *Yesod* and *Malchut* is a kind of cosmic sexual union that ultimately gives birth to all the activity in the world.

The day of the week that's connected to *Malchut* is the Sabbath. The Sabbath is the summation and accumulation of all the work of the week, and *Malchut* is the recipient of all of the *sefirot* above it on the Tree of Life (see Figure 4-1).

Malchut completes the chain of all the *sefirot*. The first three *sefirot* are an idea manifesting in the mind; the second three *sefirot* are those of the heart or the emotions, which is the place where the idea that arises in the mind begins to be evaluated. In the third triad, the idea is not only evaluated emotionally but also acted upon and brought into being in the world. Finally, *Malchut* is the real manifestation of the idea in the concrete world of reality.

The name of God connected to *Malchut* is **Shechina** (sheh-*khee*-nah; divine presence), which represents God's presence in the human world. The Shechina gathers the energies of all the other *sefirot* and offers them to the world; it creates a bridge between God and the world. The biblical character associated with *Malchut* is David, the great king of Israel.

Ways to Look at the Tree of Life

The configuration of the *sefirot* on the Tree of Life isn't as straightforward as it appears at first glance. A lot of information is packed into the Tree of Life. For example, there are three vertical lines in the Tree, each containing three *sefirot,* with each line having its own significance. There are also three *triads,* or groups of three *sefirot,* each also with its own significance.

Lots of things are going on in this depiction, and Kabbalists interpret it from a number of different angles. In this section, I show you some of the ways Kabbalists look at and analyze the chart.

Placement

The placement of each *sefirah* on the Tree of Life gives insight into its nature. For example, *Keter* is on the top of the chart, and *Malchut* is on the bottom. This placement makes sense because *Keter* is known as the *sefirah* of connection, the primary connection between God and the world, symbolically coming from above, and *Malchut* is the primary connection between humans and the world and is seen as the final *sefirah,* a summation of all the others. One can picture *Keter* pouring down from above through the crown of each person. *Malchut,* on the other hand, is on the bottom because it's the goal of creation, the physical universe and all that's contained within it.

Vertical lines

The chart of the ten *sefirot* consist of three lines:

- ✔ Middle line
- ✔ Right line, sometimes referred to as *father*
- ✔ Left line, sometimes referred to as *mother*

The location of the *sefirot* on these lines isn't haphazard. Kabbalists studying the relationships between the *sefirot* in each line can understand, for example, why *Tiferet* is on the middle line. *Tiferet* is, after all, harmony and balance. They can also see why *Chesed* and *Gevurah* are respectively on the left and right sides of the Tree of Life; these two *sefirot* constitute a pair at two extremes, just as the Tree of Life reflects.

As a Kabbalist familiarizes himself with the ten *sefirot,* he increases his insight into each of the *sefirot* and their natures by understanding why they belong on the vertical lines on which they're placed.

Horizontal lines

The horizontal lines of the Tree of Life reveal three pairs of *sefirot.* By examining each pair, each of which forms a horizontal line of the Tree of Life, the Kabbalist begins to understand how each pair is a tool for living a Kabbalistic life.

- ✔ *Chochmah* **and** *Binah:* When a Kabbalist uses his mental faculties, he employs a combination of *Chochmah* (intuition) and *(Binah)* logical analysis). A Kabbalist may say that, at any given moment as he thinks, he's going back and forth between *Chochmah* and *Binah* and between a combination of the two because some situations call for more intuition and others call for a more logical analysis.

- ✔ *Chesed* **and** *Gevurah:* In all relationships, in almost everything a Kabbalist does, she's constantly negotiating *Chesed* (giving) and *Gevurah* (receiving) and finding the proper balance for every situation. As I mention in the section "Contraction: The impulse to receive" earlier in this chapter, the pairing of *Chesed* and *Gevurah* is clearly evident in a parent's relationship with his or her child. When a parent relates to a child, in some ways it's a constant interchange between love and kindness and discipline. In the most basic sense, the parent has to find a balance between saying "yes" and saying "no."

- ✔ *Netzach* **and** *Hod:* Particularly when a Kabbalist works on something in the world, he's actively exercising the *sefirot* of *Netzach* (the urge to get things done) and *Hod* (persistence). *Netzach* prompts him to participate in the task before him, and *Hod* keeps the Kabbalist motivated and provides the power and strength to see a job through to its conclusion.

Triads

Following are the three triads on the Tree of Life:

- ✔ *Chochmah* **(wisdom),** *Binah* **(understanding), and** *Da'at* **(knowledge):** These three *sefirot* correspond to mental or intellectual activities.

- ✔ *Chesed* **(lovingkindness),** *Gevurah* **(justice), and** *Tiferet* **(harmony):** These three *sefirot* comprise emotional lives.

- ✔ *Netzach* **(eternity),** *Hod* **(splendor), and** *Yesod* **(foundation):** These three *sefirot* generally act on the physical world in which people live.

The three *sefirot* in each triad form their own groups because the three *sefirot* in each case have some common levels of connection. The *sefirot* are placed where they are on the Tree of Life because of these connections. In other words, the chart of the ten *sefirot* is a well-thought-out configuration. Every detail has an inner logic that helps to reveal the wisdom contained within the chart.

Sefirot within sefirot

Kabbalistic tradition teaches that each of the ten *sefirot* has each of the ten *sefirot* within it. For example, *Chochmah* has

- The *Chochmah* of *Chochmah*
- The *Binah* of *Chochmah*
- The *Da'at* of *Chochmah*
- The *Chesed* of *Chochmah*
- The *Gevurah* of *Chochmah*
- The *Tiferet* of *Chochmah*
- The *Netzach* of *Chochmah*
- The *Hod* of *Chochmah*
- The *Yesod* of *Chochmah*
- The *Malchut* of *Chochmah*

This same pattern applies to each of the other *sefirot*. These connections illustrate the interdependence of the *sefirot;* none of them stand alone. Here's an example of how *sefirot* within *sefirot* works: You see that your small child is about to touch a hot stove, and you realize in a split-second that the only way to protect your child from getting burned is to slap her hand and thrust it away from the stove. In that split-second, you experience the *Gevurah* of *Chesed:* Your urge to protect your child comes from the lovingkindness you feel *(Chesed),* and your decision to slap your child's hand, both to protect it and to impress upon the child that what she's about to do isn't good, is discipline and judgment *(Gevurah).* In other words, your act is one of *Chesed,* but the vehicle used to express that lovingkindness is *Gevurah.*

Pulling the Strings of Existence: The Work of the Kabbalist

Kabbalists consider the ten *sefirot,* as a group, to be an all-inclusive system depicting the entirety of reality. In addition, they see the ten *sefirot* as organic, meaning to say that just as the human body has various organs, each of which has its own function, so too do the ten *sefirot*. Each has its own function that is unique. Similarly, just as the various organs of the body complement each other and work together, so too the ten *sefirot* work together and combine in various ways. You can say that, although the ten *sefirot* are the basis of each of us, each person is different and unique based on the various combinations of *sefirot*. Some people have a tendency toward more of one *sefirah* than another, which accounts for everyone's individuality.

One of my teachers suggests that the way in which a person relates to the *sefirot* is similar to sitting in a control room: The ten *sefirot* are the "strings" of existence, and the Kabbalist uses those strings to effect change in the world. For example, suppose that I'm working on something and am getting tired. The end is in sight, though, and I just need to push myself a little to get the project done. Kabbalisticly speaking, I need to apply a little bit of *Hod* (persistence and holding on) to push through to the end of my work.

There comes a point in the study of the *sefirot* when one almost feels like a postal worker sorting mail in front of a wall full of mail slots. With each experience, the Kabbalist sees the ten *sefirot* at work more clearly and can file them into the slots on the Tree of Life.

Kabbalists conceive of the universe as a downpour of divine plenty from above that constantly creates and sustains the world. This downpour comes in the form of the ten *sefirot*, which manifest out of the pure divine light that shines from above. God contracts and forms each of the *sefirot* and their combinations, and this action results in the continuous creation of the world.

Regarding the *sefirot*, however, Kabbalists teach that the relationship goes both ways between God and humans. Not only is there a downpour of divine light in the form of the ten *sefirot*, but also there's a response from humans who use the ten *sefirot* and show God their thoughts, deeds, and actions, which are really the ten *sefirot* in various combinations. This is the basis of the idea of reward and punishment. Humans use or abuse the world and experience the consequences of their deeds. Kabbalists conceive of a universe in which God is aware of every minute detail of what is going on, so God knows how each person uses the ten *sefirot*, either for the repair of the world or for its destruction.

A Kabbalist isn't conscious of the ten *sefirot* at all times. He doesn't think to himself, "This situation calls for a little bit of *Binah*." Rather, he meditates on the ten *sefirot*, their relationships to each other, and, in general, the wisdom embedded in the Tree of Life. In doing so, the Kabbalist learns so much about the nature of the *sefirot* and their relationships that he becomes a part of the system and the Tree of Life comes alive inside him. Sooner or later, the Kabbalist puts down his books and goes out to meet the world. He doesn't carry the Tree of Life like a cookbook or a formula to tell him what the appropriate action, thought, or manipulation of a *sefirah* is at each moment. Rather, the hope is that by studying the *sefirot* in enough depth, the Kabbalist *becomes* the system of the *sefirot* and is able to apply the proper combinations spontaneously, for the most part.

Imagine, for example, that you work in an office and have specific tasks to perform for your profession. You use the ten *sefirot* constantly; here are a few examples:

- *Binah:* A task before you requires additional time to think through the matter, research it, and discuss it with others.

- *Gevurah:* As a supervisor, you notice that one coworker is getting sloppy in his work. You have to sit down with him to discuss ways to better organize his work and perform with more precision.

- *Yesod:* You realize that that coworker needs some close attention and direction and may even need to be mentored.

- *Chochmah:* You encounter a situation in which you have to react not with your head but with your intuition.

- *Tiferet:* You discover that you and your colleagues aren't getting along very well, and you need to get together to iron out your differences and solve certain common problems.

In other words, a Kabbalist can look at his or her actions and thoughts, compare them to the system of the ten *sefirot,* and recognize their correspondence. Studying the ten *sefirot* and their relationships, especially with a master teacher, begins to reveal the system of the ten *sefirot* as a profoundly insightful system for life.

Chapter 5

Everything (Even a Traffic Jam) Is for the Best

Students of Kabbalah often find one important assumption — that *everything* happens for the best — to be the most difficult to grasp. Some people never get past it and drop out of Kabbalah study as a result.

The idea that everything happens for the best sounds outrageous given all the horrific scenes on the news and family tragedies that occur every day. It doesn't take long to formulate a great resistance to such an outrageous comment. However, this statement is one of the keys of Kabbalah.

In this chapter, I explain the basic Kabbalistic mindset that leads to the view that everything that happens is for the best, and I discuss suggestions to help accustom you to see life in this way.

How Can Everything Possibly Be for the Best?

Everything is for the best? Even the Holocaust? Even the death of an innocent child? You may be thinking, "If this is Kabbalah, I want nothing of it! It's nuts!"

Throughout the study of Kabbalah, it's important to mistrust the face value of things (see Chapter 4). Everything has a deeper meaning than what's obvious at first glance. In a very real way, Kabbalah is the process of improving one's ability to see past the superficial into the depths of life itself. The Kabbalistic sages teach that people don't see everything but can improve their sight, both physical and spiritual insight, through the study and practice of Kabbalah.

One Kabbalist teaches that Kabbalah needs to be "chewed on." He makes the analogy that a baby eats liquid food and often resists the transition to solid food because he or she is forced to start chewing, and that's more difficult. But fortunately, babies learn that mastering the art of chewing food brings great benefit. Similarly, chewing on an outrageous statement such as "Everything is for the best" is tough, but it just may bring some insight and spiritual reward that doesn't show itself at first glance.

So what does it mean when the Kabbalistic sages say that everything is for the best?

Understanding how magic tricks work is a great metaphor for addressing this question. Imagine that a magician shows his hat to the audience, and it's empty. After "proving" to the audience that there's nothing in his hat, he reaches in and pulls out a rabbit. Needless to say, the stage magician didn't actually produce a rabbit out of nothing, but it appears that way to the audience because they don't see everything.

Perhaps the hat had a secret compartment that fooled the eye into thinking that the hat was entirely empty. Perhaps the rabbit was up the magician's sleeve and he dropped it into the hat as he reached in and grabbed it. Or perhaps what he took out of the hat looked like a rabbit but was actually a cleverly disguised device that could fold up into the hat as if it weren't there and then inflate as the magician revealed it to the audience.

Many theories can explain how it appears that a magician produces a rabbit out of nothing, but whatever the real reason, one thing is clear: The audience doesn't see everything.

The basic assumption of the Kabbalist is that humans only have a limited capacity to see the whole of existence. That's why there are so many unsolvable questions in the world. Kabbalists know that a paradox is one sign that they're going along the right path, and one of the primary paradoxes for the Kabbalist is understanding that the universe is beyond human understanding and that acknowledging this fact actually *increases* one's understanding.

A contemporary Kabbalist teaches that news of a knife being stuck into someone sounds horrible until you discover that the knife was in the hands of a surgeon and was being used to help cure a patient. The assumption of the Kabbalist is that even the horrible moments of life are steps in the direction of a future that will make all the suffering justified.

The student of Kabbalah encounters many metaphors, paradoxes, and stories intended to soften the soil of the mind to begin to receive this idea of everything happening for the best. Remember that the very word "Kabbalah" comes from a Hebrew word meaning "to receive." Kabbalistic tradition asks the seeker to receive an idea and try it on for size.

Getting the Words Right: Gam Zu L'Tovah

Gam zu l'tovah (gahm zoo leh-*toe*-vah; this too is for the best) is an Aramaic expression taught by Rabbi Akiva, a great Kabbalist who lived almost 2,000 years ago. Kabbalists have used this phrase for many centuries to express the idea that everything is for the best. This short expression contains an entire spiritual worldview that basically expresses the Kabbalistic assumption that God knows what's happening and why, and that all that happens will work out just fine. It's not an expression that you say lightly, and there are some important restrictions on its use. But this brief Aramaic saying sums up a philosophy of life based on faith in the eternal wisdom of God.

When bad is actually good

For centuries, Kabbalists have shared important stories that express the view that things that seem bad can, from a more complete perspective, actually be good.

These stories (and others like them) aren't meant to be taken literally; they're just stories. But in Jewish and Kabbalistic tradition, stories are vehicles for expressing profound ideas and spiritual advice. Kabbalists tell these stories as a way to integrate the ideas embedded within them, in this case that everything is for the best, into their lives and consciousness.

Rabbi Akiva looks for lodging

For centuries, the following story has served as a reminder to Kabbalists that they don't see or understand everything and that one of the sacred tasks in life is to constantly reframe their experiences to allow into their minds and hearts the possibility of a larger picture beyond human understanding.

While traveling, the great Kabbalist Rabbi Akiva found himself in a town one evening, and he inquired at the inn for a place to stay. When he was told that there was no room for him, he said, "Gam zu l'tovah, this is for the best." He inquired elsewhere in the neighborhood, and each time that he was told that there was no room for him, he responded, "Gam zu l'tovah, this is for the best."

Rabbi Akiva went to the woods on the outskirts of the town and set up a little camp for himself for the night. In the middle of the night, a wind blew out his candle, to which Rabbi Akiva responded, "Gam zu l'tovah, this is for the best." A cat came along and killed the rooster that the rabbi had with him. Rabbi Akiva reacted by saying, "Gam zu l'tovah, this is for the best." Then a wild beast came by and killed his donkey, and once again Rabbi Akiva said, "This is for the best."

The next morning, when he awoke and went back into the town, he discovered that the inn and the other places where he had looked for lodging had been attacked by a band of robbers who caused physical damage to both property and people.

If any of those places of lodging had accepted Rabbi Akiva the night before, he probably would have been a victim as well. If his candle hadn't blown out, his rooster not been killed by the cat, and his donkey not been eaten by the wild beast, he may have been detected in the woods and victimized by the robbers.

Rabbi Eliezer and Elijah the Prophet

Many times in the Talmud, Kabbalists learn that some of the great Rabbinic sages prayed with the desire to speak to Elijah the Prophet, who subsequently often appeared to them. The following story illustrates the idea that everything is for the best, even though it often doesn't seem that way. Sometimes, all that you need is a little more information, and you can turn the incident inside out and draw a very different conclusion.

One day, Rabbi Eliezer prayed to the Almighty for a vision of Elijah. Elijah the Prophet appeared before Rabbi Eliezer and said to him, "What can I do for you?" Rabbi Eliezer said, "I'd like to follow you around. I'd like to watch you do your work, your work for the Holy One, Blessed be He, in the world. I just want to follow you around and watch you do your work."

Elijah the Prophet said to Rabbi Eliezer, "Sorry, you can't follow me around. You'll have too many questions, and I don't have time for your questions." Rabbi Eliezer responded, "I promise I won't ask any questions. Will you allow me the honor of watching you do your work?" Elijah the Prophet agreed to that condition, and off they went.

That night, the two were looking for lodging and saw a dilapidated shack. They approached the shack and discovered a young, poor couple, impoverished and owning little else besides one cow, living there. Elijah the Prophet and Rabbi Eliezer approached the couple and asked them for lodging, and the young couple greeted them warmly, welcomed them in, and gathered some straw to make the two strangers as comfortable as possible. They offered their guests whatever they had, and Rabbi Eliezer and Elijah the Prophet spent the night.

When he awoke the next morning, Rabbi Eliezer overheard Elijah the Prophet praying to the Almighty, asking that the Almighty kill the cow. No sooner had Elijah the Prophet expressed this prayer than the cow suddenly died.

Rabbi Eliezer was outraged and said to Elijah, "What did you do? Why did you ask the Almighty to take the life of the cow? They were such lovely people. They have next to nothing. Why did you take their cow?" Elijah the Prophet looked at Rabbi Eliezer and said, "See, you have so many questions. You have too many questions. I don't have time for your questions." Rabbi Eliezer, though confused, quickly responded, "Please forgive me. I want to follow you. I won't ask you any more questions." Elijah gave him another chance, and off they went.

The next evening they were looking for lodging and arrived at a big mansion. They knocked on the door, and the owner of the mansion came out, greeted them coldly, and agreed that they could stay down in his cellar. He offered them no human warmth, no physical warmth, and no food, and down to the cellar they went. During the night, Rabbi Eliezer awoke upon hearing a commotion. He watched as Elijah the Prophet patched up an area of the cellar wall that was unfinished and crumbling.

The next day, they continued traveling and arrived at a synagogue of wealthy congregants. The pews were made of gold and silver, and the people in the synagogue were cold and unfriendly. When Elijah the Prophet and Rabbi Eliezer entered the synagogue, nobody greeted them, and nobody performed the mitzvah of welcoming guests. In fact, they noticed people whispering about them behind their backs. Before they left the synagogue, Elijah the Prophet looked at the congregation and said, "I pray that you should all become leaders."

They entered a neighborhood that was impoverished. The people were living in squalor, but they were very lovely, sweet, warm, gentle people. Elijah the Prophet looked at this neighborhood, looked at these people, and said, "I want to bless you that one of you should be a leader."

It was at this point that Rabbi Eliezer couldn't hold his questions in any longer. He said to Elijah the Prophet, "I know that you're going to send me away. I know that you required me not to ask questions, but I beg you, please, can you give me some understanding of what you've been doing? I don't understand anything that you're doing. I beg you. Can you offer me some kind of explanation?"

Elijah the Prophet looked at Rabbi Eliezer and said, "I'll offer you some explanation, but then you'll have to leave. Remember the first night when we encountered that lovely yet poor couple living in their shack with their cow? And remember how outraged you were the next morning when you heard me praying to the Holy One, Blessed is He, that he should kill the cow? What you didn't know was that it was time for the wife to die. But I pleaded with Hashem: Don't take the wife, take the cow."

Elijah said, "You recall the next night when we were put in that rich man's cold cellar? And you woke up puzzled when you saw that I was repairing his walls and fixing them up beautifully? I wasn't doing that. I knew that there was a treasure buried within the walls. The man who owned that mansion didn't deserve the mansion, let alone the treasure buried in the walls, so I patched and finished up the walls nicely so that no one would ever discover that treasure."

Elijah the Prophet went on. "Remember the next day, when we went to that synagogue that was so wealthy, with gold and silver pews, but all the people were so unfriendly? I noticed how confused you were when you thought that I'd offered them some big blessing by saying that they all should become great leaders. That wasn't a blessing; it was a curse. Anyone who has ever been in an organization knows the chaos that results from everyone thinking that he or she is a leader. I prayed that they all should become leaders. And then we went to that poor neighborhood, and the people were so sweet and so lovely, and you wondered, in comparison to the earlier so-called 'blessing,' why I would just say, 'I bless you that one of you should be a leader.' You see, that indeed *was* a blessing. All that neighborhood really needed was one good, strong leader who could take the people out of the poverty and squalor that they lived in."

Elijah the Prophet then said to Rabbi Eliezer, "Yes, you have to leave now, but please don't forget that what you see in the world is not the whole picture. It's only part of the grand picture in the mind of the Almighty."

A 20th-century Kabbalist who found good in everything

One of the characteristics of a Kabbalist is his or her ability to see good within everything. One of my favorite stories related to this idea has to do with Rabbi Abraham Isaac Kook, the first Chief Rabbi of Palestine during the British mandate. Rabbi Abraham Isaac Kook, more commonly known as Rav Kook, was a brilliant scholar, a great mystic, and a renowned Kabbalist.

When he was appointed to be the first Chief Rabbi, Rav Kook had many critics, and many people protested his appointment. Rav Kook responded to his critics by saying that they were right. He said that there were so many people in the world and so many scholars in the holy city of Jerusalem who were greater than he was. He expressed his situation with an analogy of shoes that are too big. He said that the shoes of the Chief Rabbi position were bigger than he could fill and therefore he needed to fill them with straw. As he explained, when straw is put into shoes to fill them out, the hard and sharp edges of the straw often irritate the feet. Rav Kook concluded that his critics who believed that he wasn't qualified to be Chief Rabbi were like straw in big shoes; just as the actual straw is irritating, the critics of Rav Kook were irritants to him. But they were necessary for him to be able to fill the shoes that he was asked to wear.

In other words, Rav Kook looked at the situation and found something positive and good in his harsh critics. He reframed the situation in a way that revealed the positive side of what was otherwise negative.

An important rule about saying "Everything is for the best"

The Kabbalistic sages certainly encourage Kabbalists to adopt the view that everything in life is for the best and express that view by saying "Gam zu l'tovah." However, the sages also insist that Kabbalists never express that phrase to others; you should only say to yourself. Kabbalists are forbidden by tradition and the basis of human compassion to say "Gam zu l'tovah" to a suffering person. Even if a person is a Kabbalist or simply a person with deep faith in God, the compassionate thing to do is to resist saying that everything is for the best.

Kabbalah recognizes human limitations; sometimes, a person's faith is shaken when something bad happens. The compassionate thing is to offer comfort, not theology, when a person is grieving.

For example, if a friend falls and hurts his knee, I don't say to him, "Gam zu l'tovah, everything is for the best." Rather, upon seeing someone who has fallen and gotten hurt, I do what I can to help my friend and relieve his pain and suffering. But if I fall and hurt my own knee, I have the right and, in fact, the obligation to take all the suffering of my own life and use it for the best.

When I fall and hurt my knee, saying "Gam zu l'tovah" is appropriate because the fall may very well be a warning from God that I need to be careful and slow down before a much larger and more devastating accident happens. The small scrapes and bruises of life actually can be used for the positive, but although a Kabbalist tries to see things for the best, he doesn't say that to a suffering person.

An exception to the rule of not saying "Gam zu l'tovah" to others is made if the person who's suffering is a deep friend. Rather than cultivate lots of friends, the sages advise that each person should invest in one good, deep friendship. Two people who are friends on the deepest and most trusting levels are permitted and even encouraged to remind each other that this is the Almighty's universe and that indeed everything is for the best.

The great sages referred to the error of saying "Gam zu l'tovah" to others who are suffering as "the sins of the friends of Job" because in the biblical book of Job, Job suffers and his friends say to him, "Don't you have faith that everything is from God?"

Don't Confuse Acceptance with Passivity

Belief that everything happens for the best, faith, trust in God, clinging to God, belief in God's individual supervision of every detail of the world, and other related notions and concepts don't mean that the Kabbalist is a passive participant in life's drama. Faith and trust in God for the Kabbalist doesn't prompt passivity or an inactive attitude.

Kabbalists believe in the following:

- **Social action:** The Kabbalist doesn't look at the ills of the world and say, "Since I believe that God supervises everything, I need to leave everything just as it is." Rather, the Kabbalist believes that his or her desire to repair the world is part of God's intention.

- **Fairness in business:** A Kabbalist doesn't believe that "whatever happens, happens" or that anything that one can get away with is obviously what God has allowed to happen. Rather, Kabbalists spend a lifetime studying, and part of that study is the study of business ethics and the fair treatment of others.

- **Animal rights:** Kabbalistic tradition has strict laws about the imperativeness of treating animals as kindly as possible, relieving their suffering, and taking steps to help animals avoid any unnecessary suffering.

- **Rights and responsibilities in marriage:** Kabbalists set high standards for this area of human experience. Marriage isn't simply a union between two people in love. Jewish law, which is the law that Kabbalists spend a lifetime studying, is quite concerned about the rights of both husband and wife. Couples fully explore these rights and agree to hold up their individual ends of responsibility before the Kabbalistic marriage ceremony takes place.

In so many aspects of life, Kabbalists walk an interesting path between trust in God and His supervision of the world on the one hand and the active pursuit of ethical behavior and the repairing of the world on the other. These two extremes aren't a contradiction but rather a profound paradox within which the Kabbalist lives his or her life.

Training Oneself to See Like a Kabbalist

One of the most important things that a Kabbalist does (and something that he or she is actually doing constantly but that nobody sees) is *inner activity*. Inner activity refers to the constant training to perceive all of life and all of existence as created by God and, therefore, for the best. As the great Kabbalist known as the Baal Shem Tov is known to have said, "Not even a single blade of grass moves without God allowing it to happen."

To be a Kabbalist is to be a reframer, to take a situation and cultivate the view that everything to do with that situation is for the best. For example, if I'm stuck in traffic, perhaps the traffic jam is preventing me from being involved in an accident farther down the road. If I have a cold and need to stay in bed for a day or two, the recovery may be strengthening my immune system so that I'm better able to fight an upcoming illness. Or the cold itself may be keeping me home to avoid some other unforeseen stumbling block.

Kabbalists learn and meditate on a number of key concepts, which I explain in this section, throughout their lives. Each concept overlaps or is connected with another, and taken together, they form the core theology of Kabbalah. But the terms that I explain in this section are more than abstract philosophical concepts. Kabbalists constantly remind themselves of these concepts (every day and throughout life) and ultimately use them as strategies for understanding their lives and the world.

Kabbalist never tire of studying these concepts or thinking about them. On the contrary, they're as vital to a Kabbalist life as air, food, and love. Meditating on these concepts is the inner activity of the Kabbalist. Focusing on these concepts daily, from the time one gets up in the morning until the time one goes to sleep at night, infuses the Kabbalist's life with a special relationship to the world.

Having faith

Emunah (eh-*moo*-nah; faith) is a broad and general term implying that a person, at the core of his or her being, believes in the existence of God.

A blessing for bad news

The great sages invented formulas for saying different blessings over the many joys of life. For example, there are blessings to say before enjoying food and a blessing to say upon all kinds of enjoyments and pleasures. But there's also a blessing to say when hearing of bad news:

Baruch Dayan HaEmet (bah-*rukh* dah-*yahn* hah-em-*et*; blessed is the true judge). This blessing implies that, from a human vantage point, the event may look and sound sad (and indeed is), but from God's vantage point, something else is going on that humans simply can't see.

A great Jewish philosopher and sage, Maimonides (also known as the Rambam), has been an important teacher to Kabbalists for centuries. His masterpiece, the Mishneh Torah, a work of 14 books that's masterfully organized and has been said to contain every concept in Jewish life, begins with the following:

> *The foundation of all foundations, and the pillar of all wisdom is to know that there is God who brought into being all of existence. All the beings of the heavens, and earth, and what is between them came into existence only from the truth of God's being.*

This primary idea is that out of which everything else grows — that God existed before existence, that God created existence, and that God is the center of all existence. The importance of getting the primary idea (a fundamental belief in God) right is much like the exactness of launching a rocket ship to the moon; if the rocket's aim is off just a little bit here on earth, by the time it gets to the vicinity of the moon, the rocket will be a tremendous distance away from its target.

Emunah implies two things:

- ✔ Faith in God
- ✔ Honesty and integrity in one's relations with others

Faith also implies a belief in the divine ownership of the world. Reminding oneself that this is God's world is an expression of faith, and therefore, those who are conscientious about treating the earth in a healthy way are expressing their faith. The Kabbalist's faith that the world is God's leads to a desire to treat the natural world with respect. Loving behavior toward others reflects the same kind of faith. If each human being is a creation of God, then treating others appropriately is an acknowledgment of the creator.

Being certain that God is perfect

Bitachon (bih-tah-*khone;* security, trust, confidence) is an aspect of the broader concept of faith and signifies the deepest certainty that God knows what He is doing, that God is perfect, that nothing happens without God allowing it to happen, and that the Kabbalist has confidence in God's infinite wisdom.

Kabbalists connect the notion of bitachon with the *sefirah* of *Netzach,* which I explain in detail in Chapter 4. It has been observed that *Netzach,* the urge to get things done, is related to bitachon because when someone is actively expressing confidence in God, he or she gets the sense that each person has a mission in life and must actively pursue that mission in order to manifest what God wants. In a sense, bitachon as confidence reflects both a confidence in God and a confidence in one's own ability to find oneself and express oneself in the way that God intended.

The concept of bitachon implies that whatever happens to a Kabbalist is ultimately for the good. Because Kabbalists believe that God is good, everything that God makes happen or allows to happen is also good.

Many books on the subject of faith and related concepts remind Kabbalists that faith and trust is really a form of service to God. The Kabbalist actively trusts in God and, through that trust, believes that his or her soul is transformed and purified. Profound trust in God opens the Kabbalist up to godliness and holiness.

Attaching yourself to God (and never letting go)

In the Christian world, the term is "communion." For the Kabbalist, it's **d'veykut** (dih-vey-*koot;* clinging), which is a similar uniting with the Holy One and not letting go. For Kabbalists, d'veykut is a high and deep stage of spiritual development where the seeker attaches himself or herself to God and exchanges individuality for a profound partnership with the Holy One. The force behind d'veykut is the love of God and desire for intimacy or closeness with God.

When a Kabbalist develops a strong sense of d'veykut, the seemingly vast number of requirements and commandments in her life transform themselves from external burdens into more and more opportunities to devote herself to God. Just as young lovers are of infinite service to their loved ones, the Kabbalist who has true d'veykut sees the requests that God makes as opportunities to express her love for the Almighty.

For example, the Kabbalist views the requirements of the Sabbath (see Chapter 10) to be part of the gift of the Sabbath, not burdensome restrictions as outsiders may see them. Similarly, Kabbalists don't see the dos and don'ts of the Torah as oppressive but rather as opportunities throughout one's day and life to connect with God.

The concept of d'veykut also informs the Kabbalist's attitude toward her own death because she believes that one of death's great rewards is the opportunity to merge with God in an even deeper and more complete way than is possible during life. D'veykut in this lifetime is fleeting and incomplete, but complete d'veykut is attainable after death.

Knowing that you're under God's supervision

Hashgacha pratit (hash-*gah*-kah *prah*-teet; private supervision, at Providence) is the Kabbalistic concept that every individual being is under the private supervision of God.

Some people believe that there is no God, whereas others believe that God created the world but then left it alone to its own devices. Kabbalists maintain that God rules the world by hashgacha pratit; the infinite God is constantly involved in every detail of existence, from the largest cataclysm to the tiniest movement of an insect. (Flip to Chapter 16 for more on God's ongoing supervision of the creation as a whole.)

As I say many times in this book, Kabbalists must reconcile the following two points of a major paradox:

- The highest expression of the Divine in the world is humankind, and humankind functions with free will.
- Nothing happens in the world without God allowing it to happen.

Hashgacha pratit doesn't contradict the belief in free will. Rather, it insists that God is actively involved in the supervision of everything, while at the same time allows for free will. Kabbalists may not always understand this paradox, but they know that it's the wisdom received from tradition.

Hoping for the best

Many people are familiar with the Hebrew word **mazal** (mah-*zal;* fate) because of the popular expression "Mazal Tov." Although the expression is commonly thought to mean "good luck," it actually means "good fate." Wishing a person mazal is a way of hoping that the person experiences only good things as his or her life unfolds.

Even though everything is for the best, wishing a person good fate is an expression of hope that what happens to the person is easy to recognize as "for the best" and not one of the challenging and difficult moments when thinking that what has happened may be tough.

Understanding that things happen for a reason

Bashert (bah-*shairt*) is a general concept that implies that things happen for a reason. Kabbalists use it most commonly in connection with matchmaking.

Within the matchmaking world, when a Kabbalist is looking for a future spouse, he says, "I'm looking for my bashert." What he means is that he's looking for the one whom God has picked out for him. A story known by all serious Kabbalah students tells of a Roman who asks one of the Jewish sages "If God created the world in six days, what has He been doing since then?" The sage's answer is that, among other things, God is making matches. To refer to somebody as your bashert is to say that you believe that this person is your partner selected by God, deliberately and for a purpose.

Of course, in today's society, people ask, "If God makes matches, why are there so many divorces?" One of my teachers of Kabbalah says that God makes matches, but no one knows why He makes the particular matches that He does. God has His own motives for doing things, and matches aren't necessarily intended to provide individuals with eternal bliss. A couple can be matched because of many things other than passion and romance. For example, many matches occur for their fruitful results (that is, for the children they produce).

Picking up the Pieces: In the Beginning a Vessel Was Shattered

The 16th-century Rabbi Isaac Luria (known among Kabbalists as the Ari; see Chapter 18) caused a revolution in Kabbalistic thought and today is considered to be, without exception, the greatest Kabbalist who ever lived. His ideas, ways of thinking, and metaphors have become the standard accepted notions that Kabbalists have studied for the last five centuries.

One of the Ari's most basic notions describes, metaphorically, the basis for the creation of the world. As the Ari explained it, God created a vessel (like a vase, cup, or container of some sort) and then poured His infinite, divine light into this vessel. The vessel couldn't contain the infinite light and shattered. The broken pieces of the vessel scattered, and the stuff of creation — all its many bits and pieces — are actually the shards produced by that cataclysmic shattering. The shards still contained evidence of the original divine light.

Being "chosen" means greater responsibility

The Torah teaches that the Jewish people are a nation of priests. This notion, which is the basis for the too often misunderstood phrase "the chosen people," in no way means that Jews are superior. This distorted idea has been spread far and wide but is nowhere to be found in Jewish literature or Jewish teachings. The idea that the children of Israel should see themselves as a "nation of priests" simply refers to Jewish consciousness that the entire world is holy and that the nation of priests is required to relate to all the details in the universe as though they were holy and in need of sanctification.

Everything has the potential for holiness, and therefore, everything needs to be related to with a certain degree of holiness. The notion of the chosen people refers to the idea that the Jewish people have a greater responsibility and burden to relate to the Divine than others do.

In other words, the world in which Kabbalists live, in each of its details, contains divine light. Whatever a Kabbalist relates to, whether it be solid, liquid, or gas, good or evil, physical or spiritual, contains divine light. And according to Kabbalistic tradition, each person is responsible for breaking open the pieces to release the light contained within. Because everything in the world contains divine light, all situations have good (divine light) hidden within them. The Kabbalist's task — and everyone else's, for that matter — is to search for or recognize that divine light and let it shine.

By integrating the shattered vessel metaphor into one's consciousness, all life and all existence has the potential for sanctity through the release of divine sparks from the divine light inside. Kabbalists make the assumption that the world needs to be repaired (see Chapters 7 and 8 for more on this concept), that God created a world that is incomplete and flawed. By revealing the divine light that's hidden in everything, the Kabbalist participates in the correcting of the world, leading to a time when God will be obvious and known to all people.

Within Kabbalistic literature, the sanctity of life is evident in the everyday act of eating. God created a world in which various species eat other species. One of the reasons that Kabbalistic tradition requires the Kabbalist to recite various blessings before eating various foods is to help to release the divine sparks embedded within the food.

For the Kabbalist, eating isn't just an effort to satisfy one's appetite. It's a releasing of divine light contained within everything. If one eats with the proper intention, the food is the source not only of physical nutrients needed to survive but also divine light that offers spiritual nourishment and the fortitude to go on to perform acts of lovingkindness.

Seeing bread as a tribute to human creativity

The blessings that Kabbalists recite before eating various foods (see Chapter 9) are divided into categories. For example, one blessing is appropriate when eating fruit from a tree, and another blessing is recited for baked goods like cookies and cakes, but not for bread. Bread has it's own special blessing.

However, if a Kabbalist sits down to a meal that consists of many different kinds of foods *and* includes bread, it's not necessary to recite the various blessings on the different kinds of foods. Rather, the Kabbalist should begin his or her meal with the blessing to be recited before eating bread and then enjoy the meal. In a sense, the blessing for bread contains all the other blessings.

So why is bread and the blessing said before eating bread of such high status? Bread represents human creativity because it's made through the creativity and ingenuity of the people who take various God-given ingredients, combine them, and create the staff of life. Eating a pear, string beans, milk, or chicken is merely taking the food that God gives. But when the Kabbalist eats bread, he's acknowledging the ability of human beings to combine the elements of the world and to create something new.

Kabbalists consider this ability to create to be a divine spark within humans. Bread is the finest example within the human diet of that expression of creativity, and therefore the blessing said before eating bread is sufficient for the entire meal regardless of how many other kinds of foods are consumed.

This example also points to the Kabbalistic notion of repairing the world. Kabbalists gather the gifts that God has given and try to combine them in a way that will improve the world. By gathering the ingredients to make bread, people exercise their ability to create the tools necessary to improve, build, and raise the level of the world. Each day, Kabbalists need to be aware that the world requires rectifying and things need to be put into their proper places. Kabbalists assume that the world is mixed up; all too often, things that are small are considered big, things that are big are considered small, things that are important are considered unimportant, and things that are unimportant are considered important. The Kabbalist's job is to put everything into its proper proportion for the sake of the health of the world.

Figuring Out Individual Divine Assignments

Kabbalistic tradition teaches that it's each person's responsibility to find his or her own place in the world. As I explain in Chapter 6, each human being is absolutely unique. In principle, each person has unique elements that belong to no one else. Of course many people share various qualities, but in totality, no two people are identical.

Growing out of this idea of divine individual assignments, of course, is the notion that each person has his or her own strengths and weaknesses, abilities and inclinations. Kabbalists relate divine assignments to the biblical story of Adam and Eve in the Garden of Eden. They teach that just as God put Adam and Eve in the garden to tend it, the world is the garden of existence, and each person has his or her own part of the garden to tend. The world is a large place, and there's lots of work to do everywhere. It isn't any individual's job to tend the entire world but rather to find that part of the world that he or she must repair.

You may be asking, "How does one discover one's true purpose in life, one's divine assignment?" One of my teachers suggests that a good first step "is simply to quiet down." Sometimes the business of life means that people actually miss hearing or seeing clearly the tasks that are obviously before them and in which they must participate.

Another method of discovering one's task is through prayer. Within personal prayers, Kabbalists often make a request to God to help reveal what they should be doing in life.

But nobody suggests that uncovering one's purpose in life is easy. Each person has free will, and the expression of that free will through the choices presented all the time can be daunting. That's where Kabbalah teachers come in. When a Kabbalah teacher is connected to his or her students in an intimate spiritual way, the teacher is often a great help in guiding his or her student. (For more on studying with a teacher, flip to Chapter 14.)

Another way to approach the question of one's true purpose in life is to recognize one's natural abilities. Natural abilities are usually a hint (or even more than a hint) of what a person should be busy doing. Ultimately, people can only hope that they've found their purposes. Kabbalists believe that through sincere prayer, and diligent study, you can attain the wisdom necessary to find the right path.

Everyone is a letter in the Torah

One of my teachers shares the metaphor that each person should see himself or herself as an individual letter in the Torah. The Torah is a scroll consisting of the Five Books of Moses, and it contains 304,805 letters. Locating oneself in the Torah is another way of saying that a person needs to find his or her place. An ancient text teaches that God looked into the Torah and created the world. The Torah is a blueprint for the world, and it's the Kabbalist's task in life to find his or her location in that blueprint.

Chapter 6

Our Bodies Don't Have Souls; Our Souls Have Bodies

Some people think that humans are just bodies; human bodies are born, they live, and they die. Some people say that humans are bodies alright — but they're bodies that have souls. Kabbalists reject both ideas and say that humans aren't bodies with souls, they're souls that have bodies.

What's the difference between a body with a soul and a soul with a body? Kabbalists believe that, contrary to what humans see on the outside, human souls are much greater than human bodies. Most important is the Kabbalistic view that that our bodies are temporary; our souls are eternal. The world that we see with our eyes and perceive with our senses is only part of creation. To be a Kabbalist is to train your senses to remember how much more you are than just your body.

Kabbalists know that their souls exist, they existed before the body they now have, and they'll exist after this current body is used up. The soul behaves in certain ways, is nourished by certain things, and must learn how to get along with its partner and instrument, the body. In this chapter, I look at the soul, how it functions, how to take care of it, and what its job is in Kabbalistic terms.

According to Kabbalistic tradition, human beings aren't just the result of two parents but rather are the product of a partnership of three. The mother and father give the baby its physical being, and God gives the baby its spiritual aspect. This idea, by the way, is alluded to in the opening chapters of the Torah, in the book of Genesis, where the description of the creation of man includes the image of God breathing into Adam's nostrils. The great sages throughout the generations have understood this divine breath to be the soul, or the spiritual aspect of the person. The two parents are responsible, however, for both a child's physical and spiritual nourishment. Just as it's important to treat your body right, your soul also needs care and attention. When a Kabbalist realizes that he or she is more soul than body, the attention focused on the soul grows in intensity.

A Spark of God in Everyone

Kabbalists believe that bodies are physical aspects and souls are spiritual aspects, and as such, bodies are temporary, and souls are eternal.

The idea that souls exist prior to birth and will also exist after death is a fundamental element of the Kabbalistic notion of the soul. According to Kabbalah, when God sends a soul into the world, God in a sense "houses" the soul in a body. The body is the instrument of the soul, and the soul uses the body during its incarnation and lifetime.

When the body is used up, so to speak, it's buried in the ground, and the soul continues on its way (see Chapter 7). Although tradition speaks of all creation being a manifestation of God, the soul in its deepest aspect is God Himself. In a sense, the world is generally considered something other than God, but the deepest part of the soul is part of God.

Kabbalistic tradition also carries the idea that, in its essence, the soul has the potential for some of the actual capacity of God. This capacity is the ability to move, to choose, to build, and to destroy — essentially, the capacity to create.

Getting to the Soul of the Matter

To begin the process of understanding the human soul, you need to understand three foundational ideas about the soul:

- ✔ The soul is ultimately beyond human understanding.
- ✔ Each human soul is really a fragment or a part of a single soul that's made up of the sum of all souls.
- ✔ Although all souls are part of one general human soul, each fragment is unique and irreplaceable and works with all the other souls to become itself.

The soul? It's beyond me

Of absolute and fundamental importance to understanding the soul is recognizing that, ultimately, grasping the true nature of the soul is absolutely and categorically impossible. Although there's much that people can say about the soul, and although many great sages have speculated on the way of the soul, the soul is one of those divinely created entities that's simply beyond human comprehension.

It's vital that the student of Kabbalah acknowledge at the outset that full comprehension of the soul is, by definition, impossible. Remember, however, that, many times in the study of Kabbalah, the acknowledgment of the impossibility of grasping a subject is a paradoxically giant step in the direction of understanding that very same impossible-to-comprehend subject.

We're all part of one great soul

In Kabbalah, human beings are part of one great soul that exists in the world. On the most fundamental level, there's only one soul in the world, and each individual soul is a part of that greater soul. That's not to say that humans shouldn't also see themselves as halves of the souls they create with their spouses. And the concept of a great soul doesn't interfere with the idea of various levels or parts of the individual soul that I talk about in this chapter.

Many Kabbalists have attempted to describe the soul in terms of light. God's divine light shines outward, and one of the rays of light that comes out of God is the one great soul. Kabbalah teachers often suggest this means that every soul is a fragment of the divine light. The soul is a spark of the Divine, and part of its task in the world is to experience and live from the humility of being but a piece of the one soul.

We're all unique, though, too

Also fundamental to the Kabbalistic view of the human soul is the basic idea that no two souls are the same. Every soul has its own function and its own path. Every soul has its own capacity, and nobody can replace another soul.

A basic principle in Judaism and Kabbalistic tradition is the profound regard for human life and the view that each person is irreplaceable. In fact, Kabbalists teach that each person has a part to play in the perfection of the world and that, even if you can do my part better than I can, my soul must complete it's journey in this lifetime by doing it's part. Nobody can replace anyone else.

Kabbalistic tradition also teaches that each individual soul is the result of special and unique combinations of the ten *sefirot* within that person. Keep in mind that the Tree of Life, the chart of the *sefirot,* is both the blueprint of the world as well as the blueprint of the structure and components of the soul. Each soul consists of the ten *sefirot* in various combinations and permutations. Kabbalists believe that the reason people are all different from each other in personality is because each is a unique combination of the *sefirot* and each soul tends toward certain *sefirot* more than others. Here are some examples (I cover the ten *sefirot* in depth in Chapter 4):

- *Netzach* is the *sefirah* that manifests as the urge to get things done. People wouldn't be productive without it, but too much *Netzach* produces a workaholic.

- *Chochmah* is intuition, and *Binah* is logical analysis. It's common to find that some people make decisions based on the feel of a situation while others gather as much information and base their decision on the "facts" they've brought together.

Descent for the Sake of Ascension — That's Life

It has been said that if only the soul were allowed to stay in heaven and bask in the divine light, its experience would be far more pleasant than it is wrapped in a human body and spending a life in the physical world. After all, without a body, the soul is free; it doesn't get entangled in the temptations of life. But it's fundamental to Kabbalistic belief that even though the soul's journey in the world is a great risk and can result in damage of the world and of the soul itself, the risk is worthwhile based on a notion described as a *descent for the sake of ascension.*

The soul descends into the world because the world gives the soul an opportunity to purify itself and raise itself to a level that it didn't exist at before it made its descent. This process, which is actually the process by which people come to know God, is the goal of life. The more people purify themselves and raise their spiritual levels, the less of a barrier there is between humans and their perception, experience, and ultimate knowledge of God. According to Kabbalah, God created humans to give them pleasure, and there's no greater pleasure than to know God. Think of the soul as a roller coaster: The only way a roller coaster can go very high is if it builds momentum by going very low very quickly.

No pain, no gain

No doubt you've heard the expression, "No pain, no gain." When people go to a gym, they usually come out with sore muscles. The sore muscles are actually broken down muscle tissue, but the breaking down of the muscle tissue during exercise leads to a rebuilding of that tissue to be even stronger than it was before.

So it is with the soul, which descends into this world of trials and tribulations and ends up with even greater spiritual achievement than it could have had without the descent. This is one of the secrets of Kabbalah: God gives people trials in life as a way for them to purify themselves and ascend to great heights of spiritual consciousness.

Leaving God only to come back again

Although describing the soul as being housed in the body paints a useful picture, Kabbalistic tradition urges students to attempt to conceive of the soul in slightly different terms.

As one of my teachers says, the soul isn't caged in the body, and humans shouldn't conceive of the soul as a point in space. Rather, the soul is a line, like the line of light created by a flashlight or a beacon, and the source of that line of light is God. When the line of light shines on a person, it goes through the person and continues on after passing through the body. In other words, the soul isn't in one particular point in space because it's a line of being.

As I mention earlier in this chapter, the soul exists before the body and will exist after the body is long gone. To extend the metaphor even farther, some Kabbalists teach that the soul is a circle. The soul is a manifestation of God that shines outward, picks up a human body, and then continues around the circle back to its source, God.

Introducing the Four Worlds of Kabbalah

Kabbalists view reality as consisting of four fundamental worlds. In Hebrew, the term used is **olam** (oh-*lam*; world). In order to understand the Kabbalistic conception of the soul, which has five levels (see the section, "Going Up? The Soul's Journey of Five Levels," later in this chapter), you first have to explore the notion of the four worlds. The four worlds correspond to the first four levels of the soul (the fifth level is the deepest level of the soul, the place where Kabbalists say that the soul is actually a part of God). Humans are a microcosm of the universe; just as the universe consists of four worlds, the human soul has four corresponding levels.

Don't think of these four worlds as four planets or four galaxies. When Kabbalists speak of "worlds," they're not talking about different locations but rather different dimensions of being. These four worlds are four general levels of reality, and Kabbalists conceive of the human consciousness as constantly going up and down and back and forth between worlds.

Following are the four worlds, according to Kabbalistic tradition:

- **Atzilut** (ah-tzee-*loot*): The world of emanation; the world of the spirit

- **Beriyah** (*bree*-ah): The world of creation; the world of the intellect, where ideas reside

- **Yetzirah** (yeh-*tzeer*-ah): The world of formation; the world of emotions

- **Assiyah** (ah-*see*-yah): The world of action; the concrete, physical world

Each of the four worlds is reflected in each person, who has a spiritual nature, an intellectual nature, an emotional side, and physicality. Each person resides in all four worlds at the same time, but one's consciousness or focus tends to go back and forth among them. For example, there are times when an individual is mostly feeling something emotionally, and at that moment, his consciousness resides in the world of emotion, which is the world of formation.

Similarly, sometimes a person is actively engaged in thinking, in which case his soul is dwelling in the world of creation. And when a person is ravenously hungry and just gobbled down a plate of food to satisfy a physical hunger, Kabbalisticly, his consciousness is residing mostly in the physical world, in the world of action.

Each of the four worlds is parallel to the others, which makes it easy for one's consciousness to bounce back and forth from one to the other over the course of each day. Interestingly, the word "parallel" in modern Hebrew comes from the same root as the word for "Kabbalah."

The progression of the four worlds

A progression exists from atzilut (emanation) to beriah (creation), to yetzirah (formation), and to asiyah (action). One way to imagine this progression is to compare it to a source of light. Imagine God as the source of divine light, with light pouring out of God in all directions. From there, the following happens:

1. In creating the world, God *emanates* divine light and begins the process of *creation.* The light emanating from God begins as a boundless emanation until God takes that boundless light and makes something out of it, which is creation.

2. God takes the process of creation a step further by beginning to form whatever it is that God has in mind. The light, therefore, goes from emanation to creation and then to *formation.* In the formation stage, God refines the creation by beginning form something.

3. The result of creation and then formation is the world or the universe itself.

4. After formation, the process is more or less complete, and the world that God has emanated, created, and formed is able to act or be. This is the world of *action.*

The world of atzilut (emanation), which is sometimes referred to as nearness to God, is the most abstract of the four worlds, but it's also considered to be the highest of the four worlds. When Kabbalists use the word "higher" to describe something, they mean that something is closer to God, more abstract, clearer, and more transparent than something that's lower. Atzilut is the most spiritual of the four worlds, and some Kabbalists go so far as to say that the world of emanation isn't really a world but is itself God.

Considering the four realms of human existence

Another way of looking at Kabbalah's four worlds in order to understand them is to relate them to the four realms of human experience: the physical, the emotional, the intellectual, and the spiritual.

Each human being exists simultaneously in these four levels:

- **Physical:** Every person has a physical aspect that includes the body and the physical senses. This aspect corresponds to the world of action, in which the human being acts within the physical world.

- **Emotional:** Every person lives within the world of emotions, which is more spiritual than the physical world. All have within them a wide array of emotions of seemingly infinite gradations. The world of emotions that each person experiences is said to reside in the world of formation.

> ✔ **Intellectual:** Every person has an intellectual life that exists above the world of emotions. Just as the world of emotions is not a physical world, so too the world of ideas is an abstract spiritual world.
>
> ✔ **Spiritual:** Above the intellectual world of each human being is the world of emanation. Sometimes this realm isn't even considered a world; because it's so abstract and transparent, some consider it to be God Himself.

You can look at the four worlds from either direction or order: from emanation to creation to formation to action, or from action to formation to creation to emanation. Similarly, when speaking of the four levels of worlds in terms of aspects of a person, you can view them from physical to emotional to intellectual to spiritual, or the other way around.

Who inhabits each world?

One of the ways to best understand each of the four words is to see the differences among them, so Kabbalists often speak of the beings that reside in each world and help to distinguish them from each other. To start, humans reside in the world of asiyah (action), and angels reside in the world of yetzirah (formation).

Kabbalists create angels constantly with every thought, deed, and inclination. Within the world of the angels, Kabbalists conceive of both positive and negative angels.

A good deed obviously creates a positive charge in the universe, and a bad deed creates a negative charge. The positive and negative angels attach themselves almost parasitically to the soul. The more positive deeds, the more positive angels are attached to the soul, and the more negative deeds, the more negative angels are attached to the soul. When a person dies and drops his or her body, the soul remains and continues its work but still carries the positive or negative nonphysical essences that the human being created. (See Chapter 8 for more on Kabbalistic angels.)

Beings referred to as *seraphs* reside in the world of beriah (creation). One way to imagine an intellectual being in the world of ideas is to think of a brainstorming session at a business that depends upon creativity. Two people each express an idea, and those two ideas connect with each other and give birth to a new idea that neither participant would have been able to think of on his or her own.

In the highest world, atzilut (emanation), there are no individual beings at all; it's a profoundly abstract world filled with clarity and transparency.

Going Up? The Soul's Journey of Five Levels

Kabbalists conceive of the soul as having five levels. Each level has a name and represents aspects of the divine soul in man. The five levels of the soul are

1. **Nefesh** (*neh*-fesh): The lowest and most basic aspect of the soul. Sometimes, the word "nefesh" is used more generally to refer to the soul. Nefesh animates existence and gives the human body its ability to move, its life force, and its ability to reproduce. The level of the soul called nefesh corresponds to the world of action.

   People living on the level of nefesh share it with animals. These people simply move, breathe, and are alive.

2. **Ruach** (*roo*-akh): The second level of the soul. Ruach is often translated as spirit. The level of the soul called ruach corresponds to the world of formation and emotions.

   People living on the level of ruach not only are alive but also experience the range of human emotions including love, compassion, humility, and awe.

3. **Neshama** (neh-*shah*-mah): The third level of the soul. The word "neshama" is sometimes used informally to refer to the soul in general, but neshama really refers to the *higher* soul, corresponding to the world of creation and ideas.

   People living on the level of neshama think, meditate on God, and reach for an intellectual grasp of the world and the Divine.

4. **Chaya** (*khah*-yah): The fourth level of the soul. The level called chaya corresponds to that which goes on in the spiritual world of emanation.

   People living on the level of chaya pierce through the worlds of emotion and ideas and enter spiritual realms that are almost impossible to describe. They begin to grasp spiritual reality and see that they're far more than bodies that are born, live, and die.

5. **Yechida** (yeh-*khee*-dah): The fifth level of the soul. This level is called the most inward point of the divine spark. Kabbalists see yechida as being beyond all the four worlds (see the section "Introducing the Four Worlds of Kabbalah") and the actual point in which the soul and the Divine make contact.

   People living on the level of yechida have reached the point of contact between the soul and God.

Proof of Kabbalah's ancient tradition

The five levels of the soul are a good example of the fact that Kabbalah is an ancient tradition. Too often, modern scholars think that Kabbalistic tradition began sometime relatively late in Jewish history — some say perhaps in the 1200s while others point to the 1500s.

Of course, they're wrong. For example, one can see a discussion of the five levels of the soul in the early Rabbinic literature, whose tradition is over 2,000 years old. A Rabbinic commentary on the book of Genesis known as *Bereshit Rabbah* talks about the Rabbinic conception of God breathing into Adam's nostrils. This commentary includes reference to these five levels of the soul and represents the fact that the ancient mystical tradition is indeed ancient.

Kabbalists teach that most people go up and down, down and up, from the lowest level of the soul upward toward God. People don't stay on one level all the time. A person can work hard spiritually and thereby raise his or her consciousness and generally live on one plane of existence. But even that person — and everyone else — has moments of consciousness that are higher and other moments that are lower. The human consciousness never stays in one place. Sometimes one is all wrapped up in his or her emotions, whereas at other times, one's consciousness resides on the level of ideas. According to Kabbalah, the world of ideas is higher than the world of emotions; emotions should be ruled by ideas, not the other way around.

As a result of great struggle and intense spiritual work, the consciousnesses of rare individuals reside on the level of chaya. Rather than be ruled by their emotions or intellectual ideas, those who are on the level of chaya have a grasp of spiritual reality. A person can't reside on the level of yechida because it's the point of intersection of a person and God. Someone fully on the level of yechida is someone who no longer exists and has fully merged into God.

What's the point of all these levels? Well, the point of the levels is the point of life, and the point of life, according to Kabbalah, is to realize one's spiritual potential and ultimately connect with the Divine within oneself. In other words, the purpose of life is for one's soul to perfect itself, and the way to that perfection is to identify with the highest level of consciousness as possible. The soul uses its instrument, the body, to travel up and back among the levels. This constant movement, up and down, back and forth, is the essence of the process of purification and results in greater and greater *Da'at,* knowledge of God.

Chapter 7

Like Déjà Vu All Over Again: Reincarnation in Kabbalah

It may (or may not) come as a surprise to you to find that Kabbalists believe in reincarnation. And not only do they believe in it, but they take it pretty seriously, too. To a Kabbalist, reincarnation explains why people are born, why they die, and how they should live their lives while they're here on earth.

Many people claim that reincarnation isn't a part of Jewish tradition. For example, if you were to ask a number of rabbis whether Jews believe in reincarnation, you'd get all kinds of answers, including the frequent responses of "No, we don't" and "A few sages did believe in this, but it isn't a central teaching of Jewish tradition." These answers are wrong, pure and simple. Scholars have documented that the greatest of the Jewish sages believed, wrote, and taught about reincarnation. The works left by the formative minds behind Kabbalah expressly teach a belief in reincarnation Even the revered and authoritative author of the standard Code of Jewish Law, Rabbi Joseph Karo, believed in reincarnation.

The first time I met my teacher, I asked him why ideas I have encountered in my dabbling in Eastern religions like Hinduism and Buddhism seem so similar to ideas in Kabbalah. Not that all the details are the same, but the Eastern and Kabbalistic sources on reincarnation generally describe the same concept and process. When I said to my Teacher, "The ideas are so similar; how can it be?" he said, "It would be stranger if it were otherwise." In other words, it would be unusual if the various world religions were *different* in many of their basic teachings. After all, truth is truth, and nobody has a monopoly on it.

In this chapter, I explain the concept of reincarnation as it relates to Kabbalistic teachings, the purpose of reincarnation, how Kabbalists view life and death, and the significance of reincarnation in a Kabbalist's daily life.

What Is Reincarnation?

The Hebrew term for reincarnation, the term used by Kabbalists over the centuries, is **Gilgul Ha-nefesh** (*gil*-gool hah-*neh*-fesh). It's made of two words: **Ha-nefesh** means "the soul," and **gilgul** actually means "rolling" or "recycling." Sometimes reincarnation is referred to in the plural, **gilgul ha'ne'shamot** (*gil*-gool hah-neh-sha-*mote;* the reincarnation of souls).

Following are basic steps in the process of reincarnation:

1. God creates your soul.

2. Your soul exists before your particular body.

3. The soul enters your body 40 days after conception.

4. Your soul tries to figure out what its job is here on earth.

5. The soul, with the help of your body, tries to complete its task and to help repair the world. At the same time, the soul, in its connection with the physical world through your body also experiences the exhilaration of life itself, and enjoys and savors it. (The opportunity to enjoy life and the ability to savor it are seen by Kabbalists as divine gifts.)

6. If you haven't finished the curriculum, which consists of the trials God gives you to solve, your soul comes back for more — it's reincarnated.

Life with a purpose

In the eyes of a Kabbalist, reincarnation is an important part of the understanding of who we humans are and what we're doing here. Kabbalah teaches that a human being isn't just the result of sex between a mother and father. As the sages have taught, the mother and father provide parts of the physical body, and God provides the life force, the soul (also known as *consciousness*). Kabbalists understand birth as a partnership of three: the mother, the father, and the Holy One. Each contributes something.

Kabbalah teaches that God's dream of a world that perfects itself is the goal of creation. One of the reasons people are born is to participate in the repairing of the world (see Chapter 8). The good news is if your soul doesn't finish its assignment, it comes back and continues its work. As it is written in the great Kabbalistic text, the Zohar, as long as a person is unsuccessful in his purpose in this world, the Holy One, blessed be He, uproots him and "replants" him over and over again. Eventually, after enough lives, enough *incarnations,* the soul fulfills its task and waits for the rest of the souls in the world to complete their tasks.

An ancient tale about the soul

A well-known story that has been told and retold by Kabbalists for almost 2,000 years involves Rabbi Meir, a student of Rabbi Akiva, one of the greatest Kabbalists of all time. The story is that one Sabbath many centuries ago, Rabbi Meir asked his wife, an extraordinary woman named Beruria, if she had seen their two sons because he didn't see them in the house of prayer. Beruria knew that their two sons had died but didn't want to tell her husband until after the Sabbath, to allow him a few more hours of the delight brought by the gift of the Sabbath given by God each week. After the Sabbath was over, Rabbi Meir once again asked Beruria where their sons were. Before answering, Beruria said that she wanted to ask her husband a legal question. She asked, "If jewels are deposited with a person for safekeeping and one day the owner comes to retrieve his gems, is there an obligation to return them?" Rabbi Meir said, "Of course." At that point, Beruria said to her husband, "He who gave us our two gems on deposit has come to retrieve them."

The soul's tasks: To repair the world and itself

One of Kabbalah's fundamental principles is that each of us has a unique task. My task isn't your task, and your task isn't mine. And even if you can do my task better than me, it still isn't yours. For example, it's my job to write a book about Kabbalah. Even if you can write a better book than I can, that may not be what you're here for.

REMEMBER

A person doesn't need to be conscious of his task in life in order to fulfill it. He can go through his entire life totally unaware of all these Kabbalistic ideas and unaware that the task of life is to figure out his task. Many people just have an intuitive sense of what they should do in the world. Regardless of their motivation, by doing what they're inclined to do, they're actually in the process of completing their divine assignments.

There are a number of possibilities for each soul:

✔ The soul enters the world, understands its assignment, and fulfills it.

✔ The soul doesn't complete its task and has to return to try to finish its work.

✔ The soul doesn't complete its task and does damage to the world.

✔ The soul enters the world and is itself damaged during its life.

The first case, in which the soul understands and fulfills its assignment, is said to be quite rare. In most cases, the soul must come back and either finish its assignment, repair the part of the world that it damaged in the past, or repair itself.

One of the issues with no consensus among Kabbalists is just how many chances each soul gets. Many say three. One of my Kabbalah teachers echoes a view held by many Kabbalists in history: As long as you make progress in a lifetime, you get another chance even if you don't finish God's assignment.

Kabbalists believe that some souls make such terrible choices and do such extreme damage to the world that they're beyond repair. The Zohar (see Chapter 13) states that those souls who are unworthy and don't achieve their purposes ultimately will be regarded as though they never even existed. They will end up as "ashes under the feet of the righteous."

In addition to its work in repairing the world, the soul also raises and purifies itself. According to Kabbalah, the soul's work on the world and its work on itself aren't two different activities — they happen simultaneously. For example, suppose you're walking down the street and see a person in need asking for a coin. By giving that person some money, you're helping to repair the world, but you're also refining yourself. The inner process of deciding to feel compassion for a person in need, as well as the decision to actually do something concrete about it, help to create new habits and patterns of behavior. You may struggle with questions such as "Should I give money to this person?" "Shouldn't the person get a job?" and "What if the person is faking it?" Ultimately, as the Kabbalistic sages have taught for centuries, it isn't your business to judge the person; it's your business to give when a seemingly needy person asks. This process of introspection and its result of giving charity is an example of the process of refining the soul, raising it up, and getting closer to the goal of the soul's final destination: basking in the Light of God.

We've all been here before

Reincarnation, for the Kabbalist, provides the framework for understanding so much about life. In fact, Kabbalists believe that the trials and challenges that people face in their lives are a result of what they may have left unfinished or may even have damaged during a previous lifetime.

Sometimes, people can recall brief glimpses of their past incarnations. For example, many people have a sense that they're reincarnations of people who were murdered during the Holocaust. *Beyond the Ashes* (A.R.E. Press) is an account of a contemporary rabbi's personal encounters with hundreds of people from all walks of life who have visions, dreams, and flashbacks that seem to be coming from another life during the Holocaust.

Reincarnation isn't a failure; most souls simply don't complete the entire curriculum in one lifetime.

Many have asked why God puts the soul through so much. Why does the soul have to figure out its assignment? Why does God allow the soul to take the terrible risk of entering the world to possibly get damaged or do damage? God's reason for the creation of the universe is to bestow pleasure on us. If all of the answers were just given to us, where would the pleasure be? But the soul descends in order to make an ascent to greater heights. It is only through work, risks, trials, and accomplishments that true joy occurs.

Birth and Death (Also known as Homecoming and Graduation)

Kabbalists believe that before a soul enters the world, it's in Heaven, basking in God's presence and learning divine wisdom. At a certain point (see the sidebar "When soul meets body" for details), God sends the soul into the world.

Most souls aren't here for the first time and bear the legacy of previous existences. But some souls are new or young souls, sent by God into the world for some divine reason.

According to Kabbalah, the process of birth causes the soul to forget the divine wisdom it has learned in Heaven. According to the Talmud, just before a baby is born, an angel taps the baby on the mouth to push it from one world to the next. The tap creates the *philtrum* (the little notch between the upper lip and nose) and also causes the soul to forget what it has learned. The message of this story is that, in life, education has more to do with remembering what one already knows rather than learning something new.

When soul meets body

Kabbalists explain that God connects the soul with its body on the 40th day after conception. This is a Kabbalistic belief that goes back over 2,000 years. Incidentally, the idea that the fetus does not have a soul until it is 40 days old has an important impact on Jewish legal opinions concerning abortion and the emerging field of stem cell research. Rabbinic authorities feel that there is a vast difference between an abortion before 40 days and after 40 days, due to the soul's arrival at that time.

After death, the soul returns to God and once again basks in God's divine light. Souls that need to return to finish their work go back into the world. Souls that have finished their work return to God and wait for the perfection of the world as a whole.

Welcome back, baby!

For a Kabbalist, a birth is really like a welcome home party. Kabbalists believe that your soul existed before the body you currently have. When a baby is born, its soul is returning to this world for another go at fulfilling its mission of completing or fixing something in the world or in itself.

When a baby boy is born, Kabbalists practice a custom known as **Shalom Zachor** (*shah*-lome zakh-*hor;* peace little boy). It's a simple enough Kabbalistic practice that you can easily do. (In fact, if you have sons, you may have already done it without even knowing it!) A Shalom Zachor is essentially a celebration marked by a festive meal that's held on the Friday night of the first Sabbath after the child's birth.

To live the life of a Kabbalist, everything you do must be enhanced and made complete with *kavanah* (consciousness and attention). So when the baby is born, just as for most other significant moments in life, a ritual helps the participants focus their attention on what the life cycle event represents. The birth of a baby isn't just a happy occasion or the answer to a couple's prayers. Rather, it's the moment that God sends another soul back into the world to do its work.

At a Shalom Zachor, family, friends, and neighbors celebrate the baby's arrival. The occasion is called a Shalom Zachor because participants, by participating in the celebration, wish the baby luck by saying, "Shalom Zachor." Kabbalists recognize that the soul of the baby has been thrust into the physical world, with its life of struggle and potential suffering. They hope that the soul navigates this life well and achieves its goals during this incarnation.

The question has often been asked: Why is there a Shalom Zachor for a baby boy and not a baby girl? One commentator points to a teaching in the Talmud stating that a woman is considered as if she is already circumcised. From birth she is considered complete. Females, according to Jewish tradition, are by definition on a higher spiritual level. The "Shalom Zachor" is for baby boys who need extra encouragement on the spiritual journey. In traditional Jewish circles today, an alternative celebration named **Simchat Bat** (*sim*-khaht bot; joy for a daughter) is a party or special spiritual gathering in honor of the birth of a girl. Even when not called a Simchat Bat, the birth of a girl is surely a cause for celebration among Kabbalists.

The Kabbalistic significance of birthdays

Perhaps the greatest teacher of Kabbalah in the past 100 years was Rabbi Menachem Mendel Schneerson, known by millions of people around the world as the Rebbe (meaning great spiritual teacher) or the Lubavitcher Rebbe (Lubavitch is the town in Russia where his ancestors came from). The Rebbe encouraged the celebration of birthdays because a birthday is the anniversary of the soul's reentry into the world. On his birthday, a person should remind himself that the soul reincarnates and gets additional chances to complete its task; he should feel as though the world was created just for him. In addition, a birthday is a time to look at one's life with extra care and introspection and to resolve to work harder to fulfill one's task in the world.

When death comes a-knockin': A Kabbalist's graduation day

Kabbalists believe that at a certain point in every person's life, he or she gets a visit from the Angel of Death, known in Hebrew as the **Malach HaMavet** (*mah*-lakh hah-*mah*-vet), whose job it is to separate the body from the soul. The body is buried in the ground, and the soul continues on in its spiritual journey.

Because death is a graduation into another life, Kabbalists follow a strict custom of burying a body within 24 hours of death. (Jews follow this custom as much as possible to this day.) This practice is connected to the belief in reincarnation. The Talmud (see Chapter 13) teaches that keeping the body unburied after the soul leaves the body and the body remains without breath is forbidden. And the Zohar adds that perhaps God decrees that a person undergoes reincarnation on the day that he dies. As long as the body remains unburied, the soul can neither go into the presence of the Holy One nor be transferred into another body.

The great Kabbalistic sages teach that when the body and soul separate, the experience varies for different types of people:

- For people who are basically good in their lives, the separation is as gentle as drawing a hair from milk.

- For people who are wicked, the separation is like the whirling waters at the entrance to a canal. Some sages teach that the separation of the body and soul of a wicked person is like pulling a rope with a spiked ball out of the throat.

Reciting a death blessing

Just as there's a Kabbalistic response to a birth, Kabbalists recite a blessing when they hear of a person's death. The blessing, in Hebrew, is **Baruch dayan emet** (bah-*rukh* da-*yahn* eh-met; blessed is the true judge). In other words, when Kabbalists find out that God has sent the Angel of Death to do its job, they acknowledge and trust that even though they don't know why it was that soul's time to leave the world, God had a good reason.

One of my Kabbalah teachers taught me that death doesn't frighten the pious Kabbalist because he or she has faith that death is simply a transition from one life into another.

Death isn't a tragedy; it's a graduation ceremony. With each incarnation, the soul learns more and continues to purify itself in order to reach its goal. Kabbalists believe that although the death of someone is a sad occasion for loved ones, God knows what He is doing.

Realizing death is not death, suffering is not suffering

When students of Kabbalah study anything, they always search for a deeper meaning and a more profound level of understanding. For example, Kabbalah asks us to believe that everything that happens in the world has a reason, and that from a Kabbalistic view, everything is for the best (see Chapter 5). So when Kabbalists hear news about a death, they first acknowledge that everything is in God's hands. God knows everything and God knows best.

Some people are on such a high level of consciousness, understand things so deeply, and have such great faith that God knows why everything happens that they don't even experience bad news as bad.

Kabbalistic tradition is, in many ways, a series of teachings designed to raise a person's consciousness, and what this often means is to see beyond the surface of things (see Chapter 4). Both death and suffering are good examples of this process.

Death is generally considered "bad news." From the point of view of family and friends of the deceased, the occasion of death can be a traumatic one. Death has acquired a sense of finality. Death, to many, means the end.

But not to a Kabbalist. Kabbalah stresses that death is a transition. It is hardly the end; it is not the end for the body, which merges into the earth, and it is not the end for the soul, which is eternal and continues on its path.

Suffering, perhaps even more than death, is thought to be a negative word. But, to a Kabbalist, everything has a purpose, everything contains God, and every descent is for the sake of ascension. Though it's easy to simply react negatively to suffering, in Kabbalah, suffering can be seen as a divine gift.

Understanding the Significance of Reincarnation to Kabbalah

Awareness of the process of reincarnation changes the whole picture of life for the Kabbalist. In particular:

- ✔ Reincarnation helps the Kabbalist see life as something other than a random event. In other words, life has meaning even though you may not see it.
- ✔ Reincarnation includes the lesson that each life has a divine purpose.
- ✔ Reincarnation gives hope and optimism to those whose lives fall short of their goals.
- ✔ Reincarnation transforms death from a tragedy into another step along the path of the soul's journey.
- ✔ Reincarnation helps explain why siblings are often so different even though they're raised in the same family by the same parents.
- ✔ Reincarnation helps explain why sometimes you may feel as if you've known someone before (we probably have!).

In this section, I explain the Kabbalistic idea that life is like a classroom. The trials, assignments, and challenges of life are the very ways that the soul makes progress.

Tending God's garden

The great Kabbalists teach that humankind must see itself as being in God's garden and then treat the garden properly by helping to perfect the world. This message is the result of Kabbalists looking closely at the details, down to the individual words and letters, of the story of Creation in the book of Genesis in the Bible (see Chapter 16). One such detail is that Adam and Eve find themselves in a garden. Their fate, as the story goes, is to tend that garden. (You can view the huge body of Jewish law as a manual for the proper care of the world. After all, the word "Torah" comes from the Hebrew root that means instruction.)

Kabbalists believe that God wants people to enjoy the world and take pleasure from life. Thus, when a soul comes back to the world to try again to achieve its task, it isn't being punished but rather is being given a great opportunity.

More to life and death than meets the eye: A reincarnation parable

When studying Kabbalah what you see is almost never what you get. Kabbalah teaches people to look beneath the surface of things. So birth isn't really birth — it's a chance to finish what you didn't complete during your last life. And death isn't really death — it's a graduation.

Kabbalistic tradition contains countless parables that teach important ideas. One parable sheds a lot of light on the subject of reincarnation.

Imagine twins who are developing nicely and peacefully in their mother's womb. The twins have it great: Things are serene, and they're both fed through a tube and are well nourished. But as nice as it is, they feel themselves dropping lower and lower and begin to wonder what will happen to them when they move too far down and fall out of their world. One of the infants believes in the spiritual tradition that promises another existence after the current one. He has faith in his belief even though there's no evidence for it. The other twin is a skeptic and doesn't believe in anything without hard evidence. He doesn't believe his brother's stories about another existence; rather, he believes that mere imagination is proof of nothing.

The first brother says, "After our death here, there will be a new great world. We will eat through our mouths. Also, we will be able to see far distances with our eyes. We will stand up straight and tall." The skeptical brother replies, "What you are saying is nonsense; it's all your imagination. There is no foundation for this belief. It is an elaborate defense mechanism. There is only this world. There is no next world." The first twin asks his nonbelieving brother what he thinks will happen to them. The second brother replies, "We will go with a bang. Our world will collapse, and we will sink into oblivion. A black void. An end to consciousness."

Suddenly the water inside the womb bursts. The womb convulses with upheaval and turmoil. Everything lets loose, and the brothers move faster and faster, lower and lower. All of the sudden, the brother with faith falls out of the womb as his nonbelieving brother watches in horror. He cries, "Why did this happen?! Why did he fall into that terrible abyss? I knew that death is horrible." While he's so filled with sorrow, he hears a cry from his brother who has fallen out of the world and exclaims, "Oh no! What a horrible end! Just as I predicted!"

The nonbelieving brother mourns his "dead" brother, but things outside the womb are much different from what he thinks. The baby's cry is a sign of health and vigor. The exit from the womb is the birth of the body; the exit from the body is the rebirth of the soul.

Viewing life as a classroom

The soul that has fulfilled its task and has done all that it's supposed to do, creating or repairing some part of the world, can bask in God's presence until the whole world is perfected. But many souls don't do all the proper things, they misuse forces in the world, or they're injured in some way. After the death of the body, these souls return to the world (entering another fetus at age 40 days) and try again to figure out their tasks and to do them successfully.

For a soul, learning how to do things properly isn't easy. The fact that it's a lifelong pursuit is the reason study is so important to the Kabbalist (see Chapter 13). Kabbalists study every day in an effort to do the following:

✔ Understand the spiritual ideas that Kabbalah teaches

✔ Apply these basic principles to improve behavior

✔ Participate with the great sages in trying to figure out what to do in life

Using reincarnation as a guide for living

Each and every day, Kabbalists ask themselves the following questions:

✔ **What is my life's work and divine assignment?**

The question, "What should I do with my life?" is one that is asked by many. For some, it's asked early in life and never revisited. For others, questioning the purpose of life is a daily occurrence. Kabbalists are encouraged to almost constantly evaluate and re-evaluate their paths to make sure that life doesn't just slip away but rather is filled with the tasks that God put you here to do and learn (see Chapter 8).

✔ **Am I doing my assignment well?**

For a Kabbalist, this question is a daily one. Every night, Kabbalists are urged to look at the day that has just passed with the hope that the actions performed and the thoughts that came to mind were healthy, appropriate, and productive. Particularly during the Days of Awe, between the holy days of Rosh Hashannah and Yom Kippur, a Kabbalist asks himself and God for an evaluation and hopes for a good one (see Chapter 10).

✔ **Is my current suffering the result of deeds done in previous incarnations?**

In Kabbalah, the advice given to a person who is suffering is to try to look at his deeds and wonder what failings have prompted the suffering. If you come up empty-handed after considering your deeds, your soul may be suffering due to misdeeds in a prior lifetime. In either case, the suffering person, according to Kabbalah, should avoid bitterness and cultivate trust that God will reveal the divine wisdom behind all events (see Chapter 9).

✔ **How can I live a life that insures the least amount of bad karma?**

A Kabbalist's life is a conscious life. Every moment a person needs to be awake and aware, and must try with the greatest efforts to integrate the wisdom that has been acquired into life's activities, all in order to avoid the negative consequences that follow from misdeeds (see Chapter 9).

Chapter 8

Instant Karma's Gonna Get You

Y ou may not be happy about this, but God knows everything that you do. Yes, everything. (Kind of makes you cringe, doesn't it?) And everything you do creates angels — good angels and bad angels. In this chapter, you discover why people give birth to angels and how this impacts both present lives and future incarnations.

In addition, you look closely at the eternal question of why suffering exists in the world. There are two main reasons for human suffering:

✔ Suffering is the result of people's misdeeds, the karma they create.

✔ God gives people suffering deliberately to test them and to provide them with the lessons that they learn from that suffering.

Everything depends on your inner attitude toward suffering. Kabbalah offers a profound perspective on suffering and provides people with strategies for coping with suffering — and using suffering for the good.

Everything Has Meaning — Everything

To put it simply, Kabbalistic tradition teaches that everything has meaning. Every thought, every inclination, every gesture, every word, and every action has significance in the universe.

One way to look at this concept is to see life as a scale in which each act that you do can tip the scale one way or the other. If the next thing you do or think is positive, the scale tips in the right direction. In the same way, if what you're about to do or think is negative, the scale tips in the wrong direction. The sages teach that this awareness of meaning must be kept in one's mind at all times.

One of my teachers offers an excellent analogy for people who feel that even if there is a God, then certainly God isn't interested in "little ol' me." After all, why would the Creator of this vast universe be interested or even aware of one small speck? Surely if there is a God, He (or She) must have far better things to do than to be concerned with one individual on a small planet in the vastness of space.

My teacher points out that the reason this line of thinking is in error is because people too often think of God and His universe in the same way that they think of the CEO of a huge corporation. Using this model, you can be fairly certain that a busy CEO is hardly interested in which pencils an assistant in one of thousands of offices is purchasing. The CEO has far more important things to focus on and almost surely doesn't even know the name of the assistant or even that this person exists. The CEO is busy with the board of directors and with the major players in the corporation and lets the people far below him on the organizational ladder worry about the little things. Applying the logic of this corporation analogy to the awareness of God and meaning in actions produces the idea that, if there is a God, He must be busy with the movement of galaxies and the creation of universes and certainly isn't concerned with the affairs of a tiny speck in the universe.

The problem lies in the fact that God isn't CEO of the universe but rather is infinite. In fact, Kabbalists often refer to God as "the Infinite, blessed is He" (see Chapter 17). In the nature of infinity, nothing is closer or farther away than anything else, and nothing is larger or smaller; against the infinite, everything is of the same proportion. Therefore, when people, as finite individuals, make even a slight gesture with their little fingers, to God it is of the same proportion as the largest cataclysm.

By seeing God as infinite, Kabbalists understand that God is aware of everything — from the largest cataclysm to the smallest gesture. The great Kabbalist and founder of the Hasidic movement Rabbi Israel, known as "the Master of the Good Name," is known to have said that not even a blade of grass moves without God being aware of it and, in fact, allowing it to happen.

While this might seem impossible or beyond our grasp, One can look to the invention of the personal computer to begin to see that such a notion is not an unreasonable at all. After all, we are really just at the very beginnings of the development of the computer, and yet a small computers sitting on a desk is able to keep track of billions and billions of pieces of information. That being case, it does not seem unreasonable at all to imagine that the Creator of the universe can do the same, and far more.

The notion that every thought, gesture, inclination, and action has meaning certainly has its impact on the decisions Kabbalists make. Human beings are believed to be the only forces in the world having free choice, so this Kabbalistic belief often serves to help people take the high road rather than the low road when a situation or choice confronts them.

Angels: The Kabbalistic Key to Karma

The Hindu belief in karma is similar to the Kabbalistic tradition. *Karma* represents the idea that the good and the evil that a person does will return with inevitable results, either in this life or in a later one. As the popular saying indicates, "What goes around comes around." This notion, in Kabbalah, is connected to the idea of angels.

In order to better understand this section's discussion of angels, you need to keep a couple of points in mind:

- ✔ For the most part, angels are beyond human comprehension. Most of what people know about angels comes not from their perceptions but rather from tradition. As one of my teachers put it, "There is no way to grasp an angel." Nevertheless, Kabbalah teaches that throughout history there have always been certain individuals who live on a higher plane of consciousness and therefore have access to information and vague perceptions. Those individuals, by sharing their visions from higher planes, help us to grasp the unknowable.

- ✔ Existence consists of four fundamental worlds that don't exist in different places but, rather, in what some Kabbalists call "different dimensions of being." These worlds intersect and interact with each other. Human beings are the inhabitants of the World of Action. Angels are the inhabitants of the World of Formation, which is the world just above the Word of Action. (Refer to Chapter 3 for a full discussion of the four fundamental Worlds.)

An angel isn't a blonde girl with wings

Often, when one wants to learn something new, the first task is to get rid of old notions in order to make room for new ones. Bob Dylan sang, "I don't want to learn what I gotta unlearn," but unfortunately, much of learning ends up being unlearning. I find that I often have to get rid of old notions to clear my mind and make room for new ideas.

At the beginning of discussions of the angels in the Kabbalistic tradition, many of my students over the years have said, "I thought that only Christians believe in angels." This misconception is in part due to angels being depicted as little creatures (usually children) with wings and appearing on Christmas trees.

In the Kabbalistic tradition, angels don't have wings. During a lecture given by one of my teachers, he gave the advice that if you ever encounter an angel sent by God, you may want to run in the other direction because unlike a common image of angels as sweet little girls with wings, the angels that appear in the holy texts studied by Kabbalists are often fierce and foreboding.

How angels are made

The Hebrew world for "angel" is **malach** (*mah*-lakh; messenger). As opposed to human beings who live in the World of Action and exercise free will, angels live on a different plane and have no such free will. Instead, the angel serves as a messenger; each angel has a particular nature and a specific assignment or task. Within this general categorization of angels, Kabbalah conceives of two kinds of angels:

- **Angels made by God:** The angels created by God serve a particular function. One such angel, for example, is the **Malach Hamavet** (*mah*-lakh hah-*mah*-vet; Angel of Death). God created the Angel of Death to enter the World of Action and to do the task of separating a person's soul from his body (see Chapter 7).

- **Angels made by humans:** According to Kabbalistic tradition, human beings produce angels, or *spiritual charges,* in the universe when they think, dream, speak, feel, and act. The angels produced are, in a sense, parasitically attached to people. So even though you can't see them, Kabbalah teaches you to think of all the angels you produce as being alive and attached to your soul.

Kabbalistic tradition speaks of *good angels* and *bad angels.* An angry word creates a different kind of spiritual charge than a kind word, but that isn't to say that an angry word is a *bad* word. Sometimes anger is appropriate, and sometimes it isn't. The same is true for love. There are times when love (and the angel it creates) is healthy and appropriate for the moment or the occasion, and there are other times when love is inappropriate.

Making corrections with the help of angels

Kabbalists believe that when a person dies, the human combination of body and soul separates. The body returns to the earth, and the soul, which is eternal, continues on (see Chapter 6). The soul carries with it the myriad of good and bad angels that it gave birth to throughout its life. The significance of this is that when a person decides to change, to improve, and to alter the course of his or her life, the change switches the direction of the bad angels that were created in the past.

Turning with teshuvah

This process of change, which is the expression of free will and creativity, is called **teshuvah** (teh-*shoo*-vah; turning). (Teshuvah is often inaccurately translated as repentance.) When a person does something regretful, God gives him or her an opportunity to change and be redeemed. Teshuvah implies that it's possible to change the past. Even though time flows in one direction, teshuvah is a spiritual concept that allows for people to go back in time, in a sense.

Needless to say, it's impossible actually to go back in time. If I punch you in the nose, there's no way that I can undo my punch. What teshuvah implies, however, is that I can change the significance of the punch. I may have punched you out of inappropriate anger, and surely there are better ways to deal with most situations than to throw a punch at someone's nose.

Teshuvah allows me to learn from my mistakes, so much so that the punch thrown in error prompts such regret within my soul that I'm transformed as a person. The very act of punching you inappropriately, followed by my deep and sincere regret, becomes the very inspiration that puts me on a positive track forever. From one point of view, the punch was surely inappropriate, but as the Kabbalists teach, with deep and sincere teshuvah, a real transformation can occur. As the great Kabbalistic sages teach, sincere teshuvah allows one's sins to become one's merits!

Transforming angels

Kabbalists throughout the ages have believed that the person who makes an error and then chooses freely and sincerely to mend his ways is actually on a higher spiritual level than a saint. How can this possibly be? How can a saint, who is the essence of goodness and purity and who experiences no temptations and therefore commits no errors, possibly be lower than a person who has made countless errors in his or her life, even if he or she does express sincere regret?

Friday night angels

An almost 2,000-year-old Kabbalist teaching tells of two angels — one good and one bad — who accompany a person home from the synagogue on Friday night. These two angels are not the kind of angel that you create through your thoughts and deeds. Rather, these angels are of the other type: They are created by God and are part of the structure of the world. When the person arrives home to find the Sabbath candles lit, the table set, and the beds made, the good angel says, "May it be God's will that the next Sabbath should be the same." And against his will, the bad angel must answer, "Amen." If the candles aren't lit and the table isn't set, the bad angel says, "May it be God's will that the next Sabbath should be the same," and, against his will, the good angel answers, "Amen." Knowledge of these two angels and how they function motivates Kabbalists to fulfill the traditional obligations on the Sabbath. After all, to get a bad angel to say "amen" when a Kabbalist fulfills the divine command to observe the traditions of the Sabbath is an extra bonus and something in which to take special pleasure.

The all-time angel hall of fame

Every night, Kabbalists recite a special prayer that refers to the four great angels: "To my right Michael and to my left Gabriel, in front of me Uriel and behind me Raphael, and over my head God's Shekhinah [the presence of God]."

One source of this prayer is a text that reads, "As the Holy One blessed be He created four winds (directions) and four banners (for Israel's army), so also did He make four angels to surround His Throne — Michael, Gabriel, Uriel and Raphael. Michael is on its right, Uriel on its left, Gabriel in front, and Raphael in the rear."

In Kabbalistic literature, the four angels surround God's throne and shed their light on the four winds of heaven.

✔ **Michael** is the guardian angel of Israel. (Each nation has a guardian angel.)

✔ **Gabriel** is God's messenger on numerous missions and the constant defender of the Jewish people.

✔ **Uriel,** meaning "light of God," is the medium by which the knowledge of God comes to man.

✔ **Raphael** is responsible for healing. His name appears repeatedly on amulets and incantations. In the Talmud, Raphael is one of the angels who visits Abraham after his circumcision.

The answer lies in the fact that people are constantly giving birth to angels of all sorts. The person who has committed many errors has given birth to countless bad, or negative, angels. However, if that person's teshuvah is sincere, then all the countless negative angels parasitically attached to his or her soul are transformed into positive angels. So the sinner who turns has at his or her disposal a vast army of formerly negative angels and can thereby work as a huge positive force in the universe. This change could never have happened if the person hadn't made errors to begin with.

Unfortunately, this notion of transforming angels is one that has been abused by certain misguided Kabbalists of the past. These Kabbalists believed that if it's possible to transform negative angels into positive ones and thereby establish themselves on a high spiritual level, then why not commit sins intentionally and then express regret after-the-fact as a way to build up one's arsenal of positive angels? The faulty logic, of course, lies in the fact that God knows everyone's thoughts and schemes and therefore can detect such a dishonest plot.

Suffering Hurts but Isn't Random: The Kabbalistic View

Perhaps the most profound questions in life and certainly the most difficult to untangle are "Why would God create a universe with so much suffering? If, in fact, God is all-powerful, why didn't He create a world of eternal bliss?" Indeed, many people have given up their beliefs in God or avoided believing altogether simply by looking at the world or turning on the evening news and seeing what troubles exist. If there's a God, they think, why in the world isn't He doing anything about this?

In this section, I clue you in to the reasons Kabbalists believe people suffer trials in their lives and how they can learn and benefit from those trials.

What goes around come around

Kabbalistic tradition explores two terms:

- **Olam ha'zeh** (oh-*lam* hah-*zeh;* this world)
- **Olam ha'ba** (oh-*lam* hah-*bah;* the world to come)

Kabbalists have taught for centuries that all deeds prompt either a reward or a punishment. With this world and the world to come in mind, you can look at a question that has challenged Kabbalists for centuries: Why do so many bad people enjoy good lives and good people encounter so much suffering?

Kabbalistic tradition is firmly planted in Judaism, which has a core belief in reward and punishment. For a few thousand years, the suggested attitude to cultivate by the great Jewish and Kabbalistic sages is this: When you see people who do evil and yet seem to be enjoying this world, you should understand that the joy they are given in this world is actually the reward that they surely deserve for some good that they've done, and that the punishment they deserve will be received by them in "the world to come."

When you see people who are good people but who suffer, you should understand that the suffering the experience in this world is actually the punishment that they surely deserve for some bad that they've done, and that the reward they deserve for being generally good people will be received in "the world to come."

"The world to come" is not the same as a next incarnation. The world to come is the final destination of the soul. The good and bad you do is part of your "account," and you cannot judge a situation by the limited period of one lifetime.

Divine punishment is not merely punitive. In fact, divine punishment, and all suffering for that matter, is never simply for the sake of causing pain. Divine punishment for bad deeds offers opportunities to refine your character traits, to prompt the introspection that is necessary to cause change in your behavior and your soul.

Misinterpreting basic Kabbalistic ideas

Some of the topics discussed by Kabbalists, such as why people experience suffering, aren't easy to explore and are often misunderstood. One of the risks in publicly discussing sensitive material is that the outsider, or the person who's satisfied with a superficial understanding of a topic, can often be misinformed and jump to conclusions that are far from accurate.

For example, a basic Kabbalistic idea is that everything is for the best. This idea is misinterpreted, however, and people think that all one really needs to do is to turn on the evening news to think that such an idea is insane. *Everything is for the best?* What about starvation? Tsunami? War? Disease? Murder? How can one possible say that everything is for the best? Another example is the idea that nothing happens without God allowing it to happen. Can any sane person actually believe this? What about torture? Rape? Starvation? Are these things that God allows to happen? And what of the people who believe these ideas to be true? Are they so callous, so glib, so insensitive?

To prevent the inevitable slander and criticism that such ideas can inspire, Kabbalists are often forced to study in private. Uninformed outsiders don't realize that Kabbalah isn't callous. On the contrary, a Kabbalist is dedicated to performing good deeds, acts of loving kindness, charity, and compassion. Kabbalists believe in medical research, in repairing the world, and in treating everyone as though they're in the image of God.

And yet, if you were to listen in on a Kabbalistic discussion of theology, specifically in relation to human suffering, you might easily conclude that Kabbalah is cruel and inhuman. I therefore beg you to consider these ideas with seriousness and sensitivity. Explore these ideas in depth, and consult wise teachers to help you to grasp these ideas.

On my bulletin board at home, I have a quote that I took from a book on physics many years ago. It reads, "In physics, you never understand a new idea, you just get used to it." Perhaps the same goes for Kabbalah: These sublime ideas are more than one can grasp in a lifetime, but as one works with them and seeks to probe them in-depth, one often emerges with rich insight and life-changing perspectives.

This is a test; this is only a test

While some of the suffering we face is the inevitable result of the misdeeds we do, Kabbalists believe that sometimes God deliberately gives us tests to overcome. In a sense, it's all about "no pain, no gain." A good analogy would be the process of building up one's muscles in the gym. When you work out with weights, for example, what is actually happening is that the muscle tissue is breaking down as a result of the workout. After the workout, the muscle tissue rebuilds and even comes back stronger than before the lifting of the weights — the test — has occurred.

Kabbalists cultivate this attitude when confronted by a trial of life. Rather than be angry with God, rather than saying "why me?," the faithful Kabbalist tries to understand that God provides medicine, sometimes bitter medicine, for the purpose of healing, growth, and refinement. The soul has a long journey, far longer than the short span of a lifetime. When God sees that a person needs to build up some muscle, a trial of some sort is offered which, if related to properly, results in something more glorious than what existed before the trial.

In Kabbalah, an important aspect of suffering is that some of the best things in life happen as a result of a bad experience or terrible occurrence. Kabbalists often look back and see that had something terrible *not* happened, something else that's glorious wouldn't have happened, either. This way of looking at suffering doesn't justify the terrible event, but it reminds one that life is on a far grander scale than the limited and immediate level that's so often the focus of attention. Kabbalah urges people to expand their perspectives in order to better handle pain.

Taking solace from trials in life

Kabbalists teach that encountering a trial or experiencing suffering prompts an opportunity to examine one's deeds closely to try to unravel the mystery of the suffering. The introspective sufferer can come to understand the negative angels that he or she has created and thereby has the opportunity to make rectification.

Can God really allow suffering?

You don't have to look very hard to see that many good people suffer. Some modern theologians have a lot of trouble, theologically, with the view that God is behind it all, either causing or allowing it to happen. One popular approach to the question, and one that goes against the views of every great Kabbalist and traditional Jewish thinker who has ever written on the subject, is to say that God is not all powerful.

Some of these modern theologians suggest that God might be "all-knowing" but that God is not "all-powerful." Another way they say it is that God created the world and left it alone. This is absolutely contrary to the fundamental conception of God in Kabbalistic tradition. God *is* all-powerful, God did not leave the world alone after creation, and everything, according to Kabbalah, comes from God.

One of the primary distinctions between Kabbalah and many modern theologians concerns the view of creation. Those theologians (and the many individuals who are not theologians but simply grapple with these questions) conceive of God as having created the universe a long time ago, whereas Kabbalah stands firm in the belief that God is intimately involved with every detail of creation and in fact creates the world anew every moment.

It's forbidden to speak theology to a suffering person. Even though the Kabbalist believes that suffering is an opportunity for introspection, she also knows that, in a time of suffering, it's profoundly difficult for a mourner to hear such reasoning. In addition, although Kabbalists believe in karma and cause and effect in the universe, no mortal fully understands this cause and effect and therefore has no right to say that a certain person is suffering because of his or her misdeeds. That person may be suffering because of bad angels created in the past, or the trial may be a gift sent by God to ultimately lift the person up to spiritual heights that never could have been reached without the suffering.

Kabbalists throughout the ages have referred to this concept of introspective suffering as "the sin of the friends of Job." Job, the Biblical character who experiences profound suffering, is visited by his friends who, when he complains of his plight, say "Don't you have faith in God? Surely you must have done something wrong because God doesn't punish righteous people; God does not pervert justice. Doesn't your faith in God bring you comfort?" Even though a person can find comfort in his or her faith, pushing that point simply isn't appropriate. If I'm suffering, I can use that suffering any way I wish, but if I see you suffering, my job is not to speak theology but rather to try to help you relieve your suffering.

One of my Kabbalah teachers taught me that the one exception to the prohibition against speaking theology to a person who's suffering is when that person is a friend. But my teacher explained that *friend* in this case doesn't mean a casual acquaintance or even one of many good friends. In life, it's highly recommended that each person have at least one extra special friendship that's so intimate, so trusting, and so close that it's permissible to speaking theology during troubled times. While a sufferer generally hopes to be surrounded by people who can offer comfort, the sufferer who's blessed by such a close friend can give that person permission to speak theology at any time. That friend is the person in the sufferer's life who can serve to remind him or her of the grand scheme of things and therefore can share the wisdom of Kabbalah.

Kabbalistic tradition also teaches — and this is profoundly important — that when souls finally achieve their goals and no longer need to be reincarnated, they bask in the Light of God and know that the pleasure of being in God's presence is so sublime and so unlike any worldly pleasure that all the human suffering endured was worthwhile.

Handling the pain

In Kabbalistic terms, the angel Raphael brings divine healing powers from Above. Explained in Kabbalistic terms or in scientific terms, it's all the same: There's a miracle of healing in the world, and people can see it on their bodies throughout their lives.

Despair, the worst sin: The advice of Rabbi Nachman of Bratslav

One of the great Kabbalists in history is Rabbi Nachman, a great-grandson of Rabbi Israel, the Baal Shem Tov — Master of the Good Name — who was the founder of the Chassidic movement. Rabbi Nachman was a great Hasidic and Kabbalistic master in his own right, and even though he died in 1810, he has the unique distinction of having a large and growing number of followers in the world today. Known as *Breslover Hasidim,* these students of Kabbalah are grateful for the many teachings of Rabbi Nachman that were written down and are available in many languages today.

Rabbi Nachman described what he considered to be the worst sin: depression. Of course, he wasn't speaking of clinical depression, which is a medical condition which requires professional attention. Rather, he referred to an attitude of depression more in line with despair, in which a person feels that he or she is so far down that

there's no hope. Remember that Kabbalah teaches that every descent is for the sake of ascension (or as one of my teachers said, "in Kabbalah there's no such thing as down"). Rabbi Nachman taught that no one should ever despair because every fall occurs for the sake of the next ascent.

To Rabbi Nachman's message, one of my teachers adds that the distance between a person and God is always the same. What *is* different is the spiritual orientation. The person who is farther away from God merely needs to turn around and approach the Almighty. A contemporary musician, Rabbi Jack Gabriel, wrote and performs a beautiful song called "Up with Joy." This song is a musical version of Rabbi Nachman's philosophy. Rabbi Gabriel sings, "Fake it 'til you make it: up with joy." Ultimately, the song, like Rabbi Nachman, urges people to take control of their emotions and put joy into their lives.

A teacher of mine once told me that he actually enjoyed getting a minor cut or scratch on his hands because it was always a miracle to watch his body heal. As a Kabbalist, this observation trained him to see that there are miracles all around. When skeptics asked him, "Why are there no longer any miracles?," he would say, "There are miracles everywhere." He'd point to a spot on one of his fingers or hands and explain, "Just the other day, I had a little paper cut in that place, and now there's absolutely no evidence of it. It healed completely."

Of course, physical healing doesn't always occur in your lifetime. Remember that Kabbalists believe that each person is a soul that has a body, and just as a bird's egg cracks and drops away to give birth to a new fledging, so too does the body of the human being drop away and give birth to the next stage on that soul's journey.

When it comes to someone else's pain, a Kabbalist's duty is to try and relieve that pain and help that person heal. But when it comes to one's own pain, one can construct an entirely different relationship with it. Kabbalistic tradition teaches that some pain is like a fire of purification. In order to understand this concept of pain as purification, you need to keep in mind that Kabbalistic tradition recognizes that human experience transcends this world. Your soul existed before this current incarnation and will exist after the current incarnation (see Chapter 7 for the scoop on reincarnation).

Part II

Cutting to the Core of Kabbalah

In this part . . .

*I*n order to go a little deeper into Kabbalah, you have to let go of some beliefs and open yourself up to some new ideas (actually, they're quite old!). This part first looks at the seemingly audacious idea that everything happens for the best. Then it explores the Kabbalistic perspective on the human soul (it has five parts, by the way) before getting to the heart of a Kabbalist's task in the world — to repair it

Chapter 9

Living One Day at a Time

*B*eing a Kabbalist is no part-time job. For Kabbalists, every thought, gesture, inclination, and action has significance. In fact, every moment of every day presents spiritual opportunities, from the moment you wake up until you're sound asleep and dreaming. Also, there are things Kabbalists do every day and Kabbalistic ways to do everything.

In this chapter, I explain the three activities that are part of the Kabbalist's daily routine, and I show you how Kabbalists make all the activities in the day special.

Three Daily Tasks of the Kabbalist

A few thousand years ago, a righteous man named Shimon taught a remarkable idea that Kabbalists think about every day. What's the big idea? That the world depends on three things:

✔ The study of the holy teachings

✔ Prayer

✔ Acts of lovingkindness

The prayer book most Kabbalists have used daily for centuries quotes this teaching, and Kabbalists strive to include these three activities into their daily routines.

Prayer: You can (and should) pray just about anywhere and anytime

Going to a synagogue (or anywhere else, for that matter) to pray isn't necessary. For the Kabbalist, God is conceived of as Infinite, which means that there's no place where God is absent (for more on this topic, see Chapter 16). In fact, two of the most well-known Kabbalists in history, Rabbi Israel Baal Shem Tov and Rabbi Nachman of Breslov, are both famous for their shared preference to pray alone in the forest.

Praying is a serious activity, and you can find plenty of recommended prayers and instruction on how to pray (see Chapter 15). But the place to start is . . . wherever you are. Keep the following in mind:

✔ You don't need to get all dressed up to pray.

✔ You don't need to wait for the Sabbath or a holy day to pray.

✔ You don't need to find the right prayer book to pray.

✔ You don't need to face any special direction to pray.

✔ You don't need a rabbi to pray.

✔ You don't need to pray in any particular language.

One of my teachers wonders whether people often build big synagogues and churches because they hope to keep God inside them. But God hears people everywhere, just as God cares about human behavior everywhere — in the marketplace, in the kitchen, and even in the bedroom.

Kabbalists have a special relationship to prayer: Because the soul is a divine spark within people (see Chapter 6), and because prayer is the process of connecting with the Divine, in a way, the soul is always connected to God. It's as though the soul is always praying. The point of prayer is connection to God. Prayer helps people remember that they aren't the center of existence, but rather God is the center.

Creating individualized prayers

At any time and for any reason, a person can

✔ **Praise God:** "O God, what delicious ingredients are in this hot fudge sundae!"

✔ **Express gratitude to God:** "Thank you, God, for this delicious hot fudge sundae!"

✔ **Make requests of God:** "What I would like right now, God, is a hot fudge sundae!"

Saying a blessing upon leaving the bathroom

Kabbalah has blessings for everything: eating, studying, putting on new clothing, seeing a shooting star, and countless other activities. Generally, a person says a blessing before doing something, such as eating a piece of fruit (an activity that has its own special blessing). God is in the bathroom, too, but out of respect, Kabbalists wait to recite this blessing until they're *leaving* the bathroom:

Blessed are You, Lord our God, Ruler of the universe, who has formed humans in wisdom, and created in them a system of ducts and tubes. It is well known before Your glorious throne that if but one of these be opened, or if one of those be closed, it would be impossible to exist in Your presence. Blessed art You, O Lord, who heals all creatures and does wonders.

People who pray regularly usually discover that they have favorite prayers and get into the habit of reciting them regularly. Even though throughout history most serious Kabbalists have prayed three times a day using a fixed formula (see Chapter 15), Kabbalists are encouraged to speak to God from their hearts at all times. Eventually, Kabbalists report reaching a point at which they feel as if they're speaking to God nonstop, *all day long*.

Getting help and guidance from a prayer book

Even though Kabbalists can pray in their own languages and can pray to God by talking off the tops of their heads at any time and in any place, they may also take a little help from prayer books. A prayer book is an anthology of prayers, and over the centuries, prayer books have gotten bigger and bigger because every generation adds to them. The point of using a prayer book is not to read every word but rather to dip into it to find words of inspiration. After all, a good prayer helps people to express themselves, and a prayer that's just right for one person may not be right for the next.

A friend once told me that, when he was a little boy, he sat next to his grandfather in the synagogue and listened as his grandfather mumbled the Hebrew words from the prayer book. When my friend asked his grandfather, "Do you understand what you are saying?," his grandfather pointed upward to heaven and said, "No, but God does."

Even though God understands people and knows what's in their hearts, it's also important for people to understand what they're saying when they pray. Praying isn't about spouting incomprehensible words in a foreign language. So, although learning Hebrew (the language that Kabbalists have prayed in for centuries) certainly is meaningful, one can find authentic Kabbalistic prayer books available in bilingual editions.

Over the centuries prayer books have appeared in Yiddish, Spanish, French, Russian, and many other languages. But Kabbalists have a special relationship to the Hebrew language, known in Hebrew as **lashon hakodesh** (lah-*shone* hah-*koe*-desh; the holy language). The Torah was originally recorded in Hebrew, and Kabbalists believe that God creates the world through a combination of Hebrew letters.

Hebrew words are rich with meaning that simply can't be conveyed with a translation. So although prayer is important in any language and should be spoken in words that the speaker can understand, Kabbalists feel that Hebrew is the ultimate language for prayer. In fact, some even feel that Hebrew should only be used for prayer and Torah study. Many traditional Jews in Israel resist speaking Hebrew in everyday conversation, feeling that the holy tongue should be reserved for the sacred tasks of study and prayer.

Kabbalists also often pray by using the biblical book of Psalms. In Hebrew it's called **Tehillim** (teh-hee-*leem*). It consists of 150 psalms, most of them written by King David (who's known in Hebrew as **Dovid ha-Melekh** [*doe*-vid hah-*mel*-ekh]). If you read through the psalms, you'll see that they express just about every human emotion. For centuries, Kabbalists have used this magnificent book of spiritual poetry to express their deepest yearnings.

Study: Kabbalists do it every day, even if just for five minutes

Kabbalists don't let a day go by without studying at least one spiritual text. To a Kabbalist, just as people breathe every day and eat everyday, they also need to pray every day and study every day. Often, people who want to adopt this habit get discouraged before they even start. After all, with such busy lives, who has time to study every day?

The rule of thumb for study is the same as it is for going to the gym: Doing it for only five minutes every day is better than doing it once a week for five hours. By praying every day, God's presence is felt as an integral part of one's life; by studying every day, one's life is sewn with the holy activity of contemplating the ideas that lead to knowing the unknowable God (see Chapter 16).

Both prayer and study bring people closer to God. Whereas prayer is mainly an emotional activity, study is intellectual. Kabbalists connect with God in both ways. My teacher taught me that the way of holiness in Kabbalistic tradition is the rhythmic oscillation between prayer and study.

Study involves asking questions, questioning assumptions, probing for inconsistencies, and raising doubts. Prayer involves expressing faith, putting trust in God, and giving voice to emotions. To get stuck in either activity — prayer or study, faith or doubt — is a terrible error on the spiritual path. Prayer without study or study without prayer are both incomplete; the "back and forth" between prayer and study, between faith and doubt, is considered proper and the way of holiness.

Choosing texts for study

Kabbalistic literature is vast, and most Kabbalistic books require quite a bit of knowledge. So picking up most Kabbalistic texts and diving right in isn't very practical (see Chapter 14 for more on the study of Kabbalistic texts). In fact, one of the reasons a teacher is so important for the Kabbalist is to recommend the right book to study at the right time. Two books are particularly useful for the student who wants to get into a daily study routine:

- ✔ The Bible
- ✔ Pirke Avot

Believe it or not, the first book Kabbalists read and study on a regular basis is the Bible, also known as the Holy Scriptures. Most of the world knows it as the Old Testament, but Kabbalists don't use this term because "old" is a reference to the word "new" in New Testament, a book that's not generally on the Kabbalist's bookshelf. In Hebrew, the Holy Scriptures are referred to as **Tanakh** (tah-_nakh_), which is an acronym of three words:

- ✔ **Torah** (_toe_-rah): The Five Books of Moses, consisting of the biblical books of Genesis, Exodus, Leviticus, Numbers, and Deuteronomy
- ✔ **Nevi'im** (neh-_vee_-eem): The books of the Prophets, like Isaiah and Jeremiah
- ✔ **Ketuvim** (keh-_too_-veem): The other books of the Bible, often called the Writings, including Proverbs, the Song of Songs, and the Psalms

For the purpose of Kabbalistic study, the Bible can be read from beginning to end, but it also can be, and often is, read by jumping around from place to place. A principle of Bible study among Kabbalists is **Ein mukdam u'meuchar b'Torah** (ayn mook-_dahm_ oo-mooh-_khar_ bah-_toe_-rah; there is no before or after in the Torah), which means that the Torah isn't chronological even though the first chapters begin with creation and even though there's a certain chronology in the Bible. So although you may want to systematically read the Bible from "beginning to end," the book is really not set up that way, and jumping around is perfectly acceptable (kind of like this book, although I'm certainly not equating _Kabbalah For Dummies_ with the Bible!).

Kabbalists don't read the Bible only on the literal level (see Chapter 14), so if you're looking for an edition of the Holy Scriptures, try to find one with a commentary. Many commentaries on the Holy Scriptures are available in English. A well-stocked Jewish bookstore with a helpful staff person can guide you to the ones that may be best to begin with. There is no single "accepted" commentary. In fact, in principle, there are many levels of Torah explication. Some traditional sources say there are 70 ways to study the Torah, while other sources say that there are 600,000 different levels of Torah study! Also, many commentaries available in English focus on individual parts of the Holy Scriptures. For the Five Books of Moses, I highly recommend *The Living Torah* by Rabbi Aryeh Kaplan (Moznaim). A wonderful new multivolume set of commentaries that incorporate many Kabbalistic ideas and teachings is *The Chumash — The Gutnick Edition*. Several volumes have appeared and more are planned.

The other ideal book for daily study, Perke Avos (*peer*-kay *ah*-vohs), which means "the chapter of the sages," is available in English in many different editions. It consists of brief yet profound sayings that have been contemplated by Kabbalists for at least two millennia.

Finding the right study partner

Kabbalists have a special term for one's study partner: **khevrusah** (khehv-*roo*-sah). Although it comes from **khaver** (khah-*vair;* friend), the study partner is a *special* friend, a friend who occupies a unique roll in the life of a Kabbalist.

Finding a study partner isn't always easy. It's important to find someone who's willing to make a firm commitment to meet regularly and on schedule. Many study partnerships have fallen apart because one member doesn't make it a priority.

Often, the two members of a study partnership are on different levels. One may know Hebrew while the other doesn't. One may be more familiar with the text than the other is. Don't assume that when one person "knows" more than the other that he or she becomes the teacher. It's often the case that a newcomer to a text will raise questions and offer points of view that the more experienced partner has overlooked. In fact, one of the primary reasons to study with a partner is that when you study alone, you can easily fool yourself into thinking that you understand a passage well. The Talmud teaches that when two people study together they "sharpen each other's blades."

A teacher can often recommend a study partner, but finding just the right study partner, like finding the right spouse, is often a matter of luck. You never know what the actual dynamics will be. One person I know finally had to drop out of his study partnership because the partner was always harping on the same issue. It wasn't that the issue was unimportant, but the person whose issue it was just made too big a deal out of it constantly.

I know people who have standing telephone appointments with their study partners every day. Again, even if the studying lasts for just a few minutes a day, it all adds up.

Shopping for contemporary Kabbalistic books

In recent years, some bookstores have devoted sections of their shops to books on Kabbalah. Just because a book is in that section doesn't mean it's reliable, of course. Just because a writer finds a publisher doesn't mean that the book is accurate, insightful, or even worth the paper it's printed on. In this regard, books on Kabbalah are no different from books on any other subject. When you're in the market for contemporary Kabbalistic books, consider the following points of advice:

✔ **Books on Kabbalah by traditional Jewish publishers are generally reliable because Orthodox Jewish publishers pay particularly close attention to accuracy and authenticity**. I don't mean to suggest that Jewish publishers who aren't Orthodox are suspect, but I'm simply saying that Orthodox publishers are known to be extremely careful about who and what they publish, and they make special efforts to be certain that their authors are qualified and have sterling reputations. In fact, one rarely sees a book published by an Orthodox Jewish publisher without at least two pages of **haskamot** (hah-skah-*mote;* approbations), which are testimonies by authorities in the field who state that the manuscript was examined with great care.

✔ **Your best bet is to buy a book on Kabbalah based on the author's reputation, but you have to know what you're looking for.** If you want an academic history of Kabbalah, then obviously you should research the reputation of the author to make sure that this academic has a good reputation among his or her peers. If you want a book about Kabbalistic ideas, readability isn't enough; nor is selecting a book based on its popularity. A book can be a bestseller and be all wet.

✔ **If you see a book on Kabbalah spelled with a "C" (as in "Cabala") rather than a "K," be suspicious.** The accepted transliteration of the word among knowledgeable people is "Kabbalah."

✔ **Rely on the guidance of a teacher.** As I stress throughout this book, a student of Kabbalah must have a qualified teacher who can offer this sort of guidance.

✔ **Kabbalah has become a pop subject and one that many publishers who want to jump on the Kabbalah bandwagon try to cash in on.** There are even a number of books with the word "Kabbalah" in the title that have absolutely nothing to do with the subject of Kabbalah! It's important to read reviews and do a little research on the reviewer or the publication in which the reviews appear. The old saying, "May the buyer beware" is an important one when it comes to books of or about Kabbalah.

I once asked my teacher why so few people speak about God, even among believers. He told me that it's because speaking publicly about one's most intimate and important relationship is often difficult. That's where the study partner comes in. A student must be open to expressing his or her doubts, faith, and most pressing questions to a study partner.

Acts of lovingkindness: In principle, Kabbalists do as many as possible

The Kabbalistic term for acts of lovingkindness is **gemelut chasadim** (geh-meh-*loot* khah-sah-*deem*). This term is meant in both a general way as well as in many specific ways. Generally, a person's approach toward people should be filled with kindness. A Kabbalist is always on the lookout for opportunities to offer kindness to others. For the Kabbalist, kindness is the basis of his or her daily lifestyle.

More specifically, there are many acts of lovingkindness that are well-known and commonly discussed within Kabbalistic texts. A few of the most highly valued acts of lovingkindness in Kabbalistic tradition are:

- **Bikkur holim** (*beer*-koor *khoh*-leem; visiting the sick)
- **Nichum Avelim** (*nee*-khum ah-*vay*-leem; comforting mourners)
- **Hakhnasat Orchim** (hakh-nahs-*aht* oar-*kheem;* hospitality)
- **Hesed shel emet** (*kheh*-sed shell *eh*-met; true kindness)
- **Kevud av v'em** (keh-*vood* ahv v'eem; honoring one's father and mother)

One of life's goals for Kabbalists — perhaps life's main goal — is to become an instrument of God's will. Achieving this goal is somewhat of a paradox for Kabbalists, however, The Bible says that man is made "in God's image," and Kabbalists take this to mean that humans have free will. Kabbalists believe that the divine spark within people gives them the ability to choose freely. On the other hand, the goal of Kabbalists is to give up their will in order to do God's will.

How does the Kabbalist find out what God's will is? Through study and prayer, of course. Kabbalists study the wisdom of great sages of the past and the present in order to learn how to behave. And the Kabbalist prays to receive divine guidance when making choices. When a Kabbalist learns how to live, his or her will and God's will merge into one.

When a Kabbalist learns from the sages the righteous way to act, he abandons his will for God's will. So when a Kabbalist walks down the street and sees a person in need, for example, the Kabbalist reaches out his hand to give charity, which is an example of an act of lovingkindness. That simple act has a larger meaning, however: The Kabbalist knows that with the right inner intention (see the section "Intending to be intentional" later in the chapter) and the right understanding, his outstretched hand actually *becomes* the outstretched hand of God.

Kabbalists give charitable donations with great frequency. Some put coins into a charity box before each prayer session, and others make sure to give something to everyone who asks, whether it be a request for a donation through the mail or an approaching beggar in the street. Ancient tradition teaches that everyone has an obligation to give charity. In Hebrew, the word for "charity," **tzedakah** (tseh-_dah_-kah), really means "justice." For the Kabbalist, giving charity is actually an expression of justice.

For centuries, the great sages have discussed just about every question imaginable related to giving charity: How much money to give (at least 10 percent of one's income), how much is too much (more than 20 percent of one's income puts the giver at financial risk), how to give (quietly), how not to give (never in a way that causes a person public embarrassment), and many others. A simpler instruction comes from the great Jewish sage, Maimonides, who taught that one should develop the practice of giving a small coin to every beggar who makes a request.

For Kabbalists, God is in the details. Jewish tradition and Kabbalistic tradition examine every aspect of every subject in order to thoroughly understand the recommended behavior. With this in mind, it's not sufficient simply to believe in giving charity. One must understand all the possible ramifications and questions prompted by the act of giving charity.

Giving charity is required of every Kabbalist. The basis for it is found in the Torah (the Five Books of Moses, also known as the first five books of the Bible), which says that a person is required to give a tenth of his or her income to the poor. The Torah has other laws about giving charity as well; for example, the produce at the corners of a farmer's fields is supposed to be left for the poor.

Kabbalists give charity many times over the course of the day, including:

- Before each of the three prayer sessions (morning, afternoon, and evening)
- Before sitting down to study
- When passing a poor person on the street who asks for a coin
- Any other time that he or she is so inspired

Even if a Kabbalist thinks that a person on the street is faking need, he or she gives charity. As the sages of old taught, people should be thankful even to the fake beggars because they keep others in the habit of giving.

Figuring out how to love

Kabbalists don't assume that lovingkindness is easy to perform. They know that it's all too easy to say, "Everyone must love each other." The real questions are: How do people love each other? What _is_ love anyway?

A fundamental principle in Kabbalah is the idea that no human emotion is bad or good in and of itself. Hate isn't considered bad, and love isn't considered good. Kabbalists believe that all the emotions and potentialities of the human heart are only deemed good or bad based on how they're used. It's all about dosage and timing. As pharmacists know, a fine line separates a medicine and a poison. So, there are times when hate is called for. For example, Kabbalists are taught to "hate evil." Not just to fight it but to hate it. Jewish tradition doesn't advocate turning the other cheek. Sometimes, as one of my teachers told me, you have to hit back; sometimes, you even have to hit below the belt.

I once asked the Nobel Peace Prize winner Elie Wiesel what he learned from the Holocaust. He told me that he learned to fight evil and not to wait, not to think that "it will get better."

Sometimes love is the absolutely wrong emotion. For example, I know a photographer who created a photographic study of a battered women's shelter and its residents. She told me that, quite often, the battered women go back to the men who beat them up. When asked why, they often say, "Because I love him." Sometimes love is the wrong emotion.

I once asked one of my Kabbalah teachers the following question: If it's true that all possible emotions and feelings are only good or bad according to how they're used and that no feeling is, in and of itself, bad, then how is the heretical view denying God's existence ever good? He told me to imagine walking down the street and seeing a beggar asking for money. I'd think to myself, as Kabbalists often do, that God takes care of everyone, so therefore I don't have to give any charity to the person. My teacher suggested that in such a case I'd have to drum up "a little heresy" by thinking that God may *not* take care of everyone. In that way, I would be prompted to give charity. In a way, my heresy would inspire me to give. Sometimes even heresy has its value.

Getting in shape to perform acts of kindness

Kabbalah differs from many other forms of mysticism in that it's deeply connected to law. Kabbalists throughout history have been just as bound to Jewish law as they have been to the sublime ideas of mysticism. The study of the law and the discussions that result from the law guide Kabbalists in their behavior. Simply believing that acts of lovingkindness are important to perform isn't enough; the Kabbalist studies the holy texts in order to fully understand just what makes for a true act of kindness.

Kabbalists find the curriculum of life in the holy books, beginning with the Torah and including all other great works of spiritual literature of the Jewish people, including the Talmud, the Midrash, the Zohar, the Codes of Law, and the great commentaries up to the present (see Chapter 13). There is no way around it; to be a Kabbalist means to be a student, and to be a student means to study the sacred texts in order to learn how to live.

Smiling is very important

Every serious Kabbalist throughout history has studied the wisdom of a great sage named **Shammai** (shah-my). Shammai was known to be a rather strict person and was sometimes impatient. Nevertheless, he taught a lesson that's recorded as a law that all Kabbalists must follow. Shammai said, "Make your study regular; say little and do much; *and greet every person with a smile.*" To Kabbalists, smiling when you greet someone is the law!

But to be a Kabbalist doesn't mean that you find a book that tells you what to do and then you go and do it. Studying is like lifting weights at a gym. I go to the gym in the morning and work out with dumbbells. I'm quite good with them, but I don't go to the gym to learn how to lift dumbbells; I go there to get in shape. I just use the dumbbells to help me get into shape so that I have the strength and stamina to get through each day. The Kabbalist doesn't go to the books to find out exactly what to do. Rather, the Kabbalist studies to get "in shape," so that when a situation presents itself, the Kabbalist can apply all the wisdom he or she has learned to the situation at hand.

Feeling good about yourself and accepting praise for acts of kindness

For Kabbalists, there's always room for growth and improvement. As one of my teachers emphasizes, "If you think you've arrived, you're lost." The life of the Kabbalist is the life of someone who is constantly trying to improve himself, refine himself, and uplift himself. There's no room for smugness in the soul of the Kabbalist. On the other hand, Kabbalists know that when they perform acts of kindness, they can feel good about themselves because they're doing God's will.

An ancient saying reveals this balance between continuing improvement and praise for one's accomplishments. A few thousand years ago, a great sage taught, "He who flees from honor, honor will pursue him." People often think this teaching means that the way to obtain honor is to run away from it. But the ancient teaching has a different meaning that's based on the Hebrew word **rodef** (roe-def; pursue). A rodef is a pursuer and may even be a person who wants to murder someone. This particular teaching means that, for the person who deserves honor and runs away from it, honor will become a pursuer and will track down the deserving person until he or she accepts the honor that's deserved. Essentially, false modesty has no place. If you do something that's not right, you deserve criticism; if you do something right (such as performing an act of kindness), you deserve (and should accept) praise.

Waking Up

Kabbalah isn't a hobby or a part-time activity. To be a Kabbalist is to be alert to the principles of Kabbalah at every moment. A Hebrew phrase mounted on the wall of many synagogues says it best: **Dah lifnay me attah omed** (dah lif-*nay* mee ah-*tah* oh-*maid*; Know before whom you stand). From the moment a Kabbalist wakes up, he or she knows that God sees everything and cares about everything.

Intending to be intentional

Kavanah (kah-vah-*nah*; inner intention) is the basis of all actions made by a Kabbalist. Basically, to have kavanah is to be conscious and deliberate. A Kabbalist must be alert, awake, aware, and intentional in his or her actions so that he or she doesn't just go through the motions. Instead, every action needs to be accompanied by the proper inner intent.

Even though kavanah is a full-time job, it's especially important first thing in the morning. Starting one's day with the right inner attitude is the launching pad for the entire day the lies ahead. Kabbalistic tradition urges everyone to begin the day with an awareness of and gratitude to God.

Kabbalists believe that one's actions and one's intentions must be in sync. To use an extreme example, you can't say "I love you" to someone while feeling hostility. It's dishonest, of course, but it's also simply the wrong intention. In general, Kabbalists want to make sure that their thoughts, words, and deeds are in concert with each other. While one can do the right thing for the wrong reason, it is best to strive for each act to be pure and complete.

Cultivating gratitude at the first moment of consciousness

When a Kabbalist wakes up in the morning, one thought should be on his or her mind and lips. No, I don't mean "What's for breakfast?," "I better rush; I have an appointment," or "I'm going to make a lot of money today." I'm talking about the Modeh Ani:

I gratefully thank you, living and eternal Ruler, for You have returned my soul within me with compassion — abundant is your faithfulness.

In Hebrew, "Modeh Ani" means "I am grateful." The whole sentence is fairly easy to memorize in Hebrew. Here's the pronunciation:

Moe-deh *ah*-nee leh-foh-*neh*-kha *meh*-lekh khai v'kah-*yohm* sheh-heh-kheh-*zar*-tah *bee* nish-ma-*tee* b'khem-*lah rah*-bah eh-moo-nah-*teh*-kha.

The Kabbalist doesn't just say these words habitually without thinking of their meaning. They're said, like everything else, with kavanah (see the preceding section). By saying the Modeh Ani, the Kabbalist is

- Thanking God for restoring his or her faculties after a night's sleep
- Acknowledging that God gave a new day in order for one to become more aware of God
- Acknowledging that God is faithful to those who feel and express gratitude to God

Anything but entitled, a Kabbalist is in the habit of expressing gratitude all day long. The great sages urge everyone to recite 100 blessings a day (see Chapter 15). Those blessings are basically words of thanks. The good and the bad, pleasures and pains, happy times and sad times are all from God and are all for the best (see Chapter 5). The great sage **Reb Zusia** (reb *zoo*-shah) once said, "When I was hungry, I thanked God for giving me an appetite."

Getting Washed and Dressed

A Kabbalist's day must be filled with an awareness of God and God's presence. Even someone busy with a task as seemingly mundane as getting washed and dressed must be filled with the awareness of God. Kabbalists believe that the only Reality is God — there's nothing and no place without God. (One of the names Kabbalists have for God is **HaMakom** [hah-mah-*cohm*; the place].)

The body is holy

Kabbalists don't believe that the body is obscene or dirty in any way. *Iggeret Ha Kodesh* (ee-*geh*-ret hah-*koe*-desh; The Holy Letter), a well-known Kabbalistic book written by Rabbi Moses the son of Nachman (also known as Nachmanides), states that every detail of the human body is holy and saying that any part of the body or any normal human bodily function is unholy is an affront against God.

Washing your hands when you awake

A custom that has existed for a few thousand years and is practiced daily by Kabbalists is washing one's hands immediately upon arising in the morning. In fact, some say that you shouldn't even walk four *cubits* (an ancient measurement that's approximately the length from the tip of one's middle finger to one's elbow) after getting out of bed without washing your hands. Some people even set a large cup of water and a basin next to the bed at night in preparation for washing their hands in the morning.

Many explanations have been provided over the centuries for this custom, but all basically point to the same idea: The body is the vessel of the soul, and the soul is holy. One must treat the vessel in a special way because its function is to house the holy soul, and that's a lofty purpose.

The proper way to wash one's hands in the morning is to pour water over the right hand and then the left three times while saying this blessing:

> *Blessed are You, Lord our God, Ruler of the Universe, Who has sanctified us with His commandments and has commanded us regarding washing the hands.*

Putting on your shoes with purpose

Kabbalah teaches that there's great significance to the right side and the left sides of things (see Chapter 4). According to Kabbalah, the sides are connected to two major cosmic forces in the universe.

- **Chesed** (*keh*-sed): Signifies expansion and is related to the right side

- **Gevurah** (geh-*voo*-rah): Signifies contraction and is related to the left side

Chesed and *Gevurah* are always working in combination with each other. For example, as a parent, I must offer a certain amount of *Chesed* to my children; specifically, I must encourage them to expand in the world and become who they are to become. I must also impose a certain amount of *Gevurah,* or limitation and discipline, on my children. Presenting too much of either is a terrible mistake for a parent to make, but the proper combination of the two is the path of healthy parenting. (I discuss *Chesed* and *Gevurah* in further detail in Chapter 4.)

Kabbalists are always aware of the significance of these two cosmic forces, and putting on one's shoes — the right and the left — is a perfect opportunity to remind oneself of these two forces and the need to combine them properly.

Kabbalists disagree on the proper procedure for putting on shoes. Some say you should begin with the right shoe, whereas others say you should begin with the left. Still others offer a compromise: Put on the right shoe first but don't tie it, and then put on the left shoe. After both shoes are on, the order is reversed for tying, with the left shoe tied first followed by the right shoe. In every method, the value of the cosmic forces of right and left, *Chesed* and *Gevurah,* are evident.

Dressing with modesty

The Hebrew concept of **tzniut** (tznee-*oot;* modesty) is important in Kabbalistic tradition. Some Kabbalists apply the general concern for modesty to modesty in how a person dresses and have many specific rules about it (such as how long sleeves and hemlines should be among women), but others are willing to take a more relaxed approach and suggest that local and contemporary standards should apply. After all, a woman or a man can wear the most modest clothing and still behave inappropriately, just as people can dress in more relaxed and modern attire and yet act with exemplary behavior.

It's generally recommended that the Kabbalist dress neatly and modestly when praying in the synagogue. On the Sabbath, tradition urges Kabbalists to dress as they would if they had an audience with the King. (For more on the Sabbath, check out Chapter 10.)

Offering Prayers and Meditation

The Kabbalist must always be aware of God, which is why the morning activities have a special intensity. It's so easy to jump out of bed and get wrapped up in all the activities and demands of one's life. The Kabbalist also gets involved in the tasks of the every day, but only after beginning each day with sufficient kavanah (inner intention) to make the day a holy one. Launching the day properly involves attention to prayer and meditation.

Reciting the standard morning blessings

Included in the 100 blessings that Kabbalists are to recite each day (see Chapter 15) is a list of blessings traditionally recited in the morning, one right after the other. These blessings appear in traditional prayer books and have been recited by Kabbalists for centuries. They suggest that people express their gratitude to the Creator for all the gifts and blessings that have been bestowed upon them. Here's a sampling of the blessings:

> *Blessed are You, Lord our God, Ruler of the universe, who gave the heart the understanding to distinguish between day and night.*

> *Blessed are You, Lord our God, Ruler of the universe, who has not made me a heathen.*

Blessed are You, Lord our God, Ruler of the universe, who has not made me a slave.

Blessed are You, Lord our God, Ruler of the universe, who opens the eyes of the blind.

Blessed are You, Lord our God, Ruler of the universe, who clothes the naked.

Blessed are You, Lord our God, Ruler of the universe, who sets the captives free.

Blessed are You, Lord our God, Ruler of the universe, who straightens those who are bowed down.

Blessed are You, Lord our God, Ruler of the universe, who spread a forth the earth above the waters.

Blessed are You, Lord our God, Ruler of the universe, who has provided for all my needs.

Blessed are You, Lord our God, Ruler of the universe, who guides the steps of man.

Blessed are You, Lord our God, Ruler of the universe, who girds Israel with might.

Blessed are You, Lord our God, Ruler of the universe, who crowns Israel with glory.

Blessed art You, Lord our God, Ruler of the universe, who gives strength to the weary.

Blessed are You, Lord our God, Ruler of the universe, who removes sleep from my eyes and slumber from my eyelids.

These blessings aren't all meant literally. For example, God doesn't literally "open the eyes of the blind." The sense of this blessing is that all people are blind to some extent, and God helps people see life and understand what's truly big and truly small, what's important and unimportant. One of my teachers taught me that these traditional blessings can be interpreted by each individual in his or her own way and can be applied to suit each person's needs and desires.

Morning prayers

Kabbalists can pray any time they like, but they also have three major prayer sessions: morning, afternoon, and evening. The morning prayer session, known as **Shakharit** (*shah*-khah-reet) comes from the Hebrew word **Shakhar,** which means "morning." I discuss the afternoon and evening prayer sessions, which are quite similar to the morning prayers, in Chapter 15.

After the recitation of the morning blessings that I mention in the preceding section, one moves on to the part of the morning prayers known as Songs of Praise. Kabbalists begin their days thinking about God, meditating on God, and singing songs of praise to God. Some of those songs, as found in the prayer book, include the well-known word **Hallelujah** (praise to God).

I once led a Kabbalah prayer service for beginners and suggested that the tune of the song "Michael Row Your Boat Ashore" be used as a Song of Praise. To the tune, I sang, "I am happy to be here today," and everyone responded, "Hallelujah." I asked the others to suggest additional phrases of praise and gratitude. Someone called out, "And I am grateful to be alive," to which the group once again responded "Hallelujah." We went on like that for a while, with people calling out their words of praise precisely in the spirit of the traditional morning prayer session as Kabbalists have done for centuries.

Focusing on the oneness of the universe: A daily Kabbalistic meditation

The most famous prayer in Jewish life — and one that has been recited by Kabbalists for dozen of centuries — is called the **Sh'ma** (sheh-*mah;* hear). The Sh'ma is as follows: **Sh'ma Yisrael, Adonai Elohaynu, Adonai Echad** (sheh-*mah* yis-rah-*ehl* ah-doh-*noy* eh-loh-*hay*-noo ah-doh-*noy eh*-chahd; Hear O Israel, the Lord our God, the Lord is One).

Kabbalists recite this prayer twice a day — once in the morning and once in the evening. The prayer is rich with meaning, every word having layers of significance. But the essence of the prayer is a meditation on the oneness of the universe: God is One, everything is God, everything is One.

Grabbing a Bite

Kabbalists don't simply eat. When a Kabbalist eats, something quite profound happens. You can't see it, but it's very much on the mind of the Kabbalist. According to Kabbalah, the act of eating is part of the repairing of the world (see Chapter 8). The basic idea is that when God created the world, he poured divine light into a vessel. The vessel shattered, and the "stuff" of the world became the shards of that broken vessel, so that contained within the shards are sparks of the divine light. By eating, Kabbalists aren't just nourishing themselves, they're releasing the divine sparks that are embedded within the food. Awareness of this release is the proper kavanah for the Kabbalist who's eating.

One of the greatest Kabbalists of all times, Rabbi Israel (known as the Baal Shem Tov), had this to say on the subject of eating: "Take care that all you do is for God's sake. Regarding eating, do not say that the intention of eating shall be that you gain strength. This is a good intention, of course; but the true perfection only exists where the deed itself happens to heaven, for that is where the holy sparks are raised."

Another thing on the minds of Kabbalists as they eat is that the food is giving them the energy to do holy acts in the world, including repairing the world (see Chapter 8) and performing acts of lovingkindness. So, when a Kabbalist eats, he or she is aware that the food is contributing to the holiness of the world.

Blessings to say before eating

The theme of gratitude permeates everything for the Kabbalist, and eating is no exception. A Kabbalist never eats without first expressing gratitude for what he or she is about to eat. Even if a Kabbalist eats only a tiny piece of chocolate or a spoonful of green peas or a sip of water, the blessing for that particular food item must be said. The blessings are simply expressions of thanks and gratitude. These blessings are found in the standard prayer book.

For blessing purposes, different foods fall under different categories, and each category has a special blessing. The categories are

- ✔ Bread
- ✔ Wine
- ✔ Baked goods other than bread
- ✔ Food found in trees (fruits and nuts)
- ✔ Food from the ground (like cucumbers and strawberries)
- ✔ Everything else (like fluids, meat, cheese, and so on)

Some foods are trickier to categorize than others. For example, peanuts aren't really nuts, they're legumes. The appropriate blessing for a peanut isn't the blessing said for nuts but rather the one said for plants that come from the ground. The whole system of different blessings for different foods helps the Kabbalist to be extra conscious of just what kind of food God is providing.

Here's a personal example of a food blessing in action. In my opinion, the greatest commercially available cookie is the Mint Milano. I often eat them after a long day (I suggest freezing them first), but I don't go home, head to my freezer, and pop down a few Mint Milanos. First, I hold the cookie in my hand and recite the Kabbalist blessing for eating baked goods (something along the lines of "Thank you God for creating the ingredients that make up Mint Milanos!"). Then I blissfully toss a few back.

Braving the blessing bee

You're probably familiar with school spelling bees. Well, in the **yeshivas** (yeh-*shee*-vahs; Jewish schools) my children went to, they didn't have spelling bees — they had "blessing bees."

They were actually called **Bracha** (*brah*-khah) Bees. The teacher would name a food, and the students would have to recite the blessing appropriate for that food.

Blessings to say after eating

After finishing a meal, a Kabbalist doesn't just push away from the table. A meal isn't complete until grace is recited; it's simply another way of saying "thanks." The concept of eat and run is really unthinkable for a Kabbalist.

When a Kabbalist eats alone, he or she recites the grace after meals by himself or herself. When a group of people eat at the same table, the grace after meals has a special introduction that brings everyone's expression of gratitude together. But each person still recites the grace after meals individually. Nobody can say it for anyone else.

There are a few different forms of grace after meals:

- After a full meal (that is, one that begins with bread), a series of four blessings may be said.
- After having a snack, a shorter grace is recited.

In either case, Kabbalists know that God provides them with nourishment and therefore must be thanked. The texts of these words of thanks can be found in the traditional prayer book.

Whether one says the traditional words of thanks or not, Kabbalists believe that a "thank you" is essential.

Repairing the World

In Chapter 8, I explain the Kabbalistic idea that the world, by definition, is in need of repair. Kabbalists believe that God didn't finish the world and that humans need to participate in the creation of the world by adding to it and repairing it.

The process of repairing the world, known as **tikkun olam** (tee-*koon* oh-*lahm*), and acts of lovingkindness, known as **gemilut hasadim,** are quite similar. In fact, the two concepts overlap. I would say that acts of lovingkindness are ways to repair the world, but they're generally interpersonal in their nature.

Repairing of the world isn't an assignment for professionals or specialists — everyone participates. Every Kabbalist knows that, and every Kabbalist is supposed to be conscious, all day long, of the countless opportunities to participate in the repair process.

Of the many ways to repair the world each day, here are a few:

- Social action
- Recycling
- Making the world a better place
- Supporting medical research
- Picking up some garbage from the sidewalk
- Writing a letter to the editor of the newspaper
- Teaching one's children something important

Bed Sheets and Balance Sheets: Ending the Day

In the same way that a Kabbalist doesn't wake or navigate his or her day without thinking about God, going to bed requires special consciousness. After all, every moment of every day for a Kabbalist must be infused with God-consciousness.

Making a nightly accounting

A Kabbalist doesn't just climb into bed at the end of each day. The day that's ending was a gift from God. The day began with a statement of gratitude for providing the Kabbalist with another opportunity to enjoy the world's pleasures and to engage in holy acts (flip back to the section "Cultivating gratitude at the first moment of consciousness" earlier in this chapter). The end of the day has its appropriate Kabbalistic activity, **Cheshbon Hanefesh** (*kez*-bone hah-*neh*-fesh; an accounting of the soul), which involves looking back on the day and examining it in detail by considering these questions:

- ✔ What did I do right?
- ✔ What did I do wrong?
- ✔ What could I have improved?
- ✔ How may I have hurt someone?
- ✔ How may I have not been conscious?
- ✔ Were my ethical goals for the day met?
- ✔ What will my ethical goals for tomorrow be?

Meditating on the oneness of the universe before falling asleep

As I explain earlier in this chapter (see "Focusing on the oneness of the universe: A daily Kabbalistic meditation"), the Sh'ma is a meditation on God's oneness. This meditation happens twice a day for the Kabbalist — in the morning and at night — because of a statement found in the Torah indicating that people should meditate on God's oneness "when we lie down and when we rise up." The words of the Sh'ma are the same each time: Hear O Israel, the Lord Our God, the Lord is One.

Kabbalists always want to be deliberate about the things they say and do, so with the Sh'ma, they think long and hard about the oneness of the world. An example of this oneness lies in an ancient teaching that the reason God created Adam and didn't create many other people at the same time is so that nobody can say, "My ancestor was greater than yours." The human family, despite all the races, religions, and nations, is really one human family.

Handling bad dreams

Kabbalists take dreams seriously. They have a traditional belief that dreams often signal things to come, so if a Kabbalist has a bad dream, he or she may perform a ritual in order to express the hope that the dream is for the best despite the bad feelings it generates. The ritual consists of finding three friends and telling them the dream; the dreamer and the friends then declare that the dream should be interpreted for the good. (A specific text providing the words to this ritual can be found in the traditional prayer book used by Kabbalists.) Because Kabbalists believe that everything is for the best, it must be possible to interpret even a bad dream in a positive way.

Another aspect to the oneness of everything is reflected in environmental issues. Even 2,000 years ago, Kabbalists were keenly aware that people have an impact on the environment of their neighbors. They developed laws to protect neighbors from bad environmental practices. For example, if someone gathered a pile of animal dung to be used as fuel or fertilizer, that person had to be conscious of where that pile was put and if it was downwind from the neighbors.

Chapter 10

Living One Week at a Time

In This Chapter

▶ Grasping the Kabbalistic significance of the Sabbath

▶ Preparing for the Sabbath all week long

▶ Demystifying Sabbath rituals and activities

There's an old saying that "More than the Jews keep the Sabbath, the Sabbath keeps the Jews." This saying is surely true for Kabbalists. The Jewish Sabbath isn't only the focus of the week for Kabbalists, but its tranquility is said to be "a taste of the world to come."

The Sabbath, which starts Friday at sundown and ends Saturday at sundown, isn't simply a day that a Kabbalist just runs into. Rather, Kabbalists prepare for the Sabbath all week long. And when it comes, they savor every detail.

In this chapter, I take a close look at how Kabbalists prepare for the Sabbath, how it's observed and celebrated, and the supplies that one needs for full participation. I also briefly explore the other days of the week and how those days lead up to the holy day of the Sabbath.

The End of the Week Is also the Beginning

For Kabbalists, the week has six days, not seven. The seventh day, **Shabbat** (shah-*bot;* Sabbath), isn't really a day at all. According to Kabbalists, the Sabbath is a special entity totally unlike the six days of the week. They view it both as the launching pad for the week as well as the week's culmination. Kabbalists derive energy for the new week from the special qualities of Shabbat, and Shabbat is also the result of the week's effort, a time to enjoy and reap the benefits of six days of hard work.

Kabbalists learn about Shabbat from the first chapters of the Bible. The text tells that God created the world in six days and that on the seventh "day," God rested. According to Kabbalistic tradition, God's rest isn't like human rest because God constantly creates and sustains the world. Nonetheless, Shabbat is often referred to as "a day of rest," and, as I discuss in the section "Being busy doing nothing" later in this chapter, the notion of rest has a very special and particular meaning in Kabbalistic tradition.

The Kabbalistic view of time is different than the usual notion of linear time that flows in one direction. In Kabbalah, time isn't linear; rather, it goes in a spiral. In this way, Kabbalists return each day, week, and year to a time and place that are similar to the last round, but hopefully, because people progress spiritually, at a higher level.

The sense of nonlinear time is reflected in the fact that neither of the two most important spiritual texts studied by Kabbalists, the Torah and the Talmud, has a beginning or an end. When Kabbalists read a portion of the Torah each week and come to the end, what appears to be the end is merely a prelude to a new beginning, where the new round begins again. Similarly, the Talmud has no beginning or end, which is one of the reasons the Talmud is referred to as a "sea." Students of Talmud study in a certain sequence, and when they reach the place that looks like an end, the next moment is merely a new beginning of the same cycle.

Keeping Your Eye on the Sabbath

Kabbalists always have Shabbat in mind regardless of the day of the week. In fact, for Kabbalists the days of the week don't have their own names, like Sunday, Monday, and so on. Rather, the names of the individual days of the week relate to Shabbat. In Hebrew, Sunday is **Yom Rishon** (yohm ree-*shown;* the first day), Monday is **Yom Sheni** (yohm shay-*nee;* the second day), and the rest of the days follow this pattern.

The consciousness and the **kavanah** (kah-vah-*nah;* inner intention) of the Kabbalist is that every day of the week brings one closer to Shabbat. During the week, Kabbalists experience heightened anticipation as the special period of Shabbat approaches. The work that the Kabbalist does during the week is intended to repair the world as well as to earn a livelihood, but in its depth, the work of the six days of the week is all part of the preparation for Shabbat.

In fact, it's been said that many Kabbalists throughout history never worried or planned for any day other than the next Shabbat. Some saintly individuals have gone so far as to believe and act as though one need not make any more money than what's necessary to bring oneself and one's family through the week in order to celebrate Shabbat.

When Shabbat is over, the round of the week is renewed, and the Kabbalist again has his eye on the next Shabbat. As the days of the week roll on, Kabbalists feel a tangible ascent to the period of time known as the holy Shabbat.

One of my Kabbalah teachers often says, "If you think you've arrived, you are lost." In other words, a Kabbalist is always striving for a better future. The idea of living in the present as much as possible is certainly wise, but during each week, the Kabbalist also longs for a return of Shabbat just as during his life, the Kabbalist yearns for the coming of the Messiah.

Preparing to Receive the Gift of the Sabbath

Kabbalists see Shabbat as a gift from above. When one understands how to appropriately participate in the Kabbalistic celebration of Shabbat, one truly anticipates this special time as though it's a gift to be received. In this section, I share with you what it takes to prepare to receive the gift of Shabbat.

Countless people who begin to explore the life of the traditional Kabbalist run in the other direction when they confront the tremendous number of requirements that Kabbalistic tradition asks of the Kabbalist, especially the requirements related to preparing for and observing the Sabbath. Kabbalah isn't some New Age hobby through which one can receive a quick fix or an inspirational poem for the soul. Kabbalah is hard work. The great masters of Kabbalah participated in an almost ceaseless effort to follow the divine commandments as passed down through tradition, to understand those commandments in detail, and to ultimately align their wills with the will of God.

Don't forget that "Kabbalah" means "to receive"

Etymologically, the word "Kabbalah" comes from the Hebrew root which means "to receive." A story from Buddhist tradition captures the very idea of Kabbalah as a receiving.

A student went to a Buddhist master and asked if he would accept him as a student. The teacher consented and then said, "First let's have some tea." The Master prepared the tea and began pouring tea from the kettle into a cup. The cup slowly but surely filled to the brim, and the master continued to pour. The student, noticing the tea overflowing from the rim of the cup, exclaimed, "Master, Master! The cup is full and overflowing." The Master put down the tea kettle, smiled, and said, "You have now received your first lesson; unless you come empty, with room within you to receive, you will never make any progress as my student."

Similarly, a student of Kabbalah should be open and filled with a desire to receive the tradition. This ability to receive certainly pertains to the arrival of the Sabbath. A Kabbalist who knows that he or she is about to receive a gift must make room for that gift. Without carving out room in one's heart and soul to be a true recipient of the Sabbath, one can't feel its sanctity or experience its holiness. To be a Kabbalist is to always be prepared to receive gifts from above.

Getting in the right frame of mind

According to Kabbalistic tradition, the quality of Shabbat is the direct result of one's preparation for it. If you travel through the week with little consciousness, anticipation, or preparation for Shabbat, the result is a rather bland Shabbat. On the other hand, if you truly experience the ascent of the week towards Shabbat and truly feel that the week is an opportunity to climb to the spiritual height that Shabbat provides, the result should be a sublime Shabbat filled with joy, pleasure, and sanctity.

When the sun goes down on Saturday night, Kabbalists don't merely begin a new week. Rather, they begin their ascent to the next holy Sabbath. Although Sunday and Monday may begin slowly and without much anticipation of the Sabbath, by Tuesday and Wednesday, Kabbalists can truly feel the coming arrival of the Sabbath.

A Kabbalah teacher taught me that one of the most important preparations for the Sabbath is to cultivate a willingness to receive it and taste it. A passage from the Torah reveals an aspect of this attitude. The Torah says that when the Children of Israel accepted the Torah from above, they responded with an unusual phrase, **Na'aseh V'nishmah** (nah-ah-*seh* vah-nish-*mah;* We will do and we will hear or We will do and we will understand [Exodus 24:7]).

This phrase reflects the opposite of what people usually do in life, which is say that they want to understand something before they do it. Essentially, they stand with their arms folded and say, "First prove it to me, and then I'll consider tasting it or doing it." The Kabbalist, however, says, "First I'll do it, and then I'll understand it." Understanding, represented by the second *sefirah* of *Binah,* leads to knowledge, which is the third *sefirah* of *Da'at* (see Chapter 4). According to Kabbalah, true *knowing* comes from the experience itself.

Visiting and using a 500-year-old mikvah

The mystical city of Tzfat, Israel, is where Rabbi Isaac Luria, known as the greatest Kabbalist who ever lived, resided. (On maps, it is often spelled "Safed," but "Tzfat" is closer to its correct pronunciation.) Tzfat has a mikvah that's believed to have been used by Rabbi Isaac Luria himself. This mikvah, which is located in a cave, has attracted countless people over the centuries. When I visited Israel recently, I tracked down an old friend of mine who used to be a devoted Grateful Dead fan and who now lives in Tzfat with his wife and children and leads the life of a Kabbalist. The very first thing we did was walk to the mikvah of Rabbi Isaac Luria and submerge ourselves in that ritual bath. The water was icy, but the experience was sublime. Knowing that countless Kabbalists (including Rabbi Isaac Luria) and others throughout the ages had used the mikvah made the experience deeply meaningful.

WORDS OF WISDOM

It's what's inside that counts

A Kabbalist related to his teacher that his little town had two bakeries. He explained that because his town was small and both bakers struggled to make a living, he felt that it was important to do business with both bakers and to buy his challah from both.

One baker wove beautifully braided challah, but his recipe wasn't that great. The other baker seemed unable to create beautifully braided challah, but his recipe was quite exceptional and delicious.

The Kabbalist asked his teacher, "For the honor of Shabbat, would it be more appropriate to use the beautifully braided challah whose recipe is mediocre or the delicious challah whose shape is unattractive?" The teacher responded that the student should use the unattractive challah with a delicious taste because the inner beauty of something — not its superficial external beauty — is of greatest importance.

Dipping in a ritual bath

Since time immemorial, Kabbalists have submerged themselves in a ritual bath known as a **mikvah** (*mik*-vah). It's generally known among Jews that women who observe the Jewish laws of family purity visit a mikvah each month. What's not generally known is the Kabbalistic tradition of submerging oneself in a mikvah every day of the year or, if that frequency is impractical, at least once a week (either before the Sabbath on Friday afternoon or on the morning of the Sabbath). Countless Hasidim throughout the world observe this Kabbalistic practice.

Similar to a baptism, submersion in a mikvah isn't a physical cleansing (no scrubbing behind the ears) but rather is a spiritual cleansing. One enters and submerges in a mikvah completely naked. Even rings are removed so that the water touches every part of the body without any barrier.

Most communities that are home to a significant number of traditional Jews have mikvahs. Specifications must be met for the construction of an acceptable traditional mikvah. It must be built in the ground or as a part of a building. Therefore, a portable receptacle, like a bathtub or Jacuzzi, can never function as a mikvah. A mikvah must contain a minimum of 200 gallons of rainwater gathered into the mikvah in accordance with a specific set of traditional regulations. Where the acquisition of rainwater isn't possible, ice or snow originating from a natural source may be used to fill the mikvah.

Checking off Sabbath essentials

In the same way that a hunter must gather his supplies for a hunting trip, a baseball player must gather his equipment in preparation for a game, and a chef must gather his tools and utensils for the kitchen, a Kabbalist needs to make some specific preparations in order to be well-equipped and prepared for the arrival of Shabbat. The following items are required:

- **Fresh clean clothes:** Kabbalists anticipate the Sabbath each week by designating the fine clothing that they'll wear both to greet Shabbat on Friday night and to live through the Shabbat day. It's not unusual for a Kabbalist to select his or her finest clothes and make sure that they're sparkling clean as a way of preparing for the Sabbath. After purchasing new clothing, many Kabbalists wait until Shabbat to wear them for the first time in honor of the holy Sabbath.

    Kabbalists recite a special blessing when wearing new clothing for the first time: *Blessed are You, Lord our God, Ruler of the universe, who clothes the naked.*

- **Candles:** Candles are important for the celebration of Shabbat. On Friday night, just as the Sabbath arrives, Kabbalistic households light at least two candles as a symbolic gesture of bringing the light of the Sabbath into their lives. At the close of Shabbat, Kabbalists use candles during the ceremony known as **havdalah** (hav-*dah*-lah), in which they bid the Sabbath goodbye and hope that the light of the Sabbath will remain and illuminate the days of the week to come.

    Sabbath candles are readily available in many large supermarkets. Candles used in the havdalah ritual are commonly available in Jewish bookstores and can be ordered from many Web sites. Havdalah candle makers pride themselves on designing havdalah candles that are colorful and woven together in a particularly ornate fashion.

- **The fruit of the vine:** An important item for celebrating Shabbat is either grape juice or wine, which are interchangeable when a Kabbalistic ritual calls for "the fruit of the vine." Other than on the holy day of Purim (see Chapter 11), which traditionally encourages the drinking of wine or other alcoholic beverages (and when it's okay to get a little tipsy), the wine the Kabbalist drinks on Shabbat isn't meant to be consumed excessively. A Kabbalist should surely avoid getting drunk on Shabbat.

- **A cup:** Kabbalists use a special cup at least three times during the Sabbath:

    - They fill the cup with grape juice or wine at the beginning of the Sabbath on Friday evening.

    - They drink grape juice or wine from the cup during lunch on the Sabbath.

- They drink grape juice or wine from the cup during the goodbye ceremony (havdalah) at the end of the Sabbath.

Cups used during the Sabbath are often ornate or decorative. Most Kabbalists who can afford it use one cup exclusively for Shabbat and other holy days.

Kabbalists are known to use beautiful cups in the **Kiddush** (kih-*doosh*) ritual, but a cup used for Kiddush isn't a sacred object — it's merely a cup (see Figure 10-1). Nevertheless, Kabbalists have a time-honored tradition known as **hidur mitzvah** (hih-*dur* mitz-*vah;* beautification of the mitzvah). This tradition calls for an effort to make all the items used for sacred purposes as beautiful as possible. Therefore, Kabbalists try to find particularly attractive cups. Throughout Jewish history, there have been a number of efforts to encourage sumptuary laws when it comes to spending, or rather overspending, on ritual objects as well as general objects and events. For example, rabbis have criticized the excessiveness of lavish wedding parties for centuries. Nonetheless, an effort to beautify ritual objects is always appropriate and encouraged.

✔ **Two loaves of bread:** A careful reading of the Torah results in a number of ritual actions. One such ritual is the presence of two loaves of bread to complete the Shabbat dinner table. Ordinarily, a table may or may not have a loaf of bread as part of the meal. But on the Sabbath, Kabbalists make sure to have two loaves of bread on their tables as a reminder that, when the children of Israel fled Egypt and wandered in the desert, one of the miracles they experienced was the manna (food) that they gathered each day and ate. The Torah explains that on Friday, in order to prevent the need to gather manna on the Sabbath, the children of Israel gathered two portions for themselves.

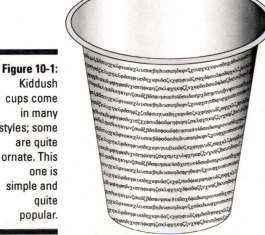

Figure 10-1: Kiddush cups come in many styles; some are quite ornate. This one is simple and quite popular.

Loaves of **challah** (*khah*-lah; egg bread; see Figure 10-2) used on Shabbat are often quite beautiful. Often, they're made from two or three strands of dough that are braided. Although this design isn't essential, the braided loaves have become customary among Kabbalists. Kabbalists display the challah on the Sabbath dinner table underneath a cloth covering referred to as a *challah cover*. The challah cover represents the layer of dew that, the Torah states, the children of Israel found each day on the manna.

The Sabbath table is considered an altar. In fact, it's a substitute location for the Temple that once stood in Jerusalem. The home of the Kabbalist is an intimate temple, and the challah and its braids may be viewed as the braiding together of the souls present in holy dialogue in the sacred center of the Kabbalist's life, the home.

- **A white tablecloth:** It's traditional among Kabbalists to cover the Shabbat dinner table with a white tablecloth. The combination of the white tablecloth and the lit candles help to transform the weekday household into a sanctuary and a holy space. The white color of the tablecloth conveys purity to the space; in Judaism, white is the color of transformation, as worn by a bride.

- **Sweet-smelling spices:** Kabbalists need to have cloves or some other sweet fragrant spices on hand to be used during the havdalah ceremony at the end of the Sabbath. It's customary for the Kabbalist to obtain a beautiful spice box that holds the spices for the havdalah ceremony. Judaica stores, of which there are dozens throughout the United States and online, sell extremely attractive havdalah sets consisting of a decorative cup, an equally decorative holder for the havdalah candle, and a beautiful spice box.

Figure 10-2:
Loaves of braided bread are an essential part of the Shabbat table.

Greeting the Sabbath the Kabbalistic Way

Friday afternoon is filled with great anticipation and busy preparation to welcome the arrival of Shabbat. For instance, Kabbalists make sure to bathe or shower before putting on their fresh and fancy clothing (see the preceding section), and they finish up the preparation of the festive meals (because Kabbalists don't cook food on the Sabbath). As well, Kabbalists make sure that proper and practical lighting is already set before sundown on the Sabbath so that one doesn't have to turn lights and lamps on or off during the holy time (lighting fires or turning on and off lights in prohibited on the Sabbath), and some even have an extra supply of hot water available in order to avoid having to heat water, which is considered work and is therefore prohibited on the Sabbath. Modern Kabbalists even have special urns that keep water hot so that it's available if and when needed during the holy time of Shabbat.

With all these activities taking place, one senses a hustle and bustle among Sabbath observers, sometimes at a frenzied pace, filled with enthusiasm and anticipation. When Shabbat arrives, however, the frenzied pace quickly turns to an aura of tranquility.

In this section, I clue you in on two activities — lighting candles and singing songs — that kick off Shabbat the right way.

Lighting the Sabbath candles

To inaugurate the Sabbath, signifying that the sun has gone down Friday afternoon and that the week is over, a Kabbalist lights two candles and recites the following blessing: *Blessed are You, Lord our God, King of the Universe, who has sanctified us by His commandments, and has commanded us to kindle the Sabbath lights.* The phrase "who has sanctified us by His commandments" appears in many blessings that refer to specific ritual acts; it acknowledges that the commandment from God is a gift offered from above. God sanctifies people by giving this commandment. Kabbalists don't experience commandments as a bunch of rules. Rather, a Kabbalist sees every commandment as a gift of sanctification given by God to those ready to receive it.

Kabbalists report that the act of lighting candles to inaugurate the Sabbath and the presence of those candles in the home lends an aura of sanctity to the space. As one Kabbalist said, "When candles are lit on the eve of the Sabbath, one can see how a plain room can be transformed into a spiritual sanctuary."

Lighting candles during a ritual is an act of particularly special significance because one of the strongest images among Kabbalists comes from the book of Proverbs: "The soul of man is a candle of God" (Proverbs 20:27).

The candle is both a popular and serious object of Kabbalistic meditation. Many Kabbalists have written books over the centuries addressing the significance of light and, in particular, the light that rises from the wick of a candle. The various colors of the flame, the upward reach of the flame, and the candle as a vessel that contains the light (a parallel to the vessel of the body that contains the soul) are just a few examples of the symbolic significance of candles.

Kabbalists go to a synagogue to participate in a special Kabbalistic prayer service welcoming the Sabbath. When they come home from the synagogue, they return to a new space lit by the Sabbath candles, signaling that the divine gift of the Sabbath has been given and is being received.

The candles that are lit to inaugurate the Sabbath don't serve any utilitarian purpose — they aren't intended to light a room, create a romantic mood, or make it possible to read in a dark room. They have a spiritual and symbolic nature; ultimately, they serve as a reminder of the primary goal of all Kabbalists, which is to bring God's divine light into the world. Always paramount for the Kabbalist is this idea that God's light is hidden in the world and the Kabbalist's job is to help to reveal it.

Singing special songs

Throughout the centuries, Kabbalists have followed the practice of singing a number of songs week after week. One such song, which is usually sung in the synagogue service that welcomes the Sabbath, is called **"L'cha Dodi"** (leh-*chah* doe-*dee*). It was written by a rabbi named Shlomo HaLevi Alkabetz. Here are the lyrics:

"Keep" and "Remember," a single word the Only God caused us to hear. The Lord is One, and his Name is One, in renown and glory and praise.

Come, let us go to meet Shabbat, for she is the fountain of blessing, poured from the beginning, from of old, the last deed, [but] first in intention.

Royal sanctuary, kingly city, arise, leave the ruins. Long enough have you sat in a valley of tears — for with compassion He will pity you.

Shake yourself free! Rise from the dust! O my people, be clothed in garments of splendor! Nearby, the son of Jesse, the Bethlehem-ite, my soul's redemption, has approached her.

Awake, awake, for your light has come! Arise and shine, rise, awake, sing; the glory of the Lord has revealed itself over you.

Be not ashamed; feel no disgrace. Why are you cast down? Why do you groan? In you the afflicted of my people will seek refuge. The city will be [re]built on its mound of ruins.

Your plunderers will be plundered, and those who devoured you will be gone; your God will rejoice over you, as a bridegroom exults over a bride.

You will overflow north and south, and you will fear the Lord. Nearby, the promised one! Let us rejoice and exult!

Enter in peace, O crown of your husband, with gladness and rejoicing, among the faithful of [God's] treasured people! Draw near, O bride; approach, O bride!

The metaphor of the Sabbath as a bride is fitting in that the special inner attitude that the Kabbalist must cultivate in preparation for receiving the Sabbath is comparable to the excitement and anticipation a husband has for his new bride. The Kabbalist renews his Sabbath anticipation and excitement each week, and songs like "L'cha Dodi" inspire such an inner attitude, or kavanah.

Transforming the Shabbat Dinner Table into a Holy Altar

For the Kabbalist, eating is a holy act connected to God, the source of all holiness. A salt shaker sits on the dining table of every Kabbalist and accompanies every full meal. The presence of the salt shaker is directly connected to the holy altar located within the holy Temple in Jerusalem, which always included a source of salt. Keeping a source of salt on the dining table is the Kabbalist's way of transforming the table into a holy altar. With salt on a table, the mundane surface takes on a higher purpose.

Whereas a salt shaker is always present at the Kabbalist's table, other items and activities are special to Shabbat celebrations. This section covers some of the most important ones.

Blessing the children

Kabbalists firmly believe in the power of blessings. They believe that the conscious transfer of blessing from one person to another, although intangible, is real, perhaps even more so than physical reality.

It has been a custom among Kabbalists for many centuries to raise one's hands over the heads of one's children and to bless them at the dinner table at the beginning of the Sabbath. The text of the blessing is: *The Lord bless you, and keep you; The Lord make His face shine upon you, and be gracious to you; The Lord lift up His countenance upon you, and give you peace* (Numbers 6:24–26).

If this blessing sounds familiar to you, it's probably because the very same blessing that Kabbalists have offered to their children over the centuries has been recited at the inauguration of American presidents from time to time. During one inauguration, the Reverend Billy Graham was invited to offer a blessing, and he chose this one. It's also the priestly blessing recited by the priesthood in the holy Temple in Jerusalem.

Singing a Kabbalistic love song to your partner

Kabbalists recite the very last chapter from the book of Proverbs at the Shabbat dinner table. On its surface, the text of this chapter appears to be a tribute to the wife, the woman of the household, the beautiful, capable, and a holy marriage partner. Indeed, husbands often recite this chapter to their wives on the eve of the Sabbath. Even when there are no women present at a Shabbat table, these verses are sung in honor of Jewish women everywhere.

A worthy woman who can find? For her price is far above rubies.

The heart of her husband safely trusts in her, and he shall have no lack of gain.

She will do him good and not evil all the days of her life.

She seeks wool, and flax, and works willingly with her hands.

She is like the ships of the merchant; she brings her food from far away.

She rises also while it is yet night, and gives food to her household, and a portion to her maidens.

She considers a field, and buys it; with the fruit of her hands she plants a vineyard.

She girds her loins with strength, and makes her arms strong.

She perceives that her merchandise is good; her candle does not go out by night.

She puts her hands to the distaff, and her hands hold the spindle.

She stretches out her hand to the poor; she reaches forth her hands to the needy.

She is not afraid of the snow for her household; for all her household are clothed with scarlet.

She makes herself coverlets; her clothing is fine linen and purple.

Her husband is known in the gates, when he sits among the elders of the land.

She makes linen garments, and sells them; and delivers girdles to the merchant.

Strength and dignity are her clothing; and she shall rejoice at the time to come.

She opens her mouth with wisdom; and in her tongue is the Torah of lovingkindness.

She looks well to the ways of her household, and does not eat the bread of idleness.

Her children rise up, and call her blessed; her husband also, and he praises her.

Many daughters have done virtuously, but you excel them all.

Charm is deceitful, and beauty is vain; but a woman who fears the Lord shall be praised.

Give her of the fruit of her hands; and let her own deeds praise her in the gates.

Reciting the 23rd Psalm

At the Sabbath table on Friday night, Kabbalists read from the book of Psalms, specifically the 23rd Psalm, popularly known as "The Lord is my Shepherd." As moving and as beautiful a poem as King David ever wrote, the 23rd Psalm reflects the steadfast and unwavering faith that the Kabbalist has in God.

The Lord is my shepherd; I shall not want.

He makes me lie down in green pastures; he leads me beside still waters.

He restores my soul; he leads me in the paths of righteousness for his name's sake.

Even though I walk through the valley of the shadow of death, I will fear no evil; for you are with me; your rod and your staff comfort me.

You prepare a table before me in the presence of my enemies; you anoint my head with oil; my cup runs over.

Surely goodness and lovingkindness shall follow me all the days of my life; and I will dwell in the house of the Lord forever.

God is the Shepherd of the Kabbalist, as the very first words of the Psalm indicate. The next statement acknowledges God as an eternally wise provider who knows just what a person needs and provides for those needs. When reciting the 23rd Psalm, the Kabbalist acknowledges God's generosity and the great bounty that God offers.

Perhaps the most famous line from this Psalm is "Even though I walk through the valley of the shadow of death, I will fear no evil; for you are with me." This statement dramatically reflects the Kabbalistic attitude toward both death and God: Death shouldn't be feared but rather acknowledged as God's will, and God didn't create the world and leave it alone but rather is always with his people.

With the startling words "your rod and your staff comfort me," the Kabbalist expresses the belief that whatever God allows to happen is actually known in God's wisdom to be for the best — even to the point that a rod and a staff are sources of comfort.

The 23rd Psalm is a deep and exquisitely beautiful poem, and by reciting it week after week, year after year, the Kabbalist etches these words and their meaning indelibly into his or her heart, mind, and soul.

Getting wet up to the wrists

It's an ancient Kabbalistic belief that a person's hands are particularly susceptible to spiritual impurity. So it should come as no surprise to find out that Kabbalists practice a very specific symbolic ritual when they wash their hands at the beginning of a meal.

Have you ever noticed that sometimes your hands get wet but the water simply rolls off and doesn't seem to have an impact on the skin? The skin may retain no evidence of outside moisture because of body oils that prevent the water from actually touching the skin. For this reason, when Kabbalists pour water over their hands before eating, they pour water over each hand at least twice and sometimes three times. The first time is merely to get the hands a little wet so that the second pouring can hopefully contact the hands in their entirety. Also, Kabbalists are careful to make sure that the entire hand, from the wrist to the tips of the fingernails, gets wet. They also always remove finger rings to guarantee that the water touches the hands in their entirety. In many households, a traditional cup with two handles is used to make it easier to pour water over each hand one at a time (see Figure 10-3).

Figure 10-3: Each hand needs to be completely wet; the two handles allow you to easily wet one hand at a time.

The washing of the hands also includes a lifting of the hands — the hands are raised up after they're washed and dried. In fact, the blessing recited upon washing one's hands refers not to washing them but lifting them. Symbolically, it may be seen as a lifting up of one's intentions.

What is this hand-washing all about? Simply put, preparing one's hands and symbolically cleansing them of spiritual impurity enhances the spiritual nature of the meal. Kabbalists don't wash their hands with soap and water and then dig in. Rather, they immerse their hands symbolically in an act of spiritual purification and then return to the table for a meal that's far more than physical nourishment. The ritual transforms a mundane dinner table into a holy altar. At the altar in the Holy Temple in Jerusalem, the priests washed their hands in this manner, so performing the ritual in one's home on the Sabbath connects the home with the Holy Temple.

Knowing the choreography of the Sabbath evening meal

At the Kabbalist's Sabbath table (see Figure 10-4), after blessing the children and reciting the 23rd Psalm and the last chapter of the book of Proverbs, the meal officially begins with a recitation of the **Kiddush** (kih-*doosh*).

Every detail of the Kiddush ritual, which involves a blessing over the fruit of the vine (grape juice or wine), has Kabbalistic significance: the color of the wine, the specific number of words in the blessing, the cup filled to the brim, and the way in which the cup is held in one's hands. The ritual is rich with symbolism; each detail reflects ideas and images from Kabbalistic tradition.

For example, the cup of wine, which is filled to the very top, reflects back to the line in the 23rd Psalm, "My cup runs over." On the Sabbath eve, with the tranquility of the Sabbath present and the rewards of the workday week manifesting in a delicious meal, the almost-overflowing cup of wine reflects the bounty that God bestows upon his people and prompts gratitude.

A Kabbalist would never eat a meal with someone else without "talking Torah." That is, Kabbalists are taught to elevate the activity of eating in many ways, one of which is by bringing God's teachings into the conversation. Particularly during the Sabbath meal, the conversation shouldn't focus on the latest headlines or recent films in the local theater. Rather, conversation during the Sabbath meal should focus on the holy, whether it be teachings from sacred texts or the retelling of stories with eternal, spiritual messages. Additionally, every Shabbat table is surrounded by people with sacred songs on their lips. The traditional Jewish prayer book (as well as other books published for the occasion) contains songs that are particularly popular for singing on Shabbat.

Figure 10-4:
A family welcoming Shabbat with candles, wine, and two loaves of challah. The father puts his hands on the children's heads while blessing them, and the mother covers her eyes.

Every meal that a Kabbalist eats, which traditionally includes a fish appetizer followed by a meat or chicken dish, concludes with grace after meals, known as **Birchat Hamazon** (beer-*khaht* hah-mah-*zone;* see Chapter 15). The Kabbalistic grace after meals is a series of four blessings plus an expression of gratitude by the recipients of the food to its creator for the bounty that God has provided.

Observing and Enjoying the Sabbath

Kabbalists refer to the Sabbath with two terms: **shamor** (shah-*more;* guarding) and **zachor** (zah-*khor;* remembering). Guarding the Sabbath and remembering the Sabbath are two distinct activities. The terms go back to the first books of the Torah, where the Children of Israel are commanded to guard the Sabbath (Deuteronomy 5:12) and remember the Sabbath (Exodus 20:8). Despite the distinctions, both activities connect with the general injunction to receive the Sabbath from God as a gift.

Kabbalists throughout the centuries have taken the tradition of guarding and remembering the Sabbath quite seriously, even to the extent of being careful to observe a great number of laws pertaining to Sabbath observance. For example, the Kabbalist doesn't light two candles to inaugurate the Sabbath and then go to a Las Vegas hotel for the evening to gamble at the blackjack table. Even if gambling is the most restful and relaxing activity a person can think of, it isn't in the spirit of the Sabbath and isn't permissible according to the Jewish laws that Kabbalists have observed for many centuries.

In this section, I explain a few of the most importance ways Kabbalists observe the Sabbath and how these observances bring peace and joy to a Kabbalist's life.

Being busy doing nothing

People often mistakenly think that the biblical prohibition against doing work on the Sabbath only pertains to physical labor and that it's permissible and appropriate to work on one's self, one's inner life, and one's character traits. On Shabbat, no work is done — neither on the physical world nor on one's self.

One of my Kabbalah teachers points out that it's such a pity to see the number of people in the world who are eager for peace of mind. Some people take classes to attain peace of mind, some take drugs, and some try meditation and other techniques, all of which are a waste of time if the goal is to attain peace of mind. As my teacher points out, a fundamental principle of Kabbalah is that peace of mind is actually quite unattainable during one's life because the human soul has two aspects:

- ✔ **Yetzer hatov** (*yay*-tzer hah-*tov*; the good urge)
- ✔ **Yetzer harah** (*yay*-tzer hah-*rah*; the evil urge)

These two aspects of the human soul are in constant battle with each other. However, the evil urge, the yetzer harah, isn't really evil in and of itself. The great sages tell the story (as it appears in the Talmud) that when some people decided to capture the yetzer harah and lock it up in prison, the result was that houses weren't built and babies weren't born. This metaphorical story implies that the yetzer harah isn't actually evil but rather is an impulse that may be used for constructive or destructive purposes.

There's no way to stop the battle between the yetzer hatov and yetzer harah, nor would one want to. According to Kabbalistic tradition, a goal of life is to use the battle between the two urges as a source of creativity. The tension between these two urges and hopefully the ultimate victory of one over the other (the good over the evil) results in the repairing and the building of the world. As my teacher points out, the goal of life isn't to end that battle but rather to raise that battle to the highest level possible, where the strife that the soul experiences results in purification, ethical living, acts of lovingkindness, and profound connection to God.

During the week, the soul has no peace thanks to both the hard work that one does and the creative tension between the yetzer harah and yetzer hatov. But then comes Shabbat, when physical work is put on hold and, although one doesn't turn off the mind, striving to reach goals isn't the order of the day.

The primary directive: The Sabbath is grounded in stillness

During the week, most people, including Kabbalists, are busy working in the world, at jobs away from home or in the home. Some people travel far and wide commuting to work or traveling for one reason or another. But on Shabbat, Kabbalists always stay close to home.

For the Kabbalist, the spirit of Shabbat is to do little, if any, tampering with the world. The Kabbalist is busy repairing the world during the six days of the week because the world is unfinished or even broken (see the section "Keeping Your Eye on the Sabbath" earlier in this chapter). But as the sages teach, Shabbat is a taste of the world to come: a world without strife or great toil.

Dance steps, not dos and don'ts

Many people who have attempted to take on the myriad commandments and restrictions incumbent upon the Kabbalist have found the task to be daunting and perhaps nearly impossible. One of the difficulties for the practitioner is the list of thousands upon thousands of teachings about every human activity, each of which has its own set of commandments and prohibitions. To outsiders, the tens of thousands of commandments incumbent upon the Kabbalist seem like a vast collection of unrelated tasks.

My Kabbalah teacher points out that if you get up close to a tree and look at the intricate details of the leaves, branches, bark, and root system, you very easily can get lost in the great number of individual parts. But when you step back, the details of the tree all come together into a wondrous whole.

The same is true for the system of Jewish law incumbent upon the Kabbalist. Individually, the laws seem cumbersome and overly demanding. But when you enter the system, you stop seeing the commandments and laws as annoyances from the outside and instead see them as dance steps of an exquisite cosmic, spiritual choreography.

In addition, most teachers instruct that it isn't necessary to take on the entire tradition at once. Not only is that next to impossible, but it's almost surely not healthy. A slow and steady progress is much more reliable when building a spiritual practice. Ultimately, the practice isn't a matter of how much one does but rather one's inner attitude and connection to God.

Many people find this Kabbalistic practice to be quite difficult and challenging because radically changing the pace of one's life every seven days isn't exactly easy. But people who take on this spiritual practice after having not been Sabbath observers often look back and wonder how they did without it. The Sabbath is nourishing for the body and, more profoundly, the soul.

39 different ways not to work on the Sabbath

For Kabbalists, the traditional prohibition against work on the Sabbath isn't a simple matter because this prohibition doesn't merely imply that one takes a holiday or a weekend without going to work. Special prohibitions define what work is for the Kabbalist and therefore define what's prohibited on Shabbat. Here's a list of the 39 activities prohibited on the Sabbath:

- Sowing
- Plowing
- Reaping
- Binding sheaves
- Threshing
- Winnowing
- Sorting
- Grinding
- Sifting
- Kneading
- Baking
- Shearing wool
- Washing wool
- Beating wool
- Dyeing wool
- Spinning
- Weaving
- Making two loops
- Weaving two threads
- Separating two threads

- Tying
- Untying
- Sewing two stitches
- Tearing
- Trapping
- Slaughtering
- Flaying
- Salting meat
- Curing hide
- Scraping hide
- Cutting up hide
- Writing two letters
- Erasing two letters
- Building
- Tearing a building down
- Extinguishing a fire
- Kindling a fire
- Hitting with a hammer
- Taking an object from the private domain to the public, or transporting an object in the public domain

As you may have guessed, these 39 activities have more than a superficial meaning — they actually reflect abstract ideas that the Kabbalist can apply to many situations. Take the category called threshing as an example. According to tradition, one is forbidden to participate in the activity of threshing on Shabbat. A modern Kabbalist may think that this is an easy one to avoid because threshing isn't something the average person does on a regular basis (or at all!). Farmers tend to handle the job. However, according to Kabbalistic tradition, the prohibition against threshing on Shabbat doesn't really apply to the specific and narrow activity of threshing as it would occur on a farm; rather, threshing reflects the abstract idea of separating one thing from another or extracting one thing that's useful from what's left behind and isn't useful. In modern terms, the notion of threshing extends, for example, to the activity of squeezing the juice from a lemon. The person squeezing the lemon extracts what he or she wants (the lemon juice) and leaves behind what's unwanted (the rind).

This abstract description still applies to the concrete and specific activity of threshing, though, because it's an activity whereby one separates a stalk of wheat, taking its fruit and leaving behind the rest. So, although at first glance squeezing the lemon and threshing seemed to be distinctly different activities, they're essentially the same.

The study of the 39 prohibited activities is a deep and complex one that has been quite familiar to serious Kabbalists throughout the centuries.

Reading from the Holy Scrolls

Kabbalists almost always participate in one particularly special Shabbat activity: listening to the public reading of a portion from the Torah scroll, the Five Books of Moses. The central book for Kabbalist, without question, is the Torah, and that special status is reflected in this custom.

Enjoying the oneg Shabbat

In many synagogues throughout the world, a time for refreshments follows the Friday night prayer service welcoming the Sabbath. Many synagogues call this refreshment time the *oneg* or *oneg Shabbat*. And many who don't know any better surely have come to the conclusion that "oneg Shabbat" means coffee and cake (or perhaps bagels and herring!). In fact, "oneg Shabbat" means the "delight of Shabbat," and although tasting and enjoying good food is certainly a delight, an oneg Shabbat for a Kabbalist is simply an extension of the great delight of receiving the Sabbath.

The Five Books of Moses are divided up so that the entire thing can be read in one year's annual cycle. Each week, a small portion is read. This public reading has continued in the same cycle year after year for centuries, and every Jewish community throughout the world is always focusing on the same Torah portion. Kabbalists make every effort either to attend a synagogue to hear the public reading or, if that isn't possible, to read the portion along with the commentaries in private each week.

Making sure you experience delight

According to Kabbalistic tradition, an essential component of the experience of the Sabbath is **oneg** (*oh*-neg; delight). On the chart of the ten **sefirot** (seh-*fear*-oat; divine channels), the first *sefirah*, *Keter* (crown), is said to be both the source of "will" and "delight." You can see the idea behind this dual significance of *Keter* by looking at the notion of will. When somebody wants something and uses her will to achieve it, the goal is always the same: delight. When a person desires something, she desires it because of the ultimate pleasure it will provide. This is the connection between will and delight. She *wills* something because it brings her what she want, and what she wants, at its root, is always enjoyment or pleasure, or as Kabbalists say, oneg. (For more on the *sefirot*, check out Chapter 4.)

Just as people do things for pleasure, God created the universe to bring Himself pleasure. For the Kabbalist, nothing's more meaningful than the idea that God created the world because He wanted to. But, in fact, Kabbalistic tradition goes one step farther and combines the two notions of will and delight: God created the world because He wanted to, but the source of that wanting was pleasure.

According to Kabbalah, this pleasure has duality: Not only is creation God's pleasure, but more significantly for humans, God created the world and humans in particular so that humans could receive. And what is it that God wants humans to receive? Pleasure! Therefore, the Sabbath as a gift from the Divine is the pinnacle of all God's giving. God *wills* it that humans should experience pleasure, and by receiving the Sabbath, Kabbalists receive a divine gift that brings delight.

According to Kabbalistic tradition, the highest form of pleasure is knowledge of God. In fact, knowledge of God and connection to God is the heart's desire and the reason that God created humans in the first place. Even beneath the disbelief of the nonbeliever is a profound and fundamental desire to approach God, to connect with God, and to experience the oneg that such knowledge and connection brings. The oneg experienced through true connection with the Infinite One is different from any earthly delight.

Saying Goodbye to the Sabbath: A Fond and Fragrant Farewell

When the sun goes down on Friday evening, Shabbat begins. And when the sun goes down on Saturday evening, Shabbat ends. Traditionally, the setting of the sun followed by the appearance of the first three stars in the sky marks the official end to Shabbat for the Kabbalist, but this is merely a guideline. Many Kabbalists, particularly in Hasidic communities, prefer that the Sabbath lingers; they're in no rush to end the sweetness of the Sabbath and begin the busy work week. Who could blame them?

Just before the Sabbath ends, Kabbalists perform an ancient ritual known as **havdalah** (*hahv*-dah-*lah*). The term implies separation, and the ritual is a separation between the seventh day and the work week that's about to begin. The havdalah prayer that Kabbalists recite is as follows:

> *Behold, God is my salvation; I will trust, and will not be afraid: for God the Lord is my strength and song, and he is become my salvation. Therefore with joy shall ye draw water out of the wells of salvation. Salvation belongs unto the Lord: thy blessing be upon thy people. The Lord of Hosts is with us; the God of Jacob is our refuge. (Lord of Hosts, praised is the man who trusts in you. Lord save! May the King answer us on the day we call.) The Jews had light and joy and gladness and honor. So be it with us. I will lift the cup of salvation, and call upon the Name of the Lord.*

Kabbalists also light an intertwined candle and make some special blessings appropriate to the moment. After all, the peace and tranquility of the Sabbath is about to end and the Kabbalist needs to jar himself or herself into another round of the week. Every standard Jewish prayer book contains the details of the havdalah ritual.

Gearing Up for the Sabbath All Over Again

Kabbalistic tradition teaches that the world is created through divine emanations known as *sefirot* (see Chapter 4). These fundamental building blocks of the universe and the human soul combine in a vast number of combinations and permutations to result in the diversity of the universe. The ten *sefirot* are often divided into the top three and the bottom seven. For Kabbalists, the bottom seven *sefirot* on the Kabbalistic chart correspond to the seven days of the week. This teaching implies that each of the days of the week has its own nature and its own tendencies.

The rhythm of the week

The Kabbalist views the week as a perpetual round that begins and ends on each Shabbat. When one Shabbat ends, the following six days become, in a sense, a ladder that the Kabbalist climbs day by day to arrive once again at the next holy Sabbath. The week has a Kabbalistic rhythm thanks to the seven *sefirot,* each of which corresponds to a day. Also contributing to the rhythm of the week is the inner attitude of the Kabbalist, who brings his or her understanding of the day to its experience with the hope and prayer that the two will resonate with each other.

- ✔ **Sunday, the Kabbalistic Day of Reaching Out:** The *sefirah* for Sunday is that of **Chesed** (*kheh*-sed), which signifies lovingkindness. *Chesed* is an expansive thrust, an expansion outward. It naturally corresponds with the first day of the week, Sunday, when the Kabbalist bids goodbye to the stillness of the Sabbath and ventures outward into the new week.

- ✔ **Monday, the Kabbalistic Day of Discipline:** Monday corresponds to the *sefirah* of **Gevurah** (geh-*voo*-rah), which signifies strength, judgment, and discipline. It stands to reason that *Gevurah* is the *sefirah* for Monday because, by Monday, the worker who sets out on Sunday is fully in the flow of the week and is beginning to flex his muscle to accomplish what he sets out to accomplish.

- ✔ **Tuesday, the Kabbalistic Day of Harmony:** The *sefirah* of Tuesday is **Tiferet** (tih-*feh*-ret), which signifies beauty and harmony. It appears as the central *sefirah* on the chart of the *sefirot,* just as Tuesday ends the first half of the week and ushers in Wednesday, which begins the second half.

- ✔ **Wednesday, the Kabbalistic Day of Motivation:** The *sefirah* of Wednesday is **Netzach** (neh-tzakh). *Netzach* implies in the urge to get things done. Wednesday, as the start of the second half of the week, is a day of motivation to complete the week successfully in anticipation of the arrival of the Sabbath.

- ✔ **Thursday, the Kabbalistic Day of Persistence:** The *sefirah* for Thursday is **Hod** (hoed), which reflects the abstract notion of persistence, bearing down, and holding on. With Friday night and the welcoming of the Sabbath bride in sight, Thursday carries the need for a rededication to finish the tasks of the week by connecting into the spirit of *Hod,* mustering up one's final energies in order for the week to be fulfilled.

Thursday night is a time for an accounting of the soul; the Kabbalist looks at any issues of the week and works for resolution or makes a plan for them to be worked on after Shabbat so that the soul and relationships can be more free and open on Shabbat.

✔ **Friday, the Kabbalistic Day of Connection:** Friday is the *sefirah* of **Yesod** (yeh-*sowd*), which reflects connecting and connection. The connection may be between teacher and student, parent and child, husband and wife, or lovers. It's no surprise that, according to Kabbalah, a Friday evening is the recommended time of the week for a husband and wife to make love, manifesting the spirit of the *sefirah* of *Yesod,* which also connects to the human genitals.

The Sabbath: The ultimate receptacle

Finally, the *sefirah* of the Sabbath is that of **Malchut** (mal-*khoot;* the kingdom). The Sabbath is the culmination of the week and the time to reap the rewards of six hard days of work. On the Sabbath, the Kabbalist sits with his or her family like royalty — princes, kings, and queens. Thus, the Sabbath is more than a day; it's an exalted and holy experience. And just as the kingdom is one whole entity, the Sabbath, as the culmination of the week, completes the wholeness of the round of days for the Kabbalist.

Chapter 11

A Year in the Life of a Kabbalist

*B*eing a Kabbalist is a full-time job — not only every day and every week, but throughout the year as well. During the year, Kabbalists travel lots of different spiritual terrain, including holy days, memorial days, and countless opportunities to connect with God. Ultimately, every day a Kabbalist is either celebrating a holiday or looking forward to the next one because the year of the Kabbalist is filled with days of sanctification of all kinds.

The special holy days of Kabbalah are the same as the holy days on the Jewish calendar. Kabbalistic tradition helps those who participate in the holy days to focus on what's important to the Kabbalist, namely his or her relationship with the Holy One. The great Kabbalists in history have had their impact on the holy days of the Jewish year by

✔ Developing special Kabbalistic rituals for the holy days

✔ Interpreting tried and true rituals in a Kabbalistic way

✔ Adding Kabbalistic significance to traditional customs

Kabbalists don't see holy days simply as historical commemorations or days to take off work; rather, holy days are particularly focused spiritual experiences. Each holy day has its own quality: Some are happy, some are sad, some are more serious, and some are lighter. But all share the constant awareness that God is the center of all things and of all being.

In this chapter, I share with you the important holy days Kabbalists (along with other Jews) observe throughout the year. I also include information on how to celebrate your birthday like a Kabbalist.

Each of the holy days in the Kabbalist's year has seemingly countless details, including lots of customs and dos and don'ts. Unfortunately, it's easy to get bogged down by these details and to be so distracted by them and so eager to fulfill them that one forgets the basic essences of the holy days.

Ringing in the New Year without a Noisemaker

The mood of the secular New Year that begins at midnight on December 31 is clearly visible on TV — surely you've noticed all the parties, noisemakers, and boisterous behavior. A Kabbalist welcomes the New Year with joy, but the mood is quite serious, not boisterous. The Kabbalist's New Year, which appears in the fall, is called **Rosh Hashanah** (rowsh hah-*shah*-nah; the head of the year).

But before Rosh Hashanah, Kabbalists participate in a month-long preparation to observe the New Year. Each year, in the Hebrew month of Elul, a number of customs are popular among Kabbalists.

- One of the most moving customs is the blowing of the **shofar** (show-*far*; ram's horn) each morning, usually in the synagogue. The sound of the ram's horn is ancient and moving, and it tends to reinforce the introspective and self-examining mood of the month.

- In accordance with the teachings of the great Kabbalist, the Ari, Kabbalists fast on the first two days of the Hebrew month of Elul in order to prepare themselves for the serious introspection done during this month.

- Kabbalists meditate on some of the names of God (in particular the most holy name, the four-letter name of God).

- In recent centuries, many Kabbalists celebrate the 18th day of the month of Elul (12 days before Rosh Hashanah), which is the birthday of the Rabbi Israel Baal Shem Tov, the founder of the Hasidic movement.

- In the Hasidic world, it's customary to visit one's spiritual teacher during the month of Elul, even if it means traveling great distances.

- Giving charity, while practiced throughout the year, is especially common among Kabbalists during the month of Elul.

According to tradition, the New Year is the time that God looks into the Book of Life and makes decisions for the coming year. So it isn't surprising that the month leading up to Rosh Hashanah is filled with serious examination of one's deeds in the past year as well as a resetting of priorities for the coming year. Kabbalists hope that God finds pleasure in this activity and is prompted to inscribe them for another year in the Book of Life.

On Rosh Hashanah, Kabbalists participate in the following special customs and practices:

- ✔ **Reciting the very first prayer service on the first night of Rosh Hashanah with particular intensity:** Starting off the year's first prayer session with extra special inner intention is a fine spiritual launch of the new year.

- ✔ **Sharing a special New Year's greeting, Shana tova umetuka (*shah*-nah *toe*-vah oo-meh-*too*-kah; a good and sweet year) with others**

- ✔ **Crying tears of longing for closeness to God:** The great Kabbalist, Rabbi Isaac Luria taught that if a person doesn't manage to cry at least a little on Rosh Hashanah or during the days after it, his or her soul may be in need of extra introspection.

The synagogue service for Rosh Hashanah is long and intense. The prayers of introspection and self-examination of one's deeds and behavior dominate the holy day prayer book known as the **Rosh Hashanah machzor** (*mahk*-zoar). Essentially, the same set of prayers has been recited by Kabbalists for centuries, and the modern Rosh Hashanah machzor contains the precise prayers that Kabbalists have used over this time.

Teshuvah in the New Year

In the secular world, people welcome and celebrate the New Year with parties. Kabbalists mark the arrival of the New Year with intense prayer and study. For centuries, Kabbalists have spent extra time throughout the month of Elul leading up to Rosh Hashanah studying and praying. This study usually centers on the profound concept of **teshuvah** (teh-*shoo*-vah).

The word "teshuvah" has a number of meanings. One is "turning," which implies that the activity of teshuvah is an inward, spiritual process whereby the Kabbalist turns his attention to the proper focal point of all existence, the Divine. Teshuvah in this sense is a realignment of one's priorities away from the distractions of the world. Teshuvah also means "a response" because of the hope that God will respond positively to one's introspection and efforts to do good deeds and think holy thoughts. Teshuvah is often translated as "repentance," but unfortunately that term has negative connotations. Although teshuvah certainly contains a sense of contrition and regret, the great sages urged their students to be less preoccupied with regret and more preoccupied with turning and setting their sights on a higher level.

Important books to check out

The following two books — one classic and one modern — are important tools for Kabbalists during the month of Elul, the month before Rosh Hashanah:

> ✔ *Shaarei Teshuvah:* This classic text translates to *The Gates of Repentance*. It was written by Rabbeinu Yonah Gerondi in the 13th century and has been studied by countless Kabbalists since.
>
> ✔ *Teshuvah:* This modern classic was written by Rabbi Adin Steinsaltz, who's known throughout the world as a master of Kabbalah. It's a detailed guidebook for the modern individual who wants to understand the intricacies of the process of change. The book is written for beginner as well as advanced students and isn't bogged down with technical terminology.

Ten Days in the Early Fall for Introspection and Turning

The ten days between Rosh Hashanah and the next significant holiday on the Kabbalist's calendar, **Yom Kippur** (yohm kee-*poor*), are days of particular intensity. Kabbalists spend time every day of the year examining their deeds and are preoccupied with these things during the month before Rosh Hashanah, but the ten days between Rosh Hashanah and Yom Kippur are the most intense of all.

These days are often referred to as *The Days of Awe*. Kabbalists use these ten days to peer as keenly as possible into their hearts and minds, taking inventory of their past deeds and character traits. The ten days leading up to Yom Kippur shouldn't be dominated by fear or concern that one has made too many errors in one's life or has sunk to a low place spiritually or ethically. Rather, for the Kabbalist, they're days of increased hope that one is being successful in the process of introspection and that, on the day of judgment, Yom Kippur, one's prayers will be answered and God will look favorably upon all the efforts that have been made up until that point.

The Day of "At-One-Ment"

Yom Kippur is certainly the most intense day of the year for the Kabbalist; it's dominated by prayer and marked by fasting for over 24 hours. In addition, the Kabbalist doesn't bathe and attempts to avoid all preoccupation with worldly matters during Yom Kippur. Yom Kippur is primarily a spiritual day.

Kabbalists give charity just before Yom Kippur because they believe that the merit of charity is protection against evil decrees. Kabbalists also believe that the sounds of the coins of charity given before the afternoon meal on Yom Kippur (after which the Yom Kippur fast begins) creates such a significant sound in heaven that the forces of impurity make way for the prayers recited during the holy day.

In many synagogues that aren't dominated by a Kabbalistic spirit, the day of Yom Kippur is a somber one. But in synagogues that are nourished by Kabbalistic tradition, the mood isn't somber at all. On the contrary, when one enters such a synagogue on Yom Kippur, one thing that's striking is that everyone is dressed in white, a symbol of purity and purification. Wearing white reflects the belief that God hears one's prayers, acknowledges one's sincere regrets, and accepts one with love and enthusiasm.

The great Kabbalistic master, the Baal Shem Tov, asked, "How can we ever think that we can pray on Rosh Hashanah and change God's mind or inspire God to grant our requests?" He suggested that each person receives blessings from God and that his or her sins can cause those blessings to stop. But when Kabbalists pray, they change themselves, not God. And then, when they change themselves, a new decree comes from heaven that once again opens up the channels of blessings. Through sincere prayer, a person can even become a different person in the eyes of heaven, prompting a shower of abundant blessings.

Yom Kippur isn't a day when a Kabbalist worries about whether God will accept his prayers. For the Kabbalist, Yom Kippur is a day of confidence, a day that concludes the intense month of Elul (see "Ringing in the New Year without a Noisemaker" earlier in this chapter for more) and the intense ten days between Rosh Hashanah and Yom Kippur (see "Ten Days in the Early Fall for Introspection and Turning" earlier in this chapter).

Acknowledging with Joy That Life Is Temporary

In the fall, Kabbalists celebrate an seven-day holiday known as **Sukkot** (sue-*coat*). The word "sukkot" is the plural of the word **sukkah** (sue-*kah;* booth), which is a direct reference to temporary dwelling places (or small huts) that are referred to in the Torah (see Figure 11-1 for an illustration of a sukkah).

Verses in the Torah describing Sukkot read:

> *And you shall keep it a feast to the Lord seven days in the year. It shall be a statute forever in your generations; you shall celebrate it in the seventh month.*

> *You shall dwell in booths seven days; all who are Israelites born shall dwell in booths;*

> *That your generations may know that I made the people of Israel to dwell in booths, when I brought them out of the land of Egypt; I am the Lord your God.*

> —Leviticus 23:41–43

Figure 11-1:
The sukkah
is an
essential
component
of the
holiday
Sukkot.

The central story that Kabbalists study during Sukkot is that of the Children of Israel's Exodus from Egypt and dwelling in the desert for 40 years until they reached the Holy Land, the Promised Land. In an effort to simulate their experience, the Torah commands that temporary dwellings be created, and for centuries Kabbalists have spent time building temporary huts and dwelling in them during the seven days of Sukkot. By eating in these huts, studying holy books in these huts, and even sleeping in them, Kabbalists symbolically participate in living as the Children of Israel did in temporary huts in the desert. One of the central ideas of the Sukkot holy days is the notion that human life is fleeting. By living in a temporary dwelling, Kabbalists get the sense that life is fragile and that each day is a blessing.

One of the rituals performed each day during the holy days of Sukkot involves holding four specific species of vegetation in one's hands and lifting them in all six directions: east, west, north, south, up, and down. These six directions reflect the Kabbalist's belief that God is everywhere and that there's no place where God is not.

Kabbalists observe a custom known as **ushpizen** (*oo*-shpee-zen; guests) in the sukkah each of the seven days because the Zohar teaches that each of the seven shepherds of the Jewish people visits the sukkah on a different night and leads the group of visitors. The traditional Jewish prayer book provides a format for welcoming these seven guests. All the people in the sukkah greet the guests out loud with traditional words of welcome. Each of the shepherds is symbolic of one of the seven lower *sefirot* (see Chapter 4). Table 11-1 matches the days of Sukkot with the appropriate shepherds and *sefirot*.

Table 11-1	The Seven Shepherds of Sukkot	
Day of Sukkot	*Shepherd of the Jewish People*	*Corresponding Sefirah*
1	Abraham	*Chesed*
2	Isaac	*Gevurah*
3	Jacob	*Tiferet*
4	Moses	*Netzach*
5	Aaron	*Hod*
6	Joseph	*Yesod*
7	David	*Malchut*

Another name for the holy days of Sukkot is **z'man simchataynu** (dzi-*mahn* sim-khah-*tay*-new; the season of our joy). Sukkot is supposed to be a happy and joyful time historically connected to the harvest period, when all the wonderful growth from the summer months is ready for harvesting; the appreciation of the harvest's abundance, the joy that's spoken about on Sukkot, is a spiritual joy.

When Kabbalists look back on the intense period from the month of Elul to Yom Kippur, they know that they've begun a new year with gratitude for the life and gifts that God provides.

The day after Sukkot is a holy day known as **Simchat Torah** (*sim*-khat *toe*-rah; the joy of the Torah). On this day, Kabbalists literally dance with the Torah scroll as the yearly round of the public reading of the Torah ends and begins again. It's a holiday marked by great joy, dancing, singing, and celebration.

Meditating on Light for Eight Days

Many people think that the Jewish holiday of **Chanukah** (*chah*-new-kah) is the Jewish Christmas. This misconception isn't so surprising considering that the two holidays often coincide on the calendar. In reality, though, Chanukah is an eight-day holiday that commemorates an historic event in the history of the Jewish people. The event is the ancient Jews' victory in their struggle against being swallowed up culturally and spiritually by the Greek culture around them.

A candle-lighting controversy (No, I'm not kidding)

Kabbalists throughout the ages have dealt with an interesting and ancient dispute pertaining to the lighting of the Chanukah menorah. The Chanukah menorah consists of eight candles, or eight flames, each representing a day. The eight flames come from a miracle that occurred in ancient times having to do with oil and its use in the Holy Temple in Jerusalem. The Jews found their Temple desecrated after achieving victory over their enemy, and they saw that there was only one measure of oil suitable for lighting. The oil was only enough to last for a single day. The miracle, as recorded and passed down through the generations, is that the oil that was sufficient only for one day actually lasted eight days. Therefore, those who observe the holy days of Chanukah light a candle each day for eight days.

Here's where the controversy comes in. Two illustrious sages named Hillel and Shammai had a dispute regarding the proper way to light the flames on each night of Chanukah.

- Shammai believed that eight candles should be lit on the first day of Chanukah, seven should be lit on the second day, six should be lit on the third day, and so forth until the 8th day, when one candle should be lit.

- Hillel argued that one candle should be lit on the first day of Chanukah, two candles on the second day, three candles on the third day, and so on until the 8th day, when all eight candles would be burning.

Hillel's position won out based on the argument that the light should increase and not decrease. After all, that's what one's task in life is all about— increasing the light in the world, specifically the divine light. Symbolically, an increase of light, with one candle being added each day throughout the eight days of Chanukah, more accurately reflects the spirit of the holy day and the Kabbalist's intention to add light to the world.

The well-known Chanukah activity is the lighting of candles (for more on this custom, see the sidebar "A candle-lighting controversy (No, I'm not kidding)." Among Kabbalists, this lighting of candles is the central activity of these holy days. Yet even more important than the lighting of the candles is the period of time immediately after they're lit each evening, when Kabbalists meditate on the light from the Chanukah flames.

The **menorah** (meh-*no*-rah; candelabra) that's lit during Chanukah (see Figure 11-2) is rich with symbolism and has been the subject of much discussion in Kabbalistic texts. The original menorah was a seven-branch candelabra that stood in the Holy Temple in Jerusalem, and Kabbalists associate each of the seven lights on their own menorahs with each of the seven lower *sefirot*. Lighting the candles of Chanukah one by one is an opportunity for Kabbalists to focus on the meaning of the *sefirot*.

Because of the association of Chanukah with Christmas, giving gifts to children after lighting the Chanukah candles is common among Jews. But gift-giving isn't a traditional part of Chanukah, and it certainly isn't customary among Kabbalists.

Figure 11-2:
A Chanukah
menorah.

Seeing God in Everything

One of the most intriguing holy days on the Kabbalah calendar, **Purim** (*poor-eem*; lottery or lots), is one that doesn't appear in the Five Books of Moses and originally commemorated an historic event. The story of the event is told in some detail in one of the books of the Holy Scriptures, the book of Esther.

Kabbalists consider the holy day of Purim to be an historic commemoration of a miracle. When reading the book of Esther, it appears from the story that the Jewish people were in bitter trouble with no way out. But the story takes a radical turn, and the Jewish people emerge victorious. It isn't a stretch to call this event a miracle, but Kabbalists throughout the centuries have pointed out that the miracle isn't just the major turning point in the story; rather, in a real way, every moment of life is miraculous, from the most mundane to the most spectacular.

Celebrating the book of Esther

On the surface, the book of Esther is a story of victory over anti-Semitism. The wicked king of Persia, King Ahasuerus, held a beauty contest in order to select a wife. All the women from the kingdom came and presented them-selves for inspection and evaluation. The victor was Esther, a young Jewish woman who eventually became Queen Esther, King Ahasuerus' wife.

According to the story, the chancellor in the kingdom, a wicked man named Haman, concocted a plot that would have resulted in King Ahasuerus authorizing the killing of the Jews in Persia. Queen Esther's cousin, Mordecai, got involved and helped the king recognize Haman for the evil man that he was. Haman was hanged, and Mordecai was offered an important leadership position within the king's regime. All of this is considered to be a miracle.

For centuries, Jews (including Kabbalists) have celebrated the holy day of Purim with many interesting customs. Adults and children dress up in cos-tumes, and the mild drinking of alcoholic beverages — not to get drunk but to get a little joyful buzz — is encouraged. These customs are a part of the joyous mood of victory as described in the book of Esther.

To outsiders, Purim looks something like Halloween because in Jewish neigh-borhoods, children go door-to-door wearing interesting and often humorous costumes. One profound difference between Halloween and Purim, though, is that on Halloween children go door-to-door asking for gifts, and on Purim one of the spiritual requirements is to go door-to-door (or at least to seek out friends and neighbors) and *give* gifts.

Purim is a time of giving and gratitude. This custom comes from the book of Esther when Mordecai declared the holiday of Purim as a time "of feasting and gladness and of sending food to one another, as well as gifts to the poor."

Including God in everything — without mentioning God at all

Perhaps the most profound aspect of Purim, however, is clear upon a close examination of the biblical book of Esther. Of the many books that make up the Bible, only the book of Esther has a unique characteristic: God's name isn't mentioned in the book even once. It's hard to believe that there could possibly be a page in the Bible, let alone an entire book, that doesn't have a single mention of God. It seems unbelievable, but it's true.

The great sages throughout the centuries drew this profound conclusion from the absence of God's name: God is so present in every detail of life that the absence of his name doesn't indicate his absence but rather his presence. In a sense, it would be impossible to mention God at every single moment of the story, so rather than His name appearing constantly, it doesn't appear at all.

The message is clear and reflects a pivotal idea at the heart of Kabbalah: Nothing happens in the world without God allowing it to happen. Not a blade of grass moving, not a leaf falling from a tree, not a single event large or small is outside the influence of God.

The great master of Kabbalah, the Vilna Gaon, pointed out that the word "Purim" shares the same letters as "Yom HaKippurim," which is the biblical name for Yom Kippur. He taught that Yom Kippur is essentially a spiritual holy day filled with great introspection and intense prayer, whereas Purim is largely a physical holy day rooted in history, with customs that are quite physical in nature. The Vilna Gaon said that these two holy days are actually two sides of the same coin. Just as humans have two sides, physical and spiritual, these two holy days comprise the physical and the spiritual.

Also, the word "pur" means lottery, implying that a person's fate is beyond him or her and is in the hands of God. On Yom Kippur, God makes a final decree about each person's fate for the coming year, and on Purim, the story in the book of Esther reminds Kabbalists that God is behind all events.

On the holy day of Purim, Kabbalists participate in the following activities:

- ✔ Hearing a public reading of the book of Esther in the evening of the holy day and then again during the following day.

- ✔ Celebrating a festive meal during the day with food and wine or other spirits. The Talmud and the Code of Jewish Law give instruction to drink until we can no longer differentiate between "Blessed is Mordecai" and "Cursed is Haman." Mordecai is the hero of the book of Esther, and Haman is the villain. This custom serves to emphasize the celebration at the victory of the Jews over its enemies.

- ✔ Giving charity to at least two people in need.

- ✔ Delivering or sending a gift of two or more kinds of foods or drink to a minimum of one friend.

Liberating Oneself from Narrowness

A popular series of holy days on the Jewish calendar is **Passover.** Many laws and customs guide Jews through the celebration of this eight-day holiday. On the first two days, families sit down to a festive meal known as a **Passover seder** (*say*-der); during the meal, members of the family and other participants read from an ancient book known as the **Haggadah** (hah-*gah*-dah). The Haggadah tells the story of the slavery experience of the Children of Israel during their time in ancient Egypt as well as the subsequent exodus from Egypt, when God, through his messenger Moses, led the Children of Israel to Liberation.

Many Kabbalistic customs are part of the Passover seder. In fact, it's probably true that most Jews who celebrate Passover and sit down to a Passover seder aren't even aware of the Kabbalistic origins of the customs. For example, the *seder plate* features various food symbols meant to remind people of details from the Exodus story. Unbeknownst to most, customs concerning the way in which these symbols are placed on the seder plate have been handed down throughout the generations by the great Kabbalists.

Perhaps the major theme of Passover, and one that Kabbalists focus on throughout the eight days of the holy season, is reflected in the Hebrew word for "Egypt," **Mitzrayim** (mitz-*rah*-yeem). Etymologically, the word for "Egypt" is almost identical to the word for the phrase "narrow place." People often find themselves in narrow places, not so much physically as psychologically and spiritually. The spirit of Passover is meant to inspire people to break free, to be liberated, and to reach higher.

Many commentaries explain the Kabbalistic significance of each of the details and rituals performed at Passover. For example, one part of the seder recounts the ten plagues that God inflicted on the ancient Egyptians. In the writings of the great Kabbalist, Rabbi Isaac Luria (see Chapter 18), the ten plagues correspond to the ten *sefirot*. The connection is quite esoteric and is explained through the use of the numerical values of the letters of each of the plagues. It's a good example of Kabbalistic details far beyond the grasp of a novice.

Another example of a Passover practice with Kabbalistic significance is **bedikat chometz** (beh-*dee*-khat *khum*-atz; search for leaven). The day before Passover, ten small pieces of bread or other food that's forbidden to be eaten on Passover is gathered and prepared to be discarded in preparation for the holy days. For Kabbalists, these ten pieces bring to mind the ten *sefirot*. Each *sefirah* has positive aspects and negative aspects, which participants symbolically discard with the bread or other forbidden food.

A 49-day Kabbalistic Meditation on the Ascent to God

The spiritual calendar observed by Kabbalists throughout the centuries has a 49-day period between Passover and **Shavuot** (shah-voo-*oat;* weeks), the next holy day on the Jewish calendar. Whereas Passover is the commemoration of the liberation of the Children of Israel from slavery in Egypt, Shavuot is the celebration of God giving the Torah to Moses on Mount Sinai.

The 49-day period between Passover and Shavuot is know as **sefirat haomer** (seh-*fee*-rat hah-*oh*-mare). Although the entire year is filled with opportunities to focus on the deep ideas in Kabbalistic tradition, these 49 days offer the Kabbalist an opportunity to focus intensely on the ten *sefirot* and, in particular, their meaning in one's life.

Kabbalistic tradition urges one to look with particular care at the seven lower *sefirot* on the chart of the ten *sefirot* (refer to Chapter 4) and to recognize that each of the seven lower *sefirot* is a fundamental human emotion that comprises human experience. Each of the seven weeks between Passover and Shavuot is dedicated to one of these seven, as follows:

- Week 1: *Chesed*
- Week 2: *Gevurah*
- Week 3: *Tiferet*
- Week 4: *Netzach*
- Week 5: *Hod*
- Week 6: *Yesod*
- Week 7: *Malchut*

After the seven weeks are over, Kabbalists symbolically arrive at Mount Sinai and are prepared to receive the Torah. A deeper understanding of each of the *sefirot* includes the notion that each *sefirah* has within it every other *sefirah*. For example, Week 1 focuses on the *sefirah* of *Chesed,* which is often translated as lovingkindness and has a sense of expansiveness. Week 1 proceeds as follows:

- **Day 1: The *Chesed* of *Chesed.*** The *sefirah* of *Chesed,* lovingkindness, has a loving aspect to it.

- **Day 2: The *Gevurah* of *Chesed.*** One of the many aspects of lovingkindness is discipline. Love that has no restraints and no boundaries can be dangerous and unhealthy.

- **Day 3: The *Tiferet* of *Chesed.*** *Tiferet* is the *sefirah* of harmony and beauty. There's a beautiful aspect to kindness, such as the kindness offered to people one meets during the day. For example, when a Kabbalist goes into a shop, she doesn't simply make a transaction and leave. She offers some affection, warmth, and friendliness to the shopkeeper, using words like "please" and "thank you" as well as making eye contact and smiling.

  An ancient Kabbalah text requires Kabbalists to greet people with a smile. This isn't just friendly advice on the part of the sage from centuries ago; it's part of the law.

✔ **Day 4: The *Netzach* of *Chesed*.** *Netzach,* which can be described as the urge to get things done, reflects the aspect of love that endures and isn't short-lived.

✔ **Day 5: The *Hod* of *Chesed*.** *Hod* represents bearing down and sticking it out, surely an important aspect within a love relationship. Sometimes a love relationship encounters rocky waters, and that's when persistence and holding on is necessary.

✔ **Day 6: The *Yesod* of *Chesed*.** In order for love to be complete between two people, there needs to be a profound emotional and intimate connection that nourishes both people.

✔ **Day 7: The *Malchut* of *Chesed*.** *Malchut,* which is the summation of all things and the physical manifestation of life, makes sure that love isn't just abstract and intangible but is real in the world.

This list contains extremely brief explanations of the *sefirot* within the *sefirot.* For more detailed information, check out Chapter 4.

Each week of sefirat haomer focuses on a different *sefirah,* and each day's focus differs as well, as shown in the preceding example. Kabbalists who participate in this activity year after year have created a number of books and Web sites to share their personal meditations on the combinations of *sefirot.* Each person has his or her own slant and perspective on both the *sefirot* themselves and the combinations of *sefirot.*

In accordance with the Torah, Kabbalists count each of the 49 days between Passover and Shavuot. This period is known as *the Counting of the Omer.* An omer is a unit of measure. On the second day of Passover, in the days of the Temple, an omer of barley was cut down and brought to the Temple as an offering. This grain offering was referred to as the Omer.

From the second night of Passover to the night before Shavuot, Kabbalists recite a blessing every night. For example, of the 10th day, one would say, "Today is ten days, which is one week and three days of the Omer." The counting connects Passover, which commemorates the Exodus, and Shavuot, which commemorates the giving of the Torah, and the counting reminds Kabbalists that the redemption from slavery wasn't complete until the Torah was received.

In the middle of the 49 days of the Counting of the Omer is a day that's of particular interest to Kabbalists. It's is known as **Lag B'Omer** (lahg beh-*oh*-mare; the 33rd day of the Omer). Lag B'Omer celebrates the great Kabbalist and author of the Zohar, Rabbi Shimon bar Yochai. Although Lag B'Omer is the anniversary of his death, he specifically requested that the day be celebrated with joy.

An entire book could be written on the seven *sefirot* and the seven aspects of each one, and in fact, such books have been written. In the final analysis, however, it's up to each Kabbalist to do the inner work necessary to prepare and refine oneself to be able to receive the Torah.

Receiving God's Teachings Constantly

As I mention in the preceding section, Shavuot is the Jewish holy day commemorating the historic events of God giving the Torah at Mount Sinai and the Children of Israel receiving the Torah. However, Kabbalists see another dimension of this holy day and its message: They believe and act as though they're always standing at Mount Sinai and always receiving the Torah. One can say that although the Torah was given at a certain moment in time many centuries ago, God is, in fact, constantly giving the Torah to the world, and at any time one can stand at Mount Sinai and receive it.

Kabbalists believe that suitable preparation is necessary in order to receive the Torah. The Torah is available for everyone, but intense preparation is necessary in order to receive the Torah more fully. Kabbalists must be ready at all times to receive the Torah from God, and in a sense, all the spiritual activities of the Kabbalist are nothing other than preparation to connect with God on higher and higher levels.

After the seven intense weeks of introspection, self-examination, prayer, and study between Passover and Shavuot (see the preceding section), the Kabbalist is ready to receive the Torah from God. The holy day of Shavuot offers a forum for that receiving of the Torah, although as I explain in this chapter, for Kabbalists the Torah is constantly being given and constantly being received in one's mind and heart. One of the customs observed on Shavuot is the reading of the book of Ruth publicly in the synagogue.

I didn't sleep at all last night

An ancient legend records that the morning of the day the Torah was given at Mount Sinai, the Jews overslept. To wake them, a ram's horn sounded, thunder rumbled, and lightning flashed. In the 16th century, the Kabbalists of Tzfat created the custom of staying up all night and studying from the various books of Torah and reading the portion of the Five Books of Moses, which tells of the giving of the Ten Commandments. This custom is called **Tikkun**

Leil Shavuot (tee-*koon* leh-*eel* shah-*voo*-oat; repairing the eve of Shavuot). Rooted in Kabbalistic tradition, this custom is still practiced and is quite popular. Some Kabbalists study a small portion of each of the books of the Bible as a way of fulfilling this custom, and others choose to read various suitable texts of a spiritual nature. In general, Kabbalists love Torah study and never tire of this activity.

Mourning the Loss of Wholeness

Jews observe **Tisha B'Av** (*tish*-ah bah-*ahv*), a memorial to the destruction of the Holy Temple in Jerusalem, on the 9th day of the month of Av in the Hebrew calendar, which corresponds to the month of July or August on the secular calendar. This day commemorates a number of national calamities for the Jewish people, including:

- ✔ The destruction of the First and Second Temples in Jerusalem
- ✔ The fall of Bar Kochba's fortress
- ✔ The expulsion of the Jews of Spain in 1492

On Tisha B'Av, Kabbalists read the biblical book of Lamentations along with other dirges. Because it's a day of mourning, Kabbalists refrain from eating, cutting their hair, and wearing nice clothing on this day. In the synagogue, Kabbalists sit on low stools or on the ground as a sign of mourning. In a real way, Kabbalists put all their sorrows into this bitterly sad day; this day of mourning signifies internal strife within the Jewish community.

With regard to Tisha B'Av, the Talmud asks the question "Why was the Temple in Jerusalem destroyed?" The answer's given in the following story, which recounts the events leading up to the Roman conquest of Jerusalem. A man had a friend whose name was Kamza and an enemy named Bar-Kamza. The man held a big banquet that was attended by many rabbis and sent an invitation to his friend Kamza. By mistake, the invitation went out to Bar-Kamza. When the man who sponsored the banquet saw Bar-Kamza at the meal, he demanded that his enemy leave. Bar-Kamza begged to be allowed to stay and even offered to pay the entire cost of the feast. The host insisted that Bar-Kamza leave and then threw him out. Hurt and angry that the rabbis at the banquet had kept silent, Bar Kamza decided to slander them to the Roman Emperor. He brought the Emperor false evidence indicating that the Jews were rebelling against him, which led to the Roman conquest of Jerusalem.

This passage from the Talmud indicates that the primary source of human troubles comes from human failures, particularly the baseless hatred that people often display toward others in the form of prejudice, gossip, backbiting, and so on. Kabbalists believe that the divine presence is absent when people display such negative activities and emotions.

The goal of the Kabbalist is to repair the world, to repair individual relationships, and to repair and refine personality traits to result in the return of the divine presence (see Chapter 7). Kabbalists believe that when they're worthy, the divine presence lives with them. This connection to God and invitation for God to dwell within oneself is said to be the primary goal of all Kabbalistic tradition.

Celebrating Birthdays Kabbalisticly

Traditionally, Kabbalists put more emphasis on an anniversary of death than an anniversary of birth. After all, as I explain in Chapter 7, they view death as a day of graduation, not a tragedy. The Angel of Death arrives and separates the body from the soul, and survivors put the body in the ground while the soul goes on to continue its work, either being reincarnated into the body of another person or waiting for the perfection of the world.

In a sense, a death is considered to be a spiritual victory for the individual. Those left behind feel sadness and sorrow because they miss the individual, but for the soul that leaves his or her body and continues on its way, the moment of death is commemorated.

This attitude is reflected in the ancient literature studied by the Kabbalists. There's a teaching, for example, that rather than celebrate a birth, we should celebrate a death in the same way that a ship returning home to port is celebrated. After all, when the ship takes off on its journey, no one knows if that journey will be a safe, peaceful, and productive one. But when the ship returns to its port after experiencing a successful journey, it's time for celebration. This teaching, which appears in the Midrash, is a perfect analogy for the Kabbalistic attitude towards death.

Nevertheless, particularly in recent times, many Kabbalists celebrate birthdays with at least as much fervor as they do deaths.

One of the greatest Kabbalistic teachers of modern times was Rabbi Menachem Mendel Schneerson, who was clearly one of the major teachers within the Jewish world in general and Kabbalah in particular. Rabbi Schneerson, who was the head of a group of Hasidic Jews known as Lubavitch and therefore was known frequently as the Lubavitcher Rebbe, frequently spoke about the importance of each individual celebrating his or her birth. He taught that a birthday is the anniversary of the day that God sent a soul into the world. This anniversary is indeed an auspicious occasion, and the Lubavitcher Rebbe urged Kabbalists to acknowledge the day with gratitude to God for providing one with another opportunity to live life.

The Lubavitcher Rebbe also urged his followers and people everywhere to use the anniversaries of their births as occasions to rededicate themselves to increased Torah study and increased deeds of lovingkindness and charity. He also urged students to take on additional projects or spiritual obligations on the anniversaries of their births.

A birthday isn't a day for surprise parties and the receiving of gifts. Rather, for some Kabbalists, celebrating the anniversary of a birth is the acknowledgment that the center of all being is God and that God creates, supports, and sustains his people throughout their gifts of life.

Chapter 12

A Kabbalist's Life Cycle

The Kabbalistic lifestyle begins even before birth and continues through-out one's life to the last breath and beyond.

From birth through adolescence, to marriage and then death, the Kabbalist uses traditional and time-honored customs to reinforce his or her beliefs, always keeping in mind that the center of all existence is God, that one's primary relationship is the relationship to God, and that whereas the body is temporary, the soul is eternal.

In this chapter, I walk you through the Kabbalist's life cycle, explaining all the key customs and celebrations along the way.

Beginning with a Bang: Birth

According to Kabbalistic tradition, three partners come together to create a newborn child: the mother, the father, and God. Kabbalists believe that a birth introduces a soul into the world through its vehicle, the body. For some souls, birth is the first time the soul is in the world. But according to Kabbalistic tradition, the souls of most people have been here before.

Greeting the newborn

On the occasion of a birth, Kabbalists participate in a special celebration called **shalom zachor** (*shah*-lowm *zah*-khar; peace little boy). The celebration usually occurs on the first **Shabbat** (shah-*bot;* Sabbath) after a birth. (For more on Shabbat, flip to Chapter 10.) Traditionally, shalom zachor is held on the occasion of the birth of a boy.

As a matter of principle, a girl's soul is on a higher spiritual level than a boy's soul. The Talmud teaches that a girl is born with more of the sefirah of *Binah* (see Chapter 4), which is understanding and the ability to analyze. One explanation offered for why a newborn boy gets a shalom zachor and a newborn girl does not is that the boy needs more help than the girl. Instead of a shalom zachor, it's customary to publicly announce the name of the newborn girl in front of an open Torah scroll in the synagogue. On the occasion of a girl's naming, words of Torah (known as divrei Torah) are also shared to honor the moment.

The idea behind shalom zachor, which often occurs in either a synagogue or in one's home, is twofold:

- ✔ **It's simply a celebration.** For a husband and wife, the birth of a baby is a profoundly joyous occasion that calls for celebration.

- ✔ **It's a way of recognizing the fact that the soul that has just entered the world is going to confront many trials and tribulations.** Before birth, a soul is in heaven, standing before God and basking in divine light. But when a soul is put into a body and sent into the world, it's no longer in the blissful state of God's presence. Rather, the soul has a body that gets hungry, cold, hot, tired, and so on. Life presents all kinds of challenges, so when Kabbalists greet a new baby boy, they wish the baby peace, and they hope that his life will be smooth and joyful.

The most important elements in a shalom zachor celebration are

- ✔ Joy
- ✔ Delicious food and drink
- ✔ Spiritual songs
- ✔ Ecstatic dancing
- ✔ Words of Torah

With regards to the last element in the list, it's traditional at a shalom zachor celebration for at least one person (if not many) to offer what are known as **divrei Torah** (*div*-rey *toe*-rah; words of Torah). A **devar Torah** (deh-*var toe*-rah; the singular form) is the sharing of an inspirational message that's connected to the Torah and uplifting. Kabbalists wouldn't dream of celebrating a shalom zachor on the occasion of a birth without sharing some words of inspiration with the others who are present.

Getting a tap on the mouth from an angel

Kabbalists believe that every detail of the human body is divine revelation. In other words, Kabbalistic tradition urges the Kabbalist to look closely at the body as a microcosm of the universe. The fact that humans have ten fingers, two arms, earlobes, hair, toes, and every other part of the body prompts the Kabbalist to search for rich meanings that the body parts, in all their detail, suggest.

An ancient text known and studied by Kabbalists refers to an interesting part of the body, the filtrum, the notch between the upper lip and nose. This ancient text asks the question "What is the divine revelation and significance of the filtrum?"

The sages suggest that, on the occasion of the baby's birth, an angel taps the baby on the month in an effort to jolt it out of paradise and into the world. That tap creates the filtrum. But the text goes on to offer another interesting and powerful insight: The angel's tap on the baby's mouth also causes the soul to forget all the Torah it has learned.

The idea behind this theory is that the soul absorbs God's wisdom, the Torah, when the soul is in God's presence before birth. But the angel's tap on the mouth not only jolts the baby into a new dimension (the world) but also jolts the baby into forgetting all the wisdom it absorbed from God. Kabbalists conclude that when a person learns things throughout his or her life, the learning isn't really an act of acquiring new information as much as it's an act of remembering what's already known.

Kabbalists also believe that each person embodies a tremendous amount of profound wisdom acquired from each incarnation. So even though a baby is born seemingly ignorant, in fact, it has learned a tremendous amount throughout its previous incarnations, and the child proceeds to recognize and remember things throughout its life.

Naming the baby — it's no minor feat

Kabbalists believe in a phenomenon called **ruach hakodesh** (*roo*-akh hah-*koe*-desh; holy spirit). According to Kabbalah, it's possible for a divine spirit, a message from God, to speak through a person.

Sometimes the spirit from God that speaks through an individual results in an entire book. The great 16th-century Kabbalist Joseph Karo, for example, is said to have participated in what today is called *automatic writing* or *channeling*. The channeler goes into a trance but remains active during the trance, even to the extent of being able to write a book while in the trance. Rabbi Joseph Karo claimed that some of his writings weren't really written by him but rather *through* him, and other great rabbis at the time made supporting observations. One of the great libraries in the Jewish world, the library of the Jewish Theological Seminary, has in its collection some rare manuscripts that are said to be the result of Rabbi Joseph Karo's ruach hakodesh.

What does all this mean for modern-day parents? Kabbalistic tradition teaches that when parents have a child and participate in a discussion of what to name the baby, unbeknownst to them, their strongest ideas of what to name the child aren't really independent thoughts. Rather, ruach hakodesh comes down from above with a message from God regarding the baby's name.

Parents don't experience lightning and thunder or hear voices; they simply experience natural thought processes. Kabbalists believe that these thought processes come from a higher source and prompt the decisions that parents make regarding a baby's name.

The importance of listening to intuition

Kabbalists believe that sometimes parents resist their natural inclinations regarding a baby's name, which results in the baby having the "wrong" name. If parents give a child the "wrong" name, one of the important tasks in life is to find one's real name and rename oneself. Many people dislike their names; this dislike, according to Kabbalah, isn't merely an issue of personal taste. Rather, the person carrying around a name that he or she shouldn't have experiences discomfort and often a deep inner desire to change the name and acquire the right one.

Renaming a sick baby

One aspect of baby-naming for the Kabbalist is renaming. When an infant or even an older child is suffering from an illness, the parents may bring that child to a synagogue and rename the baby in front of an open Torah scroll. One explanation for this custom is that it's an attempt to fool the Angel of Death.

Imagine that the Angel of Death has been given an assignment to bring about the gentle death of an individual on earth. The assumption is that the Angel of Death searching for the seriously ill individual becomes confused when a child is renamed. The Angel of Death is looking for a soul with one particular name and finds that individual with a new name. Causing this disorientation is thought to be a curative effort.

Coming of Age Kabbalistically

The first significant life cycle moment for an individual is his or her birth; the second is puberty. According to Kabbalistic tradition, profound changes occur in an individual going through puberty, and those changes are not only physical but also spiritual.

Puberty: More than hormones and acne

Kabbalists see puberty as a long, drawn-out process, not merely one day or even a short period of time. Puberty is marked by some rather specific physiological developments, but there's more to it. Spiritually, puberty marks the beginning of a slow but steady process with the ultimate goal of achieving independence and claiming full responsibility for one's actions, thoughts, and deeds.

Kabbalists practice the common Jewish celebrations that recognize the occurrence of puberty; these celebrations are

- **Bar mitzvah** (bar *mitz*-vah) for boys
- **Bat mitzvah** (baht *mitz*-vah) for girls

Generally, boys have bar mitzvahs at age 13, and girls have bat mitzvahs at age 12. However, ancient texts indicate that the bar mitzvah actually occurs with the presence of pubic hair. For Kabbalists, this physiological phenomenon marks the beginning of a process of independence and individual responsibility. Even more specifically, the bar or bat mitzvah marks the beginning of a lifelong struggle between two urges: the good urge and the evil urge.

Good and evil urges, in Kabbalah, are complicated. The good urges of humankind are the pure emotions, the holy impulses to do good. Evil urges have a different nature in that they can always be transformed into good. For the Kabbalist, nothing is evil by definition. Evil arrives when an action or thought is out of proportion or occurs at the wrong time or the wrong dosage.

It's a common misconception among many Jews that on the occasion of the bar mitzvah, a young person is suddenly responsible for the observance of ritual law. The bar and bat mitzvah merely marks the beginning of a process whereby the community recognizes the gradual process of adopting responsibilities. Teenagers who are going through puberty assume a different status in Kabbalistic culture and are closer to becoming independent adults, but Kabbalists understand that this process takes time and doesn't happen overnight.

Marking the beginning of the battle of good and evil

The Kabbalistic view of life includes the belief that the human soul contains two urges in eternal conflict:

  ✔ The **yetzer hatov** (*yay*-tzer hah-*toev*), which is the inclination for good

  ✔ The **yetzer hara** (*yay*-tzer hah-*rah*), which is the inclination for evil

One of my Kabbalah teachers stresses the importance of recognizing that life isn't a quest for peace of mind but rather a recognition that a war between the good and evil urge rages within the depths of the soul. That potential creative tension exists within one at every moment in his or her life. So the spiritual life is a war, and as my teacher puts it, the task of the spiritual seeker is deciding "at what level to wage the war." This process begins at puberty.

Before puberty, a child isn't responsible for his or her actions and thoughts. But Jewish tradition teaches that with the arrival of puberty a child can begin to be expected to join the struggle of good and evil and to learn how to be victorious in that battle.

An illuminating passage from the Talmud offers a deep understanding of the yetzer hara. The Talmud says that when the yetzer hara was "captured," houses weren't built and babies weren't born. The important implication of this metaphor is that the evil urge isn't actually evil but rather has the potential for evil. Ironically, the source of the potential for evil is the source of creativity.

For Kabbalists, evil is creativity gone sour. The original energy was there to do good and to create something positive, but that initial energy for positive creativity can also be the fuel for something evil. This potential is the reason many of the most infamous villains of history were quite creative people.

Good and evil: A matter of timing and dosage

The Kabbalistic view of all human traits is that all have their own times and places — none are good or bad.

You may be familiar with the popular song "Turn! Turn! Turn!" recorded by The Byrds in the 1960s. The lyrics to this song come directly from the Holy Scriptures that Kabbalists study all their lives. The passage comes from **Kohelet** (koe-*heh*-let; Ecclesiastes) 3:1–8 and is as follows:

> *To every thing there is a season, and a time to every purpose under the heaven;*
>
> *A time to be born, and a time to die; a time to plant, and a time to pluck up that which is planted;*
>
> *A time to kill, and a time to heal; a time to break down, and a time to build up;*

A time to weep, and a time to laugh; a time to mourn, and a time to dance;

A time to cast away stones, and a time to gather stones together; a time to embrace, and a time to refrain from embracing;

A time to seek, and a time to lose; a time to keep, and a time to cast away;

A time to rend, and a time to sew; a time to keep silence, and a time to speak;

A time to love, and a time to hate; a time of war, and a time of peace.

Kabbalists view both love and hate as neutral emotions; each is appropriate at some times and inappropriate at others. For example, erotic or romantic love isn't appropriate between an adult and a child, and slavery and injustice are situations to root out and hate.

Life is a constant challenge, and Kabbalistic tradition asks the Kabbalist to constantly weigh questions of timing and dosage as they relate to feelings of love and hate. *Dosage* refers to the degree of an emotion; for example, on some occasions, love is appropriate but perhaps overwhelming, passionate love is not. And some situations call for a gentler or more cautious love. As any pharmacist can tell you, there's a fine line between a medicine and a poison, and it usually has to do with timing and dosage. The same goes for the attributes of the soul.

According to Kabbalistic belief, girls under the age of 12 and boys under the age of 13 aren't responsible for their decisions regarding timing and dosage of emotions and navigation through the battle between good inclinations and evil inclinations. Upon the occasion of the bar mitzvah and bat mitzvah, the Kabbalist recognizes that over the next number of years (some say until the age of 21), a young person should work on the development of his or her soul because responsibility kicks in during this period.

Kabbalistic Marriage

Marriage is a serious and solemn event for Kabbalists. Kabbalistic marriage goes far beyond the performance of a ritual; it ultimately connects with the very nature of the soul.

Joining two halves to make a whole

Many people affectionately refer to their spouse as their "other half." Kabbalists don't just say that, they mean it.

According to Kabbalistic tradition, each soul is actually half a soul that needs another half to be complete; this is the spiritual basis of marriage. Marriage is certainly a partnership on a mundane level, with rights and responsibilities, but at its core, marriage for a Kabbalist is the combining of two "half souls" to make a whole.

Bringing the divine presence (or presents, if you register)

The result of joining two half souls to create one whole is a sacred marriage that brings with it the divine presence. Although Kabbalists believe that the divine presence is always with them in some way, they also believe that a special part of the nature of the divine presence shines its light on a married couple.

The joining of two souls in a marriage is a divine dance, and when the choreography is proper and beautiful, the married couple can feel the presence of God. Kabbalists also believe that the glow of the divine presence that comes from a loving marriage shines upon all who are around the couple, and they receive blessings as well.

Kabbalists know that marriage has to do with far more than love, however divine it may be. The joining together of two souls is also the joining together of two individuals in the world. Kabbalists have been studying the issues surrounding one's obligations in a marriage for many centuries.

An important aspect of a marriage in the spirit of Kabbalah is that the two people know that the most important relationship each person has is his or her relationship with God. Marriage is an opportunity for each member of the marriage to help the other with the most primary relation of all — the relationship with God.

Husband and wife each have rights and obligations, and before marriage, they must be aware of and in agreement with the rights and obligations that they've decided to share.

Additionally, in the traditional wedding ceremony, the contract that the bride and groom sign includes a reference to the obligations and rights that each party has if the marriage ends in divorce. The marriage contract, called the **ketubah** (keh-*too*-bah), requires the signatures of two witnesses who testify to the fact that they've consulted with both the bride and the groom and are confident that both parties agree that the marriage should occur and that each of the two marriage partners, under their own free will, agrees to the terms of the marriage. In Jewish law, before two people get married, they must agree to various matters — financial (the terms of a divorce) as well as emotional and sexual.

The Holy Letter: A Kabbalistic Kama Sutra

If you've ever seen the film *A Stranger Among Us,* you may remember a scene in which Melanie Griffith's character asks a student of Kabbalah what he's reading. He identifies the Kabbalistic book in his hands and quotes from it. It's an authentic Kabbalistic text called **Igeret Hakodesh** (ee-*geh*-ret hah-*koh*-desh; The Holy Letter). (Traditional belief is that this book was written by Moses Ben Nachman, known as Nachmanides or the Ramban.)

Igeret Hakodesh offers a treatise on human sexuality and teaches that sex is a holy activity. Nachmanides also states emphatically that believing that the human body is dirty is heresy.

This Kabbalistic book teaches that every detail of the human body is a result of divine intention and that sexuality has the highest potential to have an impact on one's soul. The book also suggests some physical, how-to advice, such as:

- "You should begin with words that will draw her heart to you and will settle her mind and make her happy."

- "Tell her things which will produce in her desire, attachment, love, willingness, and passion."

- "Win her heart with words of charm and seduction."

Gettin' busy the Kabbalistic way

In the Kabbalistic worldview, God is everywhere. Because every aspect of human life has the potential for holiness and the potential for the opposite of holiness, sex with one's partner can go in many directions. The task of the Kabbalist is to raise up the level of the world and reveal God in everything.

The issues that Kabbalists raise regarding the sexual component of a marriage are based on the assumption that sexuality isn't solely for procreation. Rather, marriage partners have a need and expectation for sexual intimacy with one another that's independent of the urge to procreate. For the Kabbalist, the sexual urge isn't just an animal instinct; it's a means of expression between marital partners that has great spiritual potential for intimacy, trust, and love.

Kabbalists study the following issues related to sexual relationships:

- **Pleasantness:** Kabbalists believe that a primary requirement for the sexual encounter is that it be pleasant. Kabbalists maintain that the proper attitude to cultivate during lovemaking is the desire to please one's partner.

- **Frequency:** According to a well-known text that Kabbalists have studied for centuries, husbands and wives need to be sensitive to each other when it comes to how often they make love.

For example, if changing one's occupation will directly impact how often a spouse will be at home, the change needs to be mutually agreed upon by both partners. If the couple is accustomed to a certain pace and level of intimacy, a change of occupation that rattles that pace must have unanimous approval.

✔ **Gentleness:** Kabbalistic tradition doesn't dictate which sexual positions are "acceptable" and which are not. It declares that consenting adults can do whatever they want with each other with the exception of causing physical or emotional harm.

Marriage partners must do their utmost to respect their partners in all areas, including sexuality. For example, prompting one's marital partner to cry may be considered a profoundly unfortunate offense.

WORDS OF WISDOM

Erotic imagery and Kabbalah

When one of my children was coming-of-age and asked me to teach her about sexuality, the first thing I did was to go to a book of the Holy Scriptures called **Shir Hashirim** (sheer hah-sheer-*eem*; the Song of Songs). Shir Hashirim is the famous erotic love poem of the Torah. (It's often called the Song of Solomon.) Controversy once raged over its appropriateness as part of the Bible, with the question being, "Should an erotic love poem be part of the Holy Scriptures?" The answer given by the great Jewish mystic Rabbi Akiva was, "If the Bible is holy, then the Song of Songs is the holy of holies."

This view that the erotic verses found in the Bible are of a holy nature is a clue to the way in which humans should understand their relationship to God. When mystics talk about merging with God, their imagery has an obvious sexual component.

Here's a sampling from the text that illustrates the erotic nature of the Shir Hashirim:

✔ Let him kiss me with the kisses of his mouth: for thy love is better than wine. (Song of Songs 1:20)

✔ His left hand is under my head, and his right hand doth embrace me. (Song of Songs 2:6)

✔ Thy lips, O my spouse, drop as the honeycomb: honey and milk are under thy tongue; and the smell of thy garments is like the smell of Lebanon. (Song of Songs 4:11)

✔ How beautiful are thy feet with shoes, O prince's daughter! The joints of thy thighs are like jewels, the work of the hands of a cunning workman. Thy navel is like a round goblet, which wanted not liquor: Thy belly is like an heap of wheat set about with lilies. Thy two breasts are like two young roes that are twins. Thy neck is as a tower of ivory; Thine eyes like the fishpools in Heshbon, by the gate of Bath-rabbim: Thy nose is as the tower of Lebanon which looks toward Damascus. Thy head upon thee is like Carmel, and the hair of thine head like purple; the king is held in the galleries. How fair and how pleasant art thou, O love, for delights! This thy stature is like to a palm tree, and thy breasts to clusters of grapes. (Song of Songs 7:1–7)

I wanted to show my child the Song of Songs because I wanted to make the point that, for Kabbalists, human sexuality offers perhaps the best metaphors for describing the relationship to the Divine. This relationship is described with erotic and passionate imagery. My instinct and my studies directed me to associate sexuality with the highest spiritual ideas and belief.

Of course, Kabbalists know that their relationships with God aren't sexual in the way that relationships are between husbands and wives, but the erotic connection between husband and wife is parallel to the relationship that each person cultivates with God. This intimate, deeply private, and profound relationship often is best described by verses in the Song of Songs and their commentary, which helps explain why Kabbalists have studied this section of the Bible in great detail for many centuries.

Many people have insisted that the Song of Songs is simply an ancient erotic poem that found its way into a gathering of books now called the Bible. But as all Kabbalists know, the Song of Songs, including the most detailed verses of eroticism, have been interpreted by the great sages as ways of describing the many sublime and intimate ways people relate privately with God.

What about divorce?

Kabbalah's holy texts express the belief that the holy altar in heaven weeps on the occasion of a divorce. After all, when two souls marry, they merge. When those same two souls disconnect, the pain reaches the heavens.

Nevertheless, Kabbalists study the laws of divorce just as they study the traditional laws of marriage. If a marriage must dissolve, traditional procedures and issues serve to protect the parties. These procedures are part of traditional Jewish law as codified by the great Kabbalist, Rabbi Joseph Karo.

Death and Dying in Kabbalah

According to Kabbalah, death is a natural process, not a tragedy. One of the great texts, **Pirke Avot** (peer-*kay* ah-*vote;* the Chapters of the Sages) describes life as a lobby for the world to come, and the Kabbalist sees his or her earthly existence as just one stage in the soul's evolution. (For more on the Kabbalistic soul and its journey, flip to Chapter 7.)

Kabbalists believe that at the moment of death, the two parts of the individual — the body and the soul — separate. The body is buried in the ground, and the soul continues on its way. Kabbalistic tradition teaches reincarnation with the understanding that, in most cases, the soul is reincarnated in the body of another person who then tries to continue to correct what the soul injured in the past or to create what that soul is destined to create. (Refer to Chapter 7 for more on the Kabbalistic belief in reincarnation.)

Deathbed customs

It's customary that a dying Kabbalist be kept company during his or her transition from this world to the next world. Being with a dying person at that moment is considered an expression of great respect. Kabbalists encourage the person who's dying to make peace with this world by asking forgiveness from friends and family members and by blessing their children.

Kabbalists also encourage the person who's dying to recite a traditional prayer called **vidui** (vi-*doo*-ee), which is a prayer of confession listing many common misdeeds. (This prayer is also recited on the holy day of Yom Kippur, which I address in Chapter 11.) Kabbalists firmly believe that this recitation of the confessional prayer neither brings on an earlier death nor negates hope for complete healing. They believe that this confession is connected to an understanding that death can serve to wipe the slate clean for the individual, whose soul then can go on with its work.

Another deathbed custom is reciting from the book of Psalms in the presence of the person who's dying. Of the 150 Psalms, the ones chosen deal with hope and offer comfort. Some of the more popular Psalms for this occasion are Psalms 16, 23, 25, 51, 91, 102, and 103, but many other Psalms are also suitable in this holy moment.

When death arrives

When the moment of death arrives, it's customary among Kabbalists to close the deceased's eyes and mouth, straighten his or her limbs, keep the body covered, and treat the body with extreme care and respect. Positioning the body so that the deceased's feet face the door is also customary.

Additionally, Kabbalists light a candle and place it near the head of the deceased. (Some Kabbalists light many candles and place them around the body.) From the moment of death until burial, a friend, relative, or member of the community must remain with the deceased. One of the more popular Psalms recited during this period is the 23rd Psalm, commonly known as "The Lord is My Shepherd."

Kabbalists who are present at a death or who learn about the death recite this blessing: **Baruch Atah Ahdonai, Ehlohaynu, Mehlech Haolam, Dayan HaEhmet** (bah-*rukh* ah-*tah* ah-doe-*noy* eh-loh-*hay*-nu *meh*-lekh hah-oh-*lahm* dah-*yan* hah-eh-*met;* Blessed are You, Lord our God, King of the Universe, the true judge).

Upon learning of a death, Kabbalists acknowledge that, despite the sadness of the departure of the person that they know and love, God knows what He is doing and takes everyone at a divinely appointed time.

Famous last words

It's said that when the great Indian leader Mahatma Gandhi was assassinated, his last words weren't "They got me" but rather "Ram." *Ram* is a Sanskrit term referring to God. The traditional Hindu, as part of his or her spiritual work, desires to have God on his or her mind at that precious moment of transition from life to death.

Kabbalistic tradition has a similar custom. The best known and most often recited prayer of Jewish and therefore Kabbalistic tradition is the **Sh'ma** (sheh-*mah*). Although the Sh'ma is a number of paragraphs long, the first line is the most important: **Sh'ma Yisrael, Ahdonai Ehlohaynu, Ahdonai Ehchad** (sheh-*mah* yis-rah-*ehl* ah-doh-*noy* eh-loh-*hay*-noo ah-doh-*noy* eh-chahd; Hear O Israel, the Lord our God, the Lord is One).

One of the great Kabbalists of all time, the extraordinary Rabbi Akiva, died at the hands of the Romans almost 2,000 years ago. Kabbalists believe that when Rabbi Akiva was arrested and tortured to death, he not only recited the words of the Sh'ma prayer but actually extended the last word, **ehchad** (eh-*chahd;* one). This story has been a model for centuries of Kabbalists who, when reciting the Sh'ma prayer, also prolong the last word, "ehchad."

When reciting the Sh'ma, a Kabbalist should say the word "ehchad" as long as it takes for him or her to conceive of all six directions (north, south, east, west, up, and down). While speaking the last word of the Sh'ma, the Kabbalist conceives of God as being in all directions and everywhere and also acknowledges God's oneness.

Kabbalists don't see death as a finality. According to Kabbalists, the soul of the first man, Adam, split into hundreds of thousands of individual souls that occupy the bodies of people. Each individual has the task of finding his or her own part in the world, but at a certain point, the body gives out and is used up.

One great Kabbalist, Rabbi Baruch Ashlag, tried to explain death and the relationship of a soul to a body by saying, "Just as we change our shirts, so does a person who resides in his soul, sees his physical body, and knows that from time to time he will need to change his 'shirt.'" (Check out Chapter 7 for more on reincarnation in Kabbalah.)

Following the steps of mourning

Despite the fact that Kabbalistic theology recognizes death as a normal and a natural part of existence, death is still a great shock to close relatives, and authentic grief is neither shameful nor inappropriate. The structure of Kabbalistic mourning divides the stages of mourning into a number of levels of lessening severity.

Pulling a hair from a glass of milk

An ancient Kabbalistic text poses the question, "What does it feel like when the body and soul separate?" The answer given in this text is that, in most cases, the separation of the soul from its body is "like pulling out a hair from a glass of milk."

Before you say, "Ew, yuck!" let me explain: Pulling a hair from a glass of milk is a familiar activity in rural life, so it stands to reason that the ancient text would use this metaphor when describing the separation of body and soul a few thousand years ago. It's a task that many people would have been able to relate to.

This teaching reminds me of the months I spent living in a small fishing village in southern Spain. Each day, I went to the home of the goatherd and purchased goat's milk from his wife. Upon returning home, I often needed to pull some stray goat hairs out of the milk before I boiled it and used it for drinking or cooking. Pulling a hair from a glass of milk is a simple, painless thing to do — just as separating the body and soul is for the Angel of Death to do when God wills it.

The first day

When a parent, child, sibling, or spouse dies, the Kabbalist measures the first stage of mourning as the period between death and burial. Jewish law urges that, whenever possible, burial should take place within a day of the death. This stage requires the mourner to care for the deceased and prepare the body for burial, and this responsibility takes precedence over all other commandments within Kabbalistic tradition.

Burial

A funeral for a Kabbalist has a few notable aspects:

- **Tradition calls for the coffin to be a simple box, usually constructed of pine.** Despite the fact that one can go to a funeral home and choose from more expensive caskets with extraordinarily polished outsides and plush, lavish insides, these options aren't appropriate among Kabbalists. They recognize dignity in the simplicity of a plain pine box.

  In some ways, Kabbalists view death as the great equalizer. Regardless of how rich or influential a person is in life, upon death everyone is in the same situation, and luxurious caskets are inappropriate. Kabbalists also tend to dress the deceased in a white shroud and wrap him or her in the prayer shawl used during life.

- **The eulogy must not contain any exaggerations.** There are always good things to say about individuals without having to speak falsehoods. More importantly, Kabbalistic tradition doesn't want to encourage mourners to think ill of the deceased. If a eulogy states that the deceased was a very charitable person when, in fact, he wasn't, such an exaggeration could

> prompt someone in attendance to walk away thinking, "He wasn't as gen-
> erous as they said."

> ✔ **Kabbalists recite traditional prayers when the coffin is lowered into
> the grave, and they participate in filling the grave with soil (rather
> than leaving it up to a stranger employed by the cemetery).** These
> intense acts bring psychological wisdom, impressing upon the mourners
> the finality of the individual's life on earth.

The first week after death

The Hebrew word **shiva** (*shih*-vah; seven) refers to a seven-day period of
intense mourning that begins after burial, which is counted as the first day.
During this week, Kabbalists sit on low stools or on the floor to symbolize
being "brought low" emotionally by their grief. They're also subject to the following restrictions, many of which involve a prohibition against attention to
the bodies and pleasures of the mourners themselves, whose grief prompts
them to forget about their own comforts and physical delight:

> ✔ Leather shoes aren't worn. (In ancient times, leather was a symbol of
> comfort and wealth.)

> ✔ Hair isn't cut, and men don't shave.

> ✔ Women don't wear cosmetics.

> ✔ Mourners don't work.

> ✔ Mourners don't bathe.

> ✔ Mourners don't have sexual relations.

> ✔ Mourners don't put on fresh clothes.

> ✔ Mourners don't study holy texts other than those that relate specifically
> to mourning and grief. (Studying holy texts provides great pleasure and
> therefore isn't appropriate during the week of mourning.)

> ✔ The mirrors in the homes of mourners are covered to avoid giving atten-
> tion to one's own vanity.

From the time of the funeral of a parent or another member of the immediate
family circle, surviving relatives recite a traditional prayer known as the
Kaddish (*kah*-dish). Mourners recite the Kaddish three times daily. An interesting aspect of the Kaddish is that there's no mention of death in the prayer.
Although the Kaddish is known as a mourner's prayer, the text of it has more
to do with the expression of one's faith in God. The text of the Kaddish is as
follows:

> *Glorified and sanctified be God's great name throughout the world which He
> has created according to His will. May He establish His kingdom in your
> lifetime and during your days, and within the life of the entire House of
> Israel, speedily and soon; and say, Amen.*

May His great name be blessed forever and to all eternity.

Blessed and praised, glorified and exalted, extolled and honored, adored and lauded be the name of the Holy One, blessed be He, beyond all the blessings and hymns, praises and consolations that are ever spoken in the world; and say, Amen.

May there be abundant peace from heaven, and life, for us and for all Israel; and say, Amen.

He who creates peace in His celestial heights, may He create peace for us and for all Israel; and say, Amen.

The first month

After the first week of intense mourning (shiva), the next and less severe level of mourning, **shloshim** (shih-low-*sheem;* 30), begins.

During this 30-day period, mourners don't attend celebrations, listen to music, or shave, but most of the other severities of the first week are suspended. (See the preceding section for a list of shiva restrictions.) Mourners continue reciting the Kaddish three times daily.

The first year

During the first 12 months after a burial, mourners don't attend celebrations of any kind. Mourners continue to recite the Kaddish prayer three times daily for 11 out of the 12 months that follow. Why 11 months and not 12? Out of respect for the deceased. Kabbalists believe that it can take up to 12 months for a soul to purify itself, and by stopping the recitation of the Kaddish after 11 months, mourners imply that the deceased's soul wasn't so impure that it needed the full 12 months for purification.

Observing the death annually

Each year, Kabbalist mourners note the anniversary of a death, known as a **yahrzeit** (*yahr*-tzite). In addition to reciting the Kaddish on that day in the synagogue, the mourners also often receive an honor during the synagogue service. This honor is usually in the form of an **aliyah** (ah-*lee*-ah; ascent), which is the recitation a blessing for all the congregation to hear just before verses from the Torah scroll are read out loud. Other tasks that are part of the public worship service in the synagogue are also sometimes offered as honors. In any case, the honors are the community's gestures of recognition of the mourner and in memory of the deceased.

It's also customary for a Kabbalist to light a 24-hour candle on the one-year anniversary of a death; commemorating the death in this way reiterates the belief that death is a moment of transition and not a finality.

Part III
Livin' La Vida Kabbalah

The 5th Wave   By Rich Tennant

Who barbecues in a sukkah?

In this part . . .

Kabbalah isn't just theoretical. On the contrary, Kabbalah is in the *doing*. And Kabbalah urges its practitioners to do lots of things — every day, every week, throughout the year, and throughout one's lifetime. But there are also lots of things that Kabbalists aren't supposed to do. Ultimately, Kabbalah is a dance of cosmic proportions. So, put on your dancing shoes; it's time to do some Kabbalah.

Chapter 13

Discovering the Kabbalistic Books that Really Matter

In This Chapter

▶ Starting with centuries-old must-haves

▶ Filling up Kabbalistic bookshelves

▶ Including Hasidic texts and commentaries

Kabbalists always have books around them — in their homes, syna-gogues, and study halls. The walls of these spaces usually are lined with bookshelves, and the bookshelves usually are filled with well-worn volumes of the great books that Kabbalists study. (I daresay that if you didn't have lots of books around you, then your authenticity as a Kabbalist would certainly be in question.)

In this chapter, you discover the important books that Kabbalists study. Even though thousands of books make up the library of spiritual volumes of Judaism, I focus on the major holy books of Jewish spiritual life, with a spe-cial emphasis on the most important and vital books studied by Kabbalists over the centuries.

The Essential Kabbalah Library

Thousands of books written and published over the centuries are of interest to Kabbalists, but a much smaller number of volumes have made up a Kabbalist's basic library since the beginning of Kabbalistic tradition.

A Kabbalist spends lots of time with his or her books, and it isn't unusual to find a study table filled with books by the end of a study session. Commentaries on the **Torah** (*toe*-rah) refer to other volumes, which in turn refer to others.

For example, a Kabbalist may start a study session by reading a familiar story in the Five Books of Moses. The student typically will refer to a commentary on the verses that make up that story, and the commentary refers to a homiletic text found in a collection of insights into the Torah compiled during Rabbinic times. Those texts are quoted in commentaries by other sages, and the process goes on and on. Each commentator offers insight into an eternal discussion that usually begins with the text of the Torah.

This section introduces the books that are among the standard texts in a Kabbalist's library. The first two categories, the Tanakh and the classic Rabbinic literature, form the basis of all Torah study. The Tanakh and the Talmud represent the foundation upon which all Kabbalists and students of the Torah participate in the vital, daily activity of **Talmud Torah** (tal-*mood toe*-rah; the holy act of Torah study).

Tanakh

The word **tanakh** (tah-*nak*) is an acronym for three Hebrew letters. The first letter, which has the sound of a "t," stands for Torah, which refers to the Five Books of Moses in this case. The Hebrew letter with the "n" sound stands for the word **Nevi'im** (neh-*vee*-eem; the Prophets). The third letter, which has the sound of a "k," stands for **Ketuvim** (keh-*too*-veem; writings). Tanakh is a collection of all three: the Five Books of Moses, the biblical books of the Prophets, and the biblical books of the Writings.

Outside of the Jewish world, Tanakh is called the *Old Testament,* but Jews don't use this term because it implies the existence of a new testament, which isn't part of the Hebrew Scriptures. Sometimes Jews refer to Tanakh as the *Holy Scriptures*.

The Torah, the Five Books of Moses

Tanakh begins with the Five Books of Moses, the original written tradition representing the revelation of Moses at Mount Sinai. Kabbalists consider the Torah to be the collected permutations of divine wisdom. They believe that God deliberately contracted Himself and that the words of the Torah are one transmission of divine wisdom.

Kabbalists intensely study a portion of the Torah every week along with commentaries on the Torah portions.

The word "Torah" refers to the Five Books of Moses, the entire Bible, and also commentaries on the central texts from throughout the centuries. When a Kabbalist says that he or she is studying "Torah," it doesn't necessarily mean the Five Books of Moses. All Jewish and Kabbalistic spiritual books, in some way, grow out of the original transmission of the Five Books of Moses as received by Moses from God at Mount Sinai. That's is why the term "Torah" has both a restricted and a broad meaning.

The Five Books of Moses

- ✔ **Tell the story of the creation of the world:** Kabbalists examine every detail in the description of the Creation in the opening chapters of the Torah, and this analysis of the Torah text along with the use of the terms and vocabulary in it to express complex ideas about existence itself form the basis of a significant part of Kabbalistic discussions of the most abstract ideas about the ways of the universe.

- ✔ **Teach about the lives of the great patriarchs and matriarchs (Abraham, Isaac, Jacob, Sarah, Rebecca, Rachel, and Leah):** These biblical personalities and many others are frequent companions of the Kabbalist, who knows them deeply enough to speak of them in the present tense. For example, in the Kabbalist's mind, Abraham didn't live thousands of years ago; rather, Abraham's as present as anyone alive (and perhaps even more so). Kabbalists also often speak of the patriarchs and other biblical heroes as representing the ten _sefirot_ (see Chapter 4). These figures become part of the process and discussion of reaching to grasp the way of the world.

- ✔ **Tell of Jacob's encounter with an angel and his spiritual transformation from Jacob into Israel:** The Five Books of Moses is, if anything, a record of the human relationship with God, from the story of Adam and Eve to the encounter by Moses. A pivotal episode in these holy books is the story of Jacob, who encounters a messenger of God. He and his descendants, the Jewish people, are changed by this divine encounter forever. It's not surprising that Kabbalists, whose lives are focused on the Infinite One, are interested in looking carefully at the Torah's descriptions of these encounters with God.

- ✔ **Describe the enslavement of the Children of Israel in Egypt, their successful rebellion against that slavery, and their wandering in the desert for 40 years:** The spiritual life of the Kabbalist is an important topic in many Kabbalistic texts, which frequently explore the nature of the process of spiritual growth and refinement. The way of the Kabbalist is the way of raising one's consciousness, and the methods for reaching higher or perhaps deeper levels of understanding are often found in the study and discussions of the trials encountered by the main personalities of the Torah and the evolution of the Children of Israel. Slavery in Egypt by the Children of Israel and the ultimate exodus from that place is a major theme of Kabbalistic study.

- ✔ **Relate the great moment of revelation, when Moses received the divine teachings from God on Mount Sinai and all the Children of Israel experienced an unparalleled encounter with God:** Kabbalists say that each person can be standing at Mount Sinai at any moment to experience this revelation and that proper study, prayer, and holy deeds can purify people and open them to divine revelation. Kabbalists go on to say that each person who studies Torah stands at Mount Sinai, hears the teachings, and joins in the process of revealing God in the world.

✓ **Teach fundamental principles and basic rules for living:** The Five Books of Moses, along with the classic Rabbinic literature, teach the principles of life. A special aspect of the Rabbinic literature is that it invites every generation to join in the process of studying these principles and continuing to add new insights and commentaries. (See the section "Classic Rabbinic literature" later in this chapter for details.)

The following list contains the Hebrew names of each of the Five Books of Moses followed by the names used in most English editions. And even though every detail of every word of the Torah is rich with meaning for the Kabbalist, I also list some of the main topics in each book.

✓ **Bereishit** (buh-ray-*sheet;* in the beginning): Genesis

- The creation of the world

- Abraham, Isaac, and Jacob (the patriarchs)

- Jacob goes to Egypt with his sons

- Before his death, Jacob blesses his sons

✓ **Sh'mot** (sheh-*mote;* the names): Exodus

- The Children of Israel are enslaved in Egypt

- Moses receives the Torah at Mount Sinai

- The Children of Israel build a tabernacle in the desert

✓ **Vayikra** (vah-*yih*-krah; and He called): Leviticus

- The priestly code

- Laws of sacrifice and morality, and dietary laws

- The Land of Israel

- The major festivals

✓ **Bamidbar** (bah-*mid*-bar; in the wilderness): Numbers

- Statutes and laws

- The Children of Israel are on the way to the Holy Land

✓ **Devarim** (deh-*vah*-reem; the words): Deuteronomy

- A retelling of the laws

- Moses addresses the Children of Israel

Nevi'im, the Prophets

People often think that a prophet is someone who can predict the future, but according to Jewish tradition, in addition to possibly being such a seer, a prophet is someone chosen by God to deliver a message from God to the people. The word for "prophet" in Hebrew is **Navi** (neh-*vee*). There were many prophets in biblical times, both men and women, and the books of the prophets all contain profound messages.

The **Nevi'im** (neh-*vee*-eem; books of the Prophets) are

- **Yehoshua** (yeh-hoe-*shoe*-ah; Joshua)
- **Shoftim** (*showf*-teem; Judges)
- **Shmuel** (*shmoo*-ale; Samuel I and II)
- **Melachim** (meh-*lah*-kheem; Kings I and II)
- **Yeshayah** (yeh-*shah*-yah; Isaiah)
- **Yirmiyah** (year-*mee*-yah; Jeremiah)
- **Yechezkel** (yeh-*khez*-kill; Ezekiel)
- **Trey Asar** (tray *ah*-sar; the Twelve) (treated as one book)
  - **Hoshea** (hoe-*she*-ah; Hosea)
  - **Yoel** (*yo*-ale; Joel)
  - **Amus** (*ah*-muhs; Amos)
  - **Ovadyah** (oh-*vahd*-yah; Obadiah)
  - **Yonah** (*yoh*-nah; Jonah)
  - **Michah** (*mee*-khah; Micah)
  - **Nachum** (*nah*-khoom; Nachum)
  - **Chavakuk** (*khah*-vah-kook; Habbakkuk)
  - **Tzefanyah** (tzeh-*fahn*-yah; Zephaniah)
  - **Chagai** (*khah*-guy; Chagai)
  - **Zecharyah** (zeh-*khar*-ee-yah; Zechariah)
  - **Malachi** (mah-*lah*-khee; Malachi)

Ketuvim, the Writings

Ketuvim (keh-*too*-veem; writings) is the third section of the Holy Scriptures; it consists of some of the most well-known parts of the Bible. This section contains the book of Psalms, the book of Proverbs, the book of Job, the Song of Songs, and other books that are neither books of the Prophets nor the Five Books of Moses.

The Ketuvim are

- **Tehillim** (teh-hill-*eem;* Psalms)
- **Mishlei** (*mish*-lay; Proverbs)
- **Iyov** (*ee*-yove; Job)
- **Shir HaShirim** (*sheer* hah-*sheer*-eem; Song of Songs)
- **Rut** (ruht; Ruth)
- **Eichah** (*aye*-khah; Lamentations)
- **Kohelet** (koh-*heh*-let; Ecclesiastes)
- **Esther** (*es*-tair; Esther)
- **Daniel** (dahn-ee-*el;* Daniel)
- **Nechemyah** (neh-hem-*eye*-ah; Nehemiah)
- **Divrei Hayamim** (*div*-ray hah-yah-*meem;* Chronicles)

Classic Rabbinic literature

Classic Rabbinic literature consists of the **Mishnah** (mish-*nah;* repetition), which is the written record of the oral teachings received by Moses at Mount Sinai, and the **Talmud** (tal-*mood;* learning), which is a commentary on the Mishnah written by the generations following the writing of the Mishnah.

The Mishnah

Kabbalistic tradition believes that when Moses went up Mount Sinai, he received two Torahs: One Torah was written, and the other was oral. The oral tradition is passed from one generation to the next. Writing down the oral tradition is forbidden; it must be kept fluid and alive and not constrained by exact words and letters.

Approximately 2,000 years ago, the leader of the Jewish people, a man named Rabbi Judah (who was known as Rebbe), and his colleagues realized that so many great people had been slaughtered and that the Oral Tradition was at risk of being lost. For these reasons, Rabbi Judah recorded the Oral Tradition in writing. This work, which is divided into six sections and contains the entire Oral Tradition in a kind of concise Hebrew, is known as the Mishnah.

In a sense, a compromise was reached whereby the great sages supported Rabbi Judah in creating an extremely concise written document reflecting the vast Oral Tradition originally received from God at Mount Sinai.

Studying a little bit of the Mishnah every day has been a Kabbalistic practice for many centuries. The Mishnah is divided into small teachings that are quite suitable for this kind of study.

The Talmud

After Rabbi Judah wrote the Mishnah (see the preceding section), generations of scholars studied it intensely and sought to expand upon its concise language. The first several generations of sages after the writing of the Mishnah produced a commentary referred to as the Talmud (see Figure 13-1 for a sample page from this text).

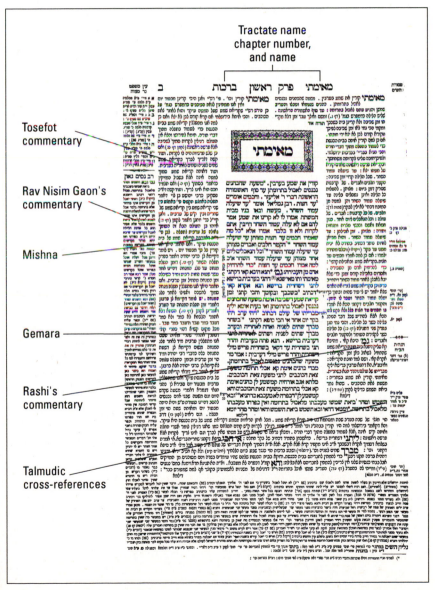

Tractate name
chapter number,
and name

Tosefot
commentary

Rav Nisim Gaon's
commentary

Mishna

Gemara

Rashi's
commentary

Talmudic
cross-references

Figure 13-1:
A sample
page from
the Talmud.

The Talmud, which consists of 63 volumes of legend, lore, and laws, is the most important holy text studied by traditional Kabbalists in their classical education. Every subject imaginable appears in the Talmud, from the most mundane to the most sublime, from the most practical to the most esoteric. Philosophical discussions, folk medicine, profound stories, fierce debates, and the probing of mystical ideas all appear within the Talmud text.

The Talmud has been growing for centuries as great commentators add to the text itself. For example, the great sage of Jewish tradition, Rashi, who lived in France and was born around the year 1000, wrote a comprehensive commentary on the Mishnah that appears in every edition of the Talmud. The commentaries of his illustrious grandsons and their students, who often disagree with Rashi, also appear. In each generation, students of the Mishnah and its commentaries (all of which is known as the Talmud) join in the eternal discussion of eternal ideas.

The Talmud is the cornerstone of the culture out of which all Kabbalists emerge. Every great Kabbalist since the beginning of Kabbalistic tradition has been a master of the study of the Talmud. Kabbalists throughout the centuries have been familiar with the Talmud and study it almost every day.

Midrashic literature: Classical compilations

Midrash (*mid*-rahsh; to seek out) is a term that's hard to define because it has several facets. It represents different ways to approach the biblical texts — sometimes understanding the laws of Tanakh and sometimes finding the moral teachings, ethical principles, mystical ideas, and profound theology embedded in the text.

The Midrash is a large and unique collection of classic spiritual literature that emerged nearly two millennia ago and continued to develop and grow for centuries. Midrashic literature may appear from the outside to be essentially a close commentary on the Bible that adds to the detail of the biblical drama, but in reality, this library of biblical commentary is far more. It contains some of the most profound and important ideas and injunctions in all of Jewish — and therefore Kabbalistic — literature.

The following books make up the midrashic literature collection:

- ✔ **Mekhilta:** The Mekhilta (meh-*khil*-tuh; measure) is a commentary on the book of Exodus.
- ✔ **Sifra on Leviticus:** The Sifra (*sihf*-rah; Aramaic for "the book") is said to be from the tradition of Rabbi Akiva, the great Rabbinic sage and mystic.

Parts of the Sifra also come from the school of Rabbi Ishmael. Although the Sifra is a commentary on parts of the book of Leviticus, it's also a commentary on parts of the Mishnah.

✔ **Sifre on Numbers and Deuteronomy:** The Sifre (*sif*-ree; writing) goes back to the schools of Rabbi Akiva and Rabbi Ishmael and focuses on the biblical verses found in the book of Numbers and the book of Deuteronomy.

✔ **The Pesikhta:** The Pesikhta (peh-*sikh*-tah) is a compilation of homiletic statements that is a commentary on the Five Books of Moses and specific teachings from the books of the Prophets.

✔ **Seder Olam Rabbah:** This book, pronounced *say*-der oh-*lahm rah*-bah, covers topics from the creation of the universe to the building of the Second Temple.

✔ **Yalkut Shimoni:** The Yalkut Shimoni (yahl-*koot* shih-*moe*-nee) is a collection of commentaries on the entire Tanakh. It was compiled in the 13th century and consists of collections of commentaries from 50 different works.

✔ **Tanna Devei Eliyahu:** This holy text, pronounced *tah*-nah *deh*-vay eh-lee-*ah*-hoo, stresses the study of Torah, prayer, and repentance as the primary activities of the spiritual seeker.

✔ **The Midrash Rabbah:** The Midrash Rabbah (*mid*-rahsh *rah*-bah) is a collection of ten volumes on different books of the Bible. They were written by different authors, in different locales, in different historical eras. The ones on Exodus, Leviticus, Numbers, and Deuteronomy chiefly consist of homilies on the Scripture selections for the Sabbath or festival; the others offer more of a critical analysis.

The following works make up the Midrash Rabbah:

- **Bereshit Rabbah (Genesis Rabbah):** A commentary on the book of Genesis that contains many parables and Rabbinic sayings

- **Shemot Rabbah (Exodus Rabbah):** A commentary on the book of Exodus

- **Vayyiqra Rabbah (Leviticus Rabbah):** A collection of commentaries on the book of Leviticus

- **Bamidbar Rabbah (Numbers Rabbah):** A commentary on the book of Numbers

- **Devarim Rabbah (Deuteronomy Rabbah):** A commentary on the book of Deuteronomy

- **Shir Hashirim Rabbah (Song of Songs Rabbah):** A beautiful collection of wisdom connected to the verses of the Song of Songs

- **Ruth Rabbah:** A commentary on the book of Ruth

- **Eicha Rabbah:** A commentary on the book of Lamentations
- **Esther Rabbah:** A commentary on the book of Esther
- **Kohelet Rabbah:** A commentary on the book of Ecclesiastes

The Zohar: The all-time Kabbalistic classic

There are four general approaches to understanding the teachings in the Torah: the literal meaning, the homiletic meaning, the hints that the text implies, and the secret, mystical meaning. The **Zohar** (*zoh*-har) contains the most concentrated and extensive gathering of mystical teachings of Judaism; these teachings explore the nature of God; the structure and origins of the universe; the nature of the human soul, sin, good, and evil; and many other spiritual subjects. (Figure 13-2 features the opening page of this great book.)

Figure 13-2:
The opening
page of the
Zohar.

After a Kabbalist has great familiarity with Tanakh, the Mishnah, the Talmud, and the Midrashic literature, the Zohar becomes a major focus of his or her study. Without a healthy familiarity with those earlier sacred books, the Zohar is nearly impossible to appreciate. But with a firm grounding in the traditional sacred books of the Jewish people, the Kabbalist can enter a mystical world with profound insights into the relationship between humans and God.

Who wrote the Zohar?

Traditionally, Rabbi Shimon bar Yochai, who lived in the early part of the 2nd century, is believed to be the author of the Zohar. However, many scholars of Jewish history and Kabbalah, including Heinrich Graetz and Gershom Scholem, have supported the view that, although tradition attributes the Zohar to Rabbi Shimon bar Yochai, 13th-century Rabbi Moses de Leon was its author. Some even believe that Rabbi Moses de Leon claimed that he was making copies of old manuscripts that he obtained from the Holy Land and supported himself, in part, by selling portions of the Zohar to those who expressed interest in the mystical tradition.

Originally, the Zohar consisted of many individual manuscripts in no particular order. Eventually much of it was arranged parallel to many of the weekly Torah portions. The text, written mostly in Aramaic with some Hebrew, has been described as a mystical novel telling of a group of rabbis who wander about the Galilean countryside exchanging the secret teachings of the Torah.

Jewish lore relates that Rabbi Shimon bar Yochai, the author of the Zohar (see the sidebar "Who wrote the Zohar?"), was pursued by the Romans. He and his son took refuge in a cave for 13 years. During that time, Rabbi Shimon and his son studied Torah, both the written Torah and the mystical teachings known as **Torat HaSod** (toe-*raht* hah-*sowd;* the secret Torah, which has come to mean "Kabbalah"). The result of these years in hiding was the writing of the Zohar.

Outsiders often think that the Zohar is the central book of Kabbalah. There's no question that the Zohar is an important Kabbalistic text, but it surely isn't the *most important* Kabbalistic text — that would be the Torah, the Five Books of Moses. My teacher offered an amusing insight on the subject. He said that people often think that the Zohar is the "secret" text and the Five Books of Moses is a text whose message is revealed on the surface. However, the opposite is true: In the Zohar, the details of Kabbalah often rest right on the surface of the text, whereas the secrets of the received tradition are hidden in the Five Books of Moses.

The English-language reader doesn't have many options when it comes to studying the Zohar. For many years, the only English translation of a significant piece of the Zohar was a literal translation done in Great Britain several decades ago and published by Soncino Press. This translation isn't famous for its usefulness and, in my opinion, isn't the best place to start a study of the Zohar.

More recently, Dr. Daniel Matt undertook an ambitious project to translate the Zohar volume by volume. Known as the Pritzker Edition, scholars have admired the work as a fine translation, but it has limited use for students who can't read the Zohar in its original language.

A number of one-volume anthologies cover portions of the Zohar, but no complete English translation with thorough commentary exists as of this writing. So the best approach to studying the Zohar is to find a qualified teacher who offers a course on the Zohar in which one can focus on brief passages and reap the rewards of Zohar study.

Other Classic Books Worth Adding to the Collection

The books and holy texts covered earlier in this chapter are all popular and well known among Kabbalists. But they aren't the only important works. A few other essential Kabbalah classics are worthy of mention and are sure to appear in (almost) every Kabbalist's library.

Sefer Bahir (The Book of Illumination)

Sefer Bahir, a classic Kabbalistic text said to be the first Jewish document to explicitly discuss reincarnation, is a brief document of less than 200 paragraphs. Each paragraph contains one or more verses from the Bible. The text also contains many references to the Talmud, the Midrash, and other books. Scholars generally agree that the book was written in the 1100s.

Three major concepts that appear in Sefer Bahir generally aren't found in earlier texts. They are

✔ The earliest explicit reference to the ten *sefirot*

✔ The designation of one of the ten *sefirot* in the feminine

✔ The depiction of the divine world as a tree

These three ideas are major ones in Kabbalistic tradition. In recent decades, the late Rabbi Aryeh Kaplan wrote a translation and commentary on Sefer Bahir called simply *Bahir* that remains the only English-language source available to help students study Sefer Bahir. It's available from many major online booksellers.

Sefer Yetzirah (The Book of Formation)

Many modern scholars consider Sefer Yetzirah to be the earliest Kabbalistic text, and its origin has long been a topic of debate. Scholarly evidence indicates that it first appeared in the tenth century, but the exact date of its origin is unknown. Some scholars say that it was created in the first century and was written before the destruction of the Holy Temple in the year 70. Other scholars say that it was written in the ninth century, and still others think that it was written in the third or fourth century. Traditionally, Sefer Yetzirah is attributed to Abraham the patriarch.

Sefer Yetzirah is a book of cosmology and includes a description of the process of creation through the power of the letters of the Hebrew alphabet. It refers to the universe as being formed by "thirty-two wondrous paths of wisdom." These paths are the pathways of connection between the ten *sefirot* and the assignment of the 22 letters of the Hebrew alphabet. Sefer Yetzirah looks closely at the letters of the Hebrew alphabet and derives cosmological significance from their combinations.

According to Sefer Yetzirah, the universe was created through the speech of God, and God speaks continuously as a way of both creating and maintaining the universe. This concept leads Kabbalists to conclude that the laws of the universe are, in a sense, the laws of the grammar of divine speech. For the Kabbalist, grammar is a part of the structure of the universe.

The late Rabbi Aryeh Kaplan wrote an English translation and commentary of Sefer Yetzirah. Another tool for studying Sefer Yetzirah is *An Introduction to Jewish Mysticism* by Leonard Glotzer. Glotzer's book addresses the commentary of the Vilna Gaon, a Jewish personality well known for his disagreement with Hasidim and its followers' approach to their faith. The Vilna Gaon was a serious student of Sefer Yetzirah, and his commentary remains perhaps the ultimate commentary for serious students of Sefer Yetzirah.

Etz Chayim (The Tree of Life)

Most Kabbalists consider Rabbi Isaac Luria, the Ari, to be the greatest Kabbalist who ever lived. He was born in Tzfat, moved to Egypt, and then returned to Tzfat in the year 1570, at which time a group of devoted disciples gathered around him. Rabbi Luria wrote very little and died at the age of 38 or 39 during a plague.

A few fragments of his writings have survived, however, thanks to one of his disciples, Rabbi Chaim Vital, who was a great scholar. One such work that offers the teachings of Rabbi Isaac Luria is known as Etz Chayim. The first part of this book was translated into English and is called The Tree of Life, but Etz Chayim hasn't been translated into English in its entirety.

The Shulchan Aruch (The Prepared Table)

The Shulchan Aruch, often referred to as the Code of Jewish Law, has become a guidebook for the behavior of every Kabbalist. It also contains the precise Jewish laws followed by traditional Jews around the world since it was written in the 1500s.

The author of the Shulchan Aruch, Rabbi Joseph Karo, was a great Kabbalist, a mystic, and a visionary. Every law in the book has a Kabbalistic commentary that illustrates that the discipline of traditional Jewish law isn't a separate realm from mysticism and spirituality but rather is its most concrete and greatest expression. For a Kabbalist, Jewish law is his or her spiritual practice.

You may be startled to see the strict Code of Jewish Law on a list of essential Kabbalistic texts, but it actually makes complete sense. From the beginning of the tradition, Kabbalists have been strict adherents of the study of Jewish law.

Tomer Devorah (The Palm Tree of Deborah)

Rabbi Moshe ben Yaakov Cordovero, one of the most important and influential Jewish mystics and a leading figure in the illustrious circle of Kabbalists in 16th-century Tzfat, wrote Tomer Devorah, an ethical work devoted to the concept of the imitation of God.

In this book, Rabbi Cordovero offers a systematic approach to the various attributes of God and explains how to work on improving oneself by imitating those attributes. A few English translations of this classic of Kabbalah are available.

The works of Rabbi Moshe Chaim Luzzatto

Rabbi Moshe Chaim Luzzatto, known as the Ramchal after his initials, is perhaps best known for his masterpiece, Messilat Yesharim (The Path of the Just).

This book has been studied in all schools of Jewish learning for centuries. In fact, some great Jewish scholars have even committed it to memory! In the words of one great sage of Jewish tradition, Rabbi Yisroel Salanter, "All the classical works of Jewish ethics demonstrate that man must fear God. Messilat Yesharim tells us how."

Rabbi Moshe Chaim Luzzatto was one of the most brilliant Kabbalists in history. One of the most prolific contemporary Kabbalists, Rabbi Aryeh Kaplan, reported that the Vilna Gaon once declared that Rabbi Moshe Chaim Luzzatto had the most profound understanding of Judaism that any human could attain. The Vilna Gaon also said that if the Ramchal had been alive during his (the Vilna Gaon's) lifetime, he would have walked from Vilna, Lithuania, to Italy to sit at his feet and learn from him.

Two of the Ramchal's greatest books, Derech Hashem (The Way of God) and Missilat Yesharim (The Path of the Just), are available in English translations

The Torah commentary of Nachmanides

Rabbi Moses ben Nachman, well known as a 12th-century Kabbalist and biblical commentator, is known both by the name Nachmanides (a Greek translation of his name) as well as the Ramban (an acronym of his Hebrew name and title.)

The Ramban stated that he wrote his commentary on the Five Books of Moses to discover the hidden meanings of the words "for in the Torah are hidden every wonder and every mystery, and in her treasures is sealed every beauty of wisdom." An English translation of his Kabbalistic Torah commentary is available.

The Thirteen Petalled Rose

Rabbi Adin Steinsaltz of Jerusalem is a master Talmudist and Kabbalist and one of the most influential rabbis of our time. In addition to his monumental commentary on the entire Talmud, a task that no single individual has accomplished for 1,000 years, Rabbi Steinsaltz is also the author of dozens of books on Judaism and Kabbalah. His masterpiece of Kabbalah is the contemporary classic, *The Thirteen Petalled Rose,* which has been described by many not as a book *about* Kabbalah but a book *of* Kabbalah.

Of all the books in the English language that I could recommend for a glimpse into the profound teachings of Kabbalah, *The Thirteen Petalled Rose* is first on my list.

Don't Forget a Few Hasidic Books

The Hasidic movement, which is firmly based on the principles of Kabbalah, was founded by the Baal Shem Tov in the 18th century. It grew to great numbers in Eastern Europe and ultimately suffered terrible and huge losses with the Holocaust. After World War II, Hasidism experienced a great revival and has continued to grow and thrive since then. Once again Hasidism has became an important and influential part of Judaism, and it's the most rapidly growing segment of the Jewish world. The Baal Shem Tov and the Hasidic leaders that have followed him have all been dedicated to bringing the teachings of Kabbalah to the masses. All texts written by or based on the teachings of the Hasidic masters are therefore Kabbalistic books, either explicitly or based on the theological assumptions of Kabbalah.

Hasidism is often an oral tradition, and there has been something of a hesitation when it comes to writing down the teachings of Hasidism. Instead, spiritual leaders encourage the transmission from spiritual master to spiritual student, from one generation to the next. Nevertheless, a number of Hasidic personalities and their writings have become well-known and popular, and these writings are available in English. In recent years, translations of texts by a wide variety of Hasidic authors have become available, but three in particular deserve special attention.

The Tanya

The Hasidic group Lubavitch has had seven leaders since its inception. The first was Rabbi Shneur Zalman of Liadi, who wrote a book that's generally known as the Tanya.

The Tanya is a book of practical and modern Kabbalah for the layperson. In it, Rabbi Shneur Zalman (also known as the Baal Ha Tanya) presents readers with a view of the structure of the human soul and offers deliberate teachings on the way in which one can master the parts of the soul in order to send it in the right direction, upward to the Divine. A challenging book, the Tanya encourages the average reader to step on the spiritual path and make progress as a student and as a spiritual entity. Members of Lubavitch study this book of Kabbalah on a regular basis, and a number of key commentaries have been published and translated into English, most notably by Rabbi Adin Steinsaltz in his two volumes, *Opening the Tanya* and *Learning From the Tanya.*

Rabbi Adin Steinsaltz's discourses

A unique set of books for Kabbalah study is Rabbi Adin Steinsaltz's *Discourses on Hasidic Thought.* (The individual titles are: *The Long Shorter Way, The Sustaining Utterance, In the Beginning,* and *The Candle of God.*) From my point of view, these books are the most valuable books in the world today for the English-language student of Kabbalah.

The books in this series allow readers to eavesdrop on a Kabbalah class that Rabbi Steinsaltz has been teaching for many years in the basement of a synagogue in Jerusalem. His classes were transcribed and edited by the late Yehuda Hanegbi and provide the English-language student with a dazzling opportunity to discover how a Kabbalist's mind works — how it analyzes the Torah text, how it speculates on the nature of life itself, and how it shares the wisdom of the ages.

These books are unique; there's nothing like them in the English language. They're Kabbalistic discourses taught by an extraordinarily gifted teacher to students who live in a Kabbalistic universe and want to follow the thoughts of one of its most creative and insightful masters.

The teachings of Rabbi Nachman

Rabbi Nachman of Breslov occupies a unique place in the world of Kabbalah. A Hasidic rabbi who lived centuries ago, his reputation not only maintained itself but grew after his death, prompting a growing movement by his followers, who to this day relate to Rabbi Nachman as though he were very much alive. These followers continue his tradition by taking direction from Rabbi Nachman's teachings for their spiritual practices, studying from the texts that teach his wisdom, and publishing and distributing these teachings to others. These Kabbalists don't believe in ghosts or that Rabbi Nachman is hiding in the flesh in this world, but they believe that his words of Kabbalah, his words of Torah, are as alive, as vibrant, and as present as those of any teacher who's physically alive.

Many of Rabbi Nachman's teachings were written down by his disciple Rabbi Nathan and are available in many volumes in English. Rabbi Nachman's focus on the joyous approach to life is legendary and is reflected in so many of his teachings. Of special note is the famous *Tales of Rabbi Nachman,* which look like simple, traditional folktales but are actually rich representations of Kabbalistic ideas regarding the worlds in which we live and the interactions of the ten *sefirot.* These ideas are all represented in a kind of code in the folktales of Rabbi Nachman.

A number of modern commentaries on these stories are available, most notably from Rabbi Aryeh Kaplan and Rabbi Adin Steinsaltz. In a volume originally published with the title *Beggars and Prayers* but later reprinted as the *Tales of Rabbi Nachman,* Rabbi Steinsaltz offers a fascinating Kabbalistic commentary on several of Rabbi Nachman's major tales. He clearly illustrates that although the folk stories are populated by kings, princes, princesses, and simple folk, they're actually profound transmissions of Kabbalistic wisdom.

Chapter 14

Hitting the Books — and Kissing Them: Studying Like a Kabbalist

*E*ven though you can take an introductory class in Kabbalah anywhere in the world these days, taking a class doesn't make you a Kabbalist. Being a Kabbalist means making a lifelong commitment to learning and practicing. Kabbalists study — every day. Not almost every day or once in a while, but every day — including weekends and holidays. Kabbalists don't have free time because any moment that's "free" is filled up with study. That's why Kabbalists almost always have at least one book of Kabbalah with them at all times. Waiting for a bus? Study. Sitting on the train? Study.

But by "studying," I don't mean that Kabbalists have to be reading every moment. They may be contemplating the things they've been learning lately; they may be thinking about God; or they may be thinking about how to apply their learning to life. But one way or another, a Kabbalist is always trying to connect with texts, teachings, and tradition.

In this chapter, you explore the importance of study and how to go about doing it. You also find out what makes a good Kabbalah teacher and how to find one. Finally, you look at the unique ways a Kabbalist studies the Bible and other Kabbalistic texts.

When Kabbalists Hit the Books, They Really Hit Them!

I'll never forget the first time I saw Kabbalists learning. I was in a **yeshiva** (yeh-*she*-vah; school of Torah study) in the Old City of Jerusalem, and I walked into a study hall full of long, narrow tables. Students were sitting on both sides of the tables, some by themselves in front of open books, some in pairs, and some in groups of three or four.

The remarkable thing was the way in which they learned. Their holy books were in front of them, and physically they related to these books in two ways:

  ✔ They kissed them.

  ✔ They hit them.

Many times throughout the study session, I witnessed students gently lifting their books to their mouths as they kissed them with affection and gratitude. It isn't unusual for a student of Kabbalah to encounter a dazzling piece of wisdom on the page that prompts him or her to lift the book and kiss it with gratitude for the enlightenment the text has offered.

But I also saw the opposite, or the apparent opposite. Students of Torah often hit pages of their books with their hands. Why? Sometimes a student gets involved in a discussion or a debate recorded in a sacred text and ends up objecting to a point of view reported in the text. At times such as these, it's not only acceptable but actually even encouraged to get so emotionally involved in the discussion or debate on the page that you hit the page as if to say, "I disagree!"

In Kabbalistic tradition, hitting a page of text shows no disrespect for the sacred book or tradition. On the contrary, one is required to get emotionally involved with what one studies. For the Kabbalist, studying and learning aren't passive activities in which one simply opens one's brain and has information poured into it. Rather, dialogue, questions, objections, and sometimes deep emotion are what make a student entangled (in the best sense of the word) in what he or she is learning.

Understanding the Importance of Study in Kabbalah

To think that Kabbalah is a body of knowledge that you can master is a huge mistake. Kabbalah requires constant and ongoing study, and mastering

Kabbalah just isn't possible. In this section, I share with you just how and why study is such an essential part of the life of a Kabbalist.

When a Kabbalist wants to spend time with a holy or sacred text, he or she generally says, "I'm going to learn," not, "I'm going to study." This may seem like an issue of semantics, but there's an important distinction between the two phrases. *Study* implies an outward thrust, to go to material, to wrestle with it, to grasp it, and to absorb it. *Learn* has a different feel to it; it implies an opening of oneself, a basic humility that recognizes a need. When you study, you go out to get information; when you learn, you open and receive information.

Receiving an ongoing benefit

Studying is like going to the gym. Just like short, regular visits to the gym are more effective than going once a week for a long session, studying briefly but regularly is better than studying for one long session and then not getting back to it for a while.

As well, just as exercise is only beneficial if you keep doing it, studying only works if you keep at it. You can exercise and get into tiptop shape, trimming away the fat and building up muscle definition, but as soon as you stop exercising, the fruits of your labor begin to deteriorate immediately. The same holds true for studying Kabbalah. One needs to review and understand the principles of Kabbalah on a regular basis. For the Kabbalist, study isn't a matter of learning a curriculum and then feeling that "I've done it, and I've learned it."

Fighting the tendency to forget

An interesting aspect of Kabbalah study has to do with the tendency people have to forget much of what they learn. This kind of forgetfulness is common when you're dealing with technical information, but it's even more common with general wisdom. Kabbalists are required to study every day to meet the need for constant reminders and review. For the Kabbalist, study is as routine and essential as the most basic bodily functions. One eats every day, one sleeps every day, and one studies every day.

Regarding the tendency to forget, one of my Kabbalah teachers taught me that forgetting something that was learned isn't necessarily a loss. Learning a new idea produces a change in one's consciousness and whole being. The mind and consciousness adjust themselves, integrating the new idea into one's being. The brain, its memory, and its ability to grasp and understand things move in order to fit in the new idea into the whole. Therefore, if and when one forgets something, it isn't really a loss because the adjustment and integration of the new idea has already taken place. Nonetheless, Kabbalists study every day, 365 days a year.

Using study to talk to God

Kabbalah teaches that when the Children of Israel stood at Mount Sinai to receive the Torah, a divine transmission occurred: God did the teaching, and the Children of Israel did the receiving. The result in its written form is the Torah, the Five Books of Moses.

Torah study for the Kabbalist is really a conversation between God and humans. It's a partnership whereby God and humankind join forces in order to solve the riddle of existence.

According to my teacher, all subsequent holy books produced by the Children of Israel and their descendents reflect a dialogue. Torah study is an effort on the part of humankind to respond to the Torah received at Mount Sinai.

Where and When Do 1 Begin?

An ancient text studied by Kabbalists records the advice of Rabbi Judah ben Teima on the question of what texts a person should study and at what age: "At five years (the age is reached for the study of the) Scripture, at ten for (the study of) the Mishnah, at thirteen for (the fulfillment of) the commandments, at fifteen for (the study of) the Talmud."

These guidelines aren't hard and fast rules, however. Some children have the capacity to begin Torah study earlier than age 5, and there are so many levels of study that one 5-year-old can begin to learn the stories in the Bible while another child pierces deeper. But the following curriculum from Rabbi Judah ben Teima makes a lot of sense and continues to be a good guide:

1. **At age 5, begin with the Holy Scriptures (Tanakh: the Five Books of Moses, the Prophets, and the Writings; see Chapter 13).**

   The Holy Scriptures is the foundation of all Kabbalah learning and is absolutely essential for serious Kabbalists.

2. **At age 10, study the Mishnah, which is the written record of the ancient oral tradition, as old as the Torah itself (see Chapter 13).**

3. **At age 13, proceed to study the commandments, Jewish law.**

   The age of 13 is advised for this study because it's the age of the bar mitzvah and bat mitzvah, when a young person becomes responsible for his or her own actions (see Chapter 12).

   4. **At age 15, study Talmud (see Chapter 13).**

   It's important to understand that the actual document called the Talmud didn't exist when Rabbi Judah ben Teima offered this curriculum advice. The term "Talmud" means "learning" but specifically means the learning of the abstract ideas at the heart of the study of Torah. This includes Kabbalah, which is the ultimate body of spiritual ideas and concepts in Jewish tradition.

Mastering or completing any of these stages is impossible; Kabbalists study them all over and over again throughout their entire lives. And one can certainly switch back and forth among these texts and ideas. But these four areas of Torah study form a structure, like a building, from the ground floor up. It's practically impossible to study the Mishnah or the commandments without being familiar with the Holy Scriptures, and the study of Kabbalah is similarly almost impossible without a solid grounding in the Holy Scriptures, the Mishnah, and the commandments.

Studying the Torah in one year

The Five Books of Moses is divided up into weekly portions that make it possible to spend one complete year studying the whole thing from beginning to end. The cycle begins and ends on the holy day of Simchat Torah (see Chapter 11).

In every synagogue throughout the world, the same portion of the Torah is read aloud on the Sabbath. Each of the portions has a name, as listed here. The list also tells you where the portions can be found in the Torah:

   1. **Bereshit** (buh-ray-*sheet;* book of Genesis)

      1. **Bereshit** Genesis 1–6:8

      2. **Noach** Genesis 6:9–11:32

      3. **Lech Lecha** Genesis 12–17:27

      4. **Vayyera** Genesis 18–22

      5. **Chayye Sarah** Genesis 23–25:18

      6. **Toledot** Genesis 25:19–28:9

      7. **Vayyetze** Genesis 28:10–32:3

      8. **Vayyishlach** Genesis 32:4–36

      9. **Vayyeshev** Genesis 37–40

      10. **Mikketz** Genesis 41–44:17

      11. **Vayyiggash** Genesis 44:18–47:27

      12. **Vayyechi** Genesis 47:28–50:26

2. **Shemot** (sheh-*mote;* book of Exodus)

    1. **Shemot** Exodus 1–6:1

    2. **Va-ayra** Exodus 6:2–9

    3. **Bo** Exodus 10–13:16

    4. **Beshallach** Exodus 13:17–17

    5. **Yithro** Exodus 18–20

    6. **Mishpatim** Exodus 21–24

    7. **Terumah** Exodus 25–27:19

    8. **Tezaveh** Exodus 27:20–30:10

    9. **Ki Thissa** Exodus 30:11–34

    10. **Vayyakhel** Exodus 35–38:20

    11. **Pekudey** Exodus 38:21–40

3. **Vayikra** (vah-*yih*-krah; book of Leviticus)

    1. **Vayikra** Leviticus 1–5

    2. **Tzav** Leviticus 6–8

    3. **Shemini** Leviticus 9–11

    4. **Thazria** Leviticus 12–13

    5. **Metzora** Leviticus 14–15

    6. **Acharey Mot** Leviticus 16–18

    7. **Kedoshim** Leviticus 19–20

    8. **Emor** Leviticus 21–24

    9. **Behar** Leviticus 25–26:2

    10. **Bechukotai** Leviticus 26:3–27

4. **Bamidbar** (bah-*mid*-bar; book of Numbers)

    1. **Bamidbar** Numbers 1–4:20

    2. **Naso** Numbers 4:21–7

    3. **Behaalotecha** Numbers 8–12

    4. **Shelach** Numbers 13–15

    5. **Korach** Numbers 16–18

    6. **Chukkat** Numbers 19–22:1

    7. **Balak** Numbers 22:2–25:9

        8. Pinchas Numbers 25:10–30:1

        9. Mattot Numbers 30:2–32

      10. Massey Numbers 33–36

    5. Devarim (deh-*vah*-reem; book of Deuteronomy)

        1. Devarim Deuteronomy 1–3:22

        2. Va-ethchanan Deuteronomy 3:23–7:11

        3. Ekev Deuteronomy 7:12-11:25

        4. Re'eh Deuteronomy 11:26–16:17

        5. Shofetim Deuteronomy 16:18–21:9

        6. Ki Thetze Deuteronomy 21:10–25

        7. Ki Thavo Deuteronomy 26–29:8

        8. Itzavim Deuteronomy 29:9–30

        9. Vayyelech Deuteronomy 31

      10. Haazinu Deuteronomy 32

      11. Vesoth Ha-Berachah Deuteronomy 33–34

If you do an Internet search for any of the names of the Torah portions listed here, you'll find many commentaries by a wide range of rabbis and teachers. Each Torah portion is rich and deep, and each can be studied endlessly, so by looking at a portion a week, year after year, students of Torah are able to make lots of progress.

Studying the Mishnah in one year

A system has been devised to get students through the six sections of the Mishnah in a year by studying two paragraphs each day. This study plan is called **Mishnah Yomi** (*mish*-nah *yo*-mee; daily Mishnah). Studying the Mishnah in one year doesn't mean mastering it; you can go deeper and deeper, but Mishnah Yomi is a good start.

Most people who study the Mishnah go at their own pace, but using the daily system can be useful. Type "Mishnah Yomi" into your favorite Internet search engine to find instructions for studying the Mishnah in Hebrew (the original language), English, and many other languages. And any good Jewish bookstore is bound to sell various commentaries on the Mishnah in English.

Studying the Talmud in 7½ years

The Talmud is huge; it has 63 sections, some of which are as long as many books. The system **Daf Yomi** (dahf *yo*-mee; a page a day) helps Kabbalah students tackle the Talmud by guiding them through it one page each day for about 7½ years. Daf Yomi is used worldwide by thousands of students and even offers phone numbers that students can call to hear a summary recording of the day's page.

Not everyone who studies the Talmud goes through a page a day. For some, even one page (they're big pages) per day is a lot, but for others, a page a day is an easy feat. Each person who studies the Talmud goes at his or her own pace. As with every other sacred text, there's no end to the depths to which a student can go.

Studying Kabbalah: Where and when do you begin?

A popular misconception about the study of Kabbalah claims that one must be 40 years old in order to study it (see Chapter 17). That isn't a rule, but just as you wouldn't study calculus before arithmetic, you really can't study Kabbalah until you have a lot of basic Torah, Mishnah, and Talmud study under your belt.

My three children (two girls and a boy) attended tradition Jewish schools and often came home with Kabbalistic ideas on their lips, eager to share them with me. In fact, since my children and I are all direct descendants of one of the most illustrious Kabbalists in history, Rabbi Isaiah Horowitz (see Chapter 18), they were always excited and eager to share when one of their teachers taught them some wisdom from one of his holy books of Kabbalah.

Can I Study Kabbalah in English? (You Already Are!)

Many people hold the point of view that unless you study a holy text in its original language, you're not really studying it. I advise you to steer clear of such a view; take it from me, it isn't true. Misunderstanding a holy text because it's in its original language is a valid risk; one can reap a far greater understanding of a text after it's translated. As my teacher once pointed out, every translation is a commentary, but a commentary isn't a crutch or a barrier to understanding; it's a common aid to understanding that every Kabbalist is involved with whenever he or she studies.

The same issue of translation comes up in the area of prayer. Unfortunately, a great number of people pray in a language that they can't understand. The great sages have taught that, regarding prayer as well as study, there's little point in doing it if you don't understand what you're doing. So a student shouldn't get intimidated by people who say that she's not really studying Kabbalah if she's studying in English.

Great experts and practitioners of Kabbalistic tradition have written many books in many languages. One example is Rabbi Adin Steinsaltz of Jerusalem, who's a master of Talmud and Kabbalah and highly revered among rabbis. His works have been translated into English, Russian, French, Spanish, Chinese, and Hebrew. One of his mottos is "Let my people know," and he's devoted much of his life to creating English-language tools and translations for serious students. His books are widely available.

Translations to consider

I advise people interested in Kabbalah to seriously investigate various translations of traditional texts. For example, any number of translations of the prayers that Kabbalists have recited and studied for centuries are available. When tracking down the classical texts, it's important to be aware of the following:

✔ **Torah texts:** Any number of translations of the Five Books of Moses are available. I prefer *The Living Torah* by Rabbi Aryeh Kaplan (Moznaim), a renowned teacher of Kabbalah and Jewish meditation, but there are lots of others.

Kabbalists consider some English translations of the Torah useless, and I tend to agree. For example, you can find translations and commentaries on the Torah written and produced by people who don't believe in divine revelation. If you also don't believe in divine revelation, don't be fooled into thinking that your best bet for study is to focus on the work of others who take the same point of view. Right or wrong, if you want to study Kabbalah, it's imperative that you study translated texts done by individuals who are believers in the tradition and therefore write from the inside.

✔ **The Talmud:** The place to start without a doubt is *The Talmud: The Steinsaltz Edition* (Random House). Now out-of-print, volumes can be found in synagogue libraries, public libraries, university libraries, and elsewhere. Used copies are also available on popular Web sites that sell used books. Also, the English *Schottenstein Edition of the Talmud* (Artscroll), which has extensive commentaries, is highly recommended, especially for the advanced student.

✔ **The Zohar:** There two translations of the Zohar in existence. One is a British translation by Maurice Simon (Soncino) that has been around for decades; it has no commentary and is of very limited value to the beginning student. The other, a clearly written and more accessible Zohar translation project underway as of this writing, is *The Zohar: Pritzker Edition* by Daniel Matt (Stanford University Press). Three volumes have appeared as of this writing, and the translator projects that there will be ten to twelve volumes in all — and that it will take him another decade to finish. The general consensus seems to be that this translation, while both monumental and groundbreaking, isn't useful for the beginner. Daniel Matt has also written *The Essential Kabbalah* (HarperCollins), a far more accessible book that I recommend.

✔ **Sefer Bahir and Sefer Yetzirah:** These two early Kabbalistic texts are translated with commentary by Rabbi Aryeh Kaplan (Weiser Books). The late Rabbi Kaplan was an extraordinary scholar and teacher, and these two books are major contributions to the small but growing collection of books in English of interest to students of Kabbalah.

I explore a number of other Kabbalistic texts of importance in Chapter 13.

Don't rule out learning Hebrew

Although studying holy books in a language that one understands is both permissible and obviously advantageous, a Kabbalist would never disregard the ultimate value of studying the Torah and other classic texts in their original language of Hebrew. When it comes to the Torah, not only are the literal meanings of the Hebrew words of the Torah of interest, but also Kabbalists are interested in

✔ The shapes of the letters

✔ The numerical value of the letters and words

✔ The linguistic roots from which the words are derived

✔ Words that have similar sounds

✔ Words that have similar spellings

✔ The spaces between the letters and words

✔ The size of the letters as written in the Torah scroll

✔ The words that are apparent misspellings

The original text of the Torah has many levels of meaning, and the serious student explores them all. The original language carries so much meaning that, from experience, students of Kabbalah understand that the more one grasps in the original Hebrew, the more profound the lessons are.

Here's just one small example of how a careful look at Hebrew words can be delightful and enlightening. The Hebrew word for "community" is **tzibor** (*tzee*-boor), which is spelled with three consonants and one vowel. The three Hebrew consonants are **tzadi** (*tzah*-dee), **bet** (bate), and **resh** (raysh). Kabbalistic tradition teaches that there are three types of people who make up a community: the saint, the sinner, and the intermediate person who struggles with his or her good and evil urges. The Hebrew word for "saint" is **tzaddik** (*tzah*-deek), the Hebrew word for "sinner" is **rasha** (*rah*-shah), and the Hebrew word for the intermediate person is **benoni** (bay-no-*nee*). The first three letters of each of these words make up the word "community." Countless other examples like this one reflect the amazing nature of Hebrew and the depth of study that a knowledge of Hebrew allows.

When the Student is Ready: Finding a Good Teacher

In the Kabbalistic tradition, a spiritual teacher, in many ways, has a higher status in a person's life than a parent. Despite the fact that one of the Ten Commandments is "Thou shall honor thy father and thy mother," the traditional understanding of what honoring one's father and mother means is quite limited, and one's spiritual teacher has elevated and exalted status in one's life. The sages say that natural parents only bring a person into this world; spiritual teachers bring that person into the world to come.

If you want to study Kabbalah, it goes without saying that finding a good teacher when you're ready is essential. You can't get far on your journey if you try to go it alone. It's never too early to look for a teacher, and there's actually a law recorded in the Mishnah that everyone is required to find a teacher.

Following is some advice regarding the search for a teacher:

✔ **Not all teachers are for everybody.** In fact, there's a Kabbalistic belief that various souls in the world are connected to other souls at their roots, meaning that two people resonate with each other because their souls have a root in common. However, people with the same personalities or the same looks don't necessarily have souls that share a common root; the matter is deeper than that.

For example, a student can find a teacher who's quite different in temperament in personality than the student is, and yet the student can resonate profoundly with the teacher and derive tremendous benefit from their relationship. If you attend a lecture and quickly decide that you don't like a certain teacher, I suggest that you not be hasty in looking for another teacher. With time, the student-teacher relationship can grow in profound ways. However, if you don't ultimately love the teacher, then he or she may not be the right one for you. A Kabbalah teacher who truly nourishes you is one whom you come to love.

✔ **Don't think that you have to understand everything in a teacher's classes in order for it to be a worthwhile experience.** In my opinion, people too often treat classes like films or theater and want to be entertained from beginning to end. If a teacher comes highly recommended, I suggest that you give him or her a chance — or more. You may sit in a class for two hours and find most of it boring except for the one sentence that strikes a chord and that just may change your life.

For a few years, I attended a Kabbalist's lectures once a week for two hours, during which this great man taught 12 of us sitting in his apartment. One advanced student in the class seemed to be able to grasp and record every word that the teacher said. I, on the other hand, was a beginner, and some weeks that went by when I only "got" one idea in the whole two-hour meeting. I sometimes felt like I was in the wrong class. However, looking back 20 years, I realize that I learned more from those classes than I thought, and some of the ideas that I picked up along the way are among the most important and profound of all my studies.

✔ **Don't be impressed by titles.** A person may have three PhDs, ordination, and be the author of a dozen books and yet have very little to teach. But a more modest individual with no official credentials can offer profound insight into a subject. Too often, teachers are criticized for having "the wrong institutional affiliation." My advice is to look beyond these superficial designations. Usually, when you find your teacher, you know it, and the other stuff doesn't matter.

✔ **Avoid teachers who think that they know everything.** A teacher who says, "I don't know" has at least one very attractive attribute: humility. In my experience, the modest teacher is usually the finer teacher.

Pairing with a Study Buddy

A **chevrusa** (khehv-*roo*-sah; study partner) is highly recommended for Kabbalah students. The study partner relationship is a very close, intimate, and important one. I remember when I was studying in Jerusalem in a traditional yeshiva, and my class was exploring some of the basic ideas of

Kabbalah in a small classroom in the Old City. After one particular class, the other students left, but I stayed behind and chatted with the teacher. A few minutes into our conversation, his own study partner, with whom he'd studied Kabbalah for years, came into the classroom. Both of their faces shone as they looked at each other with the great enthusiasm that came from meeting each day in the sublime realms of Torah study.

It's too easy for a student to fool herself into thinking that she understands what she's studying. A study partner can prevent that self-deception from occurring. In addition, study partners often challenge each other and evoke further consideration and discussion; as the sages described, "When two people study together, they sharpen each other's blades."

Another advantage to having a study partner is that he or she is an added support for regular study. A student may try to study every night for half an hour, but if she has a partner who's relying on her, she's more likely to stick to a regular study rhythm and schedule.

Finding a study partner can be as easy as meeting someone in a class or in passing who shares an interest in exploring the profound ideas of Kabbalistic tradition. Establishing a study partnership often takes no more than a simple inquiry. When two people agree to be study partners, all that's left to do is obtain two copies of a book, set a regular time, and start reading it together.

It's important that study partners want to study with the same frequency and share a seriousness about their commitment to studying Kabbalah.

Study partners may read a book sentence by sentence or paragraph by paragraph and then try to express and share what the text means before moving on to the next sentence or paragraph. Sharing understanding, insights, and free associations enriches both individuals. On the physical plane of existence, two individuals can join together and give birth to a new baby. In much the same way, two ideas can join together and "give birth" to a new idea. That new idea may never have occurred to either of the study partners individually, but their shared ideas can attach themselves to or get entangled with each other and ultimately produce a new and even deeper idea.

Studying Ancient Scripture: The Torah

Kabbalists believe that there was a time in history when Moses ascended Mount Sinai and received the Torah from God. They also believe that the giving of the Torah at Mount Sinai is an eternal event that takes place constantly; Kabbalists believe that one can place oneself at Mount Sinai and listen to the giving of the Torah at any given moment.

By studying classical Kabbalistic texts, all of which ultimately connect with the primary transmission of the Torah at Mount Sinai, one is, in a way, standing at Mount Sinai. The ancient texts are portals into a timeless realm where the ancient texts come alive and the student resides in the eternal present.

In order to study the holy texts properly, Kabbalists need to be familiar with the details in the Bible, including the basic stories and their main characters. There comes a point, as reported by all Kabbalists, when the serious student experiences these biblical characters as alive, real, and in the present.

The Torah is the most important text for every Kabbalist and any student who wants to walk the Kabbalistic path. The Torah is embedded with all of life's wisdom — sometimes explicit and sometimes hidden and just waiting to be revealed.

The secrets hidden in the story of creation

Kabbalists study the words that describe the creation of the world in great detail in order to glimpse the secrets of the workings of creation. Looking closely at this first book of the Torah has been a common one among Kabbalists. The effort to examine the book of **Bereyshit** (ber-*ray*-sheet; Genesis), particularly the creation story at the beginning, is referred to as **ma'aseh B'reyshit** (mah-ah-*seh* ber-*ray*-sheet; the work of creation). The lines in the story of creation that are of particular interest in ma'aseh B'reyshit are the following:

✔ *In the beginning God created the heaven and the earth.*

✔ *And the earth was without form, and void; and darkness was upon the face of the deep. And a wind from God moved upon the face of the waters.*

✔ *And God said, Let there be light; and there was light.*

✔ *And God saw the light, that it was good; and God divided the light from the darkness.*

✔ *And God called the light Day, and the darkness he called Night. And there was evening and there was morning, one day.*

What makes these lines so intriguing for Kabbalists? Here are a few explorations that help explain the interest:

✔ The Torah describes the universe before God said "Let there be light" as **tohu b'vohu** (*toe*-hoo beh-*vo*-who; without form and empty [Genesis 1:1]). Kabbalists see these words as technical Kabbalistic terms that allude to something that's sometimes referred to as *divine nothingness*. The process of going from formless to form is a deep concept in Kabbalah.

✔ The phrase "darkness was on the face of the deep" (Genesis 1:2) intrigues the Kabbalist because it's rich with meaning. These words are used in the same way that cosmologists attempt to find words to describe the origins of the universe.

✔ The use of the word "light" in the phrase "Let there be light" has profound meaning as well. According to the biblical story, the sun and stars weren't yet created when God said "Let there be light," so Kabbalists don't understand what's meant by the text.

Kabbalists consider the Torah to be the blueprint of the world. In fact, they've long pondered a statement claiming that God looked into the Torah and created the world. This belief implies that that the Torah is the basic root structure of everything. (For further explanation of the Torah, see Chapter 13.)

Every week, Kabbalists intensely study a portion of the Torah along with commentaries on those portions. The following sections walk you through elements of the Torah study process.

There must be 70 ways to understand the Torah

The number 70 is a significant number in Kabbalah. The Torah itself speaks of the 70 nations of the world, a basic unit of 70 parts that together constitute the whole; also, the Torah contains 70 different facets, or rays of divine light that are reflected in the text.

The Torah is unlike any other document in that it has multitudes of meanings. After all, Kabbalists conceive of God as infinite and understand that the Torah is a transmission of divine wisdom from above. Therefore, the Torah, too, is a reflection of the infinite. There's no one proper interpretation of any given text, word, phrase, sentence, or story in the Torah. The Torah text has many layers, and each layer can be peeled back to reveal dazzling images and ideas hidden within the holy text.

Does this mean that any and every interpretation is proper? Certainly not. Just because Kabbalists believe in a tremendous number of levels of meaning in the Torah doesn't mean that Torah study is a free-for-all where everybody's point of view is equally sound. The possibility for interpretation is one of the important reasons behind finding a teacher who, on the simplest level, can point out a basic mistranslation or misunderstanding.

Finding one's private gate in the Torah

Some Kabbalists teach that there aren't 70 aspects to the Torah (see the preceding section) but rather a whopping 600,000 aspects that correspond to the 600,000 primary souls said to have stood at Mount Sinai for the original revelation. Some Kabbalists interpret this as referring to the idea that there are many gates to use to enter into the world of Torah and that each of person, as one of his or her important tasks in life, is to find his or her "private gate."

Torah study isn't a free-for-all in which one can go in any direction one likes. Nonetheless, a great emphasis is placed on individuality. In fact, a special category of Torah interpretation called **chidush** (*khih*-doosh) implies a novel, new, unique perspective expressed by an individual who has been privileged to reveal still another dazzling part of the Torah. No two individuals understand the Torah in precisely the same way — nor do they have to. A basic assumption of Torah explication is that there can many simultaneous yet different interpretations of the Torah, and all can be "right." The Torah has, by definition, many levels.

The four levels of Torah study

Kabbalists relate entering the world of Torah study to entering a garden or orchard: The Kabbalist enters into the orchard of Torah study and discovers its various levels of meaning. The Hebrew word for "orchard" is **pardes** (par-*days*). In Hebrew, this word consists of four letters, and each of the four letters stands for one of the four basic Kabbalistic approaches to Torah study. The pardes becomes an acronym that reminds Kabbalists of these four approaches:

- ✔ **The literal meaning:** The first letter word of the word "pardes" is the Hebrew letter **pey,** which stands for the Hebrew word **p'shat** (puh-*shot*). P'shat indicates the literal meaning of the text. In other words, the Bible openly reveals a basic storyline at the clearest of levels.

  The word "p'shat" is used in modern conversation to refer to the literal nature of understanding. For example, two Kabbalists meet on the street, and one says to the other, "Did you go to the gathering last night?" The other person says, "Yes," and the questioner asks for a description of what happened at the gathering. The person in attendance begins to give all kinds of details, opinions, observations, and perspectives about the gathering when all the questioner really wants is a basic outline of what happened at the gathering. He says, "I don't want all of your extra observations. Just give me the p'shat."

- ✔ **The hint:** The second level of Torah analysis and explication is known as **remez** (*reh*-mez). This term indicates not what a verse says but what it implies or hints at.

- ✔ **The moral:** The third level of Torah explication is **drash** (drahsh). It focuses on neither what the verse says nor what the verse hints at but rather what lesson one can learn from the text.

- ✔ **The secret:** The last of the four general levels of Torah analysis is **sod** (sowd). The sod level is the deepest, most esoteric understanding of the Torah. This level is the most abstract level, when the details of the Torah are highly symbolic. For example, when the Torah speaks of Abraham and Isaac, the sod level can see Abraham as the personification of the

> *sefirah* of *Chesed* and Isaac as the personification of the *sefirah* of *Gevurah* (see Chapter 4 for explanations of these two important Kabbalistic terms). People often mistakenly think that sod is the Kabbalistic level of Torah analysis, but a Kabbalist is interested in all four levels and their relationship to each other. The personalities of sacred texts (the Bible, the Five Books of Moses, the Prophets, and the Writings) become archetypes for Kabbalists, representing far more than historical characters.

Discussing Life's Issues with the Sages: The Talmud

For the last few thousand years, Kabbalists have been involved in an ongoing discussion that began many centuries ago among the great sages of Jewish history. This ongoing discussion began with the compiling and editing of the Talmud, which is a written recording of various explorations on a wide range of topics by the sages. (For more on the Talmud, check out Chapter 15.)

One of my teachers taught me that if the Torah is God speaking to man, the Talmud is man speaking to God. It's essential that the student of Talmud participate actively in its study.

Talmud study isn't a passive activity in which the student opens himself up and receives wisdom or information. Rather, the study of Talmud engages the student's mind and emotions. Talmud study requires the student to probe, ask questions, object to ideas, and to generally get entangled with the text. It's been said that the act of studying the Talmud is actually God and man joining forces as they both continue to create the world.

Kabbalistic ideas appear regularly throughout the 63 volumes of the Talmud, but they usually are never explicitly stated. The student of Talmud must make an effort to understand the text and then break it open to find the eternal ideas embedded within the text. A simple parable can actually contain profound and life-changing notions. When read simply as a story, the lesson may not present itself, but when one knows that the great sages communicated some of their most profound ideas through stories, parables, and even laws, then the study of Talmud is transformed into an inquiry into the most meaningful ideas, concepts, and principles of life.

Chapter 15

Praying Like a Kabbalist

In This Chapter

▶ Finding the focal point of Kabbalistic prayer

▶ Mastering the proper inner attitudes

▶ Checking out the essential ingredients of daily Kabbalistic prayer

One of the biggest stumbling blocks that people face regarding prayer is the question of why God, who is vast beyond all vastness and the Creator of the universe, would be interested or would even care to listen to the prayers of a single individual who's no more than a tiny speck within creation. After all, if nobody's listening, why bother talking? It's tempting to abandon the whole process.

Many people pray based on habit and upbringing; they've seen their parents and grandparents pray, and like them, they go to houses of worship either routinely or on and off all their lives. And even during home rituals, many people recite the words of prayers because it's something they've always done, not because they actually believe their prayers are effective or even heard. Some people don't even understand the words of the prayers they recite!

But none of this is true for a Kabbalist. A Kabbalist prays in full consciousness and prays to a God who he knows is *always* listening and *always* responding. (Someone once aptly said, "God answers *all* of my prayers, but often the answer is 'No.'") When the Kabbalist prays, it's his soul that's praying.

This chapter offers the Kabbalistic answer to the question "Why pray?" and addresses the essential elements, both the content as well as the spiritual qualities, that people need if they want to pray as Kabbalists pray. I also explain the techniques that Kabbalists use to pray properly, with genuine understanding and feeling.

The two Hebrew words that are often used in reference to Kabbalistic prayer are

- ✔ **Tefillah** (teh-*fee*-lah; prayer)
- ✔ **Avodah** (ah-*voe*-dah; work or service)

It's interesting to note that, in Kabbalistic tradition, prayer is referred to as the "avodah of the heart."

An Overview of Prayer in the Life of a Kabbalist

If you were to ask a Kabbalist, "When do you pray?", he'd probably give you two answers: "I try to pray three times each day," and "I pray all the time."

The Kabbalistic take on prayer is that the soul is constantly praying. According to Kabbalists, in its most profound depths, the soul is part of God, and the Kabbalist's job is to raise his consciousness to the level at which he's aware of the connection humans have with God. In order to raise one's consciousness, prayer must happen constantly. The Kabbalist may be distracted at times, but at any moment, he can focus on the reality of his connection to the Almighty.

For some, prayer is easy and uncomplicated. A person for whom God is and may always have been a reality simply opens up and prays, offering words of gratitude and praise and making requests of God with the utmost sincerity. For Kabbalists (both those who have received this gift of the ability to offer prayers with full devotion as well as those who struggle with prayer), prayer requires preparation and intellectual understanding. The struggle that many have with prayer isn't a stumbling block for the Kabbalist who sees that struggle as part of the process of genuine prayer.

To pray as a Kabbalist ideally prays takes time. Sometimes years of training and preparation are necessary to achieve the kind of prayer that ultimately serves one for the rest of one's life. Children begin this process early in life, by mastering both the traditional prayer format as found in the traditional prayer book as well as the ability to maintain the kind of prolonged concentration that Kabbalistic prayer requires. The ultimate goal goes far beyond the intellectual understanding of the prayers in the prayer book or the faith that God is listening. A Kabbalist masters prayer when he or she doesn't recite the words but actually becomes the words; the words become an expression of the person reciting them.

Following roads to effective prayer

My teacher, a master of Kabbalah, suggests the following three methods to help attain an effective level of prayer:

✔ **Studying:** Regular study of holy texts and their commentaries (see Chapter 14) puts God on one's mind and in one's heart at all times. When a student of Kabbalah works hard to understand what it is that God wants of him or her, and when the student meditates and concentrates in order to go in the direction of grasping God and finding out what it means to increase one's knowledge of God, he or she is enveloped and filled with a consciousness of the Divine.

Many Kabbalists make studying before each formal prayer session a regular practice. Remember that for the Kabbalist, the study of traditional holy texts is a real dialogue with the Almighty. With great effort, concentration, and hard work during study, God is no longer just a word or a spiritual concept. God becomes real, and the student finds that he or she is actually standing before God.

✔ **Struggling with the prayer book:** This method isn't used before prayer but rather during prayer. The prayer book is full of words, concepts, and images that reflect a wide range of emotions and ideas. Too many people who pray try to keep up with the prayer leader and attempt to recite every word as though the prayers were some kind of magical formula. In a house of worship where Kabbalists pray, you can see that even though a prayer leader keeps up the pace and covers it all, the participants proceed at their own speed, often focusing on one word, one image, or one prayer; they struggle with it, trying to grasp it from all sides and hoping to squeeze it and drink its meaning.

One of the great stumbling blocks of prayer is that people are easily distracted while praying. Jewish tradition actually refers to prayer as a rime of battle. The battle is with a mind that frequently jumps from thought to thought. Prolonged concentration takes a lot of work and training and sometimes results in utter failure. But Kabbalists report that, through devoted attention and immense effort, one makes progress and achieves the inner ability to pierce through the words to reach a deep understanding with sustained concentration.

✔ **Meditating on God:** Like studying, this method occurs before a prayer session. An ancient text familiar to Kabbalists says, "The early Hasidim would set aside an hour and then pray, so that they would turn their hearts to God." Similar to study, this meditation is a preparation for prayer, but the activity isn't one of focusing on a text. Rather, meditation on God is an inner contemplation and the use of one's mind and heart in an effort to transform one's whole being into someone who stands before God.

Although, by definition, God is beyond humans' complete grasp, meditation on God and trying to conceive of the inconceivable (see Chapter 16 for more about knowing the unknowable God) brings the Kabbalist to the point where he or she is ready to stand before God in prayer.

Four kinds of prayer

So Kabbalists can pray all day, either out loud or silently in their minds and hearts. Kabbalists connect with God in prayer in the following ways:

✔ **Spontaneous prayer:** In spontaneous prayer, a Kabbalist, usually by himself or herself at home or in a quiet place (the forest or a quiet neighborhood road, for example) speaks from the heart conversationally, out loud, and directly to the Almighty. This kind of spontaneous prayer has been a common practice among Kabbalists for centuries.

✔ **Brachot (blessings):** Every moment of the day is an opportunity to recite a blessing. Kabbalists recite specially formulated blessings for almost every divine gift that they receive, be it food or good health, and they recite blessings for many other categories of human experience as well.

"Amen" is like a baseball RBI

Kabbalistic teachings include the idea that, if someone is present when someone else grabs an opportunity to connect with the Almighty, the listener can join that opportunity and take a moment to also acknowledge the presence of the Creator and His divine gifts. This acknowledgment is made by saying "Amen" (aw-*mayn*) after a blessing is spoken. Saying "amen" to a blessing is like hitting a baseball and getting to first base and sending someone on second base to home plate. In baseball, it's called an RBI (run batted in). The batter on second base scores, but he couldn't have done it without the batter who hit the single. The sages say that the "amen" response to a blessing ensures that the blessing arrives at its destination.

One teaching says that the "amen" response to a blessing has a special quality to it that's perhaps even deeper than the quality achieved by the blessing itself.

Custom teaches that the word "amen" is spoken at the same volume that the blessing was said (don't shout out "amen" if someone whispers a blessing; rather, whisper the "amen," trying to achieve equilibrium with the blessing).

As for the logistics of responding to a blessing, one should wait until a blessing is entirely finished before saying "amen." Responding before the last words of the standard blessing are spoken muffles the blessing. Also, "amen" should be spoken at the same volume that the blessing was said to achieve equilibrium with the blessing.

✔ **Standing before the King of Kings of Kings:** Three times each day (morning, afternoon, and evening), Kabbalists take an opportunity to imagine themselves standing before God in private, earnest prayer. For over 2,000 years, the recitation of the same set of prayers, collectively known as "The Prayer," has afforded the opportunity to have three unique experiences each day during which the Kabbalist actually believes that he's standing before the King of King of Kings and that his prayers are being heard.

✔ **A great declaration of faith:** Twice a day (evening and morning), Kabbalists gather deep concentration and focus on each and every word of the **Sh'ma** (sheh-*mah*), the central prayer of all Jewish tradition (see "Proclaiming the Lord is One" later in this chapter).

How to Imagine an Unimaginable God While Praying

Kabbalists conceive of God as infinite. One of the implications of this concept is that, in relation to the infinite, everything is of the same proportion. The movement of your little finger is no less significant than the largest catastrophe. You see a difference between a little flower in your front yard and the largest redwood tree in Northern California, but God views both as the same size. This idea may be difficult to grasp, but it's fundamental to the Kabbalist's conception of God as infinite.

God works in every department

Individuals who wonder about the efficacy of prayer often stumble over the false notion that God has better things to do than listen to the words of one of his tiny creatures. If the CEO of a large corporation doesn't even know the name of a clerk somewhere in his company, why would God, who is the CEO of the universe, be aware of each individual? Well, Kabbalists don't view God as a CEO. They view God as being everywhere and as a part of everything. Basically, God is equally near to everything that exists.

To a Kabbalist, God isn't a thing, a supreme being, a spiritual force, or a king on a throne, and God isn't in the heavens or somewhere else. Kabbalists understand the human temptation to objectify and limit God, so one Kabbalistic technique is to constantly reject one's limited notions and conceptions of God, lifting one's notion of God to greater and greater heights.

Knowing before whom you stand

In many synagogues throughout the world, the Hebrew expression **Dah lifnay me attah omed** (dah lif-*nay* mee ah-*tah* oh-*maid;* Know before whom you stand) is posted in the sanctuary. In the synagogue, this phrase helps to maintain decorum. Too often, people who go into the sanctuary of a synagogue and pray are distracted by conversations about mundane matters; they're unable to attend to the business of prayer. The expression Dah lifnay me attah omed serves as a reminder that, when in the sanctuary, the business at hand is the holy act of praying to the creator.

Kabbalists are always conscious of the meaning behind the phrase Dah lifnay me attah omed, and its significance goes beyond the sanctuary. Kabbalists stand before God not just in the sanctuary of the synagogue but rather everywhere, including in the bedroom, the kitchen, and the marketplace.

Shedding conceptions of God

One of my Kabbalah teachers once told me that being Jewish is difficult for many reasons, one of which being that Jewish tradition (and, in turn, Kabbalistic tradition) asks the participant to establish a personal relationship with a God that can't be conceived of. For the Kabbalist, an almost constant spiritual activity is the rejection of any limited conception of God whatsoever. You could even say that if you have a clear conception of God, one thing is sure: You're wrong.

Any image of God or conception of God can be described in finite terms, which is categorically forbidden for the Kabbalist. This point is codified most clearly in the Ten Commandments, where the second commandment reads: "Thou shall make no graven images." In some ways, the life of a Kabbalist is a continual rejection of previous conceptions of the Divine and an attempt to conceive of God in increasingly abstract and infinite ways. One Kabbalistic reference to the Divine is the phrase **Ein Sof** (ayn sowf), which implies infinity beyond all infinities.

Kabbalists don't pray to any kind of image, either physical or in one's mind. Kabbalists surely don't imagine God to be an old man with a beard on a throne holding a scepter, and they avoid any other such anthropomorphic notions of God.

Avoiding images of God is particularly difficult because the Torah continually describes God in seemingly anthropomorphic terms. Kabbalists read of God's emotions and, even more concretely, God's anatomy, as in the image of God taking the Children of Israel out of Egypt with "an outstretched arm." But God doesn't have an arm, let alone an outstretched one, because conceiving of God in any physical terms whatsoever is strictly forbidden to Kabbalists. The anthropomorphic images in the Torah and the other holy writings are merely a way to communicate sublime ideas in terms that humans can understand.

Kabbalists believe that every detail of the human form is actually divine revelation. But even though the Scriptures describe God most often in physical human terms, Kabbalists know that it's not only forbidden but also counterproductive to imagine God in any form whatsoever. By conceiving of God in increasingly abstract and nonphysical terms, a clearer apprehension of reality takes place. This is a kind of built-in function of human consciousness: When you concretize God, reality becomes distorted, but when you push your mind to understand that God is beyond all possible images and descriptions, you come to know God, everything becomes more clear.

So the Kabbalist who prays to God has to deal with two seemingly contrary concepts: On the one hand, she has all the human-like description of God from the Torah; on the other hand, she has to discard those concrete images in order to truly know God. Kabbalists find that, as time goes on and as they direct their prayers to an inconceivable God, they're able to establish and develop a relationship with God regardless of how difficult that seems. Kabbalists claim that one actually comes to the point at which one is with and conscious of God at all times.

Addressing God Directly

God is spoken to directly in Jewish *liturgy* (the actual words found in worship services and standard prayers). Even though a Kabbalist prays to a God that can't be imagined, and even though no words can possibly do God justice, words still need to be used. Two of the most popular terms in Kabbalistic prayers are "You" and " Our King."

This section examines Kabbalistic blessings and the terms and phrases commonly found in them.

Breaking down basic blessings

Jewish liturgy, which is also the liturgy of the Kabbalist, uses human imagery and down-to-earth terms in an attempt to give expression to one's deepest thoughts and yearnings. The standard form for dozens of blessings spoken by Kabbalists consists of three main phrases:

1. **Baruch atah** (bah-*rukh* ah-*tah;* Blessed are You)

   By using the term "You," which is a familiar word to all, Kabbalists attempt to make a direct connection between themselves and God. According to Kabbalistic tradition, there are no intermediaries between humans and God; prayers don't need to be delivered by a priest, an angel, or any other vehicle.

2. **Adonai Elohaynu** (ah-doe-*noy* el-oh-*hay*-new; Lord our God)

   The meaning behind this phrase is that the vast, inconceivable God is the same God who belongs to everyone and who makes Himself manifest in the world in which humans live. In other words, this part of a blessing reminds Kabbalists that the vast, infinite God, the inconceivable Lord of the universe, is also near to them and is involved in everything that they do.

   The word pronounced Adonai is the most sacred form of God's name; it's spelled with the Hebrew letters *yud* and *hey* and *vav* and *hey*. Known as the Tetragrammaton, this form of God's name, which is related to the Hebrew verb "to be," is only vocalized in prayer or when teaching prayer. According to tradition, using this name in mundane conversation is forbidden, and speaking the name at any other time besides prayer — or the teaching of prayer — is using God's name in vain. (For more on the Tetragrammaton, check out Chapter 16.) The use of Adonai makes it possible to vocalize what Jewish tradition refers to as the "ineffable name" of God.

3. **Melech haOlam** (*meh*-lekh hah-oh-*lahm;* king of the world or of the universe)

   Conceiving of God as a king or a ruler certainly brings God down to human proportion, but Kabbalists still don't pray to a human king. Rather, they pray to the King of the world.

Exploring another common phrase in Kabbalistic prayer

One of my favorite phrases also found in the liturgy used by Kabbalists is **melech malchay ha-melachim** (*meh*-lekh *mahl*-khay hahm-*lah*-kheem; the King of Kings of Kings). To get to the root of this phrase, think of an earthly king ruling over his kingdom in a world in which there are many kingdoms, each of which has a king. Now think of someone who is the head of all those kings — the King of Kings. But the Kabbalistic God is infinite — not just a king and not just a king of all kings but rather the King of the King of all Kings. This phrase is an attempt, with human language, to push the Kabbalist's conception of God as far as possible.

An unusual expression in the liturgy known to Kabbalists for many centuries is **Avienu Malkaynu** (ah-*vee*-new mal *kay*-new). This phrase is a paradox: Avienu means "our Father," and Malkaynu means "our King." Putting the two together begs the question, "Which is it? Is God our Father or is God our King?"

After all, there's a vast difference between one's father and one's king. A father is familiar; you sit on your father's lap, you touch your father's cheek, and you know your father every day. A king, on the other hand, is someone who's almost never seen. If you live in an actual kingdom with a king, it's possible to go your whole life and only glimpse the king just once for just a moment, if at all.

By addressing God as Avienu Malkaynu, Kabbalists attempt to describe something indescribable with language. Human language merely points Kabbalists in the right direction, and in this case, Avienu Malkaynu implies that God is both near and far. This idea helps the Kabbalist to maintain an intimate relationship with God while acknowledging that God is vast beyond all vastness and is beyond all conception.

Is God really listening?

Kabbalah texts are filled with the notion that God listens to prayers, and the prayers of the great personalities of Jewish tradition are recorded in the Bible, a fact that reflects their importance. Kabbalists believe that God listens to each and every prayer, but the Kabbalist who prays is caught in a paradox: If God knows everything, if God knows what is, what was, and what will be, if God knows what one need even before one asks, what is the point of asking? If God is beyond all time, if God knows the outcome of everything, isn't there something absurd about praying for the things one needs?

Actually, no. Although God does, in fact, know what the Kabbalist needs, prayer is a means helping the person who prays to figure out what he or she needs. For example, if you were asked to give a speech, you would likely prepare for it. You wouldn't be nearly as prepared and likely wouldn't say all the things you wanted to say if you just stood up and gave a speech off the top of your head rather than writing down your thoughts and practicing the speech beforehand. The very act of putting thoughts into words forms a mirror that allows the person to see himself or herself more clearly than before.

Speaking Most Public Prayer in the Plural

The prayers that Kabbalists have recited for centuries, particularly those spoken in the synagogue, are most often spoken in the first person plural (meaning, "we," "us," and "our."). Pluralized prayer reflects the notion that the Children of Israel conceive of themselves as one unit. Many holy books convey the notion that all members of the House of Israel are responsible for each other.

Synagogue prayers are central to the Kabbalist's prayer life and are said in community, but private and personal prayer shouldn't be forgotten. Personal prayers are not only permissible but recommended because each person needs to establish his or her own personal relationship with "the Lord our God."

The English word for prayer comes from a root that means "to beg," while the Hebrew verb for "to pray" is **l'hitpalel** (leh hit-pah-*lail;* to judge oneself).

Inner Attitude Is What Counts

Kabbalists are aware of the well-known teaching that "Prayer without kavanah is like a body without a soul." **Kavanah** (kah-vah-*nah*) is a Hebrew term with many levels of meaning. In regard to prayer, kavanah is inner intention, devotion, concentration, and attention. (For more on kavanah, check out Chapters 9 and 16.)

Praying with kavanah

In many houses of prayer that I've attended throughout the United States, I often see people zipping through their prayers at full speed. It hardly seems possible that these people are reading every word at such a fast speed, but even if they are, it's highly unlikely that they're actually thinking about what they're saying.

In addition, in many synagogues, all the prayers are spoken, recited, or sung in the original Hebrew. Most of the people in the congregation don't understand a word of what they're saying, but they believe that they're fulfilling their prayer responsibilities just by saying or singing the words in Hebrew.

Inner intention is not only important, it's the law

The great Kabbalistic Rabbi Joseph Karo, who lived in the 16th century, indicates in his authoritative code of Jewish law, the Shulchan Aruch, that kavanah is not only important spiritually but also is a requirement of Jewish law.

He writes, "The worshiper must inwardly intend the words uttered by his lips, and imagine himself to be in the Divine Presence. He should remove any disturbing thoughts until his mind and heart are pure and prepared for prayer. He should think that were he standing before a king of flesh and blood, he would prepare his words carefully, and address them well in order not to fail in his attempt, all the more so when he is standing before the King of Kings, Blessed is He, who searches our innermost thoughts."

Nothing could be further from the truth. Prayer is complete only if the person praying both understands and feels the power and message of the prayer and prays with kavanah. Simply saying the words — whether it's too fast to contemplate them or saying them without understanding them — just doesn't cut it.

FROM MY TEACHER

My teacher explains that, in past generations, people were so steeped in tradition that they really didn't need to understand all of what they were saying during prayer. The sound of the Hebrew prayers, along with a general sense of what the prayers were about, carried them through the prayer service. But today, most people who don't understand Hebrew aren't well versed enough and really need to understand the words they recite.

When one prays spontaneously, either walking down a road or sitting at home or strolling through the woods, the prayers are usually heartfelt because they're made up of the person's own words and feelings. But a person who prays using a prayer book and recites the words provided must do so with kavanah and with attention to the contents of the prayer in order to make the prayer complete.

Movin' on up: Levels of kavanah

Kavanah applies throughout the life of a Kabbalist. Every action, from daily chores to the celebration of holy days and the raising of one's children, requires concentration and refined inner intention. But when it comes to prayer, the entire activity of prayer requires kavanah at every moment.

Achieving kavanah is tough, and Kabbalists have identified various levels of intensity of kavanah over the centuries. Achieving kavanah is essentially a process of working through levels.

Level 1: Simple understanding

The great sages insist that a person who's praying from a prayer book needs to be able to grasp the words that he or she is saying. Of course, various degrees of intensity are possible even with a simple understanding of prayers. The amount of time that a person puts into prayer as well as his or her concentration affect intensity. Reciting a prayer rapidly without much, if any, consciousness or understanding simply can't provide the same inner intention and concentration of thought as reciting the same prayer when taking one's time and putting in greater effort. Quality kavanah is an essential part of prayer. Praying without kavanah would be like making love with your spouse while thinking of what you're going to watch on TV later — the lovemaking happens, but it just isn't the same as it would be with total consciousness.

Level 2: Identification with the prayers

On a higher level of kavanah than simply understanding the words is personally identifying with the contents of the prayer. With experience, the Kabbalist who prays notices that the prayers no longer feel external but rather help her express her inner emotions. Often, the Kabbalist finds that, over time, the prayer book is simply filled with ways in which she can express herself throughout the vast range of human emotions.

Over time, Kabbalists also find that they almost completely, if not completely, memorize the contents of the prayer book. Sound impossible? Just think of all the lyrics to popular music that you can recite from memory. I can easily type out dozens, if not hundreds, of song lyrics from my favorite artists, particularly Bob Dylan, Leonard Cohen, and Paul Simon.

Knowing these artists' song lyrics as well as I do, I daresay that I could probably relate a favorite song to almost any experience that I have. And so it is with Kabbalists who pray seriously and the prayer book: After mastering the contents of the prayer book, including its liturgical poems from the Middle Ages, psalms from King David, and standard prayers as developed by the great sages, the Kabbalist begins to see the prayer book as a personal expression of her inner feelings; the prayers in the prayer book are no longer just words to recite but rather become a way to give expression to the self.

Level 3: Mystical levels

Kabbalists are taught that, with great amounts of concentration, time, and effort, one can reach higher levels of consciousness. These higher mystical levels actually put the soul on a more sublime plane of existence.

Some prayer books even introduce what are known as **kavanot** (kah-vah-*note*). These "how to" directions help the one who is praying direct his or her concentration in the most effective of ways. You can find some of these kavanot in the popular prayer books of today. The most popular Jewish prayer book available today, *Classic Artscroll Siddur* (Mesorah Publications), includes frequent kavanot and excellent commentary on just about every prayer (including key phrases and verses).

Prayer without inner intention is empty, and prayer with the proper inner intention can raise the one who prays to a higher level of existence. Kabbalists do everything they can to fulfill their obligation to pray daily in the most effective and appropriate way possible.

Kavanah: Easier said than done

Inner intention is essential in prayer, but it's difficult to achieve. Kabbalists throughout history have offered plenty of advice to help the person who prays to achieve the deepest kavanah possible. This section shares some of that advice and direction on achieving kavanah in prayer.

No conversations

The custom among Kabbalists when preparing to pray is to abandon all mundane activity, especially conversation.

Unfortunately, some people view prayer gatherings as social gatherings and opportunities to carry on conversations with each other. Sadly, I've sat in too many synagogues where people behind me were chatting about the news of the day or discussing real estate prices instead of praying and focusing their hearts and minds on the prayers they were saying or were about to say.

The Brooklyn synagogue where I prayed regularly for ten years was a house of prayer filled with people whose lives were bound up with Kabbalistic tradition. In this synagogue, you'd never hear a conversation in the sanctuary; it simply wasn't done. Not even in a whisper.

No young children in the sanctuary

One of my ancestors, Rabbi Isaiah Horowitz (see Chapter 18), taught emphatically that young children who don't have the ability to maintain self-control shouldn't be in the sanctuary during prayer. As a Kabbalist, Rabbi Horowitz knew the requirements for utmost concentration, and the presence of children without self-control and the ability to pray on their own can be a major distraction.

Similarly, the house of prayer isn't a place where a family comes and sits together as a family unit. In traditional synagogues, men and women sit in separate sections; boys who can participate in prayer often sit with their fathers, and girls often sit with their mothers. For the traditional Kabbalist, prayer isn't a chance for families to bond and sing together. On the contrary, being with one's family during prayer often offers additional distraction and prevents kavanah.

Inner effort

The crux of achieving kavanah, particularly after external distractions are eliminated (see the two preceding sections), is giving it intense inner effort. Just as you can't go on a diet without actually eating foods with less calories and fat, the person who prays can't really achieve successful prayer without actually trying.

It's not surprising that one of the words for prayer is **avodah** (ah-*voe*-dah), which means "service" and "work." Prayer is work, and it's often hard work. One of my teachers told me that if a Kabbalist is enjoying himself too much during prayer, he's probably doing it wrong.

Use effective melodies

Kabbalists have known for centuries that chanting or singing prayers helps to focus one's attention on their content. With that in mind, certain melodies are paired with certain prayers. Melodies also help one to memorize the prayers and to internalize them.

Let your troubles go

A Kabbalist faces a paradox when it comes to prayer and personal troubles. On the one hand, tradition recommends that he bring his troubles to prayer and express them during his prayer time. Yet the great Kabbalists recommend that, when praying, the Kabbalist leave his troubles out of it by offering them to God in prayer. It's a tricky process because, on the one hand, part of the point of prayer is to ask God for help with your troubles. But your troubles shouldn't impede your ability to express your faith and trust in God.

How does one reconcile these two approaches that seem to be opposites? One of my teachers compares it to going on a vacation. When you schedule a vacation and take a trip, you make an effort to leave your work behind and not even think about it. In the same way, the Kabbalist detaches himself from his troubles when praying.

Prayer requires a great degree of trust and faith in God. It's as though the person praying is saying, "God, please listen to my troubles and help me with them so that they don't burden me and weigh me down." Ultimately, trusting that one can give God one's troubles and burdens is a major part of the essence of Kabbalistic prayer.

Avoid visual distractions

Throughout the centuries, Kabbalists didn't decorate their synagogues or put illustrations of any kind in their prayer books. Many synagogues used by Kabbalists didn't even have windows! People are often startled by the houses of prayer used by Kabbalists today because they look so drab and simple. This visual effect is a deliberate effort to aid concentration.

Most men who are Kabbalists pray with a prayer shawl called a **tallis** (*tah*-lis) over their heads. Traditionally, a tallis is made of 100 percent wool, although this isn't essential. What is essential are the items attached to each of the four corners of the tallis: The **tziztit** (*tzih*-tzeet) are ritual strings knotted in a very particular way to remind the person who prays of the 613 commandments found in the Five Books of Moses. The custom of wearing a tallis with tziztit is based on a biblical verse (Numbers 15:38). In traditional circles, a tallis is usually worn by a married man, but I've seen them used by women and unmarried men as well. Covering one's head with a soft prayer shawl creates a sort of cocoon that blocks out visual distractions and fosters additional concentration.

Upon entering a house of prayer, Kabbalists also try to situate themselves in places where they aren't forced to look at any distracting objects. It's not unusual to find a Kabbalist praying while facing a bare wall. At the Western Wall in Jerusalem, people pray with their faces almost touching the wall, blocking out all distractions so that they can pray with the deepest concentration.

Pray with the right people

Kabbalists shouldn't pray among people who are unfriendly. When people come to pray together, they need to support each other spiritually and help each other pray.

One of my Kabbalah teachers calls a gathering of individuals who have come together to pray "a circle of dancers." Along similar lines, the founder of the Hasidic movement, the Baal Shem Tov (see Chapter 18), described a gathering of people who pray as "a human ladder," with each person standing on the shoulders of the other. If any one rung on the ladder is broken, the entire ladder is weakened.

The Kabbalist's Prayer Book

A Kabbalist's prayer book is known as a **siddur** (see-*door*). The word comes from the same root as the Hebrew word **seder** (*say*-der), which is the festive meal on the first day of the holiday of Passover. In both cases, the root word refers to an ordering of things.

- ✔ During Passover, the experience around the dinner table is called the seder because rituals and discussions are conducted in a certain order.
- ✔ The siddur offers the order of prayers to the one who wants to pray.

At its core, the siddur contains the major and central prayers of the Kabbalistic prayer service. But so many additional readings, meditations, and poems have been added to the prayer book over the centuries that it's almost impossible during one prayer session to say everything provided with proper intention.

The ordering of prayer: From formless to form

When Kabbalists look back on history, they note that, in the Torah, their earliest ancestors didn't pray in a fixed format. Prayer was either spontaneous or varied from person to person. It wasn't until after the Torah was received at Mount Sinai that a tradition of a fixed format, or at least a fixed core of prayers, was established.

According to Jewish tradition, Moses received two Torahs from God at Mount Sinai: One was the written Torah, and the other was the Oral Tradition, which was forbidden to be written down but rather had to be carefully transmitted from one generation to the next. These wise and saintly people developed and taught a more formal system of prayer. Many generations later, this Oral Tradition was written down.

The keepers of the Oral Tradition were a gathering of holy individuals between the fifth and third centuries BCE known by the collective term **Knesset HaGadol** (ken-*es*-et hah-gah-*dole;* the Men of the Great Assembly).

The Oral Tradition was never supposed to be recorded formally in writing. However, the first Holy Temple in Jerusalem was destroyed, and in the year 90 CE, the rebuilt Temple was destroyed by the Romans. The great sages, including Kabbalists such as Rabbi Akiva, proceeded to gather the great teachings from past generations and record them because the hostile environment in which the Jewish people lived made it increasingly possible that these traditions would be lost if they weren't recorded.

A great compromise was undertaken whereby the tradition was recorded in a book that came to be known as the **Mishnah** (*mish*-nah). The Mishnah was supplemented by other great teachings and commentary on the fundamentals of the Oral Tradition and became known as the **Gemarah** (ge-*mah*-rah). The Mishnah and the Gemarah together form the **Talmud** (*tahl*-mood); within the pages of the 63 volumes of the Talmud, Kabbalists find the basis for the prayer book that they use today.

One of the things developed by the Knesset HaGadol and then ultimately recorded in the Talmud is the accepted order of prayers. From Talmudic times until today, the set order of prayers as detailed in the Talmud has been the basis of prayer for generations of Kabbalists.

Those who pray using the Kabbalistic prayer book tend to find that, in addition to the most essential prayers, the siddur provides many different readings and prayers for any and every occasion. Throughout the centuries, the siddur has been the first book that children and families devoted to Kabbalistic tradition ever encounter. At the earliest age, parents devoted to Kabbalistic tradition make sure that their children know how to use a prayer book, how to identify its contents, and how to establish it as a companion throughout one's life.

Generally speaking, a Kabbalist uses the same prayer book in every prayer session until it's well-worn. People who pray regularly come to be very intimate with their prayer books and are able to locate familiar words quickly when needed.

Most Kabbalists today use a siddur known as the **nusach Sfard** (*new*-sakh seh-*fard;* the Sephardic [Spanish] rite). The contents of this prayer book are quite similar to the order of prayers as recited by the greatest Kabbalist who ever lived, Rabbi Isaac Luria (the Ari). The nusach Sfard is essentially a traditional Jewish prayer book with the additions, changes, and improvements made by Rabbi Luria.

Superficially, one may notice that some of the prayers in the nusach Sfard are in a slightly different order than in other prayer books, but a more important difference is the meditations directly relating to Kabbalistic tradition that appear in the nusach Sfard. For example, the most popular prayer book among Kabbalists today is one that opens with the following introductory prayer:

> *Elijah opened his discourse and said: Master of the worlds, You are One but not in the numerical sense. You are exalted above all the exalted ones, hidden from all the hidden ones; no thought can grasp You at all. You are He who brought forth ten "garments," and we call them ten sefirot, through which to direct hidden worlds which are not revealed and revealed worlds: and through them You conceal Yourself from man. You are He who binds them together and unites them; and in as much as You are within them, whoever separates one from another of these ten sefirot, it is considered as if he had effected a separation in You. These ten sefirot proceed according to their order: one long, one short, and one intermediate. You are He who directs them, but there is no one who directs You — neither above, nor below, nor from any side. You have made garments for them, from which souls issue forth to man. You have made for them a number of bodies which are called "bodies," in comparison with the garments which cover them; and they are described [anthropomorphically] in the following manner: chesed (kindness) — the right arm; gevurah (severity, power) — the left arm; tiferet(beauty) — the torso; netzach (eternity, victory) and hod (splendor) — the two thighs; yesod (foundation) — the end of the torso, the*

sign of the Holy Covenant; malchut (kingship) — the mouth, which we call the Oral Torah; chochmah (wisdom) — the brain, that is, the thought within; binah (understanding) — the heart, by means of which the heart understands; and concerning the latter two [sefirot] it is written, "The secrets belong to the Lord our God"; supernal keter (crown) is the crown of kingship, concerning which it is said, "He declares the end from the beginning . . ."

If you're looking for a Kabbalistic prayer book, you can find one at just about every Jewish bookstore and Judaica supply Web site. You can choose from prayer books both in Hebrew and in English that reflect the Kabbalistic customs as recorded in the nusach Sfard siddur.

A Kabbalist's Daily Prayer Routine

The first words on a Kabbalist's lips each morning are a prayer, the **Modeh ani** (*moe*-deh *ah*-nee). It's a simple, one-sentence prayer that's an expression of gratitude to God for providing a new day. Flip to Chapter 9 for the prayer and its Hebrew pronunciation.

The Modeh ani is just the start of the Kabbalist's daily prayer routine, which consists of three prayer sessions and the recitation of various blessings as appropriate throughout the day. In this section, I explain the three daily prayer sessions and break down the activities that Kabbalists do during these sessions, and I also explain the additional blessings that Kabbalists recite over the course of a day and tell you when they're appropriate.

A Kabbalist's day begins at sundown and goes through the night and into the next day, as opposed to the day starting each morning.

Conducting three prayer sessions a day

Kabbalists pray at least three times a day. Because one can recite prayers at any moment and in just about any place, technically it's possible to pray all day long, almost without stopping. But the three prayer sessions established many centuries ago constitute the basic structure and rhythm of the daily prayer life of a Kabbalist. These three prayer sessions are

- The morning service **Schararit** (*shah*-kah-reet)
- The afternoon service **Mincha** (*min*-khah)
- The evening service **Ma'ariv** (*mah*-ah-reeve)

Kabbalistic tradition maintains that the patriarch Abraham introduced the morning prayers, Isaac introduced the afternoon prayers, and Jacob introduced the evening prayers.

Each of the three prayer sessions contains the same core, which is basically the recitation of a prayer called "The Prayer," which contains 19 blessings, and each session consists of 25 blessings total. I cover these elements as well as the other activities that make up each prayer session in this section.

Saying 100 blessings each day (Yes, you read that right)

The great sages taught that Kabbalists should recite 100 blessings a day. Essentially, blessings are expressions of gratitude.

The word "blessing" in Hebrew is **brachah** (brah-*khah*), its plural is **brachot** (brah-*khowt*), and the Talmud has an entire section called Brachot that deals, among other things, with the standard formula used in every blessing.

Every blessing recited by a Kabbalist begins with the same six words: **Baruch atah Adonai Elohaynu melech ha-olam** (bah-*rukh* ah-*tah* ah-doe-*noy* eh-low-*hay*-nu *meh*-lekh hah-oh-*lahm;* Blessed are You, Lord our God, King of the Universe).

Reciting 100 blessings a day isn't a difficult task for the traditional Kabbalist. Each of the three traditional prayer sessions contains over 25 blessings, which immediately brings the number to 75. The traditional **Bircat HaMazon** (beer-*cot* hah-mah-*zone;* grace after meals) consists of four blessings, so reciting it three times daily adds another 12 blessings, bringing the total to 87. (See Chapter 9 for more on the grace after meals.) The morning service contains an additional dozen or so blessings, which brings the total number of daily blessings to 100 or more. In addition, as I explain in the section "Saying a blessing for (practically) everything" later in this chapter, there are random opportunities for the Kabbalist to recite more blessings throughout the day.

The great sages' recommendation that at least 100 blessings be said each day really is intended to get Kabbalists to sprinkle their entire days with moments of gratitude and consciousness of God. Connecting with the Almighty, being conscious of the gifts God gives, and being constantly aware that the source of all things is God are the primary goals of all Kabbalists at all times. Kabbalists want to make sure that they express this awareness that prompts gratitude and don't take it for granted.

The daily morning blessings

The liturgy that Kabbalists follow includes a series of blessings that are said only in the morning. The blessings cover a wide range of aspects of life. As you can see, some of the blessings are more complex than others (I provide the exact blessings in Chapter 9):

✔ **Thanking God for the Torah.** Kabbalists recite a few blessings early every day to express gratitude to God for commanding them to involve themselves with the words of Torah, for teaching them the wisdom of the Torah, and, in general, for giving the Torah.

- **Thanking God for an understanding heart.** Kabbalists believe that God gives people three aspects of consciousness: *Chochmah* (wisdom), *Binah* (understanding), and *Da'at* (knowledge). (Refer to Chapter 4 for full coverage of these forces.) Wisdom, which is intuitive, and understanding, which is analytic, combine in a blessing called sechel (*say*-kill), which refers to both common sense and a profound grasp. Sechel implies that deep understanding is found in the heart. Specifically, the blessing thanking God for giving the Kabbalist an understanding heart also refers to the divine gift that allows human beings to distinguish between and among things.

   The blessing expresses gratitude for giving Kabbalists the ability to distinguish between day and night, which, as every Kabbalist knows, also implies light and darkness, and good and evil. So one of the first blessings recited each day by Kabbalists reminds them to examine life closely in order to increase the light and decrease the darkness.

- **Thanking God for a relationship with God.** Every morning, Kabbalists recite a prayer expressing thanks for not being among those who don't have a covenantal relationship with God based on the 613 commandments of the Torah. Every morning Kabbalists express thanks for being born into or having discovered a tradition that acknowledges and enhances one's relationship to God.

- **Thanking God that you aren't a slave.** This blessing helps the Kabbalist wake up in the morning and configure his or her day in a proper way. Serving the right goals with one's activities each day is very important.

   In this traditional blessing, the Kabbalist thanks God for not making the Kabbalist an aved (*ah*-ved; servant or slave). A slave, in the sense meant in the blessing, is someone who answers to an earthly master. This blessing contains what seems like a contradiction: On the one hand, the Kabbalist feels the great urge to acknowledge that he isn't a slave to anyone or to anything. On the other hand, a Kabbalist like the patriarch Abraham desires nothing more than to be a "servant of God."

- **Thanking God for giving sight to the blind**

- **Thanking God for clothing the naked**

- **Thanking God for releasing those who are bound**

- **Thanking God for straightening what is bent**

- **Thanking God for spreading out the earth upon the waters**

- **Thanking God for making a man's foot steps firm**

- **Thanking God for providing for everyone's every need**

- **Thanking God for giving the Children of Israel strength**

- **Thanking God for crowning the Children of Israel with splendor**

- **Thanking God for giving strength to the weary**

Reflecting on the Binding of Isaac

In the prayer book used by Kabbalists, the morning service includes the entire text of a story found in the Bible's book of Genesis. That story, known as the **Akedah** (ah-*kay*-dah; the Binding of Isaac), is essentially the story of Abraham taking his son Isaac up a mountain, as commanded by God, in order to offer him as a sacrifice. (Of course, if you were to read Genesis 22:1–19, you'd find that the literal sacrifice never took place and that, at the last moment, an animal was exchanged for Isaac.)

This chronicle of the most challenging test that God gave to Abraham is filled with symbolism and spiritual challenges of all kinds. Kabbalistic tradition, including the text of the Zohar as well as the teachings of Rabbi Isaac Luria, have established that reading and reflecting on the story on a daily basis is of profound importance. Rabbi Isaac Luria even went so far as to say that reciting the Akedah each day brings complete atonement to someone who expresses sincere regret for his or her errors.

Singing songs of praise

As part of the morning prayer session, Kabbalists spend time singing songs of praise to God. The traditional Kabbalistic prayer book contains many songs of praise, each of which follows the theme of heartfelt expression of praise for the Master of the universe, for its creation, and for the bounty that's offered to the world daily.

Kabbalists believe that the universe is created anew each moment and that God consciously wills the universe into existence at all times (see Chapter 4). With these foundational beliefs, it's easy for the Kabbalist to be eager to sing songs praising God.

Proclaiming the Lord is One

During both the morning and the evening prayer sessions, Kabbalists recite what's considered the central prayer of all Jewish tradition, the **Sh'ma** (sheh-*mah*). The Sh'ma is a public proclamation of God's oneness. Kabbalists recite the first line of the Sh'ma, **Sh'ma Yisrael, Adonai Ehlohaynu, Adonai Ehchad** (sheh-*mah* yis-rah-*ehl* ah-doh-*noy* eh-loh-*hay*-noo ah-doh-*noy* eh-chahd; Hear O Israel, the Lord our God, the Lord is One), with particular intensity every morning and every evening.

Saying "The Prayer"

All three of the Kabbalist's daily prayer sessions — the morning, afternoon, and evening sessions — contain a core prayer firmly established by the great sages dozens of centuries ago. In the Talmud, the great sages simply refer to this prayer as **Tefillah** (teh-*fee*-lah)**,** which means "The Prayer," due to its paramount importance.

Kabbalists also know "The Prayer" by two other names. One name is the **Amidah** (ah-*mee*-dah; standing), which comes from the fact that Kabbalists say Tefillah in a standing position. The inner intention while standing is to imagine that one is in the inner chambers of the palace of the King and has a private audience with the King himself. One stands before God in earnestness while reciting what are essentially 18 blessings (one more was added several centuries ago). The other name for "The Prayer" is **Shmoneh Esrai** (sheh-*moe*-nah *es*-ray; 18 blessings).

The following is a list of blessings that make up the current format of the Tefillah, the central prayer within every traditional Kabbalistic prayer service. Essentially, this prayer is a series of blessings giving

- Gratitude to God for his kindness and for everything that He creates, while recalling the great patriarchs Abraham, Isaac, and Jacob, who are either genealogical or spiritual ancestors of all Kabbalists

- Acknowledgment of God's might

- Acknowledgment of God's holiness

- Gratitude for the wisdom, insight, and knowledge that God has given the Kabbalist

- Gratitude for the gift of teshuva (see Chapter 8), which is the opportunity and capacity to change and to perfect oneself

- Gratitude to God for the forgiveness He offers

- Gratitude to God for His promise of complete redemption

- A heartfelt request to God to cure and heal Kabbalists of their afflictions and illnesses

- A heartfelt request for prosperity

- Gratitude to God for His promise to gather the shattered Jewish family together once more

- Gratitude to God for the principle of Justice

- A heartfelt request for protection from slanderers

- Gratitude to God for providing Kabbalists with righteous people among them

- A heartfelt request to God to rebuild the holy city of Jerusalem and the Holy Temple

- Gratitude to God for the future redemption and the assistance that King David and his descendents will give in the future for this redemption

- A heartfelt request that God accept Kabbalists' prayers

✔ Gratitude to God for receiving Kabbalists' prayers

✔ A heartfelt blessing of thanksgiving

✔ A heartfelt request for peace, goodness, and blessing in Kabbalists' lives

Saying a blessing for (practically) everything

In addition to the fixed order of blessings contained in the morning service, the traditional Kabbalistic siddur provides many blessings for all kinds of occasions.

The great Kabbalists teach the importance of expressing gratitude to God for everything. The wide variety of blessings provided in the Talmud and recorded in the prayer book serve the Kabbalist well in many different circumstances. According to Kabbalistic tradition, one can never express too much thanks to the Creator.

The prayer book that Kabbalists use contains blessings to be recited when Kabbalists

✔ See lightning

✔ Hear thunder

✔ See a rainbow

✔ Experience an earthquake

✔ See a comet

✔ See extraordinarily large mountains

✔ See exceptionally large rivers

✔ See the ocean

✔ See beautiful people

✔ See beautiful trees

✔ See beautiful fields

✔ See exceptionally strange-looking people

✔ See exceptionally strange-looking animals

✔ See the first fruits of the season

✔ Encounter an outstanding scholar of Torah wisdom

- Encounter an outstanding scholar of secular wisdom
- See over 600,000 people in one place
- See a friend who has recovered from a life-threatening illness
- See a synagogue that has been destroyed
- See a synagogue that was destroyed but has been restored
- Visit a place where a known miracle has occurred
- Hear good news
- Hear bad news
- Put on new clothing for the first time

In addition to the blessings that cover the circumstances listed, Kabbalists can say a general blessing at any time. They often use this blessing to express their gratitude and deepest feelings of appreciation to the Almighty. The blessing is as follows:

Baruch atah Adonai Elohaynu melech Ha-olam, she'he'che'yanu v'kee'-manu, v'hee'gee'anu la'zman ha'zeh.

bah-*rukh* ah-*tah* ah-doe-*noy* eh-low-*hay*-nu *meh*-lekh hah-oh-*lahm* sheh-*heh*-khee-yah-noo vah-*key*-ee-mahn-noo veh-*hig*-ee-yah-noo laz-*mahn* hah-*zeh*

Blessed are you Lord, our God King of the universe, Who keeps us alive, sustains us, and has permitted us to reach this moment.

Devotional poetry through the ages

A new era of Jewish history began at the end of the Talmudic period, particularly in the area of prayer. What unfolded was the beginning of a long tradition of writing beautiful songs and poems fit for inclusion in the liturgy.

The devotional poetry written by the great liturgical poets produced **piyutim** (pee-you-*teem*; devotional prayers). (The singular form is **piyut** [pee-*yoot*].) Piyutim refers to the whole body of religious poetry written throughout the ages to aid in public prayer. Piyutim have been added to the standard Kabbalistic prayer sessions and serve as interludes between the core text established by the men of the Great Assembly so many centuries ago and followed diligently by Kabbalists throughout the ages.

Although not part of the essential text, piyutim often become a Kabbalist's favorite part of prayer, and Kabbalists find that they're drawn to one piyut or another with great intensity. A single piyut may have a deep personal meaning that the Kabbalist can connect to and participate in wholeheartedly with the community in public prayer.

Piyutim continue to be written today, and from time to time, communities adopt new prayers as part of their standard prayer services. If I had a say, I'd add two modern liturgical songs to the standard prayer book: Leonard Cohen's "Halleluyah" and "If It Be Your Will." Check 'em out, and I think you'll agree.

Chapter 16

Knowing the Unknowable God

Being a Kabbalist sure has its challenges. And one of the biggest ones has to do with God. For Kabbalists, God is the center of everything, the goal of everything, and the source of everything. All study and actions are ultimately about God. In a way, God is all that there is for a Kabbalist. And yet, there's no comprehensive way to understand, know, or conceive of God, nor can one fully describe, imagine, or encounter God.

In this chapter, I fill you in on why it's impossible to fully understand God but why Kabbalists don't let that stop them from trying. I also explain how Kabbalists know God and the various names they use to refer to God.

Understanding that You Can't Understand is the First Step Toward Understanding

Kabbalists learn about God through the many verses in the Holy Scriptures that speak about God. Following is a list of some of the things Kabbalists learn about God through a careful study of the texts:

✔ **God is omnipotent; God's power is unlimited.** "All that God wishes, he does, in heaven and earth, in the seas and all the deeps" (Psalms 135:6).

✔ **God is incorporeal; God has no physical form.** "Take good heed of yourselves, for you saw no manner of form on that day that God spoke to you at Horeb." (Deuteronomy 4:15).

- **God is unique and unlike anything.** "To whom will you then liken God? To what likeness will you compare Him?" (Isaiah 40:18); "There is none like You, O God" (Jeremiah 10:6); "There are none like You among the powers (angels), O God, and there are no words like Yours" (Psalms 86:8).

- **God is absolutely unchangeable and unchanging.** "I am God, I do not change" (Malachi 3:6).

- **God is immanent, filling all creation.** "Holy, holy, holy is God of Hosts, the whole world is filed with His Glory" (Isaiah 6:3).

- **God is omnipresent; God is everywhere.** "All the earth is filled with God's Glory" (Numbers 14:21).

- **God is omniscient; God knows everything.** "Can a man hide himself in secret places so that I will not see him? Do I then not fill heaven and earth?" (Jeremiah 23:24); "God's eyes are in every place, beholding the evil and the good" (Proverbs 15:3).

- **God knows man's thoughts.** "God probes every heart and perceives every urge of thought" (1 Chronicles 28:9); "[God] knows the secrets of the heart" (Psalms 44:21).

- **God exists outside of time; God knows the future as God knows the past.** "I call the generations from the beginning; I, God, am the First, and with the last I am the same" (Isaiah 41:4).

- **God's knowledge is identical with God's infinite Essence.** "[God's] understanding is infinite" (Psalms 147:5).

- **God is impossible to comprehend.** "Can you by searching find out God? Can you probe the Almighty to perfection?" (Job 11:7); "My thoughts are not your thoughts, nor are My ways your ways" (Isaiah 48:17).

The study of Kabbalah is full of paradoxes. A long time ago, one of my teachers taught me the difference between a paradox and an absurdity: A paradox is a statement that's seemingly contradictory or opposed to common sense but perhaps is true, whereas an absurdity is ridiculously unreasonable, unsound, or incongruous. More important, my teacher taught me that a paradox is usually a sign that one is going in the right direction. When discussing the subject of God, this lesson rings very true.

Simply put, it's impossible to conceive of God. So a paradox is at work in the question, "How can a person even begin to discuss a subject that's categorically beyond his understanding?" The answer is that, in some mysterious way, the acknowledgement that something is beyond understanding is indeed a giant step in the direction of understanding the very thing that can't be grasped.

Kabbalists believe that the greatest leader who ever lived was Moses and that, of all Moses's personality traits and characteristics, the most fundamental was his humility. Kabbalists take a similarly humble stance when approaching God.

The attitude to cultivate is not that God is possible to grasp but rather that God is impossible to grasp. In this vast, infinite universe, Kabbalists see each person as a mere speck, a tiny little detail in an inconceivably gigantic universe. How could anyone even begin to dare to think that he or she could grasp the world, let alone its creator? It simply can't be done, and those who claim that they can do it are either fooling everyone else or fooling themselves.

God is beyond all possible understanding

One of the mistakes that people often make when pursuing a spiritual path is foolishly thinking that they can master a curriculum. Even though there's much to learn, one can never understand or master the ultimate subject, God. In fact, one of my teachers pointed out that any God that can be understood isn't a God worth having.

Over the years, one of my Kabbalah teachers has stressed the absolutely unbridgeable gap between each of us and God. As he put it, you would never find a Kabbalist preaching about what God is on a Sunday morning television show. If anything, a Kabbalist would preach that all he or she knows is what God is *not*.

If God is at the center of everything, and if God is the focal point of everything that the Kabbalist does, how is it possible to proceed if all one can say about God is either nothing or what God is not? Here again the paradox reveals itself: Kabbalists are able to make spiritual progress by continuously understanding that they can't understand.

Kabbalists do understand that humans can and do get glimpses of God in any number of ways. One way is through the hints and statements found in the Holy Scriptures. However, generally the sages teach that what people know about God is known mainly through the way God manifests in the world. They clarify that although people see how God manifests, they can't know God. Some Kabbalists believe that the way to know God is through the ten *sefirot,* which I cover in Chapter 4.

Kabbalists recite a well-known passage about God from the classic Kabbalah text, the Zohar (see Chapter 13), as a meditation every morning before the morning prayers. The passage, which follows, is found in the standard Kabbalah prayer book. It addresses the unknowable nature of God.

> *You are One, but not in counting. You are exalted beyond all exalted, more hidden than all hidden. No thought grasps You at all. You brought forth the ten sefirot with which to guide concealed and revealed worlds; in them You concealed Yourself from human beings . . . You guide them but no one guides you . . . You are the Reason of reasons and the Cause of causes . . . In you there is no image or likeness of anything, inside or out . . . No one knows*

You at all. And beside You there is no Oneness . . . You are known as the cause of all and the master of all . . . Each sefirah has a name . . . but You have no known name for You fill all names and You are the wholeness of all . . . You are wise but not with a known wisdom. You are understanding but not with an known understanding. You have no known place . . . But in order to make your power and might known to human beings and to show them how the world is guided with judgment and compassion there exists justice and lawfulness in accordance with the deeds of human beings . . . to demonstrate how the world functions, but not that You have a known trait of exacting justice nor a known lawfulness, which is associated with compassion, nor any of these measures whatsoever.

One of my Kabbalah teachers looks to a theorem in geometry as a way to approach the issue of knowing an unknowable God. The Desargues' Theorem in projective geometry is rather easy to grasp when one looks at the detail of it, but a problem arises in that there seems to be no way to prove this theorem . . . unless one introduces a point located in the infinite (which, of course, is impossible to grasp).

My teacher explains that so it is with life and the Kabbalist's relationship to God: Without God, the world seems to make little (if any) sense, yet when the Infinite factors into the vision of the world, a transformation occurs. So although it's true that God is beyond all possible understanding, the Kabbalist introduces the totally incomprehensible God into the formula of life and, miraculously, things begin to make some sense.

Despite the fact that understanding God is impossible, Kabbalists never give up trying. In Kabbalistic terms, the mysteries of life and efforts to understand them are an exercise in the *sefirah* of *Binah* (understanding; see Chapter 4). In fact, the Kabbalistic way of meditation is to meditate on the unknowable God, trying to use the mind as much as possible to go beyond limited concepts and limited perspectives and essentially try to leap over the boundaries of the mind. And although Kabbalists know that God can never be grasped, the effort is nonetheless profoundly worthwhile.

God is beyond time

The concept of God being beyond time is a difficult, perhaps impossible, one to grasp. Nevertheless, as I explain in the preceding section, the Kabbalist doesn't throw her hands up in helplessness. She recognizes the impossibility of the task and tries anyway, knowing that an effort to grasp the ungraspable is precisely the task of the Kabbalist.

One of the notions about God and time that appears often in Kabbalistic literature is that God was, is, and will be, and that God knows what was, what is, and what will be. The Kabbalist needs to push her mind out of the usual realm of thought in order to grasp what it means for God to be outside of time.

If God sees the future, do people have free will?

The notion that God is beyond time and that God knows what was, what is, and what will be certainly challenges usual sensibilities. If God knows what will be, the logical question is "Are people able to choose freely?" After all, if God knows what will happen, doesn't that imply that everything is preordained?

The great sage and mystic Rabbi Akiva expresses this paradox concisely when he writes, "All is foreseen and free will is given." Rabbi Akiva approaches this paradox head-on by reminding Kabbalists that although God sees what will be, the human experience is one of free will and free choice.

Remember that humans are made in God's image; just as God can create and has free will, so does the human being have freedom of choice. Keeping that point in mind, Kabbalists are able to reconcile the ideas that God is outside of time, God can see the future, and people have freedom to choose. The effort to grasp what is impossible to grasp has positive results for the spiritual seeker.

The opening words of the Torah are, **"Bereyshis boro Elohim es ha-shamayim v'es ha-ah-retz"** (ber-*ay*-shees ba-*ra* el-loh-*heem* es hah-shah-*mah*-yim *ves* hah-*ahr*-etz). The popular translation of this first Hebrew line of the Five Books of Moses is "In the beginning God created the heaven and the earth." Kabbalists look at this statement differently, breaking down the Hebrew into the following:

The first word, **Bereyshit,** means "In the beginning."

The second word, **boro,** means "created."

The third word, **Elohim,** is one of God's names.

The translation of these three words is, "In the beginning created God" or "God created in the beginning." How does this differ from the popular translation? For Kabbalists, God existed before the beginning, and therefore God created the beginning. God created time.

God is beyond matter

All Kabbalists know that one of the names of God is **HaMakom** (hah-mah-*cohm;* the place). They conceive God as "the place of the world" and often say that everything is God, and even that there is nothing else but God. But God isn't material, and any inclination to conceive of God as physical or material is a profound transgression. Since time immemorial, Kabbalists have made every effort to avoid picturing God in any physical terms whatsoever. A distinction can be made between two ways of thinking about God: pantheism and panentheism. Whereas *pantheism* equates God with the world, *panentheism* means that God is in all the worlds. A Kabbalist would say that everything resides in God.

A legend involving the patriarch Abraham reflects the Kabbalistic notion that God is beyond matter. The legends says that Abraham was the son of an idol worshipper and was given the task of watching over his father's idols. One of the idols broke, and when Abraham's father returned, Abraham explained that the idol was smashed by another idol. This clever explanation was Abraham's attempt to show his father that belief in physical objects was foolishness.

Because the Holy Scriptures state that man was made in God's image, Kabbalists go so far as to prohibit the sculpting of the human form as a three-dimensional object in an effort to prevent any possible conception of God. God isn't the sun, the moon, mountains, the universe, or anything else that can be conceived of in finite terms. The Kabbalist is urged to push his mind beyond anything ordinarily conceivable.

God is beyond the spirit

One of the most serious errors made by individuals who adopt a spiritual path is to conceive of God as "Spirit," or to say that God is spiritual, not physical. Kabbalists are emphatic about this point and say that God is not only beyond matter but also beyond spirit; God is beyond anything that can be conceived of in any terms whatsoever.

The emotion of love, for example, is a spiritual notion. One can't hold love, take a photograph of love, or contain love in any physical sense. Ideas are also spiritual when they're expressed in the abstract. Just as God isn't an emotion, God isn't an idea.

Often people make the mistake of thinking that God is spiritual. Kabbalists must always remind themselves that there's no effective way to define God and break free of any limitations that they have concerning a definition of God. Many things in the world are spiritual, including feelings, thoughts, and angels (see Chapter 8), but God isn't spiritual.

God is beyond infinity

In Kabbalah, thinking of God as infinite is a limitation. As I explain throughout this chapter, God is beyond everything that the human mind can possibly grasp. People have a tendency to make things concrete; an example is the designation of God as G-O-D, a three-letter word. No word, whether three letters or a million letters, can even begin to name or describe God.

Calling God the paradoxical name "Our Father, Our King"

One of the phrases that Kabbalists use in prayer is **Aveenu Malkaynu** (ah-*vee*-new mal-*kay*-new; Our Father, Our King). This name of God reminds Kabbalists of the paradox of existence. God is both father and king. A father is very intimate; one can sit on his lap and touch his cheek.

In contrast, a king is distant; one rarely even catches a glimpse of a king, and if so, simply for a short period of time. By conceiving of God as Aveenu Malkaynu, Kabbalists use their limited language to indicate that paradoxical nature of God.

One of my Kabbalah teachers points out that the word *infinity* still refers to something finite. For example, even though a set of numbers is infinite, the numbers themselves are finite. When Kabbalists talk about God, however, the notion of infinity expands to the infinite degree. (Am I blowing your mind yet?) God is infinite but in no way similar to an infinite set of numbers — God is infinite beyond any terms.

One of the implications of the Kabbalistic notion of God as infinite beyond all infinity is that nothing in the world is farther away from God or nearer to God. Similarly, from the vantage point of the infinite, everything is of the same proportion; the largest disaster as measured against the infinite is no larger than the brief movement of someone's little finger.

So what's the point?

If God is infinite beyond anything that people can conceive of; if God is beyond time, matter, and spirit; if God is unable to be described by any means whatsoever, then why enter into what seems to be a frustrating process (trying to understand God) with no apparent solution?

Rest assured that many a beginning Kabbalah student has thrown his or her hands up in exasperation at the intense emphasis on God being beyond everything. However, by deliberately pushing the mind in the direction of conceiving of God as inconceivable, Kabbalists ultimately come to a clearer understanding of reality. The Kabbalist wants to be absolutely honest in her explorations, and an almost constant (if not actually constant) effort to break free of limitations and to keep pushing her conception of God in the direction of the ultimate infinite nature of God is necessary to do so.

A conception of God beyond all infinite has other implications, too. For example, as I discuss in Chapter 9, a conception of God as infinite changes one's view on the question of whether God is aware of the smallest details of human lives. By seeing God as infinite, the Kabbalist is aware that nothing happens without God knowing about it and that, in fact, nothing happens without God allowing it to happen.

The conception of God as infinite makes everything significant. If God is infinite (meaning that nothing is bigger or smaller before God), then each person's next thought, inclination, or act has far more significance in the cosmos than it would if God were conceived of as anything less than infinite.

What Kabbalists Know about God, Even Though They Know Nothing about God

Kabbalah is the theology of the Jewish people, so although Kabbalistic notions about God aren't different from Jewish notions about God, the difference between Kabbalists and other Jews often is simply that Kabbalists could be said to be almost obsessed with God. Kabbalists think about God, meditate about God, struggle with ideas about God, and try to stay conscious of God constantly. Kabbalists know that God is here, right now, and not in the heavens. God is in everything we do. As one of my teachers said, "It's not that I know something you don't know; it's just that I'm busy knowing it and you're not busy knowing it."

Kabbalists are emphatic on the point that God is beyond anything that humans can conceive of, and yet, Kabbalistic tradition speaks about God in many ways. The following is what Kabbalists know and believe about God:

- **God exists.** As obvious as this may sound, belief in God's existence is considered to be a mitzvah, a Divine commandment. In fact, God's existence is the very first teaching in the great Jewish philosopher Maimonides's code of law, the **Mishnah Torah** (*mish*-neh *toe*-rah). Almost as background music to one's entire life, belief in the existence of God is fundamental and all-pervasive in the life of the Kabbalist.

- **God is one.** The oneness of God is embedded into the very root structure of Kabbalistic belief. The implication of God as one is that no other gods or beings have participated in the creation of the world. Also, God is considered to be a unity, which means that God is a single whole and complete entity; God can't be divided into parts. The most popular prayer in Jewish life is known as the **Sh'ma** (sheh-*mah*). The first statement of the Sh'ma is "Hear O Israel the Lord our God the Lord is one." Kabbalists recite this statement twice a day.

✔ **God is incorporeal (that is, God doesn't have a body).** A fundamental belief of Kabbalists is that God doesn't have a body; any reference to God's body is simply a metaphor to help make one's understanding of God's ways more comprehensible. Representing God physically is forbidden.

✔ **God is omnipresent.** Kabbalists believe that God is everywhere and is always near. One distinction that's sometimes made between the view of Kabbalah and the view of pantheism is that, whereas pantheism is marked by the notion that everything is God, Kabbalah has the point of view that everything resides in God. According to Kabbalah, in some way, the world is separate from God even though everything comes from God and God fills the universe. This paradox appears countless times in Kabbalistic literature.

✔ **God is omnipotent.** The belief that God can do everything and has unlimited power is fundamental among Kabbalists. This belief in God's omnipotence has been tested often throughout Jewish history, particularly when bad things have happened to the Jewish people, prompting the question, "Why?" Unlike some individuals who look at the suffering of the world and conclude that God isn't all-powerful, Kabbalistic tradition insists that humans simply can't understand everything; God *can* do everything, and it's through faith and trust in God that people overcome the obstacle of the suffering around them.

✔ **God is omniscient.** Kabbalists believe that God knows everything, including what people think. God knows everything that was, everything that is, and everything that will be.

✔ **God is eternal.** Kabbalists believe that God is beyond all designations of time: God had no beginning, and God will have no end. In fact, when Moses asked God for His name, the answer that came was **Ehyeh Asher Ehyeh** (*eh*-yeh *ah*-sher *eh*-yeh; I Am that I Am). The word "ehyeh" can also be translated in the future tense to mean, "I am what I will be," "I will be what I will be," or "I am becoming what I am becoming."

✔ **God is perfect.** The Kabbalistic view of God includes the notions that God has no needs, God is totally whole, and God lacks nothing.

✔ **God is neither male nor female.** Despite the fact that the Torah uses the male pronoun for God, the Kabbalistic conception of God is that God is genderless. Many languages have masculine and feminine forms built into the language, but in no way does that mean that the thing being named has a gender. Similarly, although ancient texts often refer to God in the masculine, in no way do they contradict the basic Kabbalistic notion that God has no physical form and no body and therefore is neither male nor female.

Developing a Personal Relationship with an Unfathomable God (Yes, It Can Be Done)

On my bulletin board, I've posted this quote from a book of physics: "In physics you don't understand a new idea, you just get used to it." The same goes for one's faith in God: A finite human being can never grasp the infinite and certainly can't grasp the infinite beyond all infinities. But as experienced Kabbalists have reported throughout the centuries, progress is made as one prays and meditates on God. In other words, Kabbalists get used to the idea of God being unfathomable.

Beyond that, as impossible as it seems, Kabbalists do indeed establish personal relationships with an inconceivable God. God has no face and no form, and no image could possibly be attached to one's conception of God. And yet, by meditating and praying on one's awareness of the presence of God at all times and all places, God becomes tangible. The dedicated Kabbalist arrives at the point where God is present always and is felt to be present always. This awareness leads to great faith and reliance on God as the one and only reality. For the Kabbalist, all that exists is God; everything else is an illusion.

We can't find God, but God always finds us

To deal with the challenge of thinking about a God that can't be conceived of, Kabbalists often look to one of the books of the Bible, the Song of Songs, as something of a description of the human relationship with God. The Song of Songs, which on one level is an erotic love poem, offers the senses of being hidden and flirtation. The implication is that God is a hidden God.

Among the primary teachings of Rabbi Isaac Luria, often referred to as the greatest Kabbalist who ever lived, is the notion that God needed to reduce Himself and back off in order to make room for Creation. After all, a God that's infinite in all directions and in every way leaves no room for Creation. The word for God's contraction is **tzimtzum** (*tzim*-tzoom), and it explains why God is a hidden God. In fact, Rabbi Luria presents the notion that, by definition, God is hidden and the task of life is to find God.

If God is not only hidden but also beyond all possible understanding, time, matter, and spirit, adding God to one's life is quite a challenge. The natural questions the Kabbalist asks are

✔ How is it possible to bring such a God into one's life in any kind of meaningful way?

✔ How can one pray to a God that one can't conceive of?

✔ How can one imagine a God that one can't conceive of?

✔ How can one speak of a God that one can't conceive of?

✔ What difference does it all make?

In spite of these questions, countless people of faith throughout the centuries, including Kabbalists, have stated without the shadow of a doubt that God is present in their lives, that God is real and is the most important aspect of their lives. Many people who meditate on these abstract notions even claim that they "hear" God's voice.

Kabbalistic tradition represents that some things can't be understood through words alone but rather need an experience. For example, as it's recounted in the Torah, when God offered the Torah to the Children of Israel, they said, **"Na'aseh v'Nishmah"** (nah-ah-*seh* vuh-nish-*mah*; We will do and we will understand).

My teacher has taught me quite emphatically that there's simply no way for a person to make a connection with God. No amount of meditation or yearning or reaching up to the heavens can connect a person with the Almighty. The connection can only be made from the other side. In other words, only God can reach out to humans and bridge the gap between Him and His creation. Another of my teachers used this familiar analogy: A father and his little child are walking down the street together. The child wants to hold her father's hand and reaches up to take his hand. If the father is too tall and the child too short, no amount of effort from the child can bridge the gap. The father must reach down to the child's hand in order to make contact.

So why does God want people to seek Him? According to my teachers, even though people can't bridge the gap between themselves and God, God appreciates their efforts. Keeping with the analogy of father and child, even though the child can't reach her father's hand, the father still likes to see that an effort has been made as opposed to the child holding her father's hand without putting forth any effort.

Becoming a master of return (and I'm not talking tennis)

Twentieth and twenty-first century Kabbalists are familiar with the term **baal teshuva** (bal teh-*shoo*-vah). *Baal* means "master," and *teshuva*, in this context, means "return." A baal teshuva (**baalat teshuva** for a female), therefore, describes a person who's trying to master the art of returning to God (more specifically, thinking about God, connecting with God, and reaching out to God). Although the term most often describes someone who wasn't raised in a religious environment and who has decided to become "religious" (or perhaps more precisely "observant"), all Kabbalists are **baaley teshuvah** (the plural of baal teshuvah) because they're all engaged in the constant process of returning to God.

Talking to God

A way to bring the reality of God closer is simply to talk to God. One of the great Kabbalistic masters, Rabbi Nachman of Breslov, urged his followers to recite prayers without preparation in addition to reciting the daily standard prayer sessions. He wanted them to just ad-lib it and urged people to spend a minimum of an hour alone each day talking out loud to God using their own words. Rabbi Nachman taught that the words one speaks during these prayers should be the same words that one would use when talking to a close friend.

This practice of talking to God is called **hitbodedut** (hit-bow-dih-*doot;* to make oneself be in solitude). Rabbi Nachman suggested that the best place to do this was in a forest or a field, among the world of nature. The practice, according to Rabbi Nachman should include pouring one's heart out to God about one's troubles, problems, and feelings — from personal difficulties to business woes to problems of belief and faith. He even suggested that if a Kabbalist finds it hard to talk to God, she should admit to God that she doesn't know how to do it.

Why God matters more than you may think

Establishing a close relationship with God and continuing to work on that relationship can have a huge impact on one's life. Kabbalists report that overcoming the fact that God can't be fathomed is possible only through one's sincere efforts. Studying the great sages' words about God and regular heartfelt prayer help the Kabbalist achieve a level of consciousness where he or she feels God's presence constantly. And when this happens, everything changes. The way one perceives the world, the way one looks at one's own suffering, the goals one sets in life, the way one evaluates one's life, the way one relates to others — everything changes.

In the early 18th century, the great Kabbalist, Rabbi Moshe Chaim Luzzatto, wrote a book about God that has become a classic. *Derech HaShem* (which translates to *The Way of God*) is readily available in English and is a great resource for more on the Kabbalist's personal relationship with God.

Six ways a Kabbalist relates to God

Kabbalists work on at least six different ways of relating to God. These six ways tend to overlap and are sometimes even referred to interchangeably.

Emunah: Faith

Emunah (eh-*moo*-nah; faith) is a general term for the approach that Kabbalists cultivate regarding belief in a supreme being. In this world that contains so much suffering, believing in any God is difficult, let alone a God that's the moving force behind everything. One of my Kabbalah teachers says that anyone who claims that he or she never has any doubts about God is a liar. Everyone, even the most pious people have moments of doubt. When things are going well and everything seems to be in order, faith is easy to cultivate, but when things are difficult, or worse, when tragic things happen, people grapple with their faith.

Bitachon: Trust

Bitachon (bit-ah-*khone;* trust) implies that even when Kabbalists have doubts or confusion about painful events around them, they cultivate their trust that God knows what He is doing and that everything that happens is for the best (in an often hidden way). In Kabbalistic literature, the terms "emunah" and "bitachon" are often used interchangeably, even though bitachon is actually a specific aspect of faith.

Deveikut: Clinging

Deveikut (dih-vay-*koot;* clinging) is the spiritual activity of attaching oneself to God, to the point where one feels that one has abandoned one's own will and aligned oneself with the will of God. Deveikut is sometimes seen as a smashing of the ego and merging into God. Kabbalistic discussions of deveikut often refer to unification, implying that deveikut is an effort to connect with God on such a profound level that one almost stops being aware of one's separateness from God and grasps and experiences the oneness of all things.

Kavanah: Inner intention

Kavanah (kah-vah-*nah;* inner intention) is a way of relating to God that implies that anything one does is done with God in mind. Kabbalists believe that every mitzvah (divine commandment) is actually another way to relate to God. When done with kavanah, one's consciousness is more completely filled with attention to God. In many synagogues, the statement **Dah lifnay me attah ohmayd** (dah lif-*nay* mee ah-*tah* oh-*maid;* Know before whom you stand) appears on the wall. The Kabbalist's goal is to always have awareness that he or she is standing before God.

Teshuva: Repentance

Teshuva (teh-*shoo*-vah) has many translations, including "repentance," "turning," and "turning to." The word "repentance" implies a momentary activity of regretting one's activities and reorienting oneself, but the Kabbalistic sense of teshuva is of a more constant, ongoing process of adopting a new orientation and going toward God. It ceases to be an isolated act and becomes an all-pervasive path.

Tefillah: Prayer

Tefillah (teh-*fee*-lah; praying) is the process of acknowledging, receiving, perceiving, and honoring that God is everywhere through prayer. Kabbalists pay particular attention to bringing the proper kavanah to prayer so that prayer isn't just the recitation of words, without consciousness. Tefillah should be a vehicle by which a person can increase his or her awareness of God's constant presence.

Calling God by Name (Even Though God's Nameless)

According to Kabbalistic tradition, no finite sound or combination of letters — basically, no name — could possibly come close to doing justice to the Infinite One.

Nevertheless, many names are used to refer to God. Kabbalists know that none are God's actual name; they're just terms that help humans to begin to grasp the nature of God. All the names of God are considered sacred, and Kabbalistic tradition urges great hesitation when pronouncing or writing them. The following is a summary of various names of God, as known and used by Kabbalists:

✔ **YHVH:** Sometimes referred to by scholars as *the Tetragrammaton* or *the four-letter name of God,* this name of God is often considered the most important of God's names. The four letters that make up this name are *yud, hey, vav,* and *hey.* Kabbalistic tradition forbids the pronunciation of this term unless one is the High Priest in the Holy Temple in Jerusalem on the holy day of Yom Kippur. Additionally, it's believed that the correct pronunciation of this four-letter name of God has been lost; Hebrew only includes consonants and not vowels, so a precise pronunciation is somewhat of a mystery. However, the four letter name of God is often transliterated as **Yahweh.**

- **Hashem** (hah-*shem*): Modern Kabbalists often use the designation Hashem, which means "the Name," to refer to God. Paradoxically, Kabbalists often avoid speaking God's name by calling God "the Name."

- **Adonai** (ah-*doe*-noy): This term that appears in every Kabbalah blessing is technically the plural form of "my Lord." According to tradition, the pronunciation of this name is forbidden unless it's used in prayer. When one reads this name of God outside of prayer, one usually replaces it with Hashem.

- **Ehyeh Asher Ehyeh** (*eh*-yeh *ah*-share *eh*-yeh): This phrase, which appears in the book of Exodus (3:14), is often translated as "I will be Who I will be" or "I am that I am." According to the Torah, it's the precise response given when Moses asks God for His name.

- **El** (el): A designation for "God," it's often paired with other terms, such as **El Elyon** (God Most High), **El Olam** (the Everlasting God), and **El Gibbor** (the God of Strength). El also appears as the suffix of many of the names of angels (such as Gabriel and Raphael) because they're messengers for God (see Chapter 8).

- **Elohim** (el-oh-*heem*): Frequently found in the Torah, this name of God is grammatically a plural form and, because it can also be translated as "judges," it refers to God's attribute of justice.

- **Shaddai** (shah-*die*): Sometimes Shaddai appears by itself, and sometimes it's expressed in combination with El. Often translated as "Almighty" and "Guardian," Shaddai connects to the sense of God as protector. It is interesting to note that when a Kabbalist puts a **mezuzah** (meh-*zuz*-ah) on his or her doorpost, the housing for the mezuzah frequently has the Hebrew letter **Shin** on it, standing for the name Shaddai; the mezuzah taps into the idea of Shaddai as protector in that the mezuzah is placed on the doorpost of a home as a kind of amulet for protection. Shaddai is also seen as an acronym for the three Hebrew words **Shomer Daltot Yisroel**, which mean "Guardians of the doors of Israel."

- **Yah:** This name for God is taken from the first two letters of the Tetragrammaton (see the first name in this list). Interestingly, Yah is the source of the Rastafarian name for God, *Jah,* which is heard in contemporary reggae music.

- **Tsva'ot** (tzih-vah-*oht*): This name, which means "host," appears often in the prophetic literature, not in the Five Books of Moses. It's used in the sense that God is the Host of creation. Tsva'ot also implies that all the details of creation are connected to God in the sense that they're God's army.

- **HaMakom** (hah-mah-*comb*): Kabbalists frequently refer to the universe as residing in the place of God and use the term HaMakom to refer to that place with a capital "P."

Writing the names of God

Kabbalistic tradition doesn't take the names of God casually. Writing the names of God isn't prohibited, but erasing or defacing God's names is. To be on the safe side, Kabbalists avoid writing any of God's names unless it's absolutely necessary. In fact, when any of the sacred names of God appear in print, Kabbalists avoid defacing the paper to the extent that old, worn-out prayer books and other sacred texts are buried instead of discarded in the trash. For centuries, Kabbalists have maintained **geniza** (geh-*knee*-zah; cemeteries) for old texts containing the names of God.

Often, to avoid writing an exact name of God, a Kabbalists replaces letters or syllables in the exact name; the substitution produces a name that isn't accurate. For example:

- **Adonai** becomes **Hashem** or **Ahdoshem.**
- **Elohim** becomes **Elokim** (when it isn't used contextually to refer to human judges).
- **Hallelujah** becomes **Hallelukah.**

On a related note, Kabbalists don't pronounce these names accurately or fully unless they're being said for sacred purposes. Of course, when a teacher is teaching his or her students to pray or to read sacred texts, saying the full names accurately is permissible for the sake of accurate education.

Kabbalistic tradition requires that the following seven names of God be given special care by scribes who write sacred scrolls:

- El
- Elohim
- Adonai
- Yud, Hey, Vav, Hey
- Ehyeh Asher Ehyeh
- Shaddai
- Tsva'ot

Why does God have so many names?

Kabbalists understand that God is unnamable and that no name can adequately describe God or do justice to God. In some Kabbalistic texts, God is referred to as "The Infinite, Blessed is He." This is a paradoxical name because it uses the word "infinite" and also uses a word that is quite finite, "He." (Kabbalists know that God is without gender, but there's no neutral pronoun in Hebrew, so "he" is often used when referring to God.) "The Infinite, Blessed is He" implies that God is both near and far, yet this name, too, falls short, as does every other name for God.

Even though no name does God justice, in Kabbalistic tradition, God has any number of names, each reflecting the human experience of God. Some of these additional names are

- Strong One
- Our Father, Our King
- The Creator
- God of Abraham, God of Isaac, God of Jacob
- God the strong one
- Truth
- Endless, Infinite
- Shepherd of Israel
- The Holy One, Blessed be He
- Holy One of Israel
- Shield of Abraham
- The Lord will provide
- The Lord that heals
- The Lord our Banner
- The Lord our Peace
- The Lord my Shepherd
- The Lord our Righteousness
- Rock of Israel

Kabbalists believe that there's no end to the number of names for God. As is often the case in Kabbalah, this idea is a paradox: Even though no name is adequate and God is considered unnamable, God has an infinite number of names.

Part IV
Fine-tuning the Essential Skills of the Kabbalist

The 5th Wave — By Rich Tennant

"Saaay — I have an idea. Why don't we turn down the lights, put on some soft music, and curl up with the Talmud tonight?"

In this part . . .

Kabbalists communicate with God in two ways: by studying and by praying. Both are conversations with the Holy One. In studying the holy books as well as commentaries on them, the Kabbalist receives messages and teachings from God and also sees how the great sages responded to those messages. When praying, the Kabbalist is engaged in a dialogue with the Almighty. By both studying and praying, the Kabbalist encounters one of the great paradoxes of Jewish life: establishing an intimate relationship with an inconceivable God.

Chapter 17

(Almost) Ten Myths about Studying Kabbalah

Kabbalah has been and probably always will be surrounded by myths. A number of the myths about Kabbalah concern themselves with restricting the study of Kabbalah to certain individuals and excluding others from its study. Other popular myths about Kabbalah have to do with the commercialization of Kabbalah in recent years as well as simply what Kabbalah is and what it isn't. This chapter lets me play myth-buster and set you straight on the top ten myths about Kabbalah.

You Have to Be a Man

Anybody who examines the traditional Jewish texts that have been central to Kabbalah for centuries can see that men and women are viewed through different lenses. Traditional religious responsibilities, restrictions, and customs reflect many different roles for men and women in the family as well as in ritual life.

But ultimately, Kabbalah is just as available to women as to men. I only have to look to my own family experience for proof of this point. I have a son and two daughters; both of my daughters graduated from Jewish high schools and have shared with me repeatedly that Kabbalistic ideas were regularly taught in their schools. Over the years, I've heard the stories, customs, lessons, and insights grown out of Kabbalistic tradition that were shared with them by their teachers and rabbis. And I'm not just referring to an occasional tidbit of Kabbalah here and there. Jewish education for girls is taken quite seriously. I can have in-depth, high-level theological discussions with both of my daughters (and we've been having them since they were in middle school!).

The bottom line is that you don't have to be a man to study Kabbalah. I've studied Kabbalah with authentic Jewish teachers who teach Kabbalah to both women and men all the time.

You Have to Be Married

Marriage is an important institution in Kabbalistic tradition, and the sanctity of marriage is a given for the Kabbalist. Getting married is considered both a social and a spiritual achievement. A person's status rises upon marriage because the Kabbalist believes that each person has half a soul and needs to find and connect with the other half to achieve a certain level of wholeness. The person who's privileged to receive such a high level of wholeness has something of an exalted status for the Kabbalist, *but marriage isn't a prerequisite for Kabbalah study.*

You may be wondering why someone would even suggest that one has to be married in order to study Kabbalah. One reason is because Kabbalah does, in fact, require a certain level of maturity, and marriage usually imparts some maturity because of the wholeness it creates.

One doesn't have to be married to study Kabbalah, but the more mature, stable, and experienced a person is, the better able he or she is to explore the most profound notions about the meaning of life and death, good and evil, and pain and suffering. The question of whether a student should wait to study Kabbalah until he or she is mature enough has long been a concern in Kabbalistic tradition. It would be foolish to attempt the study of a difficult subject without the proper prerequisites, but what does it take to be a mature student who is ready to study Kabbalah?

- ✔ **Knowledge of the ten *sefirot* (see Chapter 4)**

- ✔ **Basic knowledge of the stories in the Torah:** For example, knowledge of the patriarchs Abraham, Isaac, and Jacob, and their wives Sarah, Rebecca, Rachel, and Leah, is essential. These seven people are major characters in stories that Kabbalists study and refer to on a regular basis.

- ✔ **Being rooted in both law as well as ideas (or concepts):** For the Kabbalist, the study of Kabbalah is never only theoretical. An important distinction that many scholars have noted about the difference between Kabbalah and other forms of mysticism is that Kabbalah isn't just a dis-cussion of ideas; instead, it's a constant effort to connect those ideas to this world. From ritual acts to social behavior, everything a Kabbalist does is rooted in an ancient tradition that's constantly looking for ways to express itself in life. The giving of charity, acts of kindness, child-rearing, traditional celebration of the Sabbath and holidays, observance of ritual law in all realms (including eating, sleeping, and sexual behavior), and relations in the marketplace are all governed by the individual's participation in the ancient process making an effort to remain conscious and to connect every breath, action, and thought to the Infinite One. A Kabbalist needs to be rooted in the knowledge and practice of Jewish law as a perquisite to the exploration of esoteric and transcendent ideas or concepts.

✔ **Dedication:** Kabbalah isn't a fad or a hobby. It isn't a self-help craze or a cult. And it isn't some far-out superstition. Kabbalah requires seriousness, commitment, perseverance, kindness, and endurance. Just as one doesn't dabble as a brain surgeon, Kabbalists must dedicate time, knowledge, and commitment to master the art and science of Kabbalah.

Can someone pick up a book of Kabbalah and randomly stumble upon an insight or piece of wisdom of value? Yes, of course. But unless that person commits to Kabbalah, he or she can't in honesty claim to be a Kabbalist. Basically, it just isn't possible to dabble in Kabbalah.

✔ **Working with a teacher:** Kabbalah is largely an oral tradition passed on from one generation to the next. The Kabbalistic texts often aren't clear enough to be meaningful unless the person studying them is aided by the commentary of a living Kabbalist. Kabbalistic wisdom doesn't apply in the same way to every person, so a student needs the insight of a teacher to get the most out of his or her study.

Certainly one can find a lot of information in books, and many of the growing number of books on Kabbalah are profoundly insightful and informative. In fact, I've been studying five such books on a constant basis for many years. I truly believe that I've learned much from my own study in solitude with these great volumes of Kabbalah in English, but nothing matches an encounter with a contemporary teacher who can offer his or her special guidance or blessings in a way that a book never can.

You Have to Be an Orthodox Jew

This myth is rooted in the reasonable idea of prerequisites. As with many of the other myths in this chapter, the trend in Kabbalistic history is to require that the serious student be rooted in tradition, experienced with the broad range of traditional practices, and mature and knowledgeable enough to grasp and creatively participate in discussions of basic and complex ideas. But being an Orthodox Jew doesn't guarantee any of these skills or abilities.

The rigors of Orthodox life require a great deal of knowledge and ongoing study, both of which are important prerequisites for the serious student. But one easily can be an Orthodox Jew without understanding and insight, just as one can be far from the tradition of Orthodoxy and yet have the personality traits and the talents to both study and teach Kabbalah.

You Have to at Least Be Jewish

Make no mistake about it: Kabbalah is the theology of the Jewish people and has been seen and accepted as such for at least the last 500 years. Its symbols, values, customs, and history are all part of the Jewish experience. The great Kabbalists were all practicing traditional Jews, and each held encyclopedic knowledge of Jewish tradition. Their behavior reflected that tradition.

Throughout history, people have made attempts to mix Kabbalistic ideas with other approaches and philosophies and call these efforts Kabbalah. For example, a *Christian Kabbalah* that borrowed freely from the Kabbalistic tradition of the Jewish people emerged as recently as the last few centuries in Kabbalistic history. Best described as watered-down Kabbalah, Christian Kabbalah certainly never retains authentic Kabbalah's fundamental requirement of being rooted in ritual law and traditional religious behavior.

You can go into any spiritual bookstore or the spiritual section of a general bookstore and find books that claim to teach Kabbalah and sometimes even explicitly refer to Christian Kabbalah. These efforts may or may not be worthy of study, but they certainly aren't authentic representations of Kabbalistic tradition.

But does the student of Kabbalah need to be Jewish? The answer is "no." Books, lectures, classes, and magazine articles about Kabbalah are available to everyone, not just Jews. And anyone can fall victim to misinformation and distortions of the subject. As one of my Kabbalah teachers says, "There is so much misinformation available about Kabbalah that teachers of Kabbalah almost have an obligation today to write accurate books on Kabbalistic tradition." This, along with the widespread access to information throughout the world, makes any restriction absurd.

However, there's a profound difference between the way a Jewish person relates to Kabbalah and the way a person who isn't Jewish relates to it. Traditional Kabbalistic belief places a heavy burden on the Jewish people; the tradition doesn't require the same of someone who isn't Jewish. The more a Jewish person reads, learns, and understands the obligations imposed upon Jews by the tradition, the more his or her obligation grows.

According to biblical tradition, the Jewish people are to view themselves as "a nation of priests." This notion is often referred to in shorthand as "the chosen people." From the outside, the notion of the chosen people seems strange until one realizes that the term "chosen" doesn't mean greater status but rather greater responsibility for learning and performing the divine commandments. As priests in the world, the Jewish people relate to everything as sacred. So although you don't have to be Jewish to study Kabbalah, for a Jewish person, studying Kabbalah is learning the way the Jewish family has sought to understand God for many centuries.

You Have to Be Over 40

One can trace a tendency throughout Kabbalistic history to put off the study of Kabbalah until after a student masters the basics of Jewish learning and tradition. Kabbalists often refer to the following passage (Ethics of the Fathers 5:24) in the Mishnah (see Chapter 13):

> *At five years (the age is reached for the study of the) Scripture, at ten for (the study of) the Mishnah, at thirteen for (the fulfillment of) the commandments, at fifteen for (the study of) the Talmud, at eighteen for marriage, at twenty for seeking (a livelihood), at thirty for (entering into one's full) strength, at forty for understanding, at fifty for counsel, at sixty (a man attains) old age, at seventy the hoary head, at eighty (the gift of special) strength, at ninety (he bends beneath) the weight of years, at a hundred he is as if he were already dead and had passed away from the world.*

Many books about Kabbalah refer to a requirement that a student of Kabbalah needs to be over 40, but no such absolute age requirement exists. Some of the great sages in Jewish history mastered Kabbalah at a young age, whereas others never felt ready to enter into its study. The greatest Kabbalist who ever lived, Rabbi Isaac Luria (known as the Ari), died at the age of 39. He never even reached the age of 40.

Even though there's no age requirement for Kabbalah students, Kabbalistic tradition is much more welcoming to the student who has done the proper preparation in order to enter the spiritual realms of Kabbalah.

You Have to Buy Expensive Books in Hebrew

Over the past several years, I've been asked many times whether I think that there's any truth to the notion being perpetuated by a major merchandiser of new-age Kabbalah that merely having a Hebrew set of the multivolume holy work, the Zohar, in one's home will bring good fortune.

I'm a book person. I have over 3,000 books in my home collection, I've been involved with Jewish book publishing for over 25 years, and I've served as a librarian in addition to authoring several books. The presence of the books that surround me in my home, both those that I've read and those that I haven't, unquestionably enhance my life. As one of my teachers put it, "Just the title of a book and the aesthetics of its design are sometimes enough to have great impact on a room and its inhabitants."

The presence of a holy book in the home has a positive influence on its residents, but Kabbalah students aren't required to stock their shelves with expensive sets of Hebrew books. And purchasing such books if one can't afford them is certainly out of order. No amount of potential good luck can justify putting oneself in financial jeopardy by buying books or anything else. Kabbalists throughout the centuries have studied the legal area of law that deals with protecting oneself and not putting oneself in jeopardy — physically, emotionally, or economically. Kabbalists often rely on the libraries of local Jewish study houses to supplement their holdings, so that, ultimately, they own some and share some.

That said, one of my Kabbalah teachers said, "Simply to bring a few great Jewish books into one's living room, even without opening them, may very well do some good." And Kabbalists do believe in the power of the Hebrew letter, merely as it sits on a page. It's a time-honored belief among Kabbalists that if one merely passes her eye over certain passages in Hebrew or Aramaic, she can receive the text's blessings. Similarly, anyone who has ever been privileged to be in a synagogue and close to an open Torah (especially someone who's asked to read from the Torah or offer a blessing at the reading of the Torah) knows the awesome look of the Torah scroll. One need not know a letter of the Hebrew alphabet or a word in its vocabulary in order to feel the power of the Hebrew Torah scroll.

You Have to Follow a Dress Code

If you were able to look at portraits of each of the leading Kabbalists throughout history, you would notice that they were all male and all had beards and wore head coverings. In the world of Hasidism today, where the study of Kabbalah is alive and well, beards are common, and men study while wearing a hat or scull cap.

Does this mean that if you're a man you have to follow suit? I'd say no. Growing a beard certainly isn't a requirement for Kabbalah study.

As far as head coverings go, in Jewish tradition, wearing a head covering is a reminder of God's presence. Some men even wear two head coverings at the same time (a skull cap covered by a hat) symbolizing the two *sefirot* of the intellect, *Chochmah* and *Binah* (see Chapter 4).

So is a head covering required? On the one hand, you would never see a man in a traditional house of study or synagogue without one. Traditional Kabbalists would surely agree that covering one's head is as appropriate when studying from holy texts as it is when entering a holy space. But as my teacher insists, "all or nothing" is a false dilemma. It's unreasonable to take on every custom and law at once. You can surely pick up a book that teaches about Kabbalah and learn from it without your head being covered. And I'm confident that God hears all prayers regardless of what you're wearing on your head — or any other part of your body, for that matter.

Many people have also heard of a custom of wearing a red string tied around the wrist. This custom is often linked to the tomb of the matriarch Rachel in Israel, where you can obtain and wear a red string cut from long strands that have been wrapped seven times around the tomb. The red string is then made into a bracelet that's worn as a protective **segula** (seh-*goo*-lah; amulet). Some speculate that the red string has some positive impact because it can inspire the wearer to improve his or her character traits by recalling the fine qualities of the biblical Rachel.

Some say that wearing a red string wards off the *evil eye*. The basic idea of the evil eye is that a person's evil glance has power. There's no physical evidence of such a phenomenon, but to me it isn't a terribly far-fetched notion. A person's evil glance or evil eye may not provoke absolute cause and effect in the world, but the negative thoughts and emotions behind those glances are real. The great sages of Kabbalah designated these glances as the evil eye, or **ayin harah** (*ah*-yin *hah*-rah).

Bottom line: Although there's certainly nothing wrong with donning the red string, it's not a requirement for studying Kabbalah.

You Have to Know Hebrew

You don't have to be an expert in the complexities and beauty of Hebrew in order to be a Kabbalist. Nonetheless, it's absolutely true that unless you know Hebrew's complex grammar, whole areas of Kabbalistic teachings remain off-limits to you because the unique nature of Hebrew grammar expresses some of the most sublime ideas of Kabbalah.

But it would be inconceivable to begin studying Kabbalah in-depth without some knowledge of Hebrew. Even a basic knowledge of the ABCs — **aleph, bet, gimmel** — is a big help. For example, the details in the Five Books of Moses as well as other sacred texts are based on the notion that every Hebrew letter has a numerical equivalent; aleph = 1, bet = 2, gimmel = 3, and so on. This system is called *gematria* (see Figure 17-1). Often, Kabbalists will offer fascinating interpretations of sacred texts by using this system. Many Jewish amulets have been based on the numerical value of Hebrew letters as well. For example, an amulet might have the numerical equivalent of a lucky Hebrew word or phrase on it.

Figure 17-1: Every Hebrew letter has a numerical equivalent. There are no numbers in Hebrew; just this system.

100	ק	10	י	1	א
200	ר	20	כ,ך	2	ב
300	ש	30	ל	3	ג
400	ת	40	מ,ם	4	ד
		50	נ,ן	5	ה
		60	ס	6	ו
		70	ע	7	ז
		80	פ,ף	8	ח
		90	צ,ץ	9	ט

Even the shapes of the Hebrew letters are objects of study for Kabbalists. And the name of each letter also carries significance. For example, the Hebrew letter bet, the second Hebrew letter, means "house." The shape of the letter bet indeed looks like a house with one side open. For the Kabbalist, this letter reflects a powerful lesson about Abraham, who dwelled in a tent that was open on all sides so that he could eagerly go out and greet guests. That gesture of going out to greet guests relates to the *sefirah* of *Chesed,* which Abraham embodies. In other words, a simple drawing of the most primitive house with one side open becomes a reference point to the understanding of the wisdom of *Chesed,* giving, outpouring, charity, and acts of kindness, all of which are expanding outward, just as the *sefirah* of *Chesed* implies.

Students shouldn't be discouraged by the close relationship between Kabbalah and Hebrew, though. One of the greatest Kabbalists who ever lived, the illustrious Rabbi Akiva, is said to have begun learning the ABCs in Hebrew at the age of 40!

Chapter 18

Ten Great Kabbalists in History

The fact that "Kabbalah" means "to receive" implies that Kabbalah is a tradition that's passed from one generation and received by the next. The generations have produced hundreds, if not thousands, of great Kabbalists, many of whom are known not only by their names but by the books they wrote.

In this chapter, I explore ten "great" Kabbalists. To limit the list of great Kabbalists to ten is to distort the fact that Kabbalistic tradition has flourished throughout the world and throughout the centuries. But my editors asked for ten, so ten it is (and I snuck in a few additional greats). I've chosen individuals who I think have particularly special significance in the history of Kabbalah.

Adam

Students of Kabbalah say that the truths of Kabbalah were known to Adam. Tradition teaches that he knew more than anyone would ever know and passed his knowledge on to his descendants, including Hanoch and Methuselah (Genesis 5:21).

Hanoch and Methuselah were the teachers of Noah, and Noah taught his descendants, including Abraham, who studied in the school of Noah's son, Shem. Abraham also sent his son Isaac to study there, and Isaac sent his son Jacob to study with Shem and with Ever, Shem's great-grandson. Jacob's name was changed to Israel, and the Children of Israel, the Jewish people, received the wisdom of Kabbalah.

Adam was the first person. Period. He appears in the very first chapters of the Bible and is considered to be the father of all humankind. That makes him pretty important. But there's more to Adam's story.

The ultimate soul

God didn't first create Adam and then Eve from Adam, as is usually understood, but rather, the first human being was a dual male/female creature. God split the human into two halves representing Adam and Eve. As a result of the original separation, Kabbalistic tradition represents that each human is in some way only half a soul and that part of one's task in life is to locate the other half, to merge with it, and to emulate God by becoming one.

The implication of this image is reflected in the traditional Jewish wedding ceremony. When two individuals marry, Kabbalists believe that the souls of the bride and groom merge and become one.

Kabbalistic tradition also teaches that each individual in the world is really a part of the original Adam and that, in reality, there's only one soul in the world. In other words, on one level, each person is half a soul that must find its other half. But on another level, each person is a tiny spark of a soul, and the human family together constitutes one great soul, the soul of Adam.

The Talmud asks, "Why did God create one man rather than create many individuals throughout the world?" The answer given is that God created one man so that nobody could say, "My ancestor is greater than your ancestor." In other words, Kabbalistic tradition urges everyone to see themselves as part of one large human family.

The first being

Adam's significance in Kabbalah also comes from the notion known as **Adam Kadmon** (*ah*-dum *kahd*-mun; the primordial human). For Kabbalists, the biblical figure Adam is Adam Kadmon, the first being to emerge in the universe.

One of the ideas found in the Bible and represented throughout Kabbalistic tradition is that the primordial person, Adam Kadmon, was created in the image of God. The unusual wording of this idea in the Bible is found in the very first chapter (Genesis 1:26): "And God said, Let us make man in our image, after our likeness; and let them have dominion over the fish of the sea, and over the birds of the air, and over the cattle, and over all the earth, and over every creeping thing that creeps upon the earth."

According to Kabbalah, this statement refers to man in the plural form — "let *them* have dominion" — because the human form is a microcosm of the whole. All the aspects of the universe came together to create the human being. In fact, in Kabbalistic tradition, the words "man" and "world" are often interchangeable.

A frequently quoted verse from the Holy Scriptures found in the book of Job is the phrase, "In my flesh I see God." This phrase implies that the specific and deliberate design of the human being, Adam Kadmon, reveals profound ideas about the nature of the universe.

The Kabbalistic definition of a human being is a creature that lives in the worlds of matter and spirit simultaneously. Adam was the first human being, having both a body and a soul, and this unique combination in the world forms the basis of all the study and speculation about the nature of man.

Abraham

The patriarch Abraham holds great significance in Kabbalistic tradition. Perhaps most important is that Abraham reminded the world that God is One. Unlike other philosophies and religions of the world that conceive of many Gods or no God, Abraham's vision and realization of the oneness of God is a deep, fundamental, and profound one for the Kabbalist.

The oneness of God is a difficult concept to understand, despite its seeming simplicity. As the great Jewish philosopher Maimonides taught, "God is not two or more, but one, unified in a way which surpasses any unity found in the world." In today's world, many things are one, like one sun, one country called the United States, and so on. But the oneness of God is a different kind of unity, one that's outside of time and space. God is considered to be a simple unified existence. This concept requires a lifetime of contemplation and meditation and is addressed at length in Kabbalistic literature.

Kabbalists address the question, "Why did God create the world?" If God indeed exists, what was God's motive? One of the answers that Kabbalists emphatically indicate is *incorrect* is that God "needed" the world in some way. Kabbalists point out that the idea of God needing anyone or anything is impossible because it implies that God lacks something. Kabbalists conceive of God as being the whole and perfect, so God couldn't have created the world because of any need.

An answer offered by Kabbalists as to why God created the world is that God created the world in order to give pleasure to man, and God created the human being in order to receive the most profound pleasure possible: knowledge of God.

Abraham is represented on the Tree of Life (the chart of the ten *sefirot*), as the *sefirah* of *Chesed,* which is expansiveness, outpouring, and giving (see Chapter 4). In a sense, the fundamental nature of Abraham as a giver reflects the divine impulse to create the world and to give pleasure to its inhabitants.

According to many authorities, one of the most important Kabbalistic books, Sefer Yetzirah, was written by the patriarch Abraham (see Chapter 13). Others say that Abraham imparted the wisdom contained in Sefer Yetzirah and passed it down from generation to generation, but Rabbi Akiva (see the next section) actually wrote it all down and formed it into the book that Kabbalists study now.

The Torah records that God offered Abraham the opportunity to participate in the creation of a great nation and offered Abraham an opportunity for a special blessing. Abraham accepted God's offer, and this agreement between God and Abraham was signed and sealed through the ritual of the circumcision, known as **brit milah** (brit mee-*lah*). The word "brit" means "covenant," and all Kabbalists, male and female, enter a covenant with God. This covenant doesn't always involve ritual circumcision (which only pertains to males); it may also be made through a conscious gesture to connect oneself with God always.

A fundamental Kabbalistic notion is the belief that God tests humans. Kabbalists believe that all the trials of life are sent from God and that the ultimate purpose of these trials is to know God. An often repeated notion in Kabbalistic literature is "Without *Binah,* there is no *Da'at.*" This is translated as "Without understanding, there is no knowledge of God." The impact of many trials on the part of the person who receives the trial is a great effort to try to grasp its meaning. Kabbalists use the *sefirah* of *Binah* in an effort to understand their lives and to grasp the ungraspable God.

Abraham is the great representative of the concept of trials from God because, according to Kabbalistic tradition, Abraham experienced ten tests and persevered through each one. The ten tests are as follows:

1. God called to Abraham and urged him to leave the place in which he lived and to travel to the unknown.

2. After God promised Abraham prosperity, God created a famine in the land of Canaan. Abraham faced a feeling of abandonment (or possibly betrayal), but he held onto his faith that God knew what He was doing.

3. Abraham experienced what could be called "government-sponsored injustice" as he faced the trials regarding his wife Sarah in Egypt.

4. Abraham faced a war among the great kings of the time and had to cope with the difficult political atmosphere.

5. Abraham's wife Sarah was seemingly unable to have children.

6. Abraham was commanded to circumcise himself.

7. Abraham experienced injustice at the hands of Avimelech, as recorded in the Bible.

8. Abraham's concubine Hagar was sent away after she became pregnant.

9. Abraham had to send his son Ishmael away.

10. God commanded Abraham to bind and sacrifice his son Isaac.

These tests, the details of which appear in the Torah, are reminiscent of the trials that people face in life. Kabbalists work diligently on themselves in an effort to know within their heart of hearts that all trials ultimately come from God and that, even when they have no idea of why God is doing what He is doing, there is a reason. That reason may be beyond the Kabbalist's knowledge or even ability to understand, but ultimately the Kabbalist believes that everything comes from God.

Rabbi Akiva

Every student of Torah sooner or later falls in love with Rabbi Akiva. Rabbi Akiva was one of the greatest rabbis of all times and perhaps the greatest rabbi in the entire Rabbinic period of Jewish history (considered to be from 70 CE to 500 CE).

One of the remarkable aspects of Rabbi Akiva's personal story is that that he didn't know the ABCs of Hebrew until he was 40 years old. According to the Talmud, before Rabbi Akiva was 40, he was an ignorant shepherd who was actually hostile toward religion in general and Jewish tradition in particular. But a young woman named Rachel, who was the daughter of one of the richest men in Jerusalem, saw Akiva the shepherd and detected his great potential. Upon their meeting, Rachel said to Akiva that she would marry him if he promised to dedicate himself to learning Torah. He agreed, and they were married. Unfortunately, her father was quite unhappy with the match and disowned her, not speaking to her for over 24 years. The story ends happily with the reconciliation of father and daughter after Rachel's father learned of the greatness of Rabbi Akiva and, in turn, the insight that Rachel had into her husband's character, abilities, and potential.

Rabbi Akiva is clearly the hero for all who decide late in life to return to the spiritual path. Rabbi Akiva started late in life and grew to the very pinnacle of spiritual development.

Rabbi Akiva makes hundreds of appearances in Rabbinic literature and is known as one of the great mystics of Jewish history and tradition. In fact, a story that every Kabbalist is familiar with tells of four rabbis who entered an orchard. The Hebrew word for "orchard," **pardes** (par-*days*), is the source of the English word "paradise." Pardes is also an acronym of four letters: p, r, d, and s, each of which stands for a different level of Torah study.

- The "p" of "pardes" stands for the Hebrew word **p'shat** (puh-*shot*), which indicates the literal meaning of a text.

- The "r" stands for the Hebrew world **remez** (*reh*-mez; hint), which refers to those aspects of the Torah that aren't offered to the reader explicitly but rather are hinted at. Some things in the text are implied rather than stated explicitly.

- The "d" stands for the Hebrew word **d'rash** (duh-*rahsh*) and indicates the message or the ethical or spiritual teaching that one can derive from the text.

- The "s" stands for the Hebrew word **sod** (sowd; secret), which refers to the hidden, esoteric, Kabbalistic meaning embedded within the Torah text.

As the story goes, four great rabbis — Ben Azzai, Ben Zoma, Elisha ben Abuya, and Rabbi Akiva — entered the orchard or garden of Torah study individually. These four rabbis explored the greatest depths of the Torah and encountered the most sublime, esoteric teachings. What happened to the four rabbis indicates the danger of mystical study.

- Ben Azzai entered the mystical depths and died.

- Ben Zoma entered the mystical depths and went crazy.

- Elisha ben Abuya entered the mystical depths and became a heretic.

- Rabbi Akiva, as the text indicates, "entered in peace and left in peace."

What happened to Rabbi Akiva in this story and what happened to the other three rabbis is one basis for the explanation of why the study of Kabbalah has been discouraged over the centuries. When you enter a field of study that's over your head, you risk becoming confused and alienated from the subject. A curriculum must be designed with a certain degree of logic in mind; you need to learn the basics before entering deeper and more complex realms. If a student encounters complex Torah study prematurely, he or she may very well run away from it all.

Rabbi Akiva is also well known for a famous statement found in the **Mishnah** (*mish*-nah, see Chapter 13), the written record of the Oral Tradition passed on from Moses at Mount Sinai to the present. The statement is, "All is foreseen, and free will is given." Needless to say, this statement is a paradox that refers to God's relationship to the world. On the one hand, God sees and knows everything: what was, what is, and what will be. On the other hand, God has given humans a divine spark of creativity and free will. If God knows what was, is, and will be, how can humans possibly choose freely? Doesn't the fact that God knows what will be imply that everything is in the cards? Kabbalists have meditated on this paradox since time in memorial and continue to do so.

Rabbi Akiva also is credited with the expression **Gam zu l'tovah** (gahm zoo leh-*toe*-vah; everything is for the best), which I discuss in depth in Chapter 5. This well-known expression is the basis of Kabbalistic faith in God. (Rabbi Akiva's teacher of 22 years, Rabbi Nachum Ish Gamzu, taught him this expression, but nevertheless, most students know the expression from Rabbi Akiva himself.)

Kabbalists have much to learn from Rabbi Akiva, as evidence by the fact that he appears many times throughout the 63 volumes of the Talmud. He was the spiritual nourishment for thousands of disciples in his lifetime, and, in some ways, every Kabbalist and every Jew considers himself or herself to be a disciple of Rabbi Akiva.

Rabbi Shimon Bar Yochai

Rabbi Shimon Bar Yochai was a student of Rabbi Akiva and lived around the year 135 CE. Rabbi Shimon Bar Yochai was active in the revolt against the Romans and ultimately was forced to flee when the Romans pursued him. Both he and his son, Rabbi Elazar ben Shimon, hid in a cave where, according to legend, they remained for 13 years studying the Torah, specifically the secret hidden esoteric level of Torah study now known as Kabbalah. Rabbi Shimon wrote down the material that he and his son generated and discussed during their 13 years of Torah study, and that written material formed itself into the great Kabbalistic text known as the Zohar (see Chapter 13).

Rabbi Shimon bar Yochai was buried in the town of Meron, Israel; to this day, many people travel to Meron on a day on the Jewish calendar known as **Lag b'Omer** (lahg buh-*oh*-mehr). Lag b'Omer, which is the 33rd day of the counting of Omer (see Chapter 11), was the day Rabbi Shimon bar Yochai died. Every year on this day, thousands visit Meron to study the Zohar, pray, and think about the greatness of this extraordinary Kabbalist.

Kabbalists tell a story that when Rabbi Shimon Bar Yochai was on his deathbed, he began to teach Kabbalah to those around him, offering deep secrets of Kabbalistic tradition. He knew that it was his last day on earth, and he taught and taught, hoping to fit as much teaching as possible into that one day. Legend has it that a miracle occurred on that day: The Sun stood still and refused to set, and because of this, a fire began to burn around Rabbi Shimon Bar Yochai's house. Custom has it that when pilgrims go to Meron on the 33rd day of the Omer, a great fire is rekindled again in his memory. Visitors to Meron see many bonfires on Lag b'Omer, and the custom is also performed on that day throughout Israel.

Rabbi Isaac Luria, the Holy Ari

It's an undisputed fact of Kabbalistic history that the greatest Kabbalist of all time was Rabbi Isaac Luria. The first three letters of Ashkenazi Rabbi Isaac are A-R-I, which forms an acronym for the Hebrew of his name "The Godly Rabbi Isaac, but also is a Hebrew word in itself. The word **ari** (ah-*ree*) means "lion." And like the lion is the king of the jungle, the Ari is the undisputed king of Kabbalistic tradition.

The Ari proved his genius at a young age as a student of great rabbis. He transformed Judaism in its entirety with his teachings about God, the creation of the world, and the metaphysics of existence, and by revealing the Kabbalistic meanings of the holy days and rituals of Jewish life. His teachings spread far and reached every corner of the Jewish world. Many of the customs that he taught became essential parts of Jewish life in general. Despite his immense influence, Rabbi Isaac Luria never wrote down his teachings. They were preserved by his many students, the most important of whom was Rabbi Chaim Vital, a prolific writer in the 16th and 17th centuries.

The irony of ironies is that the Ari died when he was only 39 years old. Many have heard it said that one shouldn't study Kabbalah before the age of 40. But as I explain in Chapter 17, this isn't a rule but rather a warning that one must learn the basics before exploring the depths of Kabbalistic tradition. But one should also remember that the greatest Kabbalist who ever lived, the Ari, didn't even live to age 40. Clearly, the warning about not studying until one is 40 years old isn't meant to be a hard and fast rule.

The Shelah HaKodesh, Rabbi Isaiah Horowitz

Rabbi Isaiah Horowitz was born in Prague and died in the holy Kabbalistic city of Tzfat. Throughout his life, he was the leader of many different Jewish communities throughout Europe.

It's common in Jewish history to refer to a person not by his actual name but rather by a great book he has written. In the case of Rabbi Isaiah Horowitz, his masterpiece is **Shnei Luchot HaBrit** (sheh-*nay* loo-*khowt* hah-*brit;* the two tablets of the covenant). The acronym for this Hebrew expression is Sh-L-H, which is pronounced she-*luh.* This acronym has become the more popular way of referring to Rabbi Isaiah Horowitz.

In fact, many people who know Rabbi Horowitz's work and have studied it all their lives aren't even aware of his real name. They refer to him as the Shelah or more commonly as the **Shelah HaKodesh** (sheh-*luh* hah-*koe*-desh; the Holy Shelah).

The Shelah HaKodesh taught a Kabbalistic prayer that's recited by some Kabbalists today. What appears in Table 18-1 is an abridged version of that prayer, which contains several of the major points of Kabbalists that I explain throughout this book.

Table 18-1	Prayer Taught by the Shelah HaKodesh
Portion of Prayer	*Translation*
You were God before you created the universe and You are God after you created the universe. For all eternity You are God!	God created the universe, and God is outside of time (see Chapter 16).
You created Your world in order that man should know You.	God created humans to give them pleasure, and the greatest pleasure is to know God (see Chapter 6).
To preserve and maintain the world You gave us two mitzvot: "Be fruitful and multiply" and "Teach your children to speak of [Torah]." The purpose of these mitzvot is one: That the world be populated with people who honor You, that we and our children and every Jewish child, will know Your name and study Your Torah.	Each day, the Kabbalist is obligated to study and to perform acts of loving-kindness. Kabbalists teach this to their children and teach them how to study the wisdom of the sages (see Chapter 9).
Therefore I approach You, God, King of all Kings, to present my request. My eyes are to You, that You accept my prayer and favor me.	Learning how to pray is a major activity in Kabbalah (see Chapter 15).
Send me sons and daughters — and may they too have children and grandchildren until the last generation — so that each of us may all learn and teach it, live by its words and uphold it, out of love. Make our eyes light up from the mere mention of Torah, our hearts cling to Your mitzvot, so that we may love and revere You.	Study of the Torah and the wisdom literature that it has inspired is a daily activity for the Kabbalist (see Chapter 14).

(continued)

Table 18-1 *(continued)*

Portion of Prayer	Translation
Father, merciful Father, grant each of us a long and blessed life. I also ask and beg of You: May my children and children's until the end of time be kosher Jews. May no fault be found in them or in me. Instead, let us be filled with peace and truth, goodness and harmony, in the eyes of God and in the eyes of man.	For Kabbalists, God is infinite. The "eyes" of God are all seeing, all knowing, and all powerful (see Chapter 5).
May they be thoroughly proficient in Torah; masters of Scripture, of Mishnah, of Talmud, and of Kabbalah.	The progression from Scripture to Mishnah to Talmud and then to the study of Kabbalah has been the recommended curriculum for centuries (see Chapters 13 and 14).
May they be masters of mitzvot, of kindness and exemplary behavior. May they serve You with love and inner fear, not external fear.	The guiding principle for daily living is lovingkindness (see Chapter 9).
You are the Knower-of-all-Secrets. You know what is hidden in my heart.	A fundamental assumption of Kabbalah is that God knows everything, and God is involved with every detail of Creation (see Chapters 5 and 16).
My intention is for Your great and holy Name and for Your holy Torah.	Kabbalists pay particular attention to the subject of paying attention and knowing one's intention, which they call kavanah (see Chapter 15).
So please answer my prayer! In the merit of the holy Patriarchs, Abraham, Isaac and Jacob, answer my prayer and save the children! May the branches be like their root! In their merit and in the merit of Your servant King David, the fourth leg of Your throne.	For Kabbalists, the patriarchs and several major biblical figures have special and important meaning within Kabbalah and the system of the ten *sefirot* (see Chapter 4).
May the words of my mouth and the thoughts of my heart be pleasing to You, God, my rock and my redeemer.	When Kabbalists pray, it's like pouring out one's heart to the most trusted friend (see Chapter 15).

During his life, the Shelah was wealthy and was a very generous philanthropist. In his teachings, he stressed that life should be filled with joy and that transforming the evil inclination into good thoughts and actions should be a major activity in people's lives. His influence was profound, and in some ways, he's one of the fathers of the greatest revival movement in Jewish history, the Hasidic movement, which is grounded in Kabbalah (see Chapter 3).

On a personal note, I've done extensive genealogical research and discovered to my great surprise and delight that I'm a direct descendent of the Shelah HaKodesh. My great-great-great grandfather, Rabbi Chaim Yosef Gottlieb, was a rabbi who taught Kabbalah in Eastern Europe; he was a descendent of the Shelah HaKodesh on his mother's side, so that makes me a direct descendent as well. I have to believe that, in the same way that the Shelah HaKodesh was known as someone who popularized Kabbalah and spread its teachings throughout Poland and Eastern Europe, *Kabbalah For Dummies* is my opportunity to bring the wisdom of the great Kabbalistic sages to those who are thirsty for spiritual nourishment.

Rabbi Israel Baal Shem Tov

Rabbi Israel was born approximately 1698 in a small Ukrainian town near the Russian-Polish border. Legend has it that his parents, Eliezer and Sarah, were quite old at the time of his birth and that they died when he was quite young. According to the story, the last thing Rabbi Israel's father said to him before his death was, "Fear nothing else but God."

The young Rabbi Israel grew up immersed in the study of Kabbalah and associated with many saintly people, including the masters of Kabbalah, who nourished him in the most profound way. When Rabbi Israel was 36 years old, he revealed himself to the world and became known as a holy and righteous teacher.

With this life change, he also acquired the name **Baal Shem Tov** (bah-*ahl* shem towv; Master of the Good Name) because of his ability to use the names of God to perform miracles. (Although this title is rare, other people have held it as well.)

Rabbi Israel, the Baal Shem Tov, founded the Hasidic movement, a revolutionary movement that was the greatest revivalist movement in the history of the Jewish people. The word **hasid** (khah-sid) means "pious one." The core idea in the Hasidic movement is the Baal Shem Tov's interest in popularizing Kabbalah.

The Baal Shem Tov's teachings were mostly based on those of the Ari (see the section "Rabbi Isaac Luria, the Holy Ari" earlier in this chapter). But the big difference between the Ari and the Baal Shem Tov is that the Ari's Kabbalah was meant for a small core group of deeply pious individuals, whereas the Kabbalah of the Baal Shem Tov was intended for everyone, from the simplest person to the greatest sages. He wanted everybody to be able to reap the spiritual rewards of the profound teachings of Kabbalah. The genius of the Baal Shem Tov was his ability to bring the most abstract and sublime ideas down to a level that anyone could understand.

A commonality between the Ari and the Baal Shem Tov is that is that neither wrote down his teachings. In the case of the Baal Shem Tov, his leading disciple, Rabbi Yakov Yosef of Polonoye, began the dissemination of the Baal Shem Tov's teachings in a book called Toldot Yakov Yosef and continued the dissemination process with several other books. The Baal Shem Tov's disciples and their disciples to the present have written thousands of volumes that teach and expand upon his wisdom.

The Baal Shem Tov died on the second day of Shavuot in the year 1760, but his teachings and influence not only live on but also have grown as the decades have passed. His teachings and the movement that it spawned have had a major impact on Jewish practice and belief for all of Jewry throughout the world. Included are the tens of thousands of Hasidim around the world who base their lives on the teachings of the Baal Shem Tov, all of which are grounded in Kabbalah.

The Vilna Gaon

The Hebrew term for "genius" is **gaon** (*gah*-own), and Rabbi Elijah, the Rabbi of Vilna in Lithuania, who was born in 1720, was known far and wide for his unique genius. Ultimately, he became known as the **Vilna Gaon** (the genius of Vilna). His genius showed itself when he was very young; he was already giving public lectures and classes when he was only 7 years old!

Legend says that by age 7, the Vilna Gaon's intellect had fully blossomed, and by the time he was 10, he was recognized as one of the great teachers of all time. Legend also has it that for a time he took a vow of poverty and wandered from town to town until he once again came back to the city of Vilna.

The Vilna Gaon devoted his life to the study of Torah. He had a photographic memory as well as a profound grasp of both the revealed Torah and the esoteric Torah, and he was quite knowledgeable in secular fields of study, too. He was also known for his generosity and kindness as well as for his commentary on the Talmud and other texts, particularly in the realm of correcting mistakes that scribes had made over the centuries.

The Vilna Gaon was well-known as an opponent of some of the practices and perspectives of the Hasidic movement. He was wary of a number of changes in Jewish practice that some of the great leaders of Hasidism enacted (see the preceding section). His students and followers became known, mostly to Hasidim, as the **mitnagdim** (mit-*nahg*-deem; opponents). It's an unfortunate and commonly held myth that mitnagdim are against Hasidism. Hasidic Jews and mitnagdim are actually well-integrated in Jewish life today. Mitnagdim are merely very traditional Jews who don't consider themselves Hasidic.

It's a surprise to many that, despite his great opposition to the Hasidic movement, the Vilna Gaon was a well-known Kabbalist. In fact, he wrote perhaps the greatest commentary on the mystical text Sefer Yetzirah (see Chapter 13).

Rabbi Adin Steinstaltz

In 1937, Rabbi Adin Steinsaltz was born in Jerusalem into a secular family, and he didn't begin his serious Torah studies until he was a teenager. But his reputation as a genius and profound teacher grew rapidly, and by the tender age of 25, he was already teaching some of the elders in Jerusalem.

Rabbi Steinsaltz reports that his parents, who were secular Jews inclined toward socialism, were deep skeptics and brought him up to be one, too. As he has quipped, "My mother was a skeptic, my father was a skeptic; they taught me how to be a skeptic. I am such a skeptic that I became skeptical of skepticism."

Rabbi Steinsaltz has done something in today's generation that hasn't been done in 1,000 years: He has written a comprehensive commentary on the entire 63 volumes of the Talmud. Not since Rashi, the great biblical and Talmudic commentator who lived around the year 1000, has any one individual written a vast commentary on the entire Talmud that's considered an unparalleled work of genius.

Rabbi Steinsaltz is described by many as one of the most influential rabbis in modern times, not only for his commentary on the Talmud but also for his time spent traveling throughout the world, teaching and lecturing and trying to bring Jewish wisdom and Jewish sources to all comers. Rabbi Steinsaltz has been teaching Kabbalah in Jerusalem and elsewhere for decades, and his books in English are probably the best introductions to Kabbalah and Kabbalistic ideas available to the serious modern reader who's prepared to invest significant time and effort to absorb and understand his teachings. Lots of people (including me, with this book) write books "about" Kabbalah, but Rabbi Steinsaltz is one of few who writes books that *are* Kabbalah. His books represent authentic Kabbalistic tradition.

Among his most important Kabbalistic texts in English are *The Thirteen Petalled Rose* (Basic Books), *The Sustaining Utterance* (Jason Aronson), *The Long Shorter Way* (Jason Aronson), *In the Beginning* (Jason Aronson), and *The Candle of God* (Jason Aronson). Any English language reader who wants to encounter authentic Kabbalistic teachings by a contemporary master would do well to track down these books. In particular, *The Thirteen Petalled Rose* explores the fundamental ideas that hold up the entire edifice that is Kabbalah.

What? How Could You Have Left Out . . .

I can just hear my friends, colleagues, teachers, students, and children now: "Why did you pick *these* people when you could have picked . . .?" So to calm them down a little, here are ten more strong candidates for my list. If you're interested in Kabbalah, I strongly suggest that you check them out.

- **Rabbi Moshe Cordovero** (1522–1570) was one of the greatest Kabbalists of all time. At the age of 20, a "heavenly voice" told him to study Kabbalah. He's the author of one of the classics of Kabbalah, *Pardes Rimonim* (Orchard of Pomegranates).

- **Rabbi Abraham Isaac Kook** (1864–1935) was the first chief rabbi of modern Israel and the author of several highly regarded books, including *Orot* (Lights).

- **Rabbi Aryeh Kaplan** (1934–1983) was an American rabbi and prolific author who was known to have a deep understanding of Kabbalah and modern physics. He wrote many popular books, including *Jewish Meditation: A Practical Guide* (Schocken Books), on a variety of meditative techniques including mantra meditation (with suggested phrases and Bible verses to use as mantras), contemplation, visualization, and conversing with God.

- **Rabbi Yitzchak Ginsburgh** (1944–) is a popular teacher of Kabbalah in Israel today and a prolific writer. You can find more about his work and his teachings online, particularly at www.inner.org.

- **Rabbi Joseph Karo** (1488–1575) was author of the Code of Jewish Law, which remains an authority. He was a great Kabbalist and one of the most influential sages in all of Jewish history.

- **Rabbi Zalman Schachter-Shalomi** (1924–) is one of the most influential rabbis in the United States today. He's generally considered the founder of the Jewish Renewal Movement ("a worldwide, transdenominational movement grounded in Judaism's prophetic and mystical traditions") and is the author of *Paradigm Shift* (Jason Aronson) as well as other books that express his innovative ideas. His teachings are rooted in Kabbalah.

- **Rabbi Nachman of Breslov** (1772–1810), known as Rebbe Nachman, was one of the great Hasidic masters. His teachings, rooted in Kabbalah, are widely distributed in books and pamphlets throughout the world by his many disciples.

- **Rabbi Abraham Abulafia** (1240–1290) developed an unusual approach to Kabbalah that's sometimes called *ecstatic Kabbalah* or *prophetical Kabbalah* and involves meditative methods (using Hebrew letters and often their numerical values) to achieve higher states of awareness.

- **Rabbi Schneur Zalman of Liadi** (1745–1812) was one of the leading Hasidic masters in history. He was a student of Rabbi Dovber of Mezeritch, the leading student of the Baal Shem Tov (see "Rabbi Israel Baal Shem Tov" earlier in this chapter). Today, many Hasidim and others continue to study his masterpiece of Kabbalah, the Tanya, along with his other books, which are among the most influential in all of Judaism.

- **Elie Wiesel** (1928–) is best known as a recipient of the Nobel Prize for Peace and for his many deeply moving and profound books. But as a teenager, he was a serious student of Kabbalah. He has continued his studies throughout his life, and his many spiritual insights appear in his novels and essays.

Giving Madonna a break (yes, that Madonna)

She certainly isn't one of the greatest Kabbalists in history, but Madonna, the enormously gifted singer, actress, and show business personality, has probably done more than anyone in the world in recent times to make the word "Kabbalah" a familiar one. Madonna doesn't represent herself as a master of Kabbalah — she's never claimed that. What she has claimed, however, and what I respect her for, is that she's interested in Kabbalah.

Unfortunately, some writers and members of the press haven't been kind to her when it comes to her Kabbalistic interests, and I'm eager to go on record here and now to say that I'm disappointed in the press and in certain journalists and writers who have taken her to task for her interest. Madonna has just as much a right as anyone to explore questions like "Who am I?," "Where did I come from?," and "Where am I going?" Madonna has just as much a right as anyone to explore all kinds of philosophies and approaches to living with the hope of acquiring some true wisdom to apply to life's questions, puzzles, and riddles. And Madonna has just as much a right as anyone to look at Jewish tradition with the hope that it can offer insights and ideas that will serve her well. And apparently, that's exactly what she's done.

Chapter 19

Ten Places that Kabbalists Visit

In This Chapter

▶ Discovering the sacred places on the Kabbalistic map

▶ Paying one's respects closer to home

Kabbalisticly speaking, holiness is everywhere, but some places have a special status within the world of Kabbalah. This chapter covers some of the highlights of a Kabbalistic travelogue.

Jerusalem

When Kabbalists pray three times a day, they face toward Jerusalem. Jerusalem, which archaeological findings indicate has existed since the third millennium BCE, was the capital of the Jewish kingdoms of Israel, Judah, and Judea during both the First and Second Temple periods.

The name Jerusalem likely comes from a contraction of two words:

✔ **Yerusha** (yeh-*roo*-sha; heritage or inheritance)

✔ **Salem** (sah-*lem;* whole or peace)

According to the book of Genesis in the Bible, shalem is the original name of Jerusalem (Genesis 14:18).

Historical Jerusalem

According to Jewish tradition, Jerusalem was founded by the ancestors of Abraham, Shem, and Ever. In approximately 1000 BCE, King David conquered Jerusalem and declared it the capital of the kingdom of Israel. In 960 BCE, King Solomon built the First Temple there, but in 596 BCE, the Babylonians conquered the city, destroyed the city walls, and burned the Temple.

Eventually, the Jews who fled Jerusalem were allowed to return to the holy city and rebuild the Temple. Jerusalem was the capital of Judah and remained central to Jewish worship for centuries.

After the Second Temple was destroyed by the Romans in 70 CE, any hopes for the reestablishment of Jewish sovereignty in the land were dashed. In 135 CE, the Romans, under Hadrian, suppressed the Bar Kochva uprising (known as the fall of Bethar), killing 580,000 Jews. The Romans ran a plow over Jerusalem to completely destroy the Holy City and banned the Jews from living there. Jerusalem didn't serve as the capital of any state until 1948, when the modern state of Israel was established with Jerusalem as its capital. In spite of the city's turbulent history, Jews have been living in Jerusalem continuously for over two millennia.

Prayers of remembrance and longing for Jerusalem appear a number of times in the Jewish liturgy that Kabbalists have recited for centuries. Three times each day, Kabbalists recite traditional prayers that include the hope that Jerusalem and the line of King David are restored.

Jerusalem today

Today, visitors to Jerusalem see a crossroads of three major religious traditions: Judaism, Christianity, and Islam. Particularly visible are the great number of Hasidim who live and worship in the holy city.

Generally speaking, the fact that Jerusalem was the site of both Holy Temples is what makes it so central to Jews. The Torah, for example, defines the three major holy days of Sukkot, Pesach, and Shavuot as part of the Pilgrim Festivals, when Jews from far and wide came to Jerusalem to participate in the spiritual rituals performed in the Holy Temple. Kabbalists today hope for and imagine a rebuilding of the Holy Temple on the Temple Mount site of the previous temples.

Another interesting site in Jerusalem is the Ramban Synagogue. The famous Kabbalist, Rabbi Moshe ben Nachman, known by the acronym **Ramban** (rahm-*bahn*), established a synagogue on Mount Zion that moved to the Old City of Jerusalem in 1400. The original columns of the synagogue are still standing, and today, the synagogue functions on a regular basis and has become a popular site for those exploring Jewish history in general and the history of Kabbalah in particular.

The most famous pilgrimage site in Jerusalem today is the Western Wall, which was a huge retaining wall for the temple that was constructed on the Temple Mount. Great numbers of visitors to Israel are drawn to this ancient wall and express their heartfelt prayers there, as Jews have done for many centuries.

Tzfat

The city of **Tzfat** (tzeh-*faht*) is located in northern Israel in the mountains of the upper Galilee. Tzfat is considered to be one of the four Jewish holy cities in Israel, together with Jerusalem, Hebron and Tiberias. (You may find references to the city spelled Safed, Zefat, Tsfat, Zfat, Safad, Safes, Safet, and Tzfat.)

According to one legend, Tzfat is where Shem (the son of Noah) and Ever (the grandson of Noah) established a yeshiva in which the patriarch Jacob studied for many years.

The city flourished in the 1500s, when many great Jewish scholars and mystics made Tzfat their home following the expulsion of the Jews from Spain in 1492. Tzfat functioned as an important spiritual center during this time.

Some of the greatest Kabbalists called the city home, including Rabbi Isaac Luria (the Ari); Rabbi Shlomo Alkabetz, who wrote the famous song recited on Friday nights, "L'cha Dodi"; and Rabbi Joseph Karo, the author of the **Shulchan Aruch** (shool-*khan* ah-*rukh*); the Code of Jewish Law). As well, many of the most holy people in the history of Kabbalah are buried in and around Tzfat. For example, an ancient Jewish cemetery located in the city houses the tomb of the great Kabbalist Rabbi Isaac Luria as well as the graves of Rabbi Moshe ben Zimra, Rabbi Shlomo Alkabetz, Rabbi Moshe Cordovero, and Rabbi Joseph Karo. One can also find in Tzfat the tombs of Shem and Ever, the two descendents of Noah, and near Tzfat is the cave where the students of Rabbi Shimon Bar Yochai are buried.

You may be interested to know that the first printing press in the Middle East was set up in Tzfat, and in 1578, the first Hebrew book printed in Israel was published in Tzfat.

Unfortunately, Tzfat has been the victim of some serious earthquakes as well as plagues and attacks. Yet, in modern times, Tzfat has seen a revival, with many immigrants to modern Israel settling in the historic city. Today, Tzfat has an active community of returnees to Judaism, known as **baalei teshuva** (bah-*ah*-lay teh-*shoo*-vah) and several major centers for the study of Kabbalah, as well as artists who base their work on core images in Kabbalah, such as David Friedman's studio presents. The beautiful mountain setting of Tzfat and its magnificent views make it a beautiful place to visit or to live.

Meron, Israel

The town of Meron, Israel, contains the tombs of some of the greatest personalities of the Rabbinic period, including Rabbi Yochanan haSandlar, Rabbi Shimon Bar Yochai, Hillel, Shammai, and many of the students of Hillel and Shammai. These tombs have been pilgrimage spots for centuries.

Rabbi Shimon Bar Yochai, who was one of the great rabbis of the Rabbinic (Talmudic) period, is traditionally thought of as the author of the supreme Kabbalistic work, the Zohar. He was one of the greatest disciples of Rabbi Akiva and earned a reputation as a miracle worker.

It's generally believed that Rabbi Shimon Bar Yochai died on the holy day of **Lag B'Omer** (lahg beh-*oh*-mare). Because of this legend, a custom developed over the centuries to observe and celebrate the anniversary date of Rabbi Shimon Bar Yochai's death in Meron (his burial place as well as the burial place of his son Rabbi Elazar bar Shimon). This custom is as popular as ever today. Each year, you can see thousands of pilgrims out picnicking and celebrating in and around the city of Meron on this auspicious anniversary of the great sage's death.

Holy Gravesites in the Holy Land

Visiting the gravesites of holy individuals has been a Jewish custom since time immemorial. The Bible, the Talmud, and the Zohar contain many stories indicating the importance of visiting and praying at the graves of the great holy sages. For example, a Rabbinic legend records that the patriarch Jacob buried his wife Rachel on the side of the road at Beit Lechem (Bethlehem) in order that the site could be visited and prayers could be offered to God based on the great merits of the matriarch Rachel.

In Hebrew, a cemetery is often called a **Beit HaChayim** (bait hah-*khah*-yeem; house of life) based on the spiritual idea that the faithful are considered "living" even after they're dead. A Talmudic teaching says that studying the teachings of a sage at his gravesite is customary and that, when this is done, the lips of the sage move along with the lips of the person who's currently studying his words. On a similar note, the Zohar contains a teaching that when one prays at holy gravesites, the souls of the holy people can intercede on behalf of the one who prays.

Throughout the land of Israel are many sites containing the graves of the greatest personalities in Jewish history. The Cave of the Patriarchs, for example, located in Chevron (Hebron) includes the burial places of Adam and Eve, Abraham and Sarah, and Isaac and Rebecca. The graves of some of the greatest Talmudic personalities, including Rabbi Akiva and Nachman Ish Gamzu as well as the great medieval philosopher Maimonides, are frequently visited by tourists and the many individuals who know of the tradition to visit the graves of the great sages.

Holy Gravesites in Europe

Some of the most illustrious personalities who devoted their lives to learning and teaching Kabbalah were buried in Eastern Europe, and their gravesites have been established as pilgrimage places over the generations.

A custom of writing out prayer requests and reading them aloud at these gravesites has developed over time. Some pilgrims then tear the paper to symbolize the prayer being delivered, and they leave the scraps of paper in front of the grave. While in Hungary, I visited the grave of one of the great Kabbalists, known as the Kallover Rebbe. When I arrived at his grave, I found a large number of scraps of paper on the ground, indicating that, even in recent days, pilgrims came to pour their hearts out in prayer at the grave of this great Kabbalist.

The Baal Shem Tov (Rabbi Israel ben Eliezer), the founder of Hasidism, which spread the fundamental ideas of Kabbalah to the masses, was buried in the last town in which he lived, Medzhibus, in the Ukraine. His clearly marked grave remains there, and to this day, thousands of people devoted to the Kabbalistic teachings of the Baal Shem Tov visit his grave each year.

Another great Kabbalistic personality, Rabbi Nachman of Breslov, is buried in Eastern Europe. Shortly before he died in 1810, Rabbi Nachman arrived in the town of Uman, Ukraine, and his grave there remains a shrine and is regularly visited by his followers and admirers.

There are many other grave sites of illustrious rabbis in Eastern Europe as well.

A Holy Gravesite in the United States

Montefiore Cemetery in Queens, New York, is the final resting place of two great contemporary Kabbalists, Rabbi Joseph Isaac Schneerson and Rabbi Menachem Mendel Schneerson. Rabbi Joseph Isaac Schneerson was the sixth Lubavitcher Rebbe, and after his death, the new Rebbe, Rabbi Menachem Mendel Schneerson, frequently visited his father-in-law's gravesite with his prayers and the prayers of thousands of others.

When the seventh Rebbe, Menachem Mendel Schneerson died, he was laid to rest beside his father-in-law. Each year thousands of people visit the graves of both rabbis and pour out their hearts in prayer.

A well-known custom at the Western Wall in Jerusalem is writing a prayer to God, folding it up, and sticking it into one of the cracks in the wall. These notes are known as **kvitlach** (kvit-lakh). In a similar manner, when visiting the grave of the last two Lubavitcher Rebbes, it's customary to write kvitlach and read them before the graves. These pieces of paper usually contain heartfelt prayers and requests to these great holy men asking them to join in support of the prayers.

Today, a visitation center built adjacent to the graves of these two great Kabbalists is open 24 hours a day, and it isn't unusual to find people at the graves of these great Kabbalists at all hours of the day and night.

The Mikvah

A **mikvah** (*mihk*-vah) is a natural body of water or a gathering of water that's connected to a source of natural water. A mikvah contains about 200 gallons of water and is uniquely designed for immersion. Jewish and Kabbalistic tradition identifies water as the source of all living things, so a mikvah has to be filled with *living waters,* which means that it has to flow from a source that's never dormant. A mikvah can be filled with rainwater, fresh spring water, or melted snow.

In traditional Jewish life, a married woman uses a mikvah in conjunction with her monthly menstrual cycle. However, in the world of Kabbalah and specifically in the Hasidic world today, men as well as women use mikvahs. Some Hasidic men visit the mikvah and immerse themselves in its waters every Friday afternoon before the arrival of Shabbat, but others are known to visit the mikvah every day, 363 days a year (the days of Tisha B'Av and Yom Kippur are exempted; see Chapter 11).

Entering the mikvah and submerging one's naked self in the water brings about a symbolic purification. A mikvah isn't used for physical cleansing; there's no soap, no scrubbing, and no concern for cleanliness. Rather, submerging oneself in the waters of the mikvah is a symbolic act of immersing in the waters and emerging as in Genesis to take in the breath of God.

When I visited the city of Tzfat (see the entry earlier in this chapter), one of the places pointed out to me was the mikvah of the Ari, Rabbi Isaac Luria. According to tradition, this natural gathering of waters in a cave in the hills of Tzfat is the very mikvah used by the great Kabbalists centuries ago. Like countless people before me, I recited my prayers, prepared myself spiritually and physically, and submerged myself in the icy waters of the mikvah of the Ari. It was a particularly moving experience because

- ✔ I truly felt a sense of continuity from one generation to another, tracing back centuries to the Ari himself. So many Kabbalists and students of Jewish tradition have taken those same steps and entered the same living waters.

- ✔ By stripping down and fully submerging myself in the living waters, I truly felt a sense of purification, and that, of course, is precisely what the mikvah is about.

Most cities in the United States with significant Jewish communities maintain at least one mikvah, but these are usually reserved for women who use them in conjunction with their monthly cycles. The mikvahs are also used during conversion ceremonies, when a convert to Judaism is required to enter the mikvah and be submerged to symbolize rebirthing one's earthly spiritual identity.

Cities and neighborhoods with traditional Hasidic communities usually have mikvahs especially dedicated to use by men who wish to continue the centuries-old tradition. To use a mikvah today, it's best to contact your local Jewish Federation or Jewish Family Service, who maintain lists of Jewish programs and resources made available across the denominations and neighborhoods.

The Synagogue

A synagogue is obviously a Jewish house of worship, and certainly not all synagogues focus on Kabbalistic tradition. Nevertheless, serious students of Kabbalah have a close connection to the synagogue for a number of reasons.

- ✔ To participate in a complete prayer service, it's necessary to pray with nine other people. (In Orthodox circles, the ten people must be men over the age of 13, whereas in liberal Jewish communities, women are also counted in the **minyan** [*min*-yahn; quorum].) For example, the mourner's prayer, known as Mourner's Kaddish, must be said in the presence of a minyan. In addition, the **Kedusha** (keh-*doo*-shah), a particularly sacred part of a daily synagogue service, is recited when a minyan of ten is present.

✔ In the synagogue on Shabbat, the sacred Torah scroll is taken out of its station, known as the **aron hakodesh** (*ah*-rone hah-*koe*-desh; holy ark), and read publicly to the congregation. This custom that Kabbalists have participated in for many centuries is a moving and heart-stirring ritual and one that requires a minyan of ten, according to Jewish law.

✔ Tradition teaches that the **Shechina** (sheh-*khee*-nah; presence of God) dwells intimately among a minyan of ten or more who gather together in a synagogue.

The Bedroom

After reading about some of the sacred places in the world of interest to a Kabbalist, you may be thinking it odd to list the bedroom as one of the ten places that Kabbalist's visit. But by "bedroom," what I really mean is the marital bedroom.

Kabbalistic literature abounds with erotic metaphors, so much so that a number of studies have been written on the subject. Each points out that the great Kabbalists, when writing about the profound ideas of Kabbalistic tradition, often resort to erotic language. Remember that even the Kabbalist's weekly Sabbath observance is described as a wedding wherein Kabbalists greet the Sabbath bride.

When a husband and wife who are Kabbalists make love, Kabbalistic tradition teaches that their minds and inner intention should be directed toward heaven. The union of male and female isn't just a sexual act between two individuals; in a sense, Kabbalists see it as a symbolic act of cosmic proportions. According to Kabbalists, sexuality is in no way dirty or sinful; rather, sex is an exalted act that can have a profound impact on the human soul.

When a husband and wife who follow Kabbalistic tradition enter the marriage chamber, they're aware that sexuality, like all pleasures of life, is a divine gift from above, and therefore, great care and the highest respect is required to fulfill the encounter appropriately.

Here and Now

Perhaps the most important place for Kabbalists is right here and right now. In a sense, every moment of life has the potential for either sanctity (consciousness of the Creator who gives everything) or debasement (taking life for granted with an absence of consciousness). The Kabbalist's goal is to bring an awareness and consciousness of God to every moment without exception. When a Kabbalist wakes up in the morning, his or her first thoughts should be that of gratitude to God. And that consciousness should continue throughout the day, until the very last moment before sleep.

Every moment of every day also brings the opportunity for sensitivity to others (or lack of sensitivity). Kabbalistic tradition urges a heightened sense of morality and ethics at all times. The here and now offers abundant opportunities for acts of lovingkindness and efforts to repair the world.

Unlike some religious traditions that set aside certain times and days as sacred, Kabbalists consider every moment sacred. The observance of many holy days on the Jewish calendar doesn't contradict the basic and fundamental view that all life comes from the Divine and that God creates the world in every moment. Kabbalists don't put off religion and spirituality for some other time or place; they know that every moment is meant to be seized, that every moment has great spiritual potential, and that every moment is a gift from above.

Part V
The Part of Tens

The 5th Wave   By Rich Tennant

"You know how you're always saying we can learn a spiritual lesson when bad things happen to us? Well you're about to get a spiritual lesson from Herb's Towing & Collision and the Able Auto Insurance Co."

In this part . . .

Elsewhere in this book, I discuss the Ten Commandments as well as the ten fundamental forces in the universe, but those aren't the only "tens" in the world of Kabbalah. Here, you explore a few more. First, you review the ten biggest misconceptions about Kabbalah, and then you get acquainted with ten of the greatest Kabbalists in history. You also take a trip around the world — both the outer world and the inner world — to discover some of the places that are most important to Kabbalists. And finally, I make some suggestions for further essential reading as you continue your study of Kabbalah.

Appendix A

Books and Authors You'll Thank Me for Recommending

*I*f you've visited your local bookstore or spent some time searching for Kabbalah books online, you no doubt know that there are a lot of books out there about Kabbalah. Given the quantity and quality of available literature, I imagine that you wouldn't mind some recommendations of some books to read as you increase your interest and understanding of Kabbalah. This appendix contains my best suggestions in no particular order.

The Books of Rabbi Aryeh Kaplan

Elsewhere in this book I recommend Rabbi Kaplan's translation of the Five Books of Moses called *The Living Torah*. Rabbi Kaplan wrote many other noteworthy books in his relatively short career that you'd be well-served to read. Among them are some of the most important and revealing books on Kabbalah in English, including *Meditation and Kabbalah* and *Jewish Meditation: A Practical Guide*. I also suggest tracking down anything else written by the late Rabbi Kaplan — you really can't go wrong with his work.

The Thirteen Petalled Rose by Rabbi Adin Steinsaltz

Rabbi Adin Steinsaltz's *The Thirteen Petalled Rose* isn't a book about Kabbalah — it's a book *of* Kabbalah. The brief, 180-page volume has become a contemporary classic, piercing to the heart of the most profound ideas in Jewish theology. It's essential reading for any serious student of Kabbalah today.

Like *The Thirteen Petalled Rose,* all the books written by the incomparable Rabbi Steinsaltz are profound. In particular, you shouldn't miss *Simple Words,* a slim book about some of the most familiar words in our lives; the volume contains important spiritual principles that you can use every day.

The Way of Splendor: Jewish Mysticism and Modern Psychology by Edward Hoffman

Hoffman's *The Way of Splendor: Jewish Mysticism and Modern Psychology* is a wonderful introduction to Kabbalah through the eyes of a psychologist. Dr. Hoffman is a master at taking profound Kabbalistic ideas and reframing them in familiar and easy-to-grasp terms. He writes with great clarity and insight.

The Books of Rabbi Zalman Schachter-Shalomi

Known to his many students and admirers as Reb Zalman, Rabbi Zalman Schachter-Shalomi is the founder of the Jewish Renewal movement, which is marked by a deep interest and spiritual connection to Kabbalistic traditions. Two books in particular are essential reading to get into the creative mind of Reb Zalman:

- *Paradigm Shift: From the Jewish Renewal Teachings of Reb Zalman Schachter-Shalomi* by Ellen Singer, which contains his essential teachings
- *Wrapped in a Holy Flame: Teachings and Tales of the Hasidic Masters,* in which Reb Zalman doesn't just discuss the great Hasidic masters of Kabbalah — he almost *becomes* them as he writes!

Souls on Fire by Elie Wiesel

In his youth, Nobel Peace Prize winner Elie Wiesel studied Kabbalah. After his experiences during the Holocaust, he continued his lifelong study of Jewish tradition, as his exceptional books reflect. Of Wiesel's many extraordinary volumes, *Souls on Fire* is one of his masterpieces. In it he shares his passion for the lives and wisdom of the great Hasidic sages.

9½ Mystics: The Kabbala Today by Rabbi Herbert Weiner

Over 30 years ago, Rabbi Herbert Weiner, a modern congregational rabbi in New Jersey, went searching the world for teachers who could provide him with an understanding of Kabbalah. He met many contemporary teachers of Kabbalah, and in *9½ Mystics,* he shares his journeys and encounters with readers. This book remains fresh, beautifully written, and deceptively deep so many years later.

Kabbalah: Selections from Classic Kabbalistic Works by Rabbi Avraham Yaakov Finkel

This book is the best single-volume introduction to the great personalities of Kabbalah throughout history. Like several of Rabbi Finkel's other superb books (such as *The Great Torah Commentators, The Great Chasidic Masters,* and *Contemporary Sages*), *Selections from Classic Kabbalistic Works* introduces readers to biographical information about each personality and presents carefully selected words of wisdom and teachings from their writings.

The Artscroll Prayer Book

Every Jewish household and everyone interested in Judaism and Kabbalah needs an Artscroll Prayer Book. (When you pick up your copy, make sure it's *Nusach Sefard,* which means that it reflects Kabbalistic practice today.) This one volume contains every prayer and blessing referred to in *Kabbalah For Dummies.* It also offers a huge amount of information on the meanings of the prayers as well as instructions for participating in traditional rituals and celebrations. Also included are the Jewish wedding ceremony and many other prayers for life cycle events.

Mishneh Torah: Yesodei HaTorah by the Rambam

The great Jewish philosopher and sage Maimonides (also known as the Rambam) wrote many books. One of his most celebrated and revered works is the 14-volume Mishneh Torah, a compilation representing the essence of the entire body of Jewish teachings. Many sections of this huge work have been translated. I recommend the translation of the volume *Yesodei HaTorah* (The Foundation of the Torah) because it offers the very first chapters of the entire work. Known as "The laws which are the Foundations of the Torah," chapters one and two reveal the fundamentals of Kabbalah. Although Maimonides isn't known as a Kabbalist, his work is a beautiful illustration of how the same profound ideas of Jewish theology can be expressed in entirely different ways.

The Fundamentals of Jewish Mysticism by Rabbi Leonard Glotzer

The introduction to this book is one of the best explanations of the ten *sefirot* I've ever seen. The book itself follows the commentary of the Vilna Gaon as that great sage looked at one of the classics of Kabbalah, Sefer Yetzirah.

Appendix B

Patriarchs, Swindlers, Prophets, and Sinners: Meet 100 Torah Characters

Involving oneself in Torah study, including the commentaries (and commentaries on commentaries), is such an integral part of a Kabbalist's life that the characters actually live among the student, guiding the way and teaching profound principles of the universe. Following is a quick rundown of these characters, including a scriptural reference to help you remember where to find them when you need to.

Note: An asterisk (*) denotes that more than one character in Hebrew Scripture bears this name *and* appears in this list.

The Torah (toe-*rah*): Five Books of Moses

Name	Hebrew Pronunciation	Hebrew Scripture Source
Adam	ah-*dahm*	Genesis 1:26
Eve	chah-*vah*	Genesis 2:18
The Snake	nah-*khash*	Genesis 3:1
Cain	*kah*-yin	Genesis 4:1
Abel	*heh*-vel	Genesis 4:2
Noah	*no*-akh	Genesis 5:29
Shem	shem	Genesis 5:32
Ham	kham	Genesis 5:32
Japheth	*yah*-fet	Genesis 5:32

(continued)

The Torah (toe-*rah*) (continued)

Name	Hebrew Pronunciation	Hebrew Scripture Source
Melchizedek	mahl-key-*tseh*-dek	Genesis 14:18
Abraham	ahv-rah-*ham*	Genesis 17:5
Sarah	sah-*rah*	Genesis 17:15
Lot	lowt	Genesis 11:31
Hagar	hah-*gar*	Genesis 16:15
Eliezer*	eh-lee-*eh*-zer	Genesis 15:2
Isaac	yitz-*khok*	Genesis 17:19
Rebecca	riv-*kah*	Genesis 24:15
Jacob	ya-ah-*kov*	Genesis 27:6
Jacob's wrestling partner	eeesh	Genesis 32:25
Esau	ay-*sahv*	Genesis 27:19
Amalek	ah-mah-*lake*	Exodus 17:14
Rachel	rah-*khale*	Genesis 29:10
Leah	lay-*ah*	Genesis 30:16
Bilhah	beel-*hah*	Genesis 29:29
Zilpah	zil-*pah*	Genesis 30:9
Laban	lah-*van*	Genesis 24:29
Reuben	r-oo-*vane*	Genesis 29:32
Levi	leh-*vee*	Genesis 34:30
Simeon	sheem-*own*	Genesis 42:24
Judah	yeh-who-*dah*	Genesis 37:26
Dan	dahn	Genesis 49:17
Napthali	naf-tah-*lee*	Genesis 30:8
Gad	gahd	Genesis 30:11
Asher	ah-*sher*	Genesis 30:13

Name	Hebrew Pronunciation	Hebrew Scripture Source
Issachar	yee-sah-*khar*	Genesis 30:18
Zebulon	zvoo-*loon*	Genesis 30:20
Joseph	yoh-*sef*	Genesis 37:3
Benjamin	been-yah-*min*	Genesis 43:29
Dinah	dee-*nah*	Genesis 34:1
Tamar*	tah-*mar*	Genesis 38:24
Pharaoh	pahr-*owe*	Exodus 1:22
Moses	moe-*sheh*	Exodus 5:22
Miriam	meer-*yam*	Exodus 15:20
Aaron	ah-hah-*rown*	Exodus 7:19
Ziporah	tzi-poe-rah	Exodus 4:25
Eliezer*	eh-lee-eh-zer	Exodus 18:4
Gershom	ger-*shom*	Exodus 6:17
Caleb	cah-*lev*	Numbers 14:24
Bezalel	beh-tzahl-*ale*	Exodus 36:1
Nachshon	nakh-shown	Numbers 7:12
Balaam	bih-*lahm*	Numbers 22:5
Balaam's she-donkey	ah-*tone*	Numbers 22:28
Phineas	pin-*khas*	Numbers 25:7
Korah	*ko*-rakh	Numbers 16:5

The Nevi'im (neh-*vee*-eem): Prophets

Name	Hebrew Pronunciation	Hebrew Scripture Source
Joshua	yeh-ho-*shoe*-ah	Joshua 1:1
Jephthah	yif-*takh*	Judges 11:1
Samson	shim-*shone*	Judges 14:5

(continued)

The Nevi'im (neh-*vee*-eem) *(continued)*

Name	Hebrew Pronunciation	Hebrew Scripture Source
Eli	eh-*lee*	I Samuel 2:22
Samuel	shmoo-*el*	I Samuel 3:4
Saul	shah-*ool*	I Samuel 13:13
David	dah-*veed*	I Samuel 16:22
Absalom	av-shah-*lohm*	II Samuel 3:3
Amnon	ahm-*known*	II Samuel 13:7
Tamar*	tah-*mar*	II Samuel 13:7
Uriah	ooree-*yah*	II Samuel 11:6
Bathsheba	baht-*sheh*-vah	II Samuel 12:24
Solomon	sh-lo-*mo*	I Kings 1:13
Nathan	nah-*tan*	II Samuel 7:2
Obadiah	oh-vad-*yah*	Obadiah 1:1
Hosea	ho-*shay*-ah	Hosea 1:1
Amos	ah-*mos*	Amos 1:1
Micah	mee-*khah*	Micah 1:1
Elijah	eh-li-*yah*-hu	I Kings 17:1
Elisha	eh-lee-*sha*	II Kings 2:2
Jonah	yo-*nah*	Jonah 1:1
Isaiah	ye-shah-*yah*-hu	Isaiah 1:1
Joel	yo-*el*	Joel 1:1
Nahum	nah-*khum*	Nahum 1:1
Habakkuk	kha-vah-*kuk*	Habakkuk 1:1
Zephaniah	tz-fan-*yah*	Zephaniah 1:1
Jeremiah	yir-mi-*yah*-hu	Jeremiah 1:1
Ezekiel	yeh-khez-*kel*	Ezekiel 1:3
Haggai	khah-*guy*	Haggai 1:1

Name	Hebrew Pronunciation	Hebrew Scripture Source
Zechariah	zeh-khar-*yah*	Zechariah 1:1
Malachi	mahl-ah-*khi*	Malachi 1:1
Deborah	deh-vo-*rah*	Judges 4:5
Hannah	cha-*nah*	I Samuel 1:2
Abigail	ah-vee-*gah*-yil	I Samuel 25:23
Huldah	khul-*dah*	II Chronicles 34:22

The Ketuvim (keh-*too*-veem): Writings

Name	Hebrew Pronunciation	Hebrew Scripture Source
Job	ee-*yov*	Job 1:1
Satan	sah-*tahn*	Job 1:8
Naomi	nah-ah-*me*	Ruth 1:2
Ruth	root	Ruth 1:4
Esther	es-*tehr*	Esther 2:7
Mordechai	more-deh-*khai*	Esther 2:5
Ahasuerus	ah-khash-vey-*rosh*	Esther 1:1
Haman	hah-*man*	Esther 3:1
Charvonah	khar-vo-nah	Esther 7:9
Daniel	dah-nee-*yale*	Daniel 1:6
Ezra	ez-*rah*	Ezra 7:25
Nehemiah	neh-khem-*yah*	Nehemiah 1:1

Appendix C

A Glossary of Everything Kabbalah

Adam haRishon: The first human being

Adam Kadmon: The Kabblistic term for primordial man; the soul out of which all souls come

Akiva, Rabbi: One of the greatest Jewish sages, born 20 CE; well known for both his personal story (he and his wife Rachel are the major players in the greatest love story in the Talmud) as well as his teachings, particularly the paradox, "All is foreseen and free will is given"

Alkebetz, Rabbi Shlomo Halevi: Great Kabbalists born in 1500; author of the well-known Sabbath hymn "L'cha Dodi"

Amen: The traditional response to a Hebrew blessing, implying "it is so" or "I agree"; Kabbalists believe that responding "Amen" to a traditional blessing helps send the blessing to God; the one who responds "Amen" spiritually connects with the blessing and joins it its ascent

Ari: Acronym of Rabbi Isaac Luria, born 1534; universally considered the greatest Kabbalist in history

Aseret hadibrot: The ten utterances; although this is the term used to refer to the Ten Commandments, it's also a reference to the fundamental tenet of Kabbalah that God constantly creates the world through the sustained divine speech in the form of ten primary flows of divine plenty, the ten *sefirot*

Assiyah: The world of action; one of the four worlds

Atzilut: The world of emanation; one of the four worlds

Avinu Malkenu: An important prayer in Jewish liturgy; literally "our Father, our King," which expresses the divine paradox of God being far and near

Avraham: The biblical patriarch Abraham, who is the manifestation of the *sefirah* of *Chesed* (lovingkindness)

Ba'alaht teshuvah: A female who isn't originally an observant Jew but who becomes observant; literally a "master of return"

Baal Shem Tov: Rabbi Israel, Kabbalist and founder of Hasidism; literally "Master of the Good Name"; see *Hasidism*

Ba'al teshuvah: A male who isn't originally an observant Jew but who becomes observant; literally a "master of return"

Bamidbar: Hebrew name for the book of Numbers in the Bible

Bar Mitzvah: Coming-of-age ceremony for a 13-year-old Jewish boy when he begins a process that leads to becoming a fully responsible adult; signals the beginning of the process of the soul's maturation to a state where it's fully challenged by the temptations of good and evil

Baruch dayan emet: The blessing said upon hearing of a death or other bad news; literally "Blessed is the True Judge"

Bashert: Destined, fated; commonly used to refer to the person who is one's destined soul mate

Bat mitzvah: Coming-of-age ceremony for a 12-year-old Jewish girl when she begins a process that leads to becoming a fully responsible adult

Bereshit: Hebrew name for the book of Genesis in the Bible

Beriyah: The world of creation; one of the four worlds

Binah: Understanding; one of the ten *sefirot*

Birkat HaMazon: Traditional Jewish grace after meals

Bitachon: Trust in God

Bracha: Blessing

Brit milah: Ritual circumcision

Caro, Rabbi Yosef: Great Kabbalist born in 1488; well known as the author/compiler of the Code of Jewish Law

Chabad: The spiritual approach of Lubavitch Chasidism; literally an acronym of the three *sefirot* of *Chochmah, Binah,* and *Da'at*

Challot: Traditional Jewish braided bread eaten on the Sabbath; plural form of challah

Chanukah: Festival of Lights

Chavah: Hebrew name for the biblical Eve

Chaya: One of the five levels of the human soul

Chesed: Lovingkindness; one of the ten *sefirot*

Cheshbon hanefesh: Nighttime ritual of evaluating one's actions and thoughts of the day that's ending; literally "accounting of the soul"

Chevrusah: Torah study partner; the importance of studying Torah with a partner makes the relationship with a chevrusah one of the most cherished relationships in one's life

Chidush: An original, innovative interpretation, usually of a verse in the Torah

Chochmah: Wisdom; one of the ten *sefirot*

Chumash: The Five Books of Moses; literally "five"

Cordovero, Rabbi Moshe: Prominent Kabbalist born in 1522; author of one of the classic works of Kabbalah, Pardes Rimonim

Daat: Knowledge; one of the ten *sefirot*

Devarim: Hebrew name for the book of Deuteronomy in the Bible

Devekut: Cleaving to God

Din: Judgment; another name for one of the ten *sefirot, Gevurah*

Drash: Homiletic interpretation of the Torah; see ***Pardes***

Dvar Torah: Usually a short sermon or talk on a spiritual topic; literally "word of Torah"

Ehyeh asher ehyeh: Biblical phrase spoken by God to Moses at the burning bush (Exodus 3:14); literally "I am that I am"

Ein Sof: Kabbalistic term for God's essence; literally "without end"

Elul: Hebrew month leading up to the Jewish New Year; dedicated to introspection and examination of one's deeds and goals

Emunah: Faith in God

Gam zu l'tova: Aramaic expression meaning "this too is for the best"; literally "also this is for good"

Gaon: Genius; a title given to rare individuals of exceptional intellectual and spiritual ability

Gedulah: Greatness; another name for the *sefirah* of *Chesed*

Gemara: Rabbinic commentary on the Mishnah that's part of the Talmud; literally "completion"

Gevurah: Strength; one of the ten *sefirot*

Gilgul HaNefesh: Kabbalistic term for reincarnation; literally "revolving of the soul"

Hagaddah: Book used during the Passover meal that tells the story of the Children of Israel's exodus from Egypt

Hamakom: One of the names of God; literally "the Place"

Hanukkah: see *Chanukah*

Hashem: Hebrew term used to refer to God; literally "the Name"

Hashgacha pratit: Divine providence, meaning that God is the force behind all events; literally "private/individual supervision"

Hasidism: The greatest revival movement in Jewish history; dedicated to teaching Kabbalah to the masses; founded by the Baal Shem Tov

Havdalah: Ritual at the end of the Sabbath that ushers in the new week; literally "separation"

Hidur mitzvah: Act of enhancing the beauty of religious acts (such as setting a beautiful table for the Sabbath); literally "glorifying a commandment"

Hillel: Talmudic sage who lived in the first century BC; best known for wise sayings such as "That which is hateful to you, do not do to your neighbor. That is the whole Torah; the rest is commentary. Go and study it."

Hod: Splendor; one of the ten *sefirot*

Iggeret Hakodesh: Kabbalistic text attributed to Nachmanides that deals with human sexuality; literally "the holy letter"

Jerusalem: The holiest city in Judaism; the capital of the State of Israel

Kabbalah: The theology of the Jewish people; literally "received [tradition]"

Kaddish: A traditional Jewish prayer in a variety of forms, the best known being the mourner's prayer; literally "sanctification"

Kavanah: Inner intention

Keter: Crown; one of the ten *sefirot*

Ketubah: Jewish marriage contract

Ketuvim: One of the three major parts of the Holy Scriptures of Judaism, includes the Psalms, the Song of Songs, and Proverbs; literally "writings"

Kiddush: Hebrew prayer recited on the Sabbath and Holy Days before drinking a cup of wine; literally "sanctification"

Knesset hagadol: The main spiritual and legislative body of the post-prophetic era; Jewish council of the wisest men of the fifth century BCE, literally "the Great Assembly"

Kohelet: Hebrew name for the book of Ecclesiastes in the Bible

Lag B'Omer: The 33rd day of the Counting of Omer; commemorates a break in the plague that killed students of Rabbi Akiva; also the day of the death of Rabbi Shimon bar Yochai, author of the Zohar

Luria, Rabbi Isaac: see *Ari*

Maariv: Daily evening prayer session; literally "evening"

Maaseh bereshit: Kabbalistic study of the part of the biblical book of Genesis dealing with the Creation; literally "the work of Creation"

Maaseh merkavah: Kabbalistic study of the part of the biblical book of Ezekiel dealing with the prophet's vision of a divine chariot; literally "the work of the Chariot"

Machzor: Jewish prayer book for holy days other than the Sabbath; literally "cycle"

Malach: An angel

Malach hamavet: Angel of Death

Malchut: Kingdom; one of the ten *sefirot*

Matzah: Unleavened bread eaten on the holy days of Passover

Mazal: Luck, fate

Megillat Esther: The biblical book of Esther, read publicly on the Jewish holy day of Purim

Melech: King

Meron: City in Israel; the burial place of Rabbi Shimon bar Yochai, author of the Zohar, as well as his son Rabbi Elazar, the sages Hillel and Shammai, and other great sages of Judaism and Kabbalah

Midrash: A homily or story that expands on a biblical verse as a way of interpreting the text; also refers to any number of compilations of such interpretations; literally "inquiry"

Mikvah: Ritual bath used by married women on a monthly basis to fulfill the laws of family purity; also used daily by many pious Jews; use is a requirement for conversion

Minchah: Afternoon daily prayer session; literally "offering"

Mishnah: Compilation of the oral law of Judaism by Judah the Prince, the leader of the Jewish people; traditionally believed to be given orally by God to Moses at Mount Sinai

Mishneh Torah: Kabbalistic text comprised of 14 books written and compiled by Rabbi Moses ben Maimon (Maimonides, also known as the Rambam); intended to be a summary of the entire body of Jewish religious law; literally "the Second Law"

Mitzraim: Hebrew term for ancient Egypt, literally "a narrow place"

Modeh ani (M)/Modah ani (F): Short prayer of gratitude that's recited at the moment of awakening each day; commonly the first prayer taught to children

Naaseh v'nishmah: Phrase from the Torah (Exodus 24:7) spoken by the Children of Israel to Moses after Moses read the Book of the Covenant to them; it means "We will do and we will listen [understand]"

Nachmanides: Another name for the great Kabbalist Moshe ben Nahman, who wrote many classic works including a popular commentary on the Torah

Nefesh: One of the five levels of the soul

Neshamah: One of the five levels of the soul

Netzach: Victory; one of the ten *sefirot*

Nevi'im: The books of the Prophets

Nochosh: The biblical term for the snake in the Garden of Eden in the book of Genesis; the snake represents the evil tempter, also referred to as Satan

Nusach Sefarad: Style of praying, in content and pronunciation, used by Hasidim and other Eastern European Jews for a number of centuries; despite the reference to "Sefardic" (of Spanish and Portuguese descent), it isn't the way contemporary Sefardic Jews speak and pray

Ohel: Commonly refers to the little house sometimes built over a gravestone; literally "tent"; in modern Jewish circles, if one says that he'll visit "the ohel" in New York, he's referring to the graves of two great Kabbalists of the 20th century, the Lubavitcher Rebbe, Rabbi Menachem Mendel Schneerson, and his father-in-law, the previous Rebbe of Lubavitch, Rabbi Yaakov Yosef Schneersohn

Olam: World; in Kabbalistic terms, a world is a plane of existence, and both reality and human beings consist of four worlds: a physical world of action, an emotional world, an intellectual world, and a spiritual world

Olam haba: The world to come

Olom hazeh: This world

Oneg: Delight; commonly used in the form of *oneg Shabbat,* the refreshments served after prayer at most synagogues on Friday nights, when the Sabbath begins

Pardes: orchard or garden; forms the basis of the English word "paradise"; an acronym of four Hebrew letters that correspond to the different levels of understanding the verses of the Torah (the literal meaning, the moral message, that which is implied but not explicitly stated, and the mystical, Kabbalistic level)

Pesach (Passover): A seven-day holy day (eight days outside of Israel) commemorating the Children of Israel's exodus from Egypt (led by Moses) to escape bondage as slaves to Pharaoh; marked by many customs, including family gatherings to tell the story of the exodus and the eating of unleavened bread, *matzah,* for at least the first day (a prohibition against eating leaven remains in force for all the days). Unbeknownst to many contemporary practitioners, all the details of the laws of Pesach reflect Kabbalistic teachings.

Pirke Avot: Section of the Mishnah consisting of wise sayings of the great sages of Jewish and therefore Kabbalistic tradition; found in the Sabbath afternoon section of traditional Jewish prayer books because it's customary to study these verses on the Sabbath; literally "the Chapters of the Fathers"

P'shat: Looking at verses from the Torah in a plain, simple, literal way

Purim: The holy day in late winter when Kabbalists publicly read the book of Esther from the Torah; students of this holy day focus on a number of fundamental Kabbalistic principles including the view that God is behind all occurrences and events

Rabbi: Title given to individuals who have proven to a tribunal of well-established rabbis that they can pass certain examinations to measure aspects of their qualifications for the position, its title, and its responsibilities; literally "my teacher"

Rambam: Traditional acronym for 12th-century Rabbi Moses ben Maimon; known to have written that his masterpiece, the Mishneh Torah, contains "everything"

Rebbe: see *Schneeerson, Rabbi Menachem Mendel*

Remez: One of the four levels of approaching verses in the Torah (see *Pardes*); urges the Torah student to try to see beyond what the verse says literally to what's implied from the language of the Torah; literally "hint"

Rodef: A pursuer of peace (many synagogues in the United States are named Rodef Shalom) or a murderous pursuer (a person who's going to killing someone); literally "pursuer"

Rosh Chodesh: The New Moon; a monthly holiday celebrating the beginning of the new month (as determined by the lunar cycle); literally "the head of the month"

Rosh Hashanah: Holy day that begins a ten-day period of intense prayer and introspection called *the Days of Awe,* during which Kabbalists examine past actions and pray for the ability to improve and to choose correctly in the future; literally "the head of the year"

Ruach HaKodesh: A level of consciousness attained by certain people at certain times when the person can experience reality and speak from an extraordinarily high spiritual level, as if to say a spirit from God shines a special light on the person whose words and thoughts come from the holiest of places; literally "the holy spirit"

Satan: The evil inclination; also represented as the snake (see *Nochosh*); represents a figure in the deepest levels of spiritual discussion about the nature of good and evil and the relationship between the human soul and its various urges and appetites

Schneeerson, Rabbi Menachem Mendel: Spiritual giant of the 20th century who's known simply as the Rebbe to Jews around the world today; a great scholar of the Talmud and the works of Kabbalah whose guidance was sought by countless people during the decades of his leadership in the Jewish world

Seder: The festive family dinner of Passover (see *Pesach*) during which family members, friends, and guests gather to recount and celebrate the exodus from slavery in ancient Egypt, led by Moses; literally "order"

Sefer Bahir: An ancient Kabbalistic text of great significance to the student of Kabbalah; the first book that explicitly discusses the *sefirot* as divine attributes and powers emanating from God; literally "the Book of Brilliance"

Sefer Yetzirah: An ancient Kabbalistic text considered by some as the earliest Kabbalistic text; deals with the structure of Creation; many great scholars have written commentaries on Sefer Yetzirah; literally "the Book of Formation"

Sefirah: Singular form of *sefirot;* see *Sefirot*

Sefirat HaOmer: The period of seven weeks between the holy days of Passover and Shavuot; part of each day is devoted to a meditation on the *sefirot*, their meanings, and the ways in which they combine

Sefirot: The ten fundamental forces that are the basic instruments of the Divine; the ten are *Keter, Chochmah, Binah, Chesed, Gevurah, Tiferet, Netzach, Hod, Yesod,* and *Malkhut;* point to a profound Kabbalistic area of study having to do with the human potential for true knowledge of God; English translations include "number," "category," "sphere," "lights," and other terms

Shabbat: Also known as *the Sabbath;* the seventh day of the week; a weekly day of rest that's dedicated to prayer, Torah study, and a sense of gratitude and delight; the details of Shabbat rituals, including the precise details of Shabbat evening meal, are all of Kabbalistic significance

Shacharit: Morning daily prayer session; literally "dawn" or "daybreak"

Shalom Zachor: Traditional ritual performed for newborn boys on the first Shabbat after birth that's marked by a celebration of the birth and an awareness that the world of action into which the boy's soul has arrived; the celebration wishes tidings of peace to the newcomer; literally "peace little boy"

Shammai: Talmudic sage who lived in the first century BCE and who, with his school and his disciples, developed a counterbalance to the points of view of the sage Hillel and his school; his mutual explorations of spiritual as well as down-to-earth issues have led to students carefully weighing all sides of an issue

Shamor: One of the attitudes that Kabbalists cultivate toward the divine gift of Shabbat (the other attitude is Zachor; see *Zachor*); requires a person to be steadfast and to protect the sanctity of the Sabbath; literally "to guard"

Shavuot: Holy day observed each spring, seven weeks after the beginning of Passover (see *Pesach*); celebrates the giving of the Torah by God to Moses and his People

Shehechiyanu: A reference to a popular blessing recited on major holy days and many other milestone occasions expressing gratitude to God for one's existence and recognizing that God is sustaining the Creation at every moment; literally "who keeps us alive"

Sh'ma: The first word of a central prayer recited twice a day declaring God's Oneness, which Kabbalistic tradition contemplates; literally "hear"

Shemot: Hebrew name for the book of Exodus in the Five Books of Moses

Shimon bar Yochai, Rabbi: Colleague of Rabbi Akiva (see *Akiva, Rabbi*) who lived in the first century CE; traditionally considered the author of the Zohar

Shir Hashirim: Book contained in the section of the Holy Scriptures called Ketuvim (see *Ketuvim*); literally "Song of Songs"

Shiva: Period of one week following the death of a loved one; spent in introspection and gradual adjustment to the fact that a loved one's soul has separated from his or her body

Shloshim: Thirty-day period following the death of a loved one; spent in continued gradual adjustment to the fact that a loved one's soul has separated from his or her body

Shnei Luchot Habrit: A revered Kabbalistic text by Rabbi Isaiah Horowitz, who lived in the 17th century; literally "two tablets of the covenant"

Shulchan Aruch: Authoritative Code of Jewish Law written and compiled by Rabbi Joseph Caro, a 16th-century Kabbalist; is consulted today as the primary source of Jewish law; literally "the prepared table"

Siddur: Standard Jewish prayer book used daily by Kabbalists throughout the centuries; from the Hebrew word for "order"

Simchat Torah: Holy day in the fall when Kabbalists participate in the synagogue celebration of actually dancing with a Torah scroll and rejoicing in the love of the Torah; literally "the joys of the Torah"

Sod: Splendor; one of the ten *sefirot*

Sukkot: A fall holiday of eight days, which trace their origins to the Torah; marked by the custom of building temporary huts and living as much as possible in them, it's both a joyful time as well as a time to contemplate what's permanent and what's transitory at a time of year when one is surrounded by the fruits of one's harvest

Talmud: A literary and spiritual work comprised of 63 book-length parts that's the central pillar of Jewish culture; contains thousands of years of Jewish wisdom and has been studied by the great Kabbalists throughout the centuries, all of whom saw Talmud study as a requirement of their spiritual work

Tanach: Popular Hebrew acronym for the three parts of the Holy Scriptures: the Torah (the Five Books of Moses), Nevi'im (the books of the Prophets), and Ketuvim (the Writings)

Tefillah: Prayer

Tehillim: The biblical book of Psalms, most of which are attributed to King David; expresses a vast range of human thought and emotion; selections are often a part of the daily and holy day liturgies

Teshuvah: Profound spiritual process of refining oneself and changing; the ability to use one's mistakes to prompt movement in a good direction; tradition calls for Kabbalists to strive for Teshuvah constantly; literally "turning"

Tiferet: Beauty; one of the ten *sefirot*

Tikkun: Repair; commonly used in the phrase "Tikkun Olam," which refers to repairing the world; the Kabbalist's primary task is repairing the imperfect world

Tisha b'Av: The ninth day of the month of Av, which usually falls in August; the saddest day on the Jewish calendar in that it commemorates the destruction of both Holy Temples in Jerusalem as well as other well-known Jewish calamities and tragedies that also occurred on that day; observed by fasting and participating in communal prayer with a mood of mourning

Torah: Refers to the Five Books of Moses, the entire Holy Scriptures, the whole body of Torah literature throughout history, and more; the "place" where all Kabbalists meet as students of the holy texts

Tzfat: City in Northern Israel that was the center of the greatest flowering of Kabbalah in history; home of some of the most important Kabbalists in the 16th century

Tzimtzum: The contraction that God willed in order to make room for Creation; Kabbalists should follow this example and contract, making themselves humble; literally "contraction"

Tzedakah: The act of giving charity, which is an act of justice, of putting things right, according to Jewish thought and law; at least 10 percent of the Kabbalist's earnings should go to charity; literally "justice"

Vayikrah: The Five Books of Moses known as Leviticus

Vidui: The text spoken on one's death bed; also the name of the confessional prayers recited on the day of Yom Kippur (see **Yom Kippur**); literally "confession"

Vilna Gaon: Also known as Rabbi Elijah, a great 18th-century leader of Lithuanian Jewry and master of Kabbalah; wrote an important commentary on one of the classics of Kabbalah, Sefer Yeztirah; universally considered a genius; literally "the genius from Vilna"

Yaakov: Biblical patriarch known as Jacob; the son of Isaac

Yartzeit: The anniversary of a person's death; both a day of memory and a day when a Kabbalist confirms the belief that death is the soul's graduation to the next station in its spiritual journey; literally "year's time"

Yechidah: One of the five levels of the soul

Yeshiva: A traditional Jewish religious school; literally "place of sitting"

Yesod: Foundation; one of the ten *sefirot*

Yetzer hatov: Good inclination that's in constant struggle with the evil inclination, Yetzer hara (see **Yetzer hara**)

Yetzerah: The world of formation; one of the four worlds

Yetzer hara: Evil inclination that's in constant struggle with the good inclination, Yetzer hatov (see **Yetzer hatov**)

Yitzchak: Biblical patriarch known as Isaac; the son of Abraham and the father of Jacob

Yom Kippur: One of the Days of Awe; holy day in the fall that's marked by fasting and praying that lead the Kabbalist in the direction of joy, spiritual victory, and faith in God's acceptance of one's prayers

Zachor: One of the attitudes that Kabbalists cultivate toward the divine gift of Shabbat (the other attitude is Shamor; see *Shamor*); requires a person to recall the gift of the Sabbath each week; literally "to remember"

Zohar: Spiritual masterpiece that's structured as a commentary on the Torah; traditionally attributed to the first century CE sage Rabbi Shimon bar Yochai (see *Shimon bar Yochai, Rabbi*); considered the major work of Kabbalah

Part VI
Appendixes

The 5th Wave   By Rich Tennant

"Granted, they're both part of a long oral tradition, but Allemanding to my left and doing a Do-Si-Do never inspired me as much as the Kabbalah."

In this part . . .

Appendix A is a list of resources that I think you'll appreciate and enjoy. Appendix B is a handy list of the important characters in the Torah to help you remember who's who. Finally, Appendix C is a glossary of all the Hebrew terms, famous names, and other concepts that the fluent Kabbalist knows well.

Index

brit milah (circumcision), 336
Buddhism, 101
burial of the dead, 107–108, 201, 204–205
business ethics, 82
The Byrds, "Turn! Turn! Turn!", 196–197

• **C** •

cabal, 29
Cain, 329
Caleb, 331
candles, 154, 157–158
Cave of the Patriarchs, 317
CE (Common Era), 3
celebrations
　bar mitzvah, 195–197, 336
　bat mitzvah, 195–197, 336
　shalom zachor, 106, 191–192, 343
　Simchat Bat, 106
　weddings, 198
cemeteries, 316–318
Chabad, 25, 336
challah, 156
challah cover, 156
challot, 336
Chanukah (Festival of Lights), 179–181, 337
Chapters of the Sages (Pirke Avot), 201, 342
charity, 135
chart of the ten sefirot, 59
Charvonah, 333
Chavah (Eve), 329, 337
chaya, 99, 337
Chesed sefirah, 63, 70, 337
cheshbon hanefesh, 337
chevruta, 238–239, 337
chidush, 337
children, blessing, 159
Children of Israel, 211
Chochmah sefirah, 60–61, 70, 94, 337
chosen people, 88
Christian Cabala/Kabbalah, 30, 292
Chumash, 22, 337
circumcision (brit milah), 336
Classic Artscroll Siddur (Mesorah Publications), 257

cleaving to God (deveikut), 281, 337
clothing
　modesty, 141
　Sabbath (Shabbat), 154
Code of Jewish Law (Shulchan Aruch), 19, 222, 255, 315, 344
commandments, 18
commentaries on Holy Scriptures, 131–132
Common Era (CE), 3
communion, 85
conceptions of God, 250–251
concepts of Kabbalah, 17–18
consciousness. *See* soul
Conservative Jews, 24, 51
contemporary books about Kabbalah, 133
Contemporary Sages (Finkel), 327
continuous nature of creation, 57–58
coping with suffering, 121–122
Cordovero, Rabbi Moshe (Kabbalist), 45, 222, 310, 337
Counting of the Omer, 186
creation
　angels, 113, 116
　continuous nature of, 57–58
　partnership of three in the creation of human beings, 91–92, 102
　reason for, 15
　secrets in the story of, 240
　ten utterances, 17
　Tikkun ("repair"), 17
　tzimtzum, 17
cup (for Sabbath), 154–155
customs
　Chanukah, 180–181
　Counting of the Omer, 186
　deathbed, 202
　New Year, 174
　Passover, 184
　Purim, 182–183
　red string tied around the wrist, 295
　Rosh Hashanah, 175
　Shavuot, 187
　Sukkot, 177–179
　Tikkun Leil Shavuot, 187
　Yom Kipper (Days of Awe), 176–177

• H •

• *I* •

• *M* •

CPSIA information can be obtained at www.ICGtesting.com
Printed in the USA
BVOW01n0634211213

339395BV00024B/35/P